Frommer's™

KT-176-038   FIRST EDITION

London
Free &
dirt cheap

by Joe Fullman

WILEY

A John Wiley and Sons, Ltd, Publication

UK Publisher: Sally Smith
Production Manager: Daniel Mersey
Commissioning Editor: Fiona Quinn
Development Editor: Don Strachan
Content Editor: Erica Peters
Photo Research: David Cottingham
Cartography: Tim Lohnes
Photos Alamy: Page ii © Simon Hadley; Page 4, 98, 152, 190 © Alex Segre; Page 24 © Christopher Pillitz; Page 56 © Neil Setchfield; Page 226 © Akiko Nagahama; Page 280 © Niall McDiarmid; Page 306 © Total London.

British Library Cataloguing in Publication Data
A catalogue record for this book is available from the British Library
ISBN: 978-0-470-68377-4
Typeset by Wiley Indianapolis Composition Services
Printed and bound in Great Britain by TJ International Ltd
5 4 3 2 1

CONTENTS

LIST OF MAPS

About the Author

Like his parents and his parents' parents, **Joe Fullman** has been a London resident and bargain-hunter all his life, even if these days he lives in a slightly less central postcode than his forbears (but then he does pay a bargain rent). He occasionally leaves the city, however, to pursue his main job as a travel writer. During his 12 years in the business, he has written for most of the major guidebook publishers, including Rough Guides, Lonely Planet, AA, Cadogan and, of course, Frommer's. He is the author of guides to England, Berlin, Venice, Las Vegas, Costa Rica, Belize and Seville and has contributed to guides to Paris, Italy, Turkey, Central America and the Caribbean.

Acknowledgements

There are lots of people to thank, chief among them Fiona Quinn for giving me the gig and being so understanding and patient when things took a little longer than planned, and Donald Strachan for his careful editing, helpful suggestions and alchemic ability with my prose. Thanks also to everyone who responded to my bargain enquiries, taking the time to write back to me, sort things out for me, answer my queries, recommend things to me, point me in the right direction and generally stop me from spending too much money. Special mention too must go to all those friends and family who gave up their precious money-saving recommendations, particularly my mum and dad, my brother Sam, Anna B, Barry M, Ben and Aggie, Danny B, David H, Gary B, Greg I, Laura H, Neil D, Nick B, Nick R and Nicola M. You're all a bunch of cheapskates.

How to Contact Us

In researching this book, we discovered many wonderful places—hotels, restaurants, shops, and more. We're sure you'll find others. Please tell us about them, so we can share the information with your fellow travellers in upcoming editions. If you were disappointed with a recommendation, we'd love to know that, too. Please write to:

Frommer's London Free & Dirt Cheap, 1st Edition
Wiley Publishing, Inc. • 111 River St. • Hoboken, NJ 07030-5774

An Additional Note

Please be advised that travel information is subject to change at any time—and this is especially true of prices. We therefore suggest that you write or call ahead for confirmation when making your travel plans. The authors, editors, and publisher cannot be held responsible for the experiences of readers while travelling. Your safety is important to us, however, so we encourage you to stay alert and be aware of your surroundings. Keep a close eye on cameras, purses, and wallets, all favourite targets of thieves and pickpockets.

Free & Dirt Cheap Icons & Abbreviations

We also use five feature icons that point you to the great deals, in-the-know advice, and unique experiences that separate urban adventurers from tourists. Throughout the book, look for:

FREE Events, attractions, or experiences that cost no more than your time and a swipe of your Oystercard.

FINE PRINT The unspoken conditions or necessary preparations to experience certain free and dirt cheap events.

★ The best free and dirt cheap events, dining, shopping, living, and exploring in the city.

Special events worth marking in your calendar.

Frommers.com

Now that you have this guidebook to help you plan a great trip, visit our website at **www.frommers.com** for additional travel information on more than 4,000 destinations. We update features regularly to give you instant access to the most current trip-planning information available. At Frommers. com, you'll find scoops on the best airfares, lodging rates, and car rental bargains. You can even book your travel online through our reliable travel booking partners. Other popular features include:

- Online updates of our most popular guidebooks
- Holiday sweepstakes and contest giveaways
- Newsletters highlighting the hottest travel trends
- Podcasts, interactive maps, and up-to-the-minute events listings
- Opinionated blog entries by Arthur Frommer himself
- Online travel message boards with featured travel discussions

Other Great Guides for Your Trip:

Frommer's London Day by Day

Frommer's London With Kids

Frommer's London

Frommer's Best Day Trips From London

Suzy Gershman's Born to Shop London

London at your feet, tourists look towards Nelson's Column in Trafalgar Square from the steps of the National Gallery.

THE BEST THINGS IN LIFE ARE FREE

Not so long ago, a leading website asked 2,400 travellers to rank Europe's cities according to a number of criteria: cleanliness, friendliness of the locals, quality of the cuisine, value for money, and so on. Anyone who works for the London Tourist Board may want to look away now... because the UK's capital, you won't be surprised to hear, was considered the most expensive city in the European Union. However, it was also rated among the best for free attractions. These two results neatly sum up the London paradox. This city can be expensive, often scandalously so. Public transport costs are already the highest in Europe, and keep rising. Restaurant and hotel bills can be extraordinary, as can ticket prices and housing rents and… well, everything, really. Then again, London probably boasts more free museums and galleries than any other major city. What other capital can boast gratis collections of the quality of the British Museum, the National Gallery, and the Tates? What other leading metropolis has such a bucolic abundance of parks, all free (and rated by those polled as the best in Europe)? London's bank-breaking international reputation doesn't tell the whole story.

I'm not going to lie to you: living and exploring cheaply here is not easy. But it is possible. In order to root out the lowest prices for getting around, getting fed, finding somewhere to stay, and entertaining yourself, you'll need to be canny. Bargains are out there, but they take some sniffing out. London is not a city to do in an ad hoc, make-it-up-as-you-go-along sort of a way, unless you're a person for whom phrases such as 'overdraft', 'mortgage', and 'final demand' have little relevance. Here, parsimony means planning. It means scouring the web for the best hotel and transport deals, months before you arrive. It means travelling on public transport after 9:30am, watching films before 5pm, and turning up at markets in the dead of night. On occasion it can also mean slumming it—spending a night or two in a hostel, eating from a market stall rather than in a restaurant, and grabbing some free music in the foyers of the capital's art complexes.

There's also little you can do about your age. But here in London, there's a lot your age can do for you. If you're under 26 or over 60, you're entitled to discounts on transport and attraction admissions. It's the same if you're a full-time student of any age—remember to pack a recognised ID card so you can claim your dues.

If you fall between these generational stools, however, you'll just have to try that little bit harder to make your savings; which is where *Frommer's London Free & Dirt Cheap* comes in. The chapters that follow review the capital's cheapest hotels, hostels, restaurants, and bars. This book shows you how to make the most out of an abundance of attractions, revealing all the added-value extras: free concerts, daily talks, tours, and film screenings. It points you in the direction of cheap and free educational resources—lectures, classes, and readings—and helps you look your best, courtesy of bargain beauty treatments and half-price haircuts. It suggests dozens of options for both great low-cost nights out—be you a fan of live music, dancing, cinema, clubbing, or whatever—and quiet nights in with a good, inexpensive (or borrowed) book. There are also four walking itineraries for exploring a little of the city's rich history—on the cheap, of course.

In the end, the book doesn't give you all the answers. But it does provide quite a few of them and, even more importantly, contains a supply of ideas, tips, and information sources for finding your own path to a parsimonious paradise in one of the world's most exciting cities.

The roof of the Great Court of the British Museum, opened in 2000, spans out from the famous circular Reading Room.

THE BEST OF FREE & DIRT CHEAP LONDON

As we go about our busy, high-priced metropolitan lives, money pouring from our pockets like water from a burst main, London can seem mean and grasping, snatching at our hard-earned cash. Take the time, however, to seek out its many bargain opportunities and the city is suddenly a kinder place—at times positively generous. From gratis entry to some of the world's greatest museums and art galleries, to £10 opera tickets, 10p theatre tickets, and concerts on the house, there are plenty of ways to stem the flow of pounds. In the aftermath of a financial crisis, Londoners and visitors to London want value for money as never before, and the city is doing its best to oblige. From cheap eats to bargain seats, cut-price health treatments to reasonably rated rooms, what follows is the best of the best.

1 Best Cheap Sleeps

- **Best Budget Hotel:** In a competitive field, the **Luna & Simone** (47–49 Belgrave Road, SW1; ℂ **020 7834 5897**) ticks the greatest number of boxes—it's well located (a few minutes from Victoria station), well connected (the no. 24 bus stops outside), well turned out, and, well, just very good value with supremely friendly staff. See p. 41.

- **Best Central London Accommodation that's not a B & B or a Hostel:** The London School of Economics rents out its rooms in **Passfield Hall** (1–7 Endsleigh Place, WC1; ℂ **020 7107 5925**), a student residence set in a Georgian building in the centre of Bloomsbury. During the university holidays it costs from £34 for a single room, £55 for a twin. See p. 47.

- **Best-Decorated Budget Hotel:** The padded walls and space-age metal of the **Stylotel** (160–162 Sussex Gardens, W2; ℂ **020 7723 1026**. www.stylotel.com/stylotel.swf) have their fans, but nothing can top the kitschy wonderland of the **Pavilion's** (34–36 Sussex Gardens, W2; ℂ **020 7262 0905**) themed rooms—'Honky Tonk Afro', 'Funky Zebra', 'Monochrome Marilyn', and the like. See p. 37.

- **Best Hostel for Nightlife:** It's a toss up between **The Generator** (37 Tavistock Place, WC1; ℂ **020 7388 7666**), with its buzzing bar and happy-hour prices, and the nightclub and games room of **The Village.** The 'Gen' just gets the nod, courtesy of its sheer number of inmates (up to 800), who give it a truly intense atmosphere. See p. 30 and p. 38.

- **Best-Located Cheap Accommodation:** The **Meininger Hostel** (65–67 Queen's Gate, SW7; ℂ **020 7590 6910.** www.meininger-hotels.com.) next to the Natural History Museum, gets an honourable mention, as does the **Portobello Gold** (95–97 Portobello Road, Notting Hill, W11. ℂ **020 7460 4910;** www.portobellogold.com.) in the heart of the antique market. But top marks go to **Holland Park YHA** (Holland Walk, W8; ℂ **0845 371 9122**), set in a Jacobean mansion amid a landscaped, peacock-inhabited park. See p. 40.

- **Best YHA Hostel:** Of seven central London representatives, the recently opened **London Central YHA** (104 Bolsover Street, W1; ☏ **0845 371 9154**) emerges victorious. It's both better located (just north of Oxford Street) and better equipped (shop, cycle storage, café, self-catering kitchen, free Wi-Fi, games consoles) than its older, more staid counterparts. See p. 32.

2 Best Cheap Eats

- **Best Investment of £1.50:** With Brick Lane's **Beigel Bake** (159 Brick Lane, E1; ☏ **020 7729 0616**) open round the clock, you can enjoy a salmon and cream cheese bagel whenever the craving strikes. And if you really have a hunger on, £2.60 will buy you one of its signature hot salt-beef versions. See p. 301.

- **Best Investment of £2.30:** That's all it costs for one pie, one 'scrape' of mash, and a portion of parsley sauce ('liquor') at **M. Manze** (87 Tower Bridge Road, SE1; ☏ **020 7407 2985**), one of London's few remaining traditional pie-and-mash shops. If you're feeling adventurous, another 5p will add a bowl of jellied eels, or if you're just *very* hungry, you can have two pies and two scrapes of mash for £4.10. See p. 73.

- **Best Investment of £3.50:** I'm staying on the fence. Either a generously topped thin-crust slice from Soho stalwart **Malletti** (26 Noel Street, W1; ☏ **020 7439 4096**), or two curries, a portion of rice, and a samosa from **Mantra** (Whitecross Street, EC1; ☏ **020 7527 1761**), a bustling, bubbling, and extremely popular curry stall on Whitecross Street Market. See p. 60 & p. 92.

- **Best Meaty Investment of £4.25:** Located below the country's largest meat market, the **Cock Tavern** (Central Markets, EC1; ☏ **020 7248 2918**) can guarantee that the ingredients in its signature 'butcher's breakfast' are freshly sourced (if not practically still moving). It's a real flesh spectacular aimed at carnivorous connoisseurs—Smithfield's market workers—featuring not just the usual sausage and bacon, but kidneys, black pudding, fried calf's liver and, in the interests of balance, baked beans (and for a few pounds extra, steak). Even first thing in the morning, the market's special licensing hours allow you to wash it down with a pint. See p. 70.

● **Best Vegetarian Investment of £5:** At **Maoz** (43 Old Compton Street, W1; ☎ **020 7851 1586**) a fiver will buy you one of its famed falafel pittas, a portion of thin-cut fries, and a mint lemonade. And, as if that wasn't enough, you can also fill your plate with a range of salads and pickles (and keep refilling as many times as you like). See p. 60.

● **Best Fishy Investment of £5:** Provided you go between 3pm and 9pm, you can bag a real West End bargain at **The Chippy** (38 Poland Street, W1; ☎ **020 7434 1933**): the daily fish-and-chip special for £5. See p. 59.

● **Best BYO:** With no corkage fee and an off-licence right next door where you can buy a bottle of wine, Vauxhall's **Hot Stuff** (19 Wilcox Road, SW8; ☎ **020 7720 1480**) couldn't make saving money on your drinks any easier. The Indian food is equally low priced (mains £4–£6) and top quality. See p. 87.

● **Best Value Chain:** Get down to **Little Bay's** (228 Belsize Road, NW6; ☎ **020 7373 4699**) various exuberantly decorated dining rooms before 7pm and you'll pay just £2.25 for starters and £5.25 for mains—and that's for decent Euro-grub. Just try and avoid the weekend birthday parties. See p. 78.

● **Best Low-Cost Michelin Deal:** **Arbutus** (63–64 Frith Street, W1; ☎ **020 7734 4545**) serves up three lunchtime courses of Michelin-starred Modern European cooking for £15.50 (just over a fiver a course) from Monday to Friday at its swish Soho dining room. See p. 64.

● **Best Fine-Dining Bargain:** The **Vincent Rooms** (Vincent Square, SW1; ☎ **020 7802 8391**) offers what should perhaps be more accurately described as 'trainee fine dining' bargains. Here you'll be served up gourmet lesson plans created by the students of Westminster Kingsway Cooking College at prices way below what they'll charge when they pass their exams. See p. 75.

3 Best Exploring for Free

● **Best Free Gallery:** The competition is fierce, with the two Tates and newcomers like the Saatchi in town, but for sheer something-for-nothing value the **National Gallery's** (Trafalgar

Square, WC2; © **020 7747 2885**) combination of multiple masterpieces and freebies (talks, tours, and concerts) still leads the way. See p. 118.

- **Best Free Hidden Gem:** The **Petrie Museum of Egyptian Archaeology** (University College London, Malet Place, WC1; © **020 7679 2884**) not only contains numerous gems among its collection of ancient curiosities, but many are indeed hidden because of the museum's low, protective lighting. Borrow a torch from the front desk and pretend to be an archaeologist for the day in the collection's many shadowy corners. See p. 107.

- **Best Free Interactive Museum:** If you like your museums all-singing and all-dancing with lots of buttons to press, levers to pull, and computer puzzles to solve then the **Science Museum** (Exhibition Road, SW7; © **0870 870 4868**) is the place for you. The Launchpad Gallery alone has more than 50 hands-on experiments. See p. 113.

- **Best Free Museum:** I'd like to recommend something quirky and obscure, but that would feel forced: it has to be the **British Museum** (Great Russell Street, WC1; © **020 7323 8000**). The stats alone leave the competition standing: it's a quarter of a millennium old with a collection of more than 7 million artefacts drawn from every major civilisation in history displayed in more than 75,000 square metres of galleries. Free talks and tours guide you through its wealth of wonders from around the world. See p. 105.

- **Best Free Museum Evening:** Giving the masses a little extra after hours, be it a lecture, a live band, or a licensed bar, has recently become *de rigueur* for many museums. Perhaps the most evocative late opening is served up by **Sir John Soane's Museum** (13 Lincoln's Inn Fields, WC2; © **020 7405 2107**). Here, on the first Tuesday of each month, you can tour the great collector's hoard of art and antiquities by candlelight. See p. 101.

- **Best Free Park:** In terms of attractions on offer, **Hyde Park** (W2; © **020 7298 2100**) is the clear leader—with its great grassy lawns, areas of woodland, flower gardens, model boating pond, lake, lido, playgrounds, tennis centre, horse-riding centre, and cafés, not to mention free ranger-guided walks all summer. See p. 132.

- **Best Free Stargazing Opportunity:** Picking out the wonders of the cosmos is not something that's usually done with much success in London's brightly lit centre. However, head out to the wilds of Hampstead between October and April and the astronomers at **Hampstead Observatory** (Lower Terrace, NW3; ℂ **020 8346 1056**) will let you point their 15-cm (6-inch) refractor at whatever happens to be up there. See p. 102.

- **Best Free View:** North of the river, **Hampstead Heath** (NW3; ℂ **020 7482 7073**) offers the finest vistas over the low-rise suburbs to the skyscrapers of the centre. To the south, the heights of **Greenwich Park** (Charlton Way, SE10; ℂ **020 8858 2608**) enjoy a panoramic sweep taking in the borough's 18th-century maritime architecture and the steel-and-glass edifices of Canary Wharf. See p. 131 & p. 139.

4 Best Cheap London Living

- **Best Cut-Price Massage:** The trouble with most massages is that you're so worried about the cost, you can never get properly relaxed. At the **London School of Beauty Therapy** (47 Great Marlborough Street, W1; ℂ **020 7208 1302**) the full-body deep tissue probing is performed by students; it's £25 for a 75-minute session. Very soothing. See p. 172.

- **Best Free Class: Stitch & Bitch's** (www.stitchandbitchlondon.co.uk/join.html) knitting sessions are the free classes that keep on giving. Not just fun evenings out but, in theory at least, a new skill with which to create a new wardrobe (or, in my case, a couple of wonky scarves). See p. 162.

- **Best Free Exercise:** At the **Green Gym** (80 York Way, N1; ℂ **020 7278 4294**), you not only work on your own physical fitness, you also help keep the city in tip-top condition by taking part in a range of physical conservation projects: digging, clearing litter, and more digging. See p. 180.

- **Best Free Lectures: Gresham College** (Barnard's Inn Hall, EC1; ℂ **020 7831 0575**) has been providing free lectures to the inquisitive impoverished for more than 400 years. Eight professors give six lectures each a year on subjects ranging from music and astronomy to medicine, law, and commerce. See p. 156.

- **Best Free Meditation:** If your morning has been about as bad as it could be, bring your blood pressure back to Earth by heading to **Inner Space** (36 Shorts Gardens, WC2; ✆ **020 7836 6688**). A free half-hour meditation session should put you in the right frame of mind for the afternoon ahead. See p. 170.

- **Best Library:** London's libraries are one of its greatest free resources, providing a wealth of loanable knowledge in return for nothing but the effort it takes to apply for a library card. Of the capital's specialist libraries, the **Wellcome Collection's** (183 Euston Road, NW1; ✆ **020 7611 8722**) grisly cornucopia of medical materials—including books, paintings, and drawings—is one of the best and most easily accessible. Staff also offer free tours and workshops to explain the intricacies of this unique collection. See p. 109.

5 Best Shopping Deals

- **Best Market Bargains:** For markets, the basic rule of thumb is that the earlier they open, and the earlier you can be there, the better chance you have of snaffling a bargain. This particularly applies to the capital's three huge wholesale emporiums, **Billingsgate** (for fish), **New Covent Garden** (for fruit, vegetables, and flowers), and **Smithfield** (for meat). All begin their cut-price trading around 4am. See p. 194, p. 195 & p. 195.

- **Best Market Browsing:** With its giant antique market and sections devoted to clothes, records, books, bric-a-brac, fruit and veg, flowers, and household goods, **Portobello Market** (Portobello Road, W10) is a browser's paradise. See p. 200.

- **Best Second-Hand Bookshop: Oxfam's** Bloomsbury flagship (12 Bloomsbury Street, WC1; ✆ **020 7637 4610**) boasts more than 12,000 cut-price titles. It is such a slick operation that you can sometimes forget it's a charity shop (and you're therefore allowed to feel good about your budget browsing). See p. 210.

- **Best Thrift Store Bargains:** Like a vast evidence room for crimes against fashion, the **East End Thrift Store's** (Unit 1A, Watermans Building Assembly Passage, E1; ✆ **020 7423 9700**) warehouse-like confines are filled with vintage bargains, most going for less than £10. See p. 213.

6 Best Entertainment & Nightlife

- **Best Free Classical Concerts:** At the **LSO's** 'Discovery' concerts, the orchestra is the London Symphony, the venue is a beautifully converted church (161 Old Street, EC1; ✆ **020 7588 1116**), the time is midday (giving you the chance to fit a bit of culture into your working day), and the price is zero. What's not to like? See p. 238.

- **Best Free Music/Cheap Drink Combo:** The music is supplied by the Rough Trade Shop, an Indie legend since the late 1970s, while the venue and drinks come courtesy of the **Notting Hill Arts Club** (21 Notting Hill Gate, W11; ✆ **020 7460 4459**) every Saturday from 4 to 8pm. See p. 230.

- **Best Cheap Opera:** A tenner buys you a cheap seat for a production by the ENO at the **London Coliseum** (St. Martin's Lane, WC2; ✆ **0871 911 0200**) between Monday and Thursday. You'll be well to the rear, but thankfully opera singers tend to be quite loud. See p. 237.

- **Best 10p Theatre Ticket:** Yes, you read that right. Eight 10p theatre tickets go on sale at the **Royal Court Theatre** (50–51 Sloane Square, SW1; ✆ **020 7565 5000**) 1 hour before curtain-up. That's a ridiculous bargain. See p. 247.

- **Best Lunchtime Theatre:** Shake up your routine with a 'secret' midday performance of experimental theatre at the **Southwark Playhouse** (Shipwright Yard, SE1; ✆ **020 7620 3494**). For just £5, they even throw in a free sandwich. See p. 248.

- **Best Free World Music:** Explore the music and rhythms of foreign lands, from Chinese opera to Malinese *ngoni*, at **SOAS's** (Thornhaugh Street, WC1; ✆ **020 7637 2388**) monthly showcases. See p. 236.

- **Best Free Cinema:** Southwark's **Roxy Bar & Screen** (128–132 Borough High Street, SE1; ✆ **020 7407 4057**) serves up a mixture of classic oldies (free), recent releases (£3), and good food. Time it right and you could accompany your stroll down celluloid lane with a pair of 2-for-1 cocktails. They also screen classic TV comedies some lunchtimes for free. See p. 252.

- **Best Free Comedy:** Head to the bar of the prestigious **Theatre Royal Stratford East** (Theatre Square, E15; ✆ **020 8534 0310**) for a mixture of circuit regulars, newbies, and the occasional big name, particularly during July's Edinburgh Festival preview season. See p. 256.

- **Best Free Poetry:** Quality vegetarian cuisine and earnest rhymes are delivered at the **Poetry Café** (22 Betterton Street, WC2; ℰ **020 7420 9888**) every Tuesday at 'Poetry Unplugged', one of the capital's premier open-mic poetry events. If you've ever wanted to unleash your stanzas on the nation, this is your chance. All would-be versifiers welcome. See p. 258.

- **Best Free Clubbing:** The legendary **Dogstar** (389 Coldharbour Lane, SW9; ℰ **020 7733 7515**)

in Brixton seems to spend as much time naming its evenings as it does picking the music: Audiosushi, Dance Biscuit Live, and Deep Fried on Wednesday are just some names the marketing folk thought up. It's free throughout the week and before 10pm on Fridays and Saturdays. See p. 267.

- **Best Cheap Cabaret:** Standing tickets are just £5 from Tuesday to Thursday for some cheeky cabaret and burlesque at the **Volupté Lounge** (7–9 Norwich Street, EC4; ℰ **020 7831 1622**). It's London's very own basement Moulin Rouge. See p. 271.

FREE CALENDAR OF EVENTS

It should come as little surprise that a city of London's size and status does a lot of celebrating. The powers-that-be recognise a happy metropolis is one that regularly gets to blow off a little steam (hence the number of free events sponsored by the Mayor's office). Bread and circuses are, it seems, still official policy in modern Londinium.

Festivals also provide a great way of discovering and celebrating London's cultural variety. All of the capital's main ethnic groups have their special days, when you're invited to join the party, try the food, listen to the music, and generally help us all get along a little better. Many of the most prestigious events are centred on Trafalgar Square—no self-respecting celebration or parade ends anywhere else. In fact, should you be stuck for something to do on a weekend, it might be an idea just to pop down and see what's happening. There's usually something going on, even if it's just a confused-looking person standing on a plinth. The London Tourist Board's website has a detailed, up-to-date list of what's on when: www.visitlondon.com/events/calendar.

DAILY EVENTS

Ceremony of the Keys   During the past 700 years the Tower of London has served many purposes: it's been a royal palace, a fortress, a prison, a mint, an armoury, the repository of the crown jewels and, of course, a tourist attraction. Throughout that time, however, there has been one constant: the ritual locking of the palace gates has happened without fail at 9:53pm, save for one sorry World War II interlude when particularly fierce bombing delayed it for a few minutes. You can follow the yeoman warders on their procession around the gates for free, but to do so you'll have to apply at least 2 months in advance. Despite the brevity of the operation—arrive at 9:30pm and it's all over by 10pm, when the last post sounds—it's extremely popular. Apply in writing: you can request two tickets and will need to supply two possible dates when you can attend, and enclose a stamped addressed envelope. Ceremony of the Keys Office, Tower of London, EC3. ✆ **020 3166 6278.** www.hrp.org.uk/TowerOfLondon/WhatsOn/ceremonyof thekeys.aspx. Tube: Tower Hill. DLR: Tower Gateway. Daily 9:30–10pm.

Changing of the Guard   Replacing one set of guards with another could be done quickly, privately, and with the minimum of fuss—but where would the fun be in that? In these democratic times, royalty is all about putting on a show, and keeping the postcard industry in business. This particular performance sees 40 troops from the Foot Guards Regiment, resplendent in bright scarlet coats, swords, and bearskin hats, assemble at Wellington barracks at 11:27am, before marching down to Buckingham Palace to replace the men stationed there. It's now essentially pointless, but rather pretty. If it looks too crowded outside Buck House, try moving to a vantage point on Birdcage Walk on the south side of St. James's Park. Buckingham Palace, SW1. www.royalcollection.org.uk. Tube: St. James's Park. Tube/Train: Victoria. Daily 11:30am May–July, alternate days for rest of the year.

INTERMITTENT (AND LOUD) EVENTS

Gun Salutes   A number of state ceremonies each year are celebrated with a gun salute, when a contingent of cavalry from The Horse Artillery ride into **Hyde Park** (occasionally Green Park) at midday to unleash a fearsome 41-gun volley. Not to be outdone, the Honourable Artillery do the same, minus the horses but with 62 rounds, at 1pm at the **Tower of London.** If any of the events falls on a Sunday, the salute is held on the following Monday instead, the exception being Remembrance Sunday when one round is fired to start 2 minutes of silence at 11am, and another to finish it. Hyde Park, W2; Green Park, W1; Tower of London, EC3. www.royal parks.org.uk/tourists/gun_salutes.cfm. Tube: Hyde Park Corner (for Hyde Park), Green Park (for Green Park), or Tower Hill (for Tower of London). Accession Day (6th February), Queen's Birthday (21st April), Coronation Day (2nd June), Queen's Official Birthday (first, second, or third Saturday in June, fired in Green Park at 11am), Duke of Edinburgh's Birthday (10th June), State Opening of Parliament (November or December, fired at Green Park), Lord Mayor's Show (10th November), Remembrance Sunday (closest Monday to 11th November).

JANUARY

New Year's Day Parade   If you're anything like me, the last thing you want to experience on New Year's morning is a load of happy, dancing people making a tremendous amount of noise. For those who've paced themselves a little better the night before, an estimated 10,000 performers march, dance, and play their way with ill-fitting exuberance through London's cold winter streets. Expect marching bands, decorated floats, and colourful costumes. The parade follows a 2-mile route from Parliament Square to Green Park, via Trafalgar Square, Regent Street, and Piccadilly. There's ticketed seating at the start and end but it's free to watch at any other point. Parliament Square, Parliament Street, Whitehall, Trafalgar Square, Regent Street, Piccadilly, Green Park. © **020 8566 8586.** www.londonparade.co.uk. Tube: Green Park (for the end of the parade). 1st January, midday.

FEBRUARY

Chinese New Year   In late January or early February, depending on the lunar calendar, London plays host to one of the largest Chinese New Year festivals outside of China. The 2-week blowout sees numerous free events, including traditional lion dance parades and firework displays. It's also the most exuberant time of year to check out the restaurants of Chinatown (p. 58). Gerrard Street, W1. ⓒ **020 7851 6686.** www.chinatownchinese.co.uk. Tube: Leicester Square. Late January–early February.

The Great Spitalfields Pancake Race   Head down to Dray Walk, just off Brick Lane, on Shrove Tuesday to watch various fancy-dress teams take part in a special charity relay race, one in which they're expected to toss a pancake in a frying pan as they run. If you fancy joining them, you'll need to gather three like-minded friends, register with Alternative Arts, who organise the event, and either be sponsored or bring down a charity donation on the day. Should you prove victorious you'll be awarded with your very own frying pan. Dray Walk, Old Truman Brewery, Brick Lane, E1. ⓒ **020 7375 0441.** www.alternativearts.co.uk. Tube/Train: Liverpool Street. Shrove Tuesday, 12:30pm.

March

The Boat Race   Rowing crews from Oxford and Cambridge universities battle it out for the umpteenth time along a 4½-mile stretch of the course cheered on by 250,000 spectators. See p. 271.

St. Patrick's Day Parade   It begins with marching bands from Ireland and the UK making their tightly co-ordinated way down Piccadilly and Regent Street to Trafalgar Square. Next, things kick off properly with music and dancing on the main stage—and *plenty* of drinking. Most of the local pubs are decked out in green and, if they know what's good for them, offer deals on Guinness. Trafalgar Square, WC2. ⓒ **020 7983 4000.** www.london.gov.uk/stpatricksday. Tube/Train: Charing Cross. 17th March (or a date close).

April

London Marathon   It's both one of the world's best-attended sporting competitions, with 35,000 people slogging their way round a 26-mile course, and one of the UK's biggest fundraisers. Elite athletes aside, most of the entrants are running for charity. And, just to make things interesting, some decide to run the whole route wearing costume. See p. 273.

May

Arts Unwrapped   Over 3 weekends between May and June, 40 art studios, representing more than 1,000 individual artists, open their doors to members of the public. These weekends provide a fascinating opportunity to see a range of artworks being created—paintings, photographs, sculptures, films, furniture, animations, and more. Many studios lay on special events and host workshops where visitors can try their hand at certain crafts. Check the website for details. Venues across London. ℂ **020 7274 7774.** www.artsun wrapped.com. Mid-May–mid-June.

Bengali New Year   In Bangladesh and West Bengal, where this festival is principally celebrated, events are held on the traditional date of 14th April. London's version, the Baishakhi Mela, doesn't take place until the second Sunday in May, so as to lessen (only slightly, you'd have to say) the chance of rain. Festivities are the largest of their kind outside Bangladesh and centre on the so-called Banglatown area by Brick Lane in East London. Things start with the Grand Parade, a procession by members of the community dressed in colourful traditional clothes and accompanied by musicians and dancers, who make their way from Allen Gardens to Weavers Field by way of Brick Lane. Many of the area's curry restaurants set up stalls offering samples. Festivities continue with traditional Bengali music, plus modern examples of Bhangra and Bollywood performed on specially erected stages. Brick Lane, E1. www.melafestival.com/whatson/BaishakhiMela.php. Tube/Train: Liverpool Street. Second Sunday in May.

Covent Garden May Fayre and Puppet Festival   A whole day devoted to celebrating the dubious charms of squeaky-voiced, wife-beating Mr Punch. The event is held at St. Paul's Church (also known as the 'actors' church'; p. 126) close to the spot where Samuel Pepys made the first recorded sighting of a Punch and Judy show back in 1662. It begins sedately enough with a procession and a church service and, from midday, 5 hours are given over to a succession of Punch and Judy shows and puppet workshops. The event ends with maypole dancing and folk music. And that, apparently, 'is the way to do it'. St. Paul's Church Garden, Bedford Street, WC2. ℂ **020 7375 0441.** www.alternativearts.co.uk. Tube: Covent Garden. Second Sunday in May.

JUNE

Greenwich & Docklands International Festival   London's largest celebration of outdoor theatre takes place over 4 days at various venues in Greenwich and Docklands, including Canary Wharf, the National Maritime Museum, the Old Royal Observatory, and the Thames itself. Acts are difficult to categorise, but expect lots of dancing in strange costumes, stilt-walking, crazy-costumed jugglers, acrobats sliding down ropes, music and light shows, plus plenty of unusual sights: an 18m (60ft) caterpillar, a 6m (20ft) high queen on a penny farthing cycling along the river, and giant video projections on many of the waterfront buildings. The whole thing resembles a maritime version of Cirque du Soleil. Greenwich, SE10. ℂ **020 8305 1818.** www.festival.org. Train/DLR: Greenwich. DLR: Cutty Sark. Four days in late June.

BP Summer Screens   Opera and ballet performances beamed live from the Royal Opera House to big screens in Trafalgar Square and Canary Wharf. See p. 237.

Coin Street Festival   Three-month-long free arts festival organised by the Coin Street Community Builders, the non-profit organisation that runs the Oxo Tower and Gabriel's Wharf. It features plenty of live music as well as fancy-dress parades and arts and crafts workshops. Bernie Spain Gardens, SE1. ℂ **020 7021 1600.** www.coin street.org/coinstreet_festival.aspx. Tube/Train: Waterloo. June–August.

Exhibition Road Music Day   This celebration of music from around the world may take place in South Kensington, but its origins lie across the Channel. It's essentially a British version of France's *Fête de la Musique,* launched a few years ago by an organisation dedicated to all things Gallic, the Institut Français. The day sees performances taking place on the street, in Hyde Park, and at many prestigious local institutions, including the Natural History Museum, the Science Museum, the V&A, the Royal College of Music, Imperial College, the Ismaili Centre, the Goethe-Institut, and the Institut itself. Pretty much every style of music imaginable is represented, from folk, classical, and jazz to world music, swing, and hip hop. Exhibition Road, SW7. ℂ **020 7591 3000.** www.exhibitionroadmusicday.org. Tube: South Kensington. Closest Sunday to 21st June.

Trooping the Colour   The Queen's official birthday is celebrated by a glorious piece of pointless pomp. During Trooping the Colour (not Trooping 'of' the Colour) the Queen rides from Buckingham Palace down The Mall in a horse-drawn coach (until the 1980s, she rode side-saddle on horseback) to inspect a regiment of the Household Division displaying their flag, or colour. There's lots of stiff, smartly synchronised marching, followed by an RAF fly-past and a gun salute in Green Park (p. 14). The Mall, SW1. ⓒ **020 7414 2479.** www.royal.gov.uk. Tube: St. James's Park, Green Park. First, second, or third Saturday in June.

Paradise Gardens   Emerging out of 'Fusion East', a 3-year cultural project funded by various East End boroughs, Paradise Gardens is an annual free festival in Victoria Park. It's based *very* loosely on a Victorian village fête, albeit on a much larger scale with music from around the world, circus acts, urban dance troops, a design tent where Hoxton hipsters do their cutting-edge thing and, perhaps the only true Victorian touch, vintage steam train rides. The local community turns out in droves to support the event, which grows in popularity by the year. Victoria Park, E3. ⓒ **020 7387 1203.** www. paradisegardens.org.uk. Tube: Mile End. Third weekend in June, midday–10:30pm.

City of London Festival   If you're interested in either classical music or architecture, this festival will have something to intrigue you; if by chance you have a passion for both, then make this a red-letter event. From late June to early July various historic venues in the Square Mile play host to concerts. Venues across the City of London, E1. ⓒ **020 7583 3585.** www.colf.org. Three weeks from late June–early July.

JULY

Pride Parade   This is London's largest LGBT event and, if estimates of a million-plus participants are true, the UK's largest outdoor event. The parade is the culmination of the 2-week Pride London Festival—a mixture of films, theatre, walks, talks, and concerts—and sees a grand procession of people marching a 100m (328ft)—long rainbow flag from Baker Street through the West End to Trafalgar Square. Music continues late into the night, usually concluding with a performance by the London Gay Symphony Orchestra. Trafalgar Square, WC2. ⓒ **0844 884 2439.** www.pride london.org. Tube/Train: Charing Cross. One Saturday in early July.

The Big Dance   More a giant keep-fit class than a celebration of rhythmic grace, the Big Dance is a week-long series of events and workshops designed to get sedentary Londoners shaking their legs. Various styles are showcased at several venues, and in the past have included ballroom dancing on Regent's Park bandstand, rock 'n' rolling at Kensington Palace, contemporary dance on the steps of St. Paul's, and, the main event, a giant synchronised (to a point) 2-day dance-off in Trafalgar Square. Venues across London. www. london.gov.uk/bigdance. One week in early July.

Shoreditch Festival   Not, as you might expect, a narrowly targeted celebration of wilfully dishevelled hair and obscure underground music, but a big, family-oriented shindig. Venues in and around Shoreditch Park host tea dances, a dog show (prizes are awarded for the 'most glam dog' and the 'best old dog'), children's play areas, and picnic performances by the Royal Philharmonic Orchestra and the English National Ballet—plus a few art installations, and a bit of experimental music to keep the natives happy. Shoreditch Park, N1. ✆ **020 7033 8520.** www.shoreditchfestival. org.uk. Tube: Old Street. Four days in mid-July.

iTunes Festival   This internet generation festival books out Camden's Roundhouse for the entire month of July, staging two acts a night—that's 62 concerts over 31 days from both up-and-comers and international superstars (recently Oasis, Snow Patrol, and Franz Ferdinand). Tickets are free and available on a first-come, first-served basis from the website. For anyone who misses out, all shows are recorded and available to download from the iTunes Store for between £2.99 and £4.99. Chalk Farm Road, NW1. ✆ **0844 482 8008.** www.ituneslive.co.uk. Tube: Chalk Farm.

Edinburgh Previews   During the last 2 weeks of July, an army of comedians put their acts through basic training at venues across the capital, in preparation for full-scale Edinburgh assaults the following month. See p. 256.

More Music at the Scoop   Three weeks of free music performances at the Scoop Amphitheatre next to City Hall. See p. 234.

AUGUST

London Mela   Gunnersbury Park in West London is the venue for the world's biggest celebration of Indian culture outside India. A mixture of music, circus acts, dancing (including mass Bollywood dance-alongs), comedy, and food (lots of food) attracts an estimated 70,000 people. The main stage plays host to acts from the subcontinent, as well as home-grown talent and 'fusion' performers from across the world. There's also a special area for families and children. Gunnersbury Park, W3. ℭ **020 7387 1203.** www.london-mela.org. Tube: South Ealing. One Sunday in mid-August.

Notting Hill Carnival   Talk of its imminent demise is seemingly always premature: Europe's biggest street party keeps getting bigger. What started as a small-scale celebration of Afro-Caribbean culture back in 1964 has since grown into a loud, proud, noisy, colourful, gyrating celebration of summer. Proceedings kick off in miniature on Sunday with a Children's Day Parade, followed by the main event on the Monday. Expect over-the-top costumes, elaborate floats, pumping sound systems, exuberant dancing, plenty of food and drink, and seemingly endless crowds. Notting Hill, W11. ℭ **020 7727 0072.** www.rbkc.gov.uk. Tube: Ladbroke Grove, Westbourne Park, Notting Hill Gate. August Bank Holiday Sunday and Monday.

SEPTEMBER

Regent Street Festival   For 1 day each September, the cars and buses of Regent Street are replaced by thousands of people who come to enjoy the food, drink, and music of this decade-old street festival. Many shops offer entertainment for the crowds, including Hamleys toy store which lays on face painters, balloon artists, stilt-walkers, and even a mini Ferris wheel. Regent Street, W1. ℭ **020 7287 9601.** www.regentstreetonline.com. Tube: Oxford Circus, Piccadilly Circus. One Sunday in late September.

Thames Festival   Sponsored by the Mayor of London's office, this riverside spectacular marks the end of summer with a varied assortment of events held between Tower Bridge and Westminster Bridge, including live music, circus performances, lantern processions, and firework displays. 'Feast on the Bridge' sees Southwark Bridge closed to traffic, and lined with food stalls. ℭ **020 7928 8998.** www.thamesfestival.org. One weekend in mid-September.

Open House Weekend   Organised by Open House, a body dedicated to bringing the best of the city's architecture to the attention of the public, this weekend sees hundreds of usually private buildings open their doors—for free. The range of participating properties is huge, from domestic houses, schools, and banks to some of the capital's architectural icons, including 30 St. Mary Axe ('The Gherkin') and Mansion House. Most operate an open-access policy—just turn up and queue (expect queues for the very popular locations to be up to an hour or two). Others may require advance booking for guided tours. See p. 128.

OCTOBER

Diwali   The 5-day 'Festival of Light' is an important occasion for several London religions, including Hinduism and Sikhism. Focal points include the Shri Swaminarayan Mandir temple in Neasden and Trafalgar Square, where colourful decorations, dance performances, and floating lanterns are rolled out. The National Gallery joins in the fun with its own lantern display, and Diwali-related storytelling for children. Trafalgar Square, WC2. ℂ **020 7983 4000.** www.london.gov.uk/mayor/diwali/index.jsp. Tube/Train: Charing Cross.

NOVEMBER

Bonfire Night   Thankfully, the dodgy Catholic versus Protestant origins of the 5th November celebrations have been largely forgotten, and today it's just a good excuse to warm the winter air with bonfires and blast shed-loads of fireworks up into the night sky. Free organised displays take place throughout London at venues including Battersea Park and Alexandra Palace—the latter also provides a good vantage point for watching displays, both public and domestic, across the rooftops of the capital. Venues across the capital. 5th November.

London to Brighton Veteran Car Run   Formula 1 it's not. This gentle pootle between the capital and the coast is open only to cars built before 1905. (When first held in 1896, this must have seemed like the cutting edge of the motoring future.) The event starts early—out of necessity as the cars don't move very fast—at around sunrise from Hyde Park. Westminster Bridge is one of the best vantage points to watch the vehicles trundling along in all their retro glory—or, often as not, broken down at the side of the road. You can also see the cars parked on Regent Street the day before the race. Hyde Park, W2. ℂ **01327 856 024.** www.lbvcr.com. Tube: Hyde Park Corner. First weekend in November.

The Lord Mayor's Show   It's a venerable and time-honoured tradition and, like most of our venerable and time-honoured traditions, almost completely meaningless in the modern age. Officially, the event marks the presentation of the Lord Mayor of London (symbolic head of the City of London, not the Mayor of London) at the Royal Courts of Justice, where he swears allegiance to the monarch. Unofficially, it's an excuse for said Mayor to ride around in his big, gold coach (on display in the Museum of London for 364 days of the year) at the head of a grand parade between Mansion House and St. Paul's. All this is followed by a firework display on the Thames between Blackfriars Bridge and Waterloo Bridge. Through the City. ℭ **020 7332 3456.** www.lordmayorsshow.org. Tube: St. Paul's, Bank, Mansion House. Mid-November.

DECEMBER

Portobello Winter Music Festival   Helping to keep the winter blues away with a bit of blues (and dance, and indie, and folk, and world music), this pre-Christmas jamboree is a cross between a record fair and a mini-festival, with stalls selling rare vinyl (including one operated by the Rough Trade shop) and lots of live music and DJs. All events are free till 7pm, after which a small 'donation' is requested. The Bridge, 4–8 Acklam Road, W10. www.portobellowinterfest. com. Tube: Ladbroke Grove. Friday to Sunday in mid-December.

Christmas in London   Free festive sources of fun include the tacky lights of Oxford Street, the (usually slightly) more tasteful illuminations of Regent Street, the window displays of Hamleys, Harrods, and Fortnum and Mason, and the nightly carols sung beneath a giant Christmas tree in Trafalgar Square—donated each year by Norway as a thank you for Britain's support during World War II. The West End all month.

New Year's Eve   If you want to brave the crowds, the drunkenness, and the endless journey home, there are two main focuses for the capital's New Year's Eve celebrations: Trafalgar Square, to hear the midnight bongs of Big Ben; and, the more popular choice these days, the riverbank and bridges opposite the London Eye where the midnight firework display takes place. You'll need to claim your vantage point early. Public transport is free from midnight until around 4:30am. 31st December.

The Edward Lear Hotel, formerly the home of the Victorian artist and writer.

CHEAP SLEEPS

You probably think this is going to be a short chapter; after all, London's hotels can be fiendishly expensive, averaging around £125 a night for a double room. The good news is that this price has come down around 10% since the financial meltdown of 2008. The bad news is that it's still a long way short of what most people would consider reasonable. Still, there's plenty you can do to cut your bill even further: make sure you do your research; book as far in advance as possible (or at the last second); and remember, the further from the centre you stay, the cheaper your room is likely to be, although you will need to factor in travelling costs into town, which can quickly mount up. Perhaps most importantly, you need to settle on a minimum level of comfort. Are only the finest facilities and softest beds good enough for your pampered frame, or can you put up with a bit less, a whole lot of noise, and maybe the odd broken spring for the sake of a bargain? If it's the latter then hostelling could be the answer, providing some of the cheapest accommodation going, often right in the centre. And if you're here on an extended trip, it may be worth looking into renting an apartment or taking part in a home swap, which often provide the biggest savings of all.

1 Inn for a Penny—Hotels & B & Bs

There are no real hotel seasons in London: prices tend to stay high year round. There may be savings to be grabbed just after Christmas and away from the peak summer months, but to define these periods as a 'low season' would be to overestimate the reductions you can expect. Geography is a far more telling guide to price. London's cheapest hotels tend to cluster on certain streets like accommodating vultures. In the vicinity of major train stations—Victoria, Paddington, and King's Cross especially—they are guaranteed a steady stream of tired foreign visitors looking for somewhere cheap to stay. Bear in mind when hunting for hotels, that London is short on space, so rooms are often small, parking extremely limited (and expensive), and there are few gardens (forget outdoor pools or tennis courts). However, Wi-Fi access, often provided free, is becoming ever more widespread. For an 'affordable' hotel, we have set a limit of £90 per night for a double room with a private bathroom.

BLOOMSBURY & KING'S CROSS

The stretch of Gower Street just south of University College London is the principal thoroughfare for B & B bargains in Bloomsbury. Otherwise there are a good few hostels, which grow evermore grim and downmarket the closer to King's Cross you travel.

AFFORDABLE

★ **Arosfa** Previously a simple and rather dowdy B & B, the Arosfa has recently gone all boutiquey with new furniture and slick decor. Thankfully, prices have stayed resolutely downmarket. Some rooms are a bit on the small side (particularly the bathrooms), but everything

Dorm Free—Hostelling

YHA Hostels

If you don't mind foregoing a bit of comfort, privacy, and peace and quiet, you can find a bed in a hostel dormitory much cheaper than in a hotel. Everything is relative, of course: 'cheaper', in this instance, doesn't necessarily mean 'cheap'. London's hostels are among the most expensive in the world, typically around £12 to £18 for a bed in an independent establishment, rising to £19 to £25 (not including breakfast) for a space in one of the seven London hostels owned by the Youth Hostelling Association (www.yha.org.uk). Despite their relatively high prices, YHA hostels are extremely popular and, without pre-booking, you're unlikely to have a private room, or possibly even space in a dorm. If you're not a member of the YHA, or its affiliate Hostelling International (www.hihostels.com), you'll have to join (£15.95 or £9.95 for under 26s) if you want to avoid paying a non-member supplement of around £3 every time you stay in a hostel. Note that YHA dorms are segregated.

Independent Hostels

While YHA hostels may not be the most exciting of accommodation options, you at least know what you're getting, and can confidently expect the facilities to be of a certain standard. Independent hostels are more of a gamble. Some are the equal of anything the YHA can offer (if not superior), but quite a few are a whole smelly heap worse with fewer and shabbier amenities, tattier decor, and grimmer atmospheres. For these places, price is usually a good indicator of what to expect. The cheaper your dorm bed, the less time you may want to spend sleeping there. Having said that, many independent hostels do offer a less stuffy atmosphere than their YHA counterparts—where drinking is not usually allowed and all dorms are single-sex—which is a plus in many visitors' eyes. For user reviews of London's hostels check out www.hostelz.com, www.hostelworld.com, and www.hostellondon.com.

now feels fresh and clean. Indeed, you can find something very similar but with considerably tattier rooms and for a much higher price elsewhere on this B & B-heavy stretch of road. Extra touches, such as

Hotel Booking Websites

Visit London (www.visitlondon.com) and LondonTown.com (www.londontown.com) both have comprehensive bookable hotel databases. The sites also carry a range of advertised deals, the availability of which is often more restricted than the excited marketing copy might suggest. All the main holiday deal websites—www.lastminute.com, www.travelocity.co.uk, www.expedia.co.uk, and so on—have extensive hotel listings, and www.laterooms.com is a dedicated hotel room specialist. Perhaps the site with the best potential deals is www.priceline.co.uk. It works like this: pick the area of town and grade of hotel you want, then bid your price. How much cheaper than the standard rate you bid is entirely up to you. At this point the site asks for your credit card details and searches your chosen area. If your offer is accepted by one of the hotels, a room is automatically booked. However, the benefit of a cheaper rate means *you can't back out*. The room is non-refundable. Great savings are possible, perhaps a night in a four-star for less than £50, but you've no say which specific hotel you get. It's the luck of the draw, so pick your area of town carefully and bid wisely. While searching the web, watch out for sites proffering 'cheap deals in central London', by which many of them actually mean 'moderate deals more than 10 miles from central London'. Be sure to check the location of any hotel on a map before booking. Remember many hotels offer deals if you book direct through their websites.

free fruit and water in the room, coupled with the small garden at the rear and friendly staff, make this a genuinely outstanding property. Breakfast and Wi-Fi access are included in the room rate.

83 Gower Street, WC1. ℂ **020 7636 2115.** Fax 020 7323 5141. www.arosfalondon.com. 15 rooms. Double from £82. Credit cards JCB, MC, V. Tube: Goodge Street. **Amenities:** Lounge, internet access (Wi-Fi), garden. *In room:* TV.

Hotel Cavendish   The walk-up rate for a double at the Cavendish is a perfectly reasonable £90, but if you book online far enough in advance this can drop to £65, which is quite a deal. The rooms are a little cramped, as they always are in converted Georgian townhouses, but spotless and surprisingly stylish. There's a lounge and, best of all, a walled garden. The room rate includes full English breakfast and Wi-Fi access. FINE PRINT Wi-Fi is available from the lobby only; you pay for it in your room.

75 Gower Street, WC1. ℂ **020 7636 9079.** Fax 020 7580 3609. www.hotel cavendish.com. 18 rooms. Double £65–£90. Credit cards AE, DC, MC, V. Tube: Goodge Street. **Amenities:** Breakfast/dining room, garden, internet access. *In room:* TV, telephone, Wi-Fi, hairdryer, desk, tea and coffee facilities.

Ridgemount Hotel One of a glut of B & Bs occupying this Georgian terrace, the Ridgemount is a bit boxy and basic, with only 15 en-suite rooms. But with prices for a double starting at just £60, it's about as good a bargain as you can find around here. The friendly owners are always ready with maps and advice, and extras include free breakfast (full English of course) and Wi-Fi access.

65–67 Gower Street, WC1. ℂ **020 7636 1141.** Fax 020 7636 2558. www.ridge mounthotel.co.uk. 32 rooms, 17 with private baths. Double without/with private bath £60/£78. Credit cards MC, V. Tube: Goodge Street. **Amenities:** Lounge, garden. *In room:* TV, hairdryer.

Cheap Sleeps

Ashlee House Slickly managed, independent hostel housed in a former office block on the edge of Bloomsbury. It has a lively, youthful ambience, which it helps to foster

Flashes, Tweets & Feeds

Look out for so-called 'flash' sales on the internet. Hotel booking sites like www.hotelconnect. co.uk, and some individual hotels, sometimes offer crazy deals (I've seen four-star rooms for £5 and hostel beds for 5p). As the name suggests, these sales happen quickly; you need to get online and book as soon as they open because rooms are normally all snapped up within an hour or two of the deal going live. Finding out when sales are taking place is, of course, the hard part. The best option is to let others do the searching for you. You can subscribe to free newsletters from deal-scanning sites such as http://uk.travelzoo. com, www.dealchecker.co.uk, www.hotukdeals.com, and www. moneysavingexpert.com: they will alert you as and when flash sales, or other London deals, become available. And, depending on how much of an IT expert you are, you could also subscribe to these sites' tweets via Twitter or even customise some RSS feeds to get deals sent direct to your desktop.

by offering discounts to guests at local bowling alleys and nightclubs. Prices start at a very decent £12 for a space in a 16-bed dorm (less than half of what you'll pay at some YHA hostels), although this rises to £17 at weekends. As is usually the case, the smaller the dorm, the higher the rates. All accommodation is in the form of bunk-beds, which come with their own reading lights and safety boxes. Both mixed and single-sex dorms are available. Breakfast is included in the price, and Wi-Fi is available from 50p an hour.

261–265 Grays Inn Road, WC1. ℂ 020 7833 9400. Fax 020 7833 9677. www.ashlee house.co.uk. 171 beds in rooms sleeping 1–16. From £12 per person. Credit cards DC, JCB, MC, V, VE. Tube/Train: King's Cross. **Amenities:** 24-hour reception, luggage storage, self-catering kitchen, laundry facilities, internet access with Wi-Fi.

The Clink Hostel   Hostel living doesn't have to mean slumming it on a bare minimum. This recently opened place, set in the atmospheric confines of a former Victorian courthouse (and prison), offers a modern alternative to the backpacking norm. The building has been revamped in a very 21st-century, not to say oxymoronic, way with 'designer dorms' filled with stylish sturdy furniture, including 'pod beds' designed to provide sleepers with more privacy than typical bunks. The whole thing has been done with a great deal of wit and care – the courtrooms now house an internet café and TV room, while the old cells are private bedrooms.

78 King's Cross Road, WC1. ℂ **020 7183 9400.** Fax 020 7713 0735. www.clinkhostel. com. 100 beds. From £15 per person. Credit cards MC, V. Tube/Train: King's Cross.

The Generator   Like a giant accommodation factory, this legendary place is London's largest hostel, with a mighty 800 beds spread amid harsh neon-lit decor perhaps best described as 'futuristic industrial'. Still, you don't come here for the fittings. You come for the prices, which are pretty low, starting at £15 for a bunk in a 12-bed dorm (including continental breakfast). You come for the large bar, which is always packed and where events (pool competitions, bikini parties, and the like) are staged nightly. And, so long as you don't make too big a night of it, you come for the free 2½ hour walking tour of London's main tourist sites given daily at 10:15am. It's a great place to meet fellow partying travellers, particularly during the bar's pre-9pm happy hour when the £1 discount on most drinks helps to oil the social wheels. Both mixed and female-only dorms are available.

37 Tavistock Place, WC1. ℂ **020 7388 7666.** Fax 020 7388 7644. www.generatorhostels. com. 800 beds in rooms sleeping 1–12. From £15 per person including breakfast.

Youth (only) Hostels

The five-strong Astor hostel chain enforces a strict age limit for its guests, catering solely for 18 to 35 year olds (who upon arrival must show valid ID to prove their inexperience). Should older travellers wish to join in, they can apply to stay. Permission is granted at the discretion of the management, presumably after the applicant has performed a suitably youthful dance or demonstrated they know how to use a mobile phone. Unsurprisingly, the Astors are big on partying and socialising (in fact, maybe the older generation is better off out of it). The Astor Kensington is perhaps the most boisterous example. For somewhere a bit quieter try the Astor Museum near the British Museum, where the accommodation is functional but clean and well maintained. Extras include free continental breakfast, free luggage storage, and 40 minutes free internet access.

Locations:

Astor Kensington, 138 Cromwell Road, South Kensington, SW7. ℂ **020 7373 5138.** Fax 020 7373 5138. www.astorhostels.co.uk. 120 beds. Winter/Summer from £13/£15 per person weekdays in 10-room dorm, double from £30. Credit cards DC, JCB, MC, V, VE. Tube: Gloucester Road. **Amenities:** 24-hour reception, self-catering kitchen, internet access (Wi-Fi), telephones, luggage storage.

Astor Museum, 27 Montague Street, WC1. ℂ **020 7580 5360.** Fax 020 7636 7948. www.astorhostels.co.uk. 75 beds in 12 rooms sleeping 4–12. Winter/Summer from £15/£18 per person weekdays in a 12-bed dorm, twin rooms from £30. Credit cards DC, JCB, MC, V, VE. Tube: Holborn. **Amenities:** 24-hour reception, self-catering kitchen, internet access (Wi-Fi), telephones, luggage storage.

Credit cards DC, JCB, MC, V. Tube: Russell Square. **Amenities:** Bar, 24-hour lounge, internet access (including Wi-Fi), luggage storage.

St. Pancras YHA   This large building opposite the British Library used to be a police station and today is home to a suitably well-organised and secure hostel. Entry to its rooms and dorms is via a key-card system installed following refurbishment in the winter of 2008/9, which also saw the hostel's rooms given a lick of paint and a new café-bar added. Slightly away from London's main tourist areas, this markets itself as a quieter, family-friendly alternative to more central rivals, offering extra cots for under 3s and with triple-glazing to keep down the noise from busy Euston Road outside. FINE PRINT If you're looking to party you're better off heading to the two YHAs near Oxford Street (p. 32).

79–81 Euston Road, NW1. ℂ **0845 371 9344.** Fax 020 7388 6766. www.yha.org.uk. 34 rooms sleeping 2–6, 184 beds. £21.95 per person. Credit cards DC, JCB, MC, V, VE. Tube/Train: King's Cross, Euston. Train: St. Pancras. **Amenities:** TV lounge, cycle storage, café, laundry service, washing machines, luggage storage.

Smart NHS Russell Square Hostel The Smart Group operates six London hostels that are pretty much the exemplars of no-frills accommodation. Rooms are featureless and functional, while beds are somewhat small and often stacked three high, which can make getting into the top bunk quite an adventure at the end of the evening. However, you get what you pay for, and £7.99 for a bunk in the 24-bed dorm Russell Square branch essentially represents the best hostel deal going, especially when you consider that breakfast, bed linen, and Wi-Fi are included in the price. It's not the sort of hostel you're going to spend much time socialising in, but for a cheap stopover it does the trick.

70–72 Guilford Street, WC1. ℂ **020 7833 8818.** Fax 020 7221 9444. www.smartback packers.com. 290 beds. From £7.99 per person. Credit cards MC, V, VE. Tube: Russell Square. **Amenities:** 24-hour reception, self-catering kitchen, TV room, games room, internet access (Wi-Fi).

SOHO, PICCADILLY & FITZROVIA

Unsurprisingly, the centre of the West End can offer just a few decent budget choices, all of them hostels. You'll struggle to find a hotel double bedroom around here for under £100 at any time of year.

Cheap Sleeps

London Central YHA The newest and shiniest of the YHA's seven central London hostels, this lies a couple of minutes' walk north of Oxford Street. As you'd expect, it's modern looking and well equipped with funky decor, good showers, and free Wi-Fi. Its city-centre location, size (with room for up to 290 people), and 24-hour café-bar (complete with Nintendo Wii consoles for hire) make this a perfect choice for anyone interested in nightlife and meeting fellow travellers, but quite a poor one for anyone seeking a quiet base for a bit of gentle sightseeing.

104 Bolsover Street, W1. ⓒ **0845 371 9154.** Fax 0845 371 9155. www.yha.org.uk. 59 rooms sleeping 4–8. £24.50 per person. Credit cards DC, JCB, MC, V, VE. Tube: Great Portland Street. **Amenities:** Lounge, cycle store, shop, 24-hour café-bar, self-catering kitchen, laundry facilities, internet access (Wi-Fi), luggage storage.

Oxford Street YHA   Just off Oxford Street, this is one of the YHA's busiest, most bustling and most boisterous hostels. Having said that, most of the rooms sleep only four, so you shouldn't have too many sleepless nights. With just 75 available beds, you'll need to book well in advance, particularly in summer months.

4 Noel Street, W1. ⓒ **0845 371 9133.** Fax 020 7734 1657. www.yha.org.uk. 21 rooms sleeping 2–4, 75 beds. £24.50 per person. Credit cards DC, JCB, MC, V, VE. Tube: Oxford Circus. **Amenities:** TV lounge, shop, laundry service, washing machines, luggage storage.

Piccadilly Backpackers   First off, it has a great location right next to Piccadilly Circus. Secondly, it's pretty well equipped with room for up to 700 hostellers plus plenty of extras, such as an internet café, a TV lounge, luggage storage, and a travel shop. Thirdly, several of its dorms have pod beds which have been designed to give sleepers slightly (stress *slightly*) more privacy than is usual in a room accommodating nine other people. Fourthly, it is a bit basic, even for a hostel, with peeling paint and mattresses that are perhaps not the cleanest. But fifthly, and most importantly, prices start at £12 (minus £1 if you book online), making it perhaps the cheapest accommodation option in the entire West End.

12 Sherwood Street, W1. ⓒ **020 7434 9009.** Fax 020 7434 9010. www.piccadilly backpackers.com. 700 beds. From £11 per person. Credit cards AE, MC, V, VE. Tube: Piccadilly Circus. **Amenities:** Laundry facilities, internet café, travel shop, luggage storage, TV lounge, no curfew.

MARYLEBONE, PADDINGTON & NOTTING HILL

The streets surrounding Paddington station, particularly Sussex Gardens and Norfolk Square, are thick with budget B & Bs—some good, some indifferent, some truly awful, but all just a few minutes' walk from Hyde Park. There's also a glut of bargain places near Marble Arch, while to the west, Notting Hill has a few quirky little places on offer.

AFFORDABLE

Ashley Hotel Near Paddington Station, this is almost the archetypal budget B & B. Located on a leafy garden square filled with rival accommodation, the family-owned hotel boasts 54 rooms of all shapes and sizes spread throughout a converted Victorian house. Many are compact—think single-sized doubles and twins, often as not with adjoining beds to save space. Following a period of renovation all doubles now have en-suite facilities, even if some are on a reduced scale, and are fairly well equipped. Bathroom-less singles start at £40. The price includes continental breakfast.

15–17 Norfolk Square, W2. ℂ **020 7723 3375.** Fax 020 7723 9966. www.ashleyhotel london.com 54 rooms. Double £75. Credit cards MC, V. **Amenities:** Lounge, breakfast room. *In room:* TV, radio, telephone, tea and coffee facilities.

Columbia Hotel At £89 for a standard en-suite double or twin, this comes in just under budget. A large establishment spread over five interconnecting Victorian houses, the Columbia boasts an elegant, high-ceilinged lounge left over from when this was a well-to-do address. The bedrooms, however, are a touch more modest. Several are of a good size and well equipped, but many of the fixtures and fittings are old and a bit tatty. In truth, the hotel could do with a refit, so long as that doesn't put the prices up. On the plus side, some of the uppermost rooms have views of Hyde Park, continental breakfast is included in the room rate, and there's free Wi-Fi access in the lounge and bar.

95–99 Lancaster Gate, W2. ℂ **020 7402 0021.** Fax 020 7706 4691. www.columbia hotel.co.uk. 100 rooms. Double £89. Credit cards MC, V. Tube: Lancaster Gate. **Amenities:** Lounge, bar, breakfast room, internet access (Wi-Fi), luggage storage. *In room:* TV, telephone, tea and coffee facilities, hairdryer.

Edward Lear Hotel The former home of the 19th-century limerist and artist is now a decent budget hotel just a runcible spoon's throw from Hyde Park. It looks rather grand from the outside, with its flow-erboxes and blue plaque, but inside the rooms are a bit bare and frayed, though clean. Still, the staff are very friendly and the prices good—typically £80 for a bathroom-less double, which falls to just £63.50 in winter provided you stay at least 5 consecutive nights. Breakfast is included in the price and there's free internet access, albeit from a single computer in the guest lounge.

28–30 Seymour Street, W1. ℭ **020 7402 5401.** Fax 020 7706 3766. www.edlear.com.
32 rooms, 18 with private baths. Double without/with private bath £63.50–£80/£88.50–
£112.50. Credit cards AE, MC, V. Tube: Marble Arch. **Amenities:** Lounge, internet access,
breakfast room. *In room:* TV, radio, telephone, tea and coffee facilities.

Garden Court Hotel   Near Portobello Market, this family-run place
underwent a recent refurbishment which saw its facilities upgraded
and its rooms newly wallpapered in flowery patterns. Thankfully
prices have stayed low, starting at £76 for a bathroom-less double,
which is good value, particularly as the breakfast (buffet rather than
cooked) and Wi-Fi (access in the lounge) are included in the price.
Note that many of the rooms, especially the singles, are on the bijou
side of small. FINE PRINT If you want your own bathroom, prices shoot
up to £118 for a double.

30–31 Kensington Gardens Square, W2. ℭ **020 7229 2553.** Fax 020 7727 2749. www.
gardencourthotel.co.uk. 34 rooms, 16 with private bathroom. Double without/with
private bath £76/£118. Credit cards MC, V. **Amenities:** Breakfast room, garden, internet access (Wi-Fi). *In room:* TV, telephone, hairdryer.

Lincoln House Hotel   The longer you stay at the Lincoln House, a
cosy little place near Marble Arch, the cheaper it gets. Prices for the
smallest doubles start at £95, but drop to £89 if you book for more
than 7 nights. Its thickly carpeted, wood-panelled, iron banistered
interior has an antique, 'old London' feel. The rooms, all of which are
en suite, vary hugely from commodious family rooms to the tiny Cap-
tain's Cabin, a bizarre exercise in miniaturisation available for one
person only (as that's all that will fit, and probably then only if they
contort themselves) from £55. Free Wi-Fi is available in all rooms, but
breakfast is an extra £3.90. FINE PRINT Foreign guests can secure a 5%
discount if they pay in cash (British pounds).

33 Gloucester Place, W1. ℭ **020 7486 7630.** Fax 020 7486 0166. www.lincoln-house-
hotel.co.uk. 24 rooms. Double £89–£125. Credit cards AE, MC, V. **Amenities:** Breakfast room, internet access (Wi-Fi). *In room:* AC (in some), TV, telephone, fridge (in
some), tea and coffee facilities, hairdryer.

Portobello Gold   Above a bar-restaurant in the middle of the Portobello antique market are six decently priced rooms, sleeping two to
three people. Rates start at £70 if booked online (£80 walk-up), dropping to £60 if you stay more than 7 nights. The rooms are a touch
small with slightly worn fixtures and furniture, but no more than you'd

expect for the price. There's also a cute and cosy two-floor maison-
ette apartment with a kitchen, a bath, and even a roof garden with
great views. It's just £170 a night for four people (or £180 for six) if
booked online, which drops to £140/£150 for four/six people if
booked for more than 7 days—that's very good value. [FINE PRINT] The
location, plus the restaurant's AC units, make the rooms quite noisy.

95–97 Portobello Road, Notting Hill, W11. ☎ **020 7460 4910.** Fax 020 7243 6566.
www.portobellogold.com. Six rooms, one apartment. Double £60–£120. Credit cards
AE, MC, V. Tube: Notting Hill Gate, Ladbroke Grove. **Amenities:** Bar, restaurant, internet café, Wi-Fi. *In room:* TV, telephone.

St. David's Hotel   Remember this is a budget hotel, set your expectations accordingly, and you should be perfectly satisfied. Most rooms
are mini-sized and a bit raggedy in places, but generally fine. And, in
any case, it's the management who really make this place what it is,
with a friendly, can-I-do-anything-to-help attitude. A big full English
breakfast is included in the price, which starts at just £65 for a bathroom-less double.

14–20 Norfolk Square, W2. ☎ **020 7723 3856.** Fax 020 7723 4963. www.stdavids
hotels.com. 70 rooms. Double without/with private bath £65/£80. Credit cards AE,
MC, V. Tube/Train: Paddington. **Amenities:** Breakfast room, internet access, hairdry-
ers, irons, electrical adaptors available at reception. *In room:* TV, telephone.

Stylotel   Welcome to an attempt to combine budget accommodation, designer styling, and slightly pretentious branding in one harmo-
nious package. According to Stylotel's advertising blurb, this is 'not a
hotel' more 'a machine for living in'. You don't get that sort of meaningless vision-speak at your average B & B, which is essentially what
this is, albeit with more facilities and retro-futurist decor featuring lots
of glass, metal, and uplighting. If you ignore the decor (impossible,
but try) you're left with a superior budget hotel offering well-equipped
but rather small bedrooms (and some super-small bathrooms), English
breakfasts, and decent rates, starting at £85.

160–162 Sussex Gardens, W2. ☎ **020 7723 1026.** Fax 020 7262 2983. www.stylotel.
com/stylotel.swf. 40 rooms. Double £85. Credit cards AE, MC, V. Tube/Train: Paddington. **Amenities:** Lounge, breakfast room, 24-hour reception, internet access (Wi-Fi).
In room: TV, telephone, modem port, hairdryer, desk, wardrobe.

Wigmore Court Hotel   This Georgian townhouse just north of
Oxford Street is by no means picture perfect. The decor is a bit chintzy
and rather chipped and faded in places, plus there's the odd lock here

and there that doesn't work. But to improve things the friendly owners would probably need to bump up their prices, so let's just accept it the way it is, with a basic double with shared facilities at £70 (£89 for en suite). The hotel also regularly offers deals, particularly on longer stays, that can bring prices right down. Rates include a full English breakfast.

23 Gloucester Place, W1. (C) **020 7935 0928.** Fax 020 7487 4254. www.wigmore-court-hotel.co.uk. 44 rooms. Double without/with bathroom £70/£80–89. Credit cards MC, V. Tube: Marble Arch. **Amenities:** Breakfast room. *In room:* TV, telephone, tea and coffee facilities.

Worth a Splurge

Pavilion   On a street filled with low-end, cram-'em-in budget basics, this offers something very different. In place of the usual chipped paintwork and out-of-date furniture are rooms decorated with wonderfully glam, delightfully decadent decor. Every room is themed— 'green with envy', 'diamonds are forever', 'Casablanca nights'—each a paean to excess. Think brightly coloured walls, leopard-print sheets, and plenty of velvet. The rooms have been used as backdrops for countless magazine photo shoots—you can see pictures on the website. A hundred pounds will get you a day-glo double with en-suite facilities and a TV for when you've finished feasting your eyes on the decoration. FINE PRINT It can be a bit noisy with all the comings and goings.

34–36 Sussex Gardens, W2. (C) **020 7262 0905.** Fax 020 7262 1324. www.pavilionhotel uk.com. 30 rooms. Double £100. Credit cards MC, V. Tube: Edgware Road. Tube/Train: Paddington. **Amenities:** Breakfast room. *In room:* TV, telephone.

THE CITY, LONDON BRIDGE & EAST LONDON

This is a bit of a catch-all heading encompassing those few bargains to be found in the vicinity of the City and London Bridge, plus the YHA's largest hostel, way out in Rotherhithe Docklands.

Affordable

City Hotel   Book online 10 days in advance at the City Hotel—or, conversely, right at the last minute—and the standard £89 rate for a double room drops to £74. Booked ahead, even triple rooms come in at under £100. In contrast to many central hotels, which tend to occupy converted houses, this is a modern, purpose-built affair with decor that conforms to the international corporate template, albeit done to a slightly lower spec than you'd get in a Best Western. The rooms are well equipped and extras include parking (something of a rarity in London at this price) and the inevitable 'conference facilities'. There's also a bar and restaurant. ⟨FINE PRINT⟩ Breakfast is a far-from-bargain £9.95. Go to the local café instead.

12–20 Osborn Street, E1. ⓒ **020 7247 3313.** Fax 020 7375 2949. www.cityhotellondon. co.uk. 110 rooms. Double £74–£89. Credit cards A, BC, DC, MC, V, VE. Tube: Aldgate East. **Amenities:** Laundry, bar, restaurant, parking. *In room:* AC, TV, telephone, tea and coffee facilities, safe, hairdryer.

CHEAP SLEEPS

London Thameside YHA   This is, by quite some distance, the YHA's largest London hostel, capable of sleeping 320 people. They obviously couldn't find anywhere big enough to house it in the centre, which is why you'll find it occupying a purpose-built structure out in Rotherhithe, far from the bright lights and big city buzz. Still, it's only 20 minutes or so from the centre on the Jubilee line or (from 2010) the East London line, and about 5 minutes west of Greenwich. It has the requisite facilities, including decent showers, but is a bit tired and scruffy in places.

20 Salter Road, SE16. ⓒ **0845 371 9756.** Fax 020 7237 2919. www.yha.org.uk. 48 rooms sleeping 2–10, 320 beds. £19.95 per person. Credit cards DC, JCB, MC, V, VE. Tube: Canada Water, Rotherhithe (from 2010). **Amenities:** TV lounge, bicycle storage, shop, parking, café-restaurant, luggage storage.

St. Paul's YHA   The YHA's City hostel is located around 100m from St. Paul's Cathedral. It's large and well equipped, with room for 190 guests, most of whom stay in dorms sleeping three to eight people, but a little dog-eared and would benefit from a refurb. Its private rooms (three singles and six twins) tend to book up early. There's a café but unfortunately no kitchen. Breakfast is an extra £4.65.

36 Carter Lane, EC4. ⓒ **0845 371 9012.** Fax 020 7236 7681. www.yha.org.uk. 43 rooms sleeping 1–11, 190 beds. £24.50 per person, under 18s £18.50. Credit cards DC, JCB, MC, V, VE. Tube: St. Paul's. **Amenities:** TV lounge, games room, shop, café, laundry, internet access, luggage storage.

The Village   Three branches of the seven-strong St. Christopher's Inns' chain of hostels can be found on this stretch of road: The Orient Espresso, The Inn, and The Village, the self-proclaimed flagship. Very much from the 'backpacking means partying' school of hostelling, this is one of the capital's liveliest and best-equipped hostels with a large bar-cum-nightclub, a games room, satellite TV, and free Wi-Fi. They also throw in free breakfast. And if you've never made it onto *Big Brother*, you could book yourself into the 'live dorm', pictures of which are streamed 24/7 on the internet. Prices start at just £8.90.

161–165 Borough High Street, SE1. ℂ **020 7939 9710.** www.st-christophers.co.uk. 170 beds in rooms sleeping 2–12. Dorm beds from £10.90, private rooms from £26. Credit cards JCB, MC, V, VE. Tube: Borough. Tube/Train: London Bridge. **Amenities:** No curfew, bar, nightclub, games room, TV, laundry facilities, luggage storage, lockers, internet access (Wi-Fi).

EARLS COURT & SOUTH KENSINGTON

Earls Court is one of the capital's main budget-hotel hotspots, its Victorian terraces chock-full of cut-price B & Bs and hostels plus their attendant service industries—low-cost supermarkets, cafés, fast-food shops, launderettes—all aimed squarely at the backpacking community. Things are a bit more genteel in South Kensington where there are a number of fine hostels, many popular with school groups.

AFFORDABLE
Eden Plaza Hotel   It may bill itself as a three-star hotel but, elegant facade aside, it's really closer to a one-star. Double rooms can be had for £70, if booked online, which is pretty reasonable, but don't go expecting much beyond somewhere to stay. Pretty much everything about this place could improve—the decor, the service, the level of cleaning, the breakfasts (included in price). However, if everywhere else is full, it's perfectly acceptable for a night or two. Just don't book it for your honeymoon.

68–69 Queensgate, SW7. ℂ **020 7370 6111.** Fax 0207 370 0932. www.edenplaza kensington.co.uk. 62 rooms. Double £70–£90. Credit cards MC, V. Tube: South Kensington, Gloucester Road. **Amenities:** Lounge, breakfast room. *In room:* TV, radio, telephone, tea and coffee facilities, trouser press, hairdryer.

The Mayflower   The Mayflower offers a superior version of the Earls Court B & B norm, with everything done to a higher specification and with a more modern look and feel than most of its competitors. The well-equipped if small bedrooms are tastefully decorated with fans, wooden beds, cotton sheets, and wool blankets, and boast modern tiled bathrooms. You may have trouble swinging your cat, but at least you'll be comfortable while you try. Standard doubles start at £95 Sunday through Thursday (£99 Friday and Saturday), which is slightly beyond our price range, but the hotel runs deals in summer and at Christmas when prices drop to £79. One- and two-bed apartments with kitchens start at £120 a night.

26–28 Trebovir Road, SW5. ℂ **020 7370 0991**. Fax 020 7370 0994. www.mayflower hotel.co.uk. 48 rooms. Double £79–£115. Credit cards AE, DC, MC, V. Tube: Earls Court. **Amenities**: Lounge, juice bar, breakfast room, internet access (Wi-Fi). *In room:* TV, telephone, fan, tea and coffee facilities, Wi-Fi, hi-fi, safe, trouser press, hairdryer.

Merlyn Court Hotel   The cheapest, smallest bathroom-less double at this popular friendly little B & B is just £68, including continental breakfast. The accommodation is as basic as you'd expect for the price—rooms are small and don't have TVs or beverage facilities, and there's no lift—but everything is spruce and well maintained. And it's very handily located in an Edwardian terrace a minute or so from Earls Court Tube.

2 Barkston Gardens, SW5. ℂ **020 7370 1640.** Fax 020 7370 4986. www.merlyncourt hotel.com. 15 rooms. Double room without/with private bath £68–75/£80–85. Credit Cards JCB, MC, V. Tube: Earls Court. **Amenities:** Lounge, breakfast room. *In room:* Iron, hairdryer.

Cʜᴇᴀᴘ Sʟᴇᴇᴘs

Earls Court YHA   Refurbished following a fire a couple of years ago, Earls Court's YHA hostel is undeniably well equipped, but there's something rather austere about it. It's functional rather than homely and, bizarrely, the self-catering kitchen is located in the basement while the dining area is upstairs. There are plenty of alternative dining options in the Earls Court area.

38 Bolton Gardens, SW5. ℂ **0845 371 9114.** Fax 020 7835 2034. www.yha.org.uk. 33 rooms sleeping 2–10, 186 beds. £21.95 per person. Credit cards DC, JCB, MC, V, VE. Tube: Earls Court. **Amenities:** TV lounge, garden, shop, café, self-catering kitchen, Wi-Fi access, luggage storage.

★ **Holland Park YHA**   This not only enjoys one of the most scenic locations of any London hostel, set in the wing of a Jacobean mansion among the woods of Holland Park (p. 131), it's also cheaper than many YHA rivals. It's particularly popular in summer with school groups, when it can get noisy, in part because there are only dorms available, no private rooms; so, not a place for a bit of quiet meditation.

Holland Walk, Kensington, W8. ℂ **0845 371 9122.** Fax 020 7376 0667. www.yha.org. uk. 16 rooms sleeping 1–10, 200 beds. £19.95 per person. Credit cards DC, JCB, MC, V, VE. Tube: High Street Kensington. **Amenities:** TV lounge, garden, restaurant, internet access, luggage storage.

Meininger Hostel Occupying a 1960s' building adjacent to the Natural History Museum and metres from the Science and V&A museums, this German-owned hostel couldn't be better placed for a bit of cultural browsing. Its educational location means it attracts a fair number of school and college groups, so it's not always the quietest or most relaxing of environments, but then what hostel is?

65–67 Queen's Gate, SW7. ✆ **020 7590 6910.** Fax 020 7590 6912. www.meininger-hotels.com. 47 rooms sleeping 1–6. Dorm beds from £15, private rooms from £33. Credit cards AE, MC, V. Tube: South Kensington, Gloucester Road. **Amenities:** Luggage storage, lockers, parking, internet access. *In room:* AC, TV, key-card security system.

VICTORIA

One of the capital's most famous—if not infamous—budget areas lies just south of Victoria railway station where the streets, notably Ebury Street, are packed with simple bed and breakfast accommodation. Most places offer sub-standard variations on a minimal theme, but there are some choice picks hidden among the also-rans.

AFFORDABLE

Cartref House The Cartref's genial hosts go out of their way to guide their charges around London. A typical Victorian townhouse, it's not much to look at from the outside (or indeed from the inside) but it's clean and basic and does the job. Bedrooms are decently sized and high ceilinged, although the beds and bathrooms are less generously proportioned. The price includes Wi-Fi access and a full English breakfast, just the thing to fortify you for a bit of sightseeing.

129 Ebury Street, SW1. ✆ **020 7730 7338.** Fax 020 7730 6176. www.cartrefhouse. co.uk. 19 rooms. Double £86.50–£96. Credit cards AE, MC, V. Tube/Train: Victoria. **Amenities:** Internet access (Wi-Fi), breakfast room. *In room:* Fan, TV, tea and coffee facilities, hairdryer.

★ **Luna & Simone Hotel** This cheery little place is one of the best budget choices going. The rooms are bijou but everything within them is neat and tidy and just so, and they boast good tiled bathrooms for this class of hotel plus power showers. The staff are friendly and attentive, and cook up a mean breakfast (included in the room rate), although only until 8:30am, so set your alarm. It's just a 10-minute walk to Victoria Station, or a short hop on the no. 24 bus which stops right outside and can also take you right into Trafalgar Square.

47–49 Belgrave Road, SW1. ✆ **020 7834 5897.** Fax 020 7828 2474. www.lunasimone hotel.com. 35 rooms. Double £85–£115. Credit cards AE, MC, V. Tube/Train: Victoria.

Amenities: Breakfast room, luggage storage. *In room*: TV, tea and coffee facilities, hairdryer, safe.

Morgan House   Right behind the coach station, this is one of Victoria's (or Belgravia's, as they grandly insist on calling it) better budget B & Bs. Although set in a simple townhouse, the interior is adorned with old furniture and pictures, which makes it look a bit like the home of an aristocrat now forced to live in a modest abode following a bad run at the track. The bedrooms are prettily decorated and some have slick modern bathrooms, but they vary in size, so ask to see what you're getting. Those at the back suffer less from street noise. There's also a breakfast room and a small patio garden where very full English breakfasts (included in price) are served.

20 Ebury Street, SW1. *C* **020 7730 2384.** Fax 020 7730 8442. www.morganhouse. co.uk. 11 rooms. Double without/with private bath £72/£92. Credit cards MC, V. Tube/Train: Victoria. **Amenities:** Breakfast room. *In room*: TV, tea and coffee facilities, hairdryer.

2 Cheap Chains

Their decor may be blandly corporate and the service slickly imper-sonal, but at least with a chain hotel you know what you're getting. The same geographical rule of thumb applies: the closer you want your hotel to be to the Queen's big house, the more cash it will cost you.

EasyHotel   The Easy chain has applied the no-frills policy behind its airline, internet café, and cruise businesses (not to mention various other operations; see www.easy.com) to the hotel trade and now operates five properties in the traveller hotspots of Paddington, South Kensington, Earls Court, Victoria, and Heathrow. Room rates start at just £25 at Heathrow, which gets you a double room with a shower and not much else. All other services—including TV and breakfast—are charged separately. Note that in the traditional Easy way these prices can rise significantly in periods of high demand, so reserve early. And don't turn up unannounced: Easy hotels can be booked only via their website, www.easyhotel.com.

Express at Holiday Inn   Holiday Inn's budget offshoot isn't, in truth, terribly 'budget', particularly in the centre of town where a double is a hefty £130 to £170. This drops to £90 to £120 once you get as far out as Greenwich or Wimbledon, and comes right down to £70 to £90 in the furthest outskirts of Croydon and Newbury Park. They also

offer occasional summer deals when prices can drop below £50.
ℂ **0800 434040.** www.hiexpress.co.uk.

Ibis This French-owned, no-frills chain operates a standard expensive-in-the-centre-cheaper-on-the-outskirts pricing policy. Expect to pay around £110 for a double at the Ibis Euston St. Pancras, around £95 at the Ibis Greenwich, around £68 at the Ibis Barking, and £52 at the Ibis Wembley (though not on Cup Final weekend). www.ibis hotel.com.

Premier Inn The self-styled 'quality budget hotel' chain operates more than 30 hotels within the M25. Prices range from £110 to £120 for a double room in the city centre between Monday and Thursday (this can drop to below £90 Fri–Sun), to £75 in the week (and just £65 at weekends) in such far-flung locations as Enfield and Croydon. www.premierinn.com.

Travelodge To get the best rates from Travelodge, perhaps the country's most famous exemplar of the Alan Partridge-style cheerily bland budget hotel, you'll need to do your homework. For each night each hotel offers either a standard (or 'flexible', as they call it) rate or a 'saver' rate, which is typically around 10 to 30% cheaper but on occasion can be more expensive. The saver days are scattered throughout the calendar, which means, to get the best deal, you need to book each night individually rather than as a block. It's time consuming, but worth it. Locations outside of the centre offer the best rates—Kingston Travelodge has flexible rates of £55 to £59, which drop to £35 to £45 on saver nights, while the slightly more central Battersea Travelodge has flexible rates of £75 to £85, dropping to £62 on saver nights. www.travelodge.co.uk.

3 Flat Rate—Apartment Rental Agencies

If you're sticking around London for a few weeks, it may be worth looking into renting an apartment, particularly if you're travelling as a family. As with hotels, prices go up the closer to the action you want to be, but are typically still below what you'd pay for a hotel room. And the longer you stay, the better the deal. Expect to pay around £80 a night for a one-bed flat in the centre of town, and perhaps half that amount on the outskirts. Most places insist on a minimum stay, usually of 3 nights. The following agencies should be able to sort you out with something suitable.

AAE Shortlets   Self-contained one-bedroom apartments with kitchens and bathrooms in well-to-do areas, such as Hampstead, Swiss Cottage, and Belsize Park, from £400 per week.

℘ **020 7794 1186.** www.aaeshortlets.co.uk.

Euracom   Budget options start at £78 a night for a one-bed flat near Hyde Park, £83 for the same in Bayswater, and £413 a week for one in Bloomsbury. There's usually a minimum-stay requirement of at least 3 nights, and more typically a week.

℘ **020 8420 7666.** www.euracom.co.uk.

Holiday Serviced Apartments   Small studios or one-bed apartments in the W2 or NW1 postcodes start at around £490 a week (£70 a night), dropping to £350 a week (£50 a night) for a longer stay. The price includes all utilities and taxes.

℘ **0845 470 4477;** from outside UK ℘ **+44 1923 82 0077.** www.holidayapartments.co.uk.

London Holiday Accommodation   Offers accommodation in two complexes: self-contained apartments in a block near Tower Bridge where a two-person studio is £70 per night (facilities include Wi-Fi, TV, DVD player, safe, and iron); and rooms with a shared kitchen and living area in a building on the site of the original Globe Theatre in Southwark for £55 a night (one or two people).

℘ **020 7265 0882.** www.londonholiday.co.uk.

Outlet Holidays   One-bed apartments in Soho, just a minute or so from Oxford Street, for around £70 to £75 a night outside of the peak Christmas and summer periods.

℘ **020 7287 4244.** www.outlet4holidays.com.

4 Camp Sites

It may be one of the cheapest options, but camping will involve a fair amount of sacrifice. All of London's camp sites are a long way out of the centre, so you'll have to factor travel costs into any savings you might be making. A pitch is usually around £3, and you'll also pay £6 to £8 per person per night. For more information and user reviews of the various camp sites facilities, check out www.ukcampsite.co.uk.

Crystal Palace Caravan Club Site   Right next to Crystal Palace Park (p. 130), this is primarily a caravan park, but there are also a number of pitches for tents. It has good facilities, including large, clean showers, and is just a 45-minute trip (outside of rush hour) aboard the no. 3 bus to Oxford Street.

Crystal Palace Parade, SE19. ℂ **020 8778 7155**. www.caravanclub.co.uk. £6.10 per person. Train: Crystal Palace.

Lee Valley Camping & Caravan Park   This is a well-equipped site located near to one of the giant Lee Valley reservoirs that supply the capital with much of its drinking water. It has pitches for both caravans and tents, as well as showers, washing machines, and spin dryers. The centre of town is around a 45 minute–1½ hour journey away via train (Ponder's End) and Tube (Tottenham Hale).

Meridian Way, Edmonton, N9. ℂ **020 8803 6900**. www.leevalleypark.org.uk. £7 per person. Train: Ponder's End.

5 Home, Cheap Home

So long as you don't expect the level of facilities or service you'd get at a hotel or apartment, home stays—where you stay in a room in an individual's or family's home—can be a good bargain choice. It typically costs £25 to £50 per person to stay in or near the centre of town, dropping to £15 to £30 for the outer regions, with breakfast usually included in the price. Many places offer reduced rates for weekly or monthly stays.

At Home in London   This agency specialises in homes in well-to-do areas such as Knightsbridge, Kensington, Mayfair, and Chelsea. Prices range from £52 to £92 per night for a double room, depending on the location.

ℂ **020 8748 1943**. www.athomeinlondon.co.uk.

Host & Guest Service Ltd   Another good budget option, with prices starting at £15.50 per person per night in the suburbs, rising to around £25 in the centre of town. The agency also specialises in finding short- to medium-term accommodation for students from around £14.50 a night, or £85 a week. For more details, download a brochure from their website.

ℂ **020 7385 9922**. www.host-guest.co.uk.

London Bed & Breakfast Agency   Offers places throughout the capital from £35 per night per person.

✆ **020 7586 2768.** www.londonbb.com.

London Homestead Services   Perhaps the best budget option, LHS have a range of properties on its books, some of which go for as little as £16 per person per night. Note that this is an introduction agency only. Once you've paid a £5 booking fee, you deal directly with the homeowner for the rest of your stay.

✆ **020 7286 5115.** www.lhslondon.co.uk.

6 University Halls of Residence

Several of London's universities rent out rooms in their student halls of residence during the three main holiday periods: Christmas (typically a month from early December to early January); Easter (a month in total, falling either side of the religious weekend); and summer (late June to early September). Halls are often centrally located and provide a standard price of accommodation akin to a private room at a hostel. The rooms are fairly basic, but clean, albeit with perhaps a few stains that only a student could explain. Understandably, given the nature of the halls' principal clientele, most can offer a choice or single or twin rooms only. Some have a B & B option, some are strictly self-catering, and some even insist that you bring your own crockery and cutlery. Note that this is not a 'show up and book' option. You'll need to reserve your room well in advance. A single can be had for as little as £23 a night (£21 if you're under 26).

King's College   Prices at King's halls start at £25 per night for a single room and £40 for a double, both including breakfast. Further reductions are available if you're under 26 and/or staying longer than a week. www.kcl.ac.uk.

Locations:

● **Denmark Hill,** King's College Hall, Champion Hill, SE5. ✆ **020 7733 2166.** Single, including breakfast, from £25. Train: Denmark Hill.

● **Hampstead,** Hampstead Budget Rooms, Kidderpore Avenue, NW3. ✆ **020 7435 3564.** Single, including breakfast, less than/more than 7 nights: £32/£29, twin £53/£48. Tube: Finchley Road.

- **South Bank,** Stamford Street Apartments, 127 Stamford Street, SE1. ℰ **020 7633 2182.** Single (no doubles), not including breakfast, £40. Tube/Train: Waterloo. Train: Waterloo East.

- **Southwark,** Great Dover Street Apartments, 165 Great Dover Street, SE1. ℰ **020 7407 0083.** Single less than/more than 7 nights £40/£37, twin £60/£54. Tube: Borough.

London School of Economics   Appropriately, given its field of specialisation, this college takes fuller advantage of the summer accommodation trade than most of its rivals, operating more than a dozen properties, all either in or within easy reach of central London. Prices can be as low as £40 per night for a small twin or double room (£45 with breakfast). In 2008, **Passfield Hall,** in Bloomsbury, won the Silver Award for 'Best Budget Accommodation' from the London Tourist Board. www.lsevacations.co.uk.

Locations:

- **Bloomsbury,** Passfield Hall, 1–7 Endsleigh Place, WC1. ℰ **020 7107 5925.** Single without/with breakfast £34/£37; twin £55/£60. Tube: Euston Square. Tube/Train: Euston.

- **Clerkenwell,** Rosebery Hall, 90 Rosebery Avenue, EC1. ℰ **020 7107 5850.** Single without/with breakfast £30/£33; twin £47/£52. Tube: Angel.

- **Fitzrovia,** Carr-Saunders Hall, 18–24 Fitzroy Street, W1T. ℰ **020 7107 5888.** Single without/with breakfast £30/£33; twin £40/£45. Tube: Warren Street.

- **Holborn,** High Holborn Residence, 178 High Holborn, WC1. ℰ **020 7107 5737.** Single, not including breakfast, £37; twin £55. Tube: Tottenham Court Road, Holborn.

- **Southwark,** Bankside House, 24 Sumner Street, SE1. ℰ **020 7107 5750.** Single without/with breakfast £38/£43; twin £65/£75. Tube: Southwark. Tube/Train: London Bridge.

- **Southwark,** Butler's Wharf Residence, 11 Gainsford Street, SE1. ℰ **020 7107 5795.** Single, breakfast not included, £35; twin £55. Tube/Train: London Bridge.

7 Home Swap Agencies

This option takes preparation, but the rewards—in money saved—are worth the effort. The principle is fairly straightforward: you stay in somebody else's home while they, in turn, stay in yours. It's not a completely free option, of course. Most home swaps are arranged via agencies, who typically charge a membership fee of £50 and up. However, once on their books you have access to a database of homes and can begin negotiating a swap. The house stay is usually rent free, which means you just have to stump up for other holiday

CouchSurfing

CouchSurfing is essentially a more modern, more informal, more internet-generation friendly and, most importantly, even cheaper version of home swapping. Set up in 2004, **couchsurfing.org** is a not-for-profit global networking site on which travellers offer to put each other up for free by whatever means they can—be it in a spare bedroom, on the eponymous couch, in the garden (climate permitting), or even on the floor. Anywhere, in fact, where a tired traveller could possibly bed down for the night. The idea is to improve the 'global sense of trust', 'spread tolerance', 'facilitate cultural exchange', and, of course, save money.

It has proved hugely popular. The website now has more than a million members, with accommodation in over 200 destinations—including London—and, according to internet tracking companies, is one of the most visited travel sites on the web. It seems that people really do like a freebie (and facilitating cultural exchange, of course). It goes without saying (although we are now going to say it) that there are risks inherent in either visiting a stranger's house or letting a stranger into yours, but CouchSurfing has tried to minimise these by asking members for references and confirmation of identity and address with a credit card on registration. Still, don't get into any situation you're not comfortable with and make sure friends and family know where you are at all times.

www.couchsurfing.org

essentials: flight, food, and probably public transport as the majority of homes are likely to be located on the outskirts of the city.

- **Home Base Holidays** ✆ **020 8886 8752.** www.homebase-hols.com. Annual membership £29.

- **Homelink International** ✆ **01962 886882.** www.homelink.org.uk. Annual membership £115.

- **Intervac** ✆ **0845 260 5776.** www.intervac.com. Annual membership £49.99.

CHEAP SLEEPS IN THE WEST END

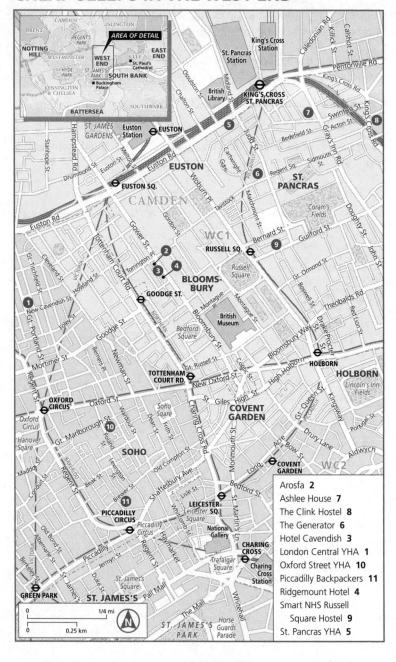

Arosfa **2**
Ashlee House **7**
The Clink Hostel **8**
The Generator **6**
Hotel Cavendish **3**
London Central YHA **1**
Oxford Street YHA **10**
Piccadilly Backpackers **11**
Ridgemount Hotel **4**
Smart NHS Russell
 Square Hostel **9**
St. Pancras YHA **5**

City Hotel **3**
St. Paul's YHA **1**
The Village **2**

CHEAP SLEEPS IN MARYLEBONE & PADDINGTON

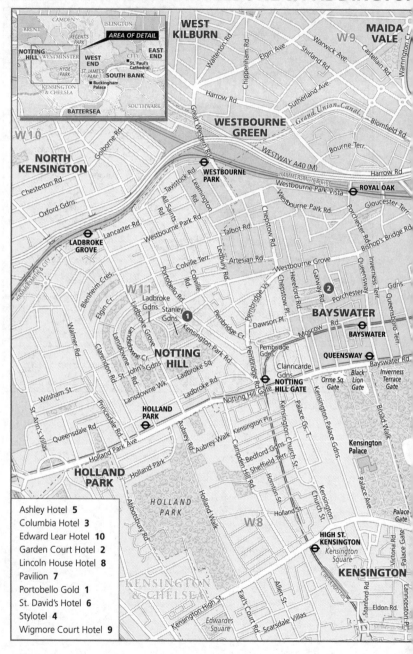

Ashley Hotel **5**
Columbia Hotel **3**
Edward Lear Hotel **10**
Garden Court Hotel **2**
Lincoln House Hotel **8**
Pavilion **7**
Portobello Gold **1**
St. David's Hotel **6**
Stylotel **4**
Wigmore Court Hotel **9**

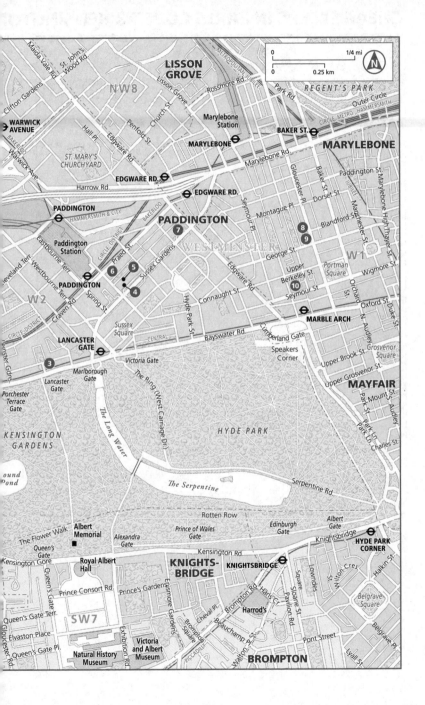

CHEAP SLEEPS IN EARLS COURT & KENSINGTON

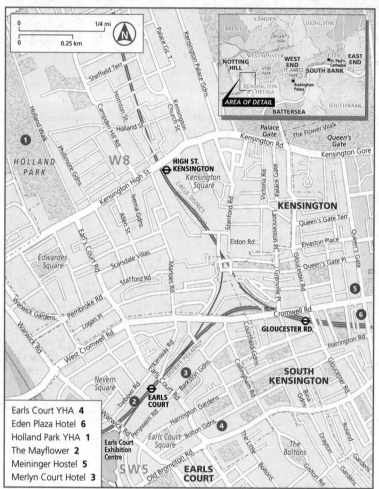

Earls Court YHA **4**
Eden Plaza Hotel **6**
Holland Park YHA **1**
The Mayflower **2**
Meininger Hostel **5**
Merlyn Court Hotel **3**

CHEAP SLEEPS IN VICTORIA

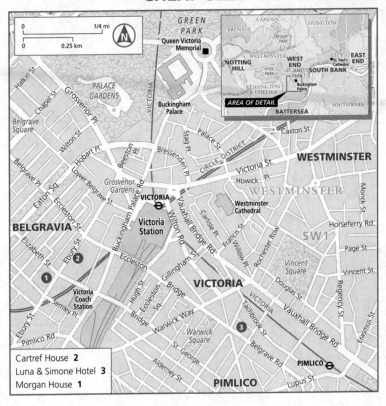

Cartref House **2**
Luna & Simone Hotel **3**
Morgan House **1**

Beigel Bake in Brick Lane is a thriving 24-hour bakery.

CHEAP EATS

When it comes to finding mealtime bargains, the key is to be as open-minded as possible about where, when, and what you eat. In general, prices in outer London are pitched a deal lower than in the tourist-oriented centre, but there are discounts to be found even there. Many of the fanciest restaurants also offer fixed-price multi-course set menus at lunch and in the early evening, sometimes for as little as £15. The capital's cosmopolitan make-up also acts as a useful break on culinary inflation. Think of a country and it's pretty much guaranteed there will be a restaurant serving its national cuisine somewhere in town, often catering to an immigrant community who expects to pay local, day-to-day prices. That's not to say you should ignore native nosh—such great British staples as fish and chips, pie and mash, and pub grub are also money-saving standbys. And street food, for so long our weak spot, has improved in recent years, with many of the capital's markets now serving up cheap tray-fuls of grub for under a fiver.

1 Soho, Piccadilly & Chinatown

Soho is a place where the posh and the low-rent happily coexist; where the gleaming offices of multinational media companies sit alongside tawdry sex shops and strip clubs. It's a dichotomy that extends to the dining scene. This is both expense-account heaven, packed with high-end gastrofests, and prime bargain-hunting territory with a great collection of value cafés, sandwich bars, and restaurants. Try not to get them mixed up. Leicester Square and Piccadilly are rife with over-priced tourist restaurants, while Chinatown is thick with bargain (and not so bargain) choices from the Far East.

Cha Cha Moon *ASIAN* This new eatery from Alan Yau shares many similarities with his previous venture, Wagamama. Diners sit side by side at long tables and choose from a mixed Asian menu—in this instance combining Hong Kong, Singaporean, and Malaysian cuisine. What's different this time are the prices. In his desire to replicate the eating experience of the Hong Kong *dong mein* ('noodle stall') of his youth, Yau has set prices more

Top Table Treats

An increasing number of websites, including www.london-eating.co.uk and www.squaremeal.co.uk, have (literally) made it their business to hunt out restaurant bargains on your behalf. **Top Table** (**www.top table.com**), the best of the lot, has a searchable database of restaurants which you can book directly through its website, and also lists any places currently running special offers—three courses for £15, 50% off, 2-for-1 deals, and so on. Reviews are user generated so you can check whether those offers are quite what they seem. You can even follow updates from the site on Twitter (http://twitter.com/top table), if you really want to keep apprised of which restaurants are currently struggling to fill their tables.

appropriate for street snacks than restaurant meals. Dishes cost between £5 and £7, and that's for surprisingly generous portions. FINE PRINT The only drawback is the noise level. A combination of bad acoustics and lots of fellow diners means you'll struggle to hold a coherent conversation. But as long as the restaurant's popularity continues to translate into low prices, you won't find too many people complaining (and even if they did, you wouldn't be able to hear them).

15–21 Ganton Street, W1. ℭ **020 7297 9800.** www.chachamoon.com. Mains £5–£7. Mon–Thurs midday–11pm, Fri & Sat midday–11:30pm, Sun midday–10:30pm. Tube: Oxford Circus, Piccadilly Circus.

The Chippy *FISH & CHIPS* The deliberately austere decor is a bit of a macguffin—this is no 1950s' survivor but a thoroughly modern eatery rendered in note-perfect retro style, from the tiled walls to the Formica table tops and tomato-shaped ketchup bottles. The food and prices are decidedly retro too—battered cod, thick-cut chips, mushy peas, and a mug of tea (with the bag left in, of course) for just £7.50. Haddock, plaice, and pollock are also available. From 3 to 9pm they offer a daily fish and chip special for just £5.

38 Poland Street, W1. ℭ **020 7434 1933.** Mains £4.50–£6. Mon–Thurs 11:30am– 9pm, Fri & Sat 11:30am–11pm. Tube: Oxford Circus.

La Porchetta Pollo Bar *ITALIAN* Now absorbed into a chain and refurbished according to corporate instructions, this legendary Soho venue nonetheless retains many of the qualities that made it a local favourite: quality pizzas tossed by a pizza chef, an informal, café-like ambience, and great prices. You can pick up a generous bowl of pasta for under £6 or a large pizza and a glass of wine for less than a tenner.

20 Old Compton Street, W1. ℭ **020 7494 9368.** Mains £4–£7. Daily midday–midnight. Tube: Leicester Square, Tottenham Court Road.

Leong's Legend *CHINESE/TAIWANESE* Leong's spicy interpretation of Taiwanese cuisine aims to offer something different to Chinatown's Cantonese norm. Dishes include *sanbei ji* (stir-fried chicken coated in rice wine, soy sauce, and sesame oil for £6.80) and the house speciality, *xin long bao*, or soup-filled dumplings (and yes, that is the right way round). The art is to create dumplings that are thin enough to be tender and yet sturdy enough to hold the pork broth without bursting. They're tasty, if a little tricky to eat, and great value at eight for a fiver. The dining room, decked out to resemble a traditional teahouse, is small and a

bit cramped—some seats are impractical for anyone other than a con-
tortionist—but perfectly serviceable for a quick sit-down meal.
FINE PRINT As with many lower-priced places that rely on constant customer turnover, the service can be a bit perfunctory. Don't expect your
every need to be catered for.

4 Macclesfield Street, W1. ℭ **020 7287 0288.** Mains £5–£6.80. Daily midday–11pm.
Tube: Leicester Square.

Malaysia Kopi Tiam *MALAYSIAN*   This place serves up the sort of
food that wouldn't seem out of place sizzling on a Malaysian night-
market stall. Prices may be a little higher than in the Far East, but still
represent great value for this part of town—under £10 for two courses
and drinks. Specialities include *nasi lemak* (coconut rice with fish,
boiled eggs, and spicy sambal sauce), Hainanese chicken rice, and
assa laksa (spicy noodle soup). FINE PRINT It's spread over two floors
but is still often packed out. Hopefully its current success will put an
end to its peripatetic existence—it has moved to several locations in
recent years—but do check first.

67 Charing Cross Road, WC2. ℭ **020 7287 1113.** Mains £2.80–£7. Sun–Thurs midday–11pm, Fri & Sat midday–11:30pm. Tube: Leicester Square.

★ **Malletti** *ITALIAN/PIZZA*   'Affordable Italian' too often means a
rubbery slice on the go. Not at Malletti, however, a tiny pizzeria in
the heart of Soho that offers a huge choice of expertly prepared thin-
crust pizzas with all the toppings you might expect (ham, mozzarella,
salami) plus a few you probably wouldn't (spinach, broccoli). It's a
no-fuss sort of place—your role is to order, pay, and then leave,
unless you want to fight for one of the two available stools—but good
value with slices starting at £3.50, calzones at £4, and pasta or risotto
from £4.50. There's also a larger branch in Clerkenwell with a seating
area. You need to be quick, however. When the last slice sells, down
come the shutters, usually by 4pm.

26 Noel Street, W1. ℭ **020 7439 4096.** Mains £3.50–£5. Mon–Sat 8:30am–5pm. Tube:
Oxford Circus, Tottenham Court Road. Other locations: Clerkenwell, 174–176
Clerkenwell Road, EC1. ℭ **020 7713 8665.** Tube: Chancery Lane. Tube/Train: Far-
ringdon.

★ **Maoz** *VEGETARIAN*   This US veggie fast-food chain serves one of
the city's great falafels—just £4 for one stuffed in a hot pitta that you
can then adorn with a vast choice of salads and pickles. Pick up a
homemade lemonade to go with it and you've got yourself a fab meal

for under a fiver. FINE PRINT It can get very crowded at lunch, but you're usually guaranteed a seat late in the evening.

43 Old Compton Street, W1. ℭ **020 7851 1586.** www.maozusa.com. Mon–Thurs 11am–1am, Fri & Sat 11am–2am, Sun 11am–midnight. Tube: Leicester Square, Tottenham Court Road.

Mother Mash *BRITISH*   MM has taken what is usually a mere supporting act, mashed potato, and brought it centre stage. It offers half a dozen varieties—with cheese, mustard, horseradish, cabbage —all custardy smooth (or lumpy and bumpy if you prefer, on request), which are served with free-range sausages (eight varieties, including veggie; £6.95 for two) or a locally sourced pie (five varieties, including veggie; £7.95) and, just to keep the options coming, a choice of five gravies. From 8:30–11am they also sell bacon sandwiches for £2.95 and a decent, albeit terribly gastro, 'British Breakfast' in which everything is grilled, free range, and hand-cut for £6.50.

26 Ganton Street, W1. ℭ **020 7494 9644.** www.mothermash.co.uk. Mains £6.95– £7.95. Daily 8:30am–11pm. Tube: Oxford Circus, Piccadilly Circus. Other location: 107– 112 Leadenhall Street, EC3. ℭ **020 7929 6158.** Mon–Fri 7am–6pm. Tube: Aldgate.

Pierre Victoire *FRENCH*   In truth, Pierre Victoire is nothing special. You're not going to come out reeling from a revolutionary taste sensation. Instead, provided you go during the set bargain periods, you'll probably come out thinking 'well, that wasn't bad, and it was pretty cheap'. And that, in the end, will have to do. The food is French— lemon sole goujons, roasted honey duck, and seafood crêpes might feature—£7.90 for two courses at lunch or £9.90 for the same 5 to 7pm. Steer clear of the à la carte.

5 Dean Street, W1. ℭ **020 7287 4582**. www.pierrevictoire.com. Daily midday–midnight. Mains £12.90–£13.90. Tube: Tottenham Court Road.

Princi *ITALIAN/BAKERY*   The London version of this venerable Milanese bakery chain is as catwalk stylish as you'd expect—all smooth marble, minimalist stools, and 'infinity' water features. The prices come as a (welcome) surprise and perhaps can be put down to the involvement of Alan Yau, the current king of stylish-yet-affordable eateries (see also Cha Cha Moon, p. 58). Its long counters are piled high with Italian treats, including olive bread, pizza slices (for £2 to take away), and salads (from £3.50). There's also a hot counter serving generous portions of pasta. FINE PRINT There seems to be no formal queuing system, which can make ordering rather chaotic.

135 Wardour Street, W1. ℂ **020 7478 8888.** www.princi.co.uk. Mains £4.50–£7.50. Mon–Sat 7am–midnight, Sun 9am–10pm. Tube: Tottenham Court Road, Leicester Square.

★ **The Stockpot** *BRITISH/EUROPEAN*   The perfect place to fill up on cheap Euro-British, school-dinner-ish stodge—lasagne, sausage and mash, spag bol and the like—before a night out in Soho. The decor, menu, and even the prices are all resolutely 1960s, which is when the venue first opened. It's a little cramped but the service is ever friendly. Most mains are around the fiver mark and nothing comes in at more than £7. The house red is a tenner. A top bargain place.

8 Old Compton Street, W1. ℂ **020 7287 1066.** Mains £3.50–£7. Mon–Sat 11:30am–midnight, Sun midday–11:30pm. Tube: Tottenham Court Road.

Viet *VIETNAMESE* This will never win any awards for decor or service, both of which are rather spartan, but it might be in with a shout when they hand out gongs for good-value food. Most dishes come in at under £6, and the *pho* (a litmus test for any Vietnamese) is tangy and satisfying. The BYO policy helps keep prices down, despite a £2.50 corkage fee.

34 Greek Street, W1. ℂ **020 7494 9888.** Mains £4.50–£7. Mon–Sat midday–11pm, Sun midday–10:30pm. Tube: Leicester Square.

Wong Kei *CHINESE* Famously cheap and famously rude, the Wong Kei hit upon a winning formula long ago and it's been sticking with it ever since: charge low prices for good, simple cooking;

Tips for Tipping

Watch out for double tipping, a dubious practice whereby establishments automatically add a 'discretionary' service charge (in other words a tip, typically 12.5%) to your bill and then cheekily ask whether you'd like to leave a gratuity. Any meal would have to be pretty special to warrant two tips. Remember, you need only leave a tip if you consider the service and food to have been worth it. If the food was sub-standard, or the service rude, you're comfortably within your rights to leave nothing at all. And, if service went really badly, you're more than justified in using your discretion and getting any automatic service charge taken off the bill. If you want to make sure your tip goes into the pocket of your waiter and not the general wages pot, use cash instead of plastic.

make diners share large round tables; get them to order almost immediately; and chivvy them out of the door once the last mouthful has been eaten. Oh, and remember never to smile. With seating for over 500 diners over two floors, this is one of the country's largest Chinese restaurants. However, despite its obvious success, rumours of a recent mellowing are greatly exaggerated. Expect service with a sneer.

41 Wardour Street, W1. ℂ **020 7437 8408.** Mains £3–£7. Mon–Sat midday–11:30pm, Sun midday–10:30pm. Tube: Leicester Square, Piccadilly Circus.

> ## Breaking the Chain
>
> Finding chain restaurants in London that deliver consistent quality at decent prices is not always an easy task. In general, standalone restaurants tend to be better at balancing the equation between ingredients, cooking standards, and price. A few chains and small groups, however, are holding their own in the budget world: **Fuzzy's Grub,** p. 72; **Little Bay,** p. 78; **Masala Zone,** p. 69; **Mirch Masala,** p. 85; **Mother Mash,** p. 61; **Sagar,** p. 88.

Yoshino *SUSHI/SASHIMI*   Its location, in a narrow, grungy alley off Piccadilly, isn't promising, but the restaurant itself more than delivers. A short menu changes daily according to the available catch. It's all super fresh tasting and, thanks to a recent round of price cutting, eminently affordable. You can get curry and rice at lunch for £5.80 or a mini bento box—cutely arranged compartments of sushi, sashimi, miso soup, rice, pickles, salad, and sweet omelette—for £7.80. FINE PRINT Last orders are at 9pm.

3 Piccadilly Place, W1. ℂ **020 7287 6622.** www.yoshino.net. Sushi pieces £2.50–£5. Mon–Sat midday–10pm. Tube: Piccadilly Circus, Green Park.

2 Marylebone & Mayfair

As one of the capital's richest and most gourmet-inclined areas, Mayfair has little to offer readers of this book, at least in the evening. At lunch, when high-rollers are thinner on the ground, many of the top-end places do drop their prices down to mere-mortal levels, offering some good-value set menus. Marylebone, to the north across Oxford Street, can offer a few budget choices, particularly along Baker Street and Marylebone High Street.

Slashing the Michelins (Low-Cost Posh Nosh)

Just like any other business, restaurants are at the mercy of the free market. When that market is booming, prices rocket and establishments at the top of the food chain feel emboldened to create lavish concoctions of caviar, truffles, and edible gold, safe in the knowledge that someone will pay. But when things start to get a little tight, even the fanciest places have to rein things in and get more price competitive. Almost every gourmet restaurant in London—even the most celebrated, Michelin-starred places—now offers a fixed-price menu, usually at lunch or pre-/post-theatre. Obviously you'll have less food choice than going à la carte, but then you'll also be spending far fewer pounds.

Ambassade de l'Ile *FRENCH* No. of Michelin stars: 1. 117/119 Old Brompton Road, SW7. ✆ **020 7373 7774.** www.ambassadedelile.com. Fixed-price menus £20 for two courses, £25 for three, available lunch only. Tube: South Kensington.

Arbutus *MODERN EUROPEAN* No. of Michelin stars: 1. Possibly the best value in town. 63–64 Frith Street, W1. ✆ **020 7734 4545.** www. arbutusrestaurant.co.uk. Fixed-price menus £15.50 for three courses at lunch (Mon–Sat midday–2:30pm, Sun midday–3pm), £17.50 for three courses pre-theatre (Mon–Sat 5–7pm, Sun 5:30–7pm). Tube: Tottenham Court Road.

Club Gascon *FRENCH* No. of Michelin stars: 1. 57 West Smithfield, EC1. ✆ **020 7796 0600.** www.clubgascon.com. Fixed-price menu £18 for three courses at lunch only (Mon–Fri midday–2pm). Tube/Train: Barbican, Farringdon.

Corrigans *MODERN BRITISH* No. of Michelin stars: 1. 28 Upper Grosvenor Street, W1. ✆ **020 7499 9943.** www.corrigansmayfair.com. Fixed-price menus £19.50 for two courses, £23.50 for three, available lunch only (Mon–Fri midday–3pm, Sun midday–4pm). Tube: Marble Arch.

Gordon Ramsay at Claridge's *MODERN BRITISH* No. of Michelin stars: 2. Claridge's Hotel, Brook Street, W1. ✆ **020 7499 0099.** www. gordonramsay.com. Fixed-price menu £30 for three courses at lunch (Mon–Fri midday–2:45pm, Sat & Sun midday–3pm). Tube: Bond Street.

Kay Mayfair *CHINESE*   No. of Michelin stars: 1. Recently voted London's best Chinese restaurant. 65 South Audley Street, W1. *✆* **020 7493 8988**. www.kaimayfair.co.uk. Fixed-price menu £19 for two courses at lunch (Mon–Fri midday–2:30pm, Sat 12:30–3pm). Tube: Marble Arch.

L'Atelier de Joel Robuchon *FRENCH*   No. of Michelin stars: 2. With 14 stars shared between eight restaurants in the UK, US, France, Japan, and Hong Kong, Robuchon is the world's most Michelin-starred chef. 13–15 West Street, WC2. *✆* **020 7010 8600**. www.joel-robuchon.com. Fixed-price menus £19 for two courses, £25 for three, available lunch (midday–3pm) and pre-theatre (5:30–7pm). Tube: Leicester Square.

Nahm *THAI*   No. of Michelin stars: 1. Europe's only Michelin-starred Thai restaurant. The Halkin Hotel, Halkin Street, SW1. *✆* **020 7333 1234**. www.halkin.como.bz. Fixed-price menu £15 for two courses at lunch (midday–2:30pm). Tube: Hyde Park Corner.

Pied à Terre *FRENCH*   No. of Michelin stars: 2. 34 Charlotte Street, W1. *✆* **020 7636 1178**. www.pied-a-terre.co.uk. Fixed-price menu £25 for two courses at lunch (12:15–2:30pm). Tube: Goodge Street.

Ristorante Semplice *ITALIAN*   No. of Michelin stars: 1. 9/10 Blenheim Street, W1. *✆* **020 7495 1509**. www.ristorantesemplice.com. Fixed-price menus £16 for two courses, £19 for three, available lunch only (Mon–Fri midday–2:30pm).

Tamarind *INDIAN*   No. of Michelin stars: 1. 20 Queen Street, Mayfair, W1. *✆* **020 7629 3561**. www.tamarindrestaurant.com. Fixed-price menus £14.95 for two courses, £18.95 for three, at lunch (Sun–Fri midday–2:45pm), £25 for three courses early evening (Mon–Sat 5:30–7pm, Sun 6–7:30pm). Tube: Green Park.

Umu *JAPANESE (KYOTO STYLE)*   No. of Michelin stars: 1. 14–16 Bruton Place, W1. *✆* **020 7499 8881**. www.umurestaurant.com. Fixed-price menu £21 for 10-piece chef's special sushi selection at lunch only (Mon–Fri midday–2:30pm). Tube: Bond Street.

★ **The Golden Hind** *FISH & CHIPS* Something of a rarity, a real neighbourhood chippie just a stone's throw from Oxford Street. This cosy little place has been operating since 1914, and has perfected the art—and it is an art—of frying its fish in crisp and crunchy, yet light and fluffy, batter. Cod, rock, haddock, plaice, skate, and even halibut (at £10.40 by far the most expensive option) are available, plus a few sides, including mushy peas and Greek salad—the last showing the influence of current owner, Dimitri. It's not as cheap as some chippies in outer London, but it's great value for the location and excellent quality. Its bargain factor is boosted by a BYO policy, with no corkage fee. Cod and chips £7.70. FINE PRINT One quibble: there's a minimum charge of £3 per person, so you can't grab a quick bag of chips (£1.30).

73 Marylebone Lane, W1. ⓒ **020 7486 3644.** Mains £5.40–£10.40. Mon–Fri midday–3pm & 6–10pm, Sat 6–10pm. Tube: Bond Street.

Maze Grill *AMERICAN/STEAKHOUSE* A near-ubiquitous media presence, Gordon Ramsey has become a culinary colossus, one big shouty, sweary icon of fine dining. He now operates 10 restaurants, all of them fairly expensive. If you fancy seeing what all the fuss is about, but are put off by the thought of paying £40 for a main, then head to the Maze Grill. This posh steakhouse offers the best value of any of Ramsey's establishments, provided you go for the set lunch: two courses for £15 or three for £18, midday to 3pm Monday to Friday and midday to 3:30pm Saturday and Sunday. Otherwise mains are £13.50 to £27.50. Of course, your meal won't actually be cooked by Ramsey himself—he'll be too busy railing at the failings of a restaurant owner on one of his numerous TV shows—but by a protégé schooled in the ways of the angry master.

10–13 Grosvenor Square, W1. ⓒ **020 7495 2211.** www.gordonramsay.com/mazegrill. Mains £13.50–£27.50. Daily 6:45–10:30am, midday–3pm & 6–11pm. Tube: Bond Street.

Ranoush Juice *LEBANESE* Avoid the pricey mains at this original branch of the popular 'luxury Lebanese' chain, and opt instead for the *shawarma* (a kebab-like wrap of chickpeas, sesame paste, and diced lamb: £6.50), meatballs (£5), or falafel (£4.50) from the hot mezze menu. If you feel like experimenting, you could also try their range of *nayeh*, made with raw lamb and herbs (£5–£7).

3 Edgware Road, W2. ☎ **020 7723 5929.** Mains £11.95–£12.95. Daily 9–3am. Tube: Marble Arch.

Titbits *VEGETARIAN*   The real bargains at Titbits, a swish vegetarian joint off Regent Street, are the buffet choices, or 'food boats' as they prefer to call them: £1.80 buys you 200g (7oz) at lunch, rising to £2 at dinner. You have a choice of more than 40 dishes, every one freshly prepared, locally sourced (up to a point), and GM free, so you can feel good about yourself as you save money.

12 Heddon Street, W1. ☎ **020 7745 6146.** www.titbits.co.uk. Mon–Wed 9am–10:30pm, Thurs–Sat 9am–midnight, Sun 10am–10:30pm. Tube: Piccadilly Circus, Oxford Circus.

3 Bloomsbury & Fitzrovia

This area is known more for its universities, museums, and hotels than its dining scene, but there are a few budget choices among the student bookshops and halls of residence. Be sure, too, to check out the stalls of the **Goodge Street Market** (p. 91) and remember, if you're in a rush, fast-food outlets line the concourses of Euston, St. Pancras and King's Cross stations.

Fryer's Delight *FISH & CHIPS* Defiantly old-school chippy in the heart of Bloomsbury. The decor is vintage 1960s, and the menu simple and traditional, consisting of the usual half-dozen fish choices (cod, rock, plaice, etc.), none of which cost more

Taste of London

Taste of London is an annual 'restaurant extravaganza', or so the press release would have you believe, held in Regent's Park over 4 summer days. Forty or so chefs from the capital's top restaurants, including several Michelin star winners, gather to provide tips and advice for budding cooks. Best of all, from a bargain-hunting perspective, they also cook up batches of their signature dishes which are then offered for sale much more cheaply than they would be at their formal restaurants. How much money you save will depend on the sturdiness of your constitution. The entrance fee is a hefty £21 per day, so you need to be sure you can fit in enough cut-price gourmet cuisine to make it worthwhile.
Regent's Park, NW1. ☎ **0871 230 7132.** www.tastefestivals.com. Four days in June, midday–9:30pm. Tube: Regent's Park.

than £4.20, plus the standard assortment of pies, sausages, and saveloys (£1–£1.60). The chips, which are fried in beef fat to give them that perfect soggy-fluffy consistency, are particularly tasty (£1.80 per portion).

9 Theobald's Road, WC1. ℂ **020 7405 4114.** Mains £4.60–£7. Mon–Sat midday–10pm, takeaway operates till 11pm. Tube: Holborn.

The Norfolk Arms *PUB/TAPAS* This once traditional and rather seedy Bloomsbury boozer has been transformed into a most tasteful gastropub-cum-tapas bar, and is all the better for it. Gone are the mouldy carpets, and horse brasses, and in their place come wooden floors, comfy furniture, and hams hanging from the ceiling. The Spanish tapas menu is extensive, at around 30 items, most of which will set you back around £2 to £4, unless you go for the £7.50 mozzarella stuffed with white truffle. Wines start at £3.20 a glass, while sherry (a traditional partner to tapas) is just £2.60.

28 Leigh Street, WC1. ℂ **020 7388 3937.** www.norfolkarms.co.uk. Tapas £1.50–£7.50. Mon–Sat 11am–11pm, Sun midday–3pm & 6:30–10:30pm. Tube/Train: Euston, King's Cross.

Ragam *INDIAN* A cheery ramshackle little place specialising in southern Indian cuisine. The big draws are the *dhosas*, flour, and lentil crêpes filled with a variety of tasty fillings, and served with *sambal* (vegetable stew) and coconut chutney for £3 to £5. FINE PRINT The decor could use an update and it can be very crowded. Booking is advisable at weekends.

57 Cleveland Street, W1. ℂ **020 7636 9098.** Mains £3.50–£7. Daily midday–3pm & 6–10:30pm, till 11pm Mon–Thurs, till 11:30pm Fri & Sat. Tube: Goodge Street.

4 Covent Garden, Trafalgar Square & The Strand

Quality low-cost dining in WC2, one of the capital's main tourist postcodes, exists, but it can take some hunting out amid a culinary landscape dominated by uninspiring, overpriced chains. The best bargains are generally found away from the busy thoroughfares.

Food for Thought *VEGETARIAN/CAFÉ* Despite its location on touristy Neal Street, this veggie stalwart has maintained a commendably fair-minded pricing policy throughout its many years of operation. The menu is extensive, and changes daily, but is always wholesome and fresh tasting—expect moussaka, veggie curries, quiches, and the like, all for around a fiver. As an extra incentive, it's BYO with no corkage. FINE PRINT It's small and rather cramped, but they do offer a takeaway service if you'd rather (or are compelled to) find an alternative venue to tuck in.

31 Neal Street, WC2. ⊘ **020 7836 907.** Mains £4–£7. Mon–Sat midday–8:30pm, Sun midday–5pm. Tube: Covent Garden.

India Club *INDIAN* Try to ignore the faded decor and chipped Formica tables, and instead concentrate on all the lovely money you're saving. With most curries coming in at under £5, and a BYO drinks policy, this redoubtable 50-year-old establishment is still leading the way for curry bargains in the capital. True, the food can be a bit hit and miss (generally more hits than misses), but it has a loyal following and exudes a warm, tatty charm.

Second Floor, Strand Continental, 143 Strand, WC2. ⊘ **020 7836 0650.** Mains £4–£6. Mon–Sat midday–2:30pm & 6–11pm. Tube: Covent Garden, Temple.

Masala Zone *INDIAN* This is something of a budget oasis in the otherwise overpriced environs of Covent Garden. The starters, all based on traditional Indian street dishes, are superb, but for real value go for a thali—a beautifully presented tray of rice, curry (vegetable or meat), two vegetable dishes, a lentil dhal, poppadom, and chutney from £7.80. It's essentially a two-course meal in itself. FINE PRINT Whatever you do, don't head to its sister restaurant, Chutney Mary, by mistake or you'll end up paying about double for similar fare. Takeaway service available.

48 Floral Street, WC2. ⊘ **020 7329 0101.** www.masalazone.com. Mains £7.80–£10.70. Mon–Sat midday–11pm, Sun 12:30pm–10:30pm. Tube: Covent Garden. Other locations: *Soho*, 9 Marshall Street, W1. ⊘ **020 7287 9966.** Tube: Oxford Circus. *Islington*, 80 Upper Street, N1. ⊘ **020 7359 3399.** Tube: Angel. *Camden*, 25 Parkway, NW1. ⊘ **020 7267 4422.** Tube: Camden Town.

Porky's Pantry *CAFF* A stone's throw from Nelson's Column lies a slightly less celebrated, but no less noble, icon of Britishness —Porky's Pantry. An old-style greasy spoon advertised by a cartoon pig in a bowtie (of course), Porky's offers a variety of sandwiches, bagels, and even croissants (it is in the heart of tourist London, after all), but it's the fry-ups that are its mainstay: £4.20 buys you a 'Full English'. An extra pound entitles you to 'Porky's Super Fry-Up', which will

BYO: Bring Your Own

Not every restaurant lets you bring your own booze, but those that do are offering a tremendous service. Providing your own refreshments saves both money—any beer or wine offered by a restaurant can typically be bought retail for less than half the price—and time spent perusing the wine list (unless, like me, you're a 'house red' kind of a person). Some restaurants do charge a couple of quid for corkage, the fancy term for taking the cork out (or unscrewing the top, you can't get round it that easily) and providing glasses, but most don't: **Amaranth,** p. 85; **Blah Blah Blah,** p. 90; **The Fish Club,** p. 84; **Food for Thought,** p. 68; **Fryer's Delight,** p. 67; **Golden Hind,** p. 66; **Hot Stuff,** p. 87; **India Club,** p. 69; **Jai Krishna,** p. 79; **Lahore Kebab House,** p. 83; **Loong Kee,** p. 81; **Ragam,** p. 68; **Rock & Sole Plaice,** p. 70; **Satuma,** p. 76; **Seafresh,** p. 74; **Tong Kanom Thai,** p. 76; **Viet,** p. 62.

require a porcine-like constitution to complete, consisting of two sausages, two eggs, bacon, beans, tomatoes, two toast, and a mug of tea.

49 Chandos Place, WC2. ⓒ **020 7836 0967.** Mains £3.50–£6. Mon–Sat 7:30am–5pm. Tube: Leicester Square. Tube/Train: Charing Cross.

Rock & Sole Plaice *FISH & CHIPS* Its central location, and cheesy name give it a touristy air, but this is the real deal, having served its first portion of chips back in 1871. The takeaway option is the cheapest—£5 for cod and chips—but eating in is more convivial, although it'll cost you a few pounds extra. A shaded outside seating area is deservedly popular in summer.

47 Endell Street, WC2. ⓒ **020 7836 3785.** Mains £5–£7. Mon–Sat 11:30am–11pm, Sun midday–10pm. Tube: Covent Garden.

5 The City

With so few City residents, the Square Mile's eateries are aimed primarily at the hordes of workers doing their weekday 9 to 5 here, many of whom, such as bankers and financial traders, have a bit less money to spend on lunch than in previous decades. Keep an eye out for set meal deals.

★ **The Cock Tavern** *BRITISH/MEAT*   Your appreciation of the Cock Tavern will hinge entirely on how in touch you are with your inner carnivore. Housed in Smithfield, London's busiest wholesale meat

Grease is the Word? The Great British Caff

It was once thought that the growing popularity of continental-style cafés in the capital would sound the death knell for a great British institution, the caff. However, our classic purveyor of fry-ups, bacon sarnies, and double egg and chips—affectionately known as 'greasy spoons' in ironic acknowledgement of a lack of refinement—is holding strong in the face of this fancy foreign competition. Outside of central London, they can still be found on every high street, serving cheap platefuls of old-fashioned grub to the faithful. To qualify as authentic, the decor must be minimal, the table tops Formica, and the plastic menu should offer what seems like a huge amount of choice, but which is revealed upon closer inspection to be permutations of the same ingredients: bacon, sausage, egg, tomatoes, mushrooms, baked beans, chips, and fried bread. Put them all together and you get the caff Holy Grail: a full English Breakfast. Despite its hearty proportions, the works usually sells for less than £5, which more than anything probably explains the caff's survival. Grown adults will argue long and hard about the merits of their favourite local. Our chosen caffs offer the biggest (and best) platefuls for the smallest cash outlay: **Alpino,** p. 77; **E. Pellici,** p. 80; **Gambardella,** p. 86; **Porky's Pantry,** p. 69; **Regency Café,** p. 74; **River Café,** p. 89; **The Shepherdess,** p. 82.

market, this is dedicated to showcasing the best of the stalls' wares—and, as the stallholders themselves are the tavern's principal customers, they take care to get things right. Full English breakfasts are generous, and meaty and reasonably priced at £4.25 (or £7.95 if you add steak). Some of the steak and pie mains are a touch pricier (the 'master steak' goes for £23.95), but they do offer a three-course lunch and dinner for £12.95. It also has a licensed bar. FINE PRINT Note that the tavern keeps rather unorthodox opening hours, to be in sync with the lives of the market traders.

Central Markets, Farringdon, EC1. ℭ **020 7248 2918.** www.thecocktavern.com. Mains £5–£23.95. Mon–Sat 6–10:30am & noon–7:30pm; drinks served Mon–Thurs 6:30am–11pm, Fri & Sat 6:30am–2am. Tube/Train: Farringdon, Barbican.

Rise of the Gastrocaffs

First the simple pub became 'the gastropub'… and recent times have seen the emergence of another new dining phenomenon, the gastrocaff. It's an attempt to take the caff, if not upmarket, then at least towards better ingredients and slightly less lard-heavy cooking methods—even if that seems to be rather missing the point. Caff eating is about challenging your arteries to a duel, and even the most modern gastrocaff daren't risk moving far away from the classic template. They might do it with fresher, and better-sourced ingredients, plus an added layer of irony, but the core elements remain. A posh 'full English' at any of our favourites will cost a little more than at a traditional establishment, typically £6 to £7.50: **Albion,** p. 80; **Frizzante,** at Hackney City Farm, p. 303; **Mother Mash,** p. 61; **River Café,** p. 89.

Fuzzy's Grub *BRITISH* In any given poll of the nation's favourite meals, it is guaranteed that roasts will come near the top, and yet the number of places that serve them—pubs aside—is laughably small. City favourite Fuzzy's Grub does its best to redress the imbalance with its range of lunchtime meat-fests. Choose from beef, lamb, pork, turkey, or chicken, served with all the trimmings for £5.50; or, if you're not up to tackling the works, you can choose a salad topped with roast meat for £3.85. They're also good for breakfast sandwiches—egg for £1.75, bacon for £2.75.

62 Fleet Street, EC4. ✆ **020 7583 6060.** www.fuzzysgrub.com. Mon–Fri 7:30am–3:30pm. Tube/Train: Blackfriars. Other locations: 22 Carter Lane, EC4. ✆ **020 7248 9795.** 10 Well Court, EC4. ✆ **020 7236 8400.** Tube: Bank, Mansion House; 56–57 Cornhill, EC3. ✆ **020 7621 0444.** Tube: Bank; 96 Tooley Street, SE1. ✆ **020 7089 7590.** Tube/Train: London Bridge.

Golden Fish Bar *FISH & CHIPS* The Golden has had 150 years to master its art, and mastery is what it has most definitely achieved. The cod—cooked to order as in all good chippies—is succulent, flaky, and encased in light, crisp batter; the chips are thick-cut, and fluffy, while the mushy peas achieve just the right balance between mass, and mush. You can get the whole works, plus a cup of tea, for less than £6.

102 Farringdon Road, EC1. ✆ **020 7837 3547.** Mains £5–£7.50. Daily 11:30am–2:30pm & 5–9:30pm. Tube/Train: Farringdon.

6 South Bank & Bankside

London's South Bank offers you the chance to fill up on both cultural fare—modern art, classical concerts, and Shakespeare plays—and decent low-cost nosh, including pie and mash, Greek *mezedes* and the free samples handed out at **Borough Market** (for which, see p. 90).

★ **Masters Super Fish** *FISH & CHIPS*   There are many people who regard this as one of London's premier fish and chip establishments, including a good proportion of the area's black taxi drivers (who know a bargain when they see one) as well as theatre goers en or post route to the nearby Old Vic. It's an orthodox, traditional place that has made a few grudging nods towards modernity—Dover sole and halibut appear on the menu—but which largely concentrates on doing the basics well: large portions of cod/rock/haddock in crispy batter on a mattress of thick-cut chips for under £7. Eating in entitles

★ M. Manze—More Mash for Less Cash

The taste of 19th-century London at (almost) 19th-century prices, pie and mash is as evocative of the capital as Big Ben or red buses. The classic meal consists of a minced beef and onion pie, soft mashed potato, and bright green (almost luminous) 'liquor', a local variation on parsley sauce. Originally popularised by labourers looking for a cheap, filling meal, it has enjoyed a revival in recent years for largely the same reasons—the works should cost less than £3. The East End boasts several establishments (p. 81), but this classic branch just south of Tower Bridge is one of the best, decked out in the traditional style with tiled walls, marble table tops, wooden benches, and a sawdust floor.

87 Tower Bridge Road, SE1. ✆ **020 7407 2985.** www.manze.co.uk. Mains £1.65–£4.10. Mon 11am–2pm, Tues–Thurs 10:30am–2pm, Fri 10am–2:30pm, Sat 10am–2:45pm. Tube/Train: London Bridge. Other locations: *Peckham*, 105 Peckham High Street, SE1. ✆ **020 7277 6181.** Train: Queens Road Peckham. *Sutton*, 26 Sutton High Street, SM1. ✆ **020 8286 8787.** Train: Sutton.

you to a range of complimentary extras, including bread, a starter of three prawns, and a pickled onion—you just can't top that for value.

191 Waterloo Road, SE1. ℭ **020 7928 6924.** Mains £7–£12.50. Mon 5:30–10:30pm, Tues–Thurs & Sat midday–3pm & 4:30–10:30pm, Fri midday–3pm & 4:30–11pm. Tube/Train: Waterloo.

The Real Greek *GREEK*   This modern bar-cum-Greek restaurant makes a great riverfront pit stop, doling out a range of hot and cold *mezedes* (£2–£5.95) and, the top draw, lamb, pork, and chicken skewers, served either on a bed of leaves (£4.75) or wrapped in pitta as a souvlaki (£5.75).

Units 1 & 2 Riverside House, 2A Southwark Bridge Road, SE1. ℭ **020 7620 0162.** www.therealgreek.com. Mains £5.75–£6.25. Mon–Sat midday–11pm, Sun midday–10:30pm. Tube/Train: London Bridge. Other locations: *Hoxton*, 14–15 Hoxton Market, N1. ℭ **020 7739 8212.** Tube/Train: Old Street. *Marylebone*, 56 Paddington Street, W1. ℭ **020 7486 0466.** Tube: Baker Street. *Putney*, 31–33 Putney High Street, SW15. ℭ **020 8788 3270.** Train: Putney. *Covent Garden*, 60–62 Long Acre, WC2. ℭ **020 7240 2292.** Tube: Covent Garden. *Spitalfields*, 6 Horner Square, Old Spitalfields Market, E1. ℭ **020 7375 1364.** Tube/Train: Liverpool Street.

7 Victoria, Westminster & Pimlico

For an area that includes both the low-rent boarding houses of Victoria and the grand offices of Westminster, it seems fitting that the bargain offerings here are equally varied, including both greasy spoons and the gourmet dining rooms of one of the capital's finest catering colleges. If neither of those tickle your fancy, there's always the fast-food court inside Victoria station.

Regency Café *CAFF*   Gingham curtains, Formica table tops, plastic seats screwed to the floor... this place has caff-chic down pat. It offers a winning combination of comforting old-school food at decent prices—pie, chips, and beans for £3.70, the breakfast works for £5—and a cheery bantering atmosphere. The whole show is presided over by Regency's booming-voiced proprietor; there's no chance you won't hear when your order is up. FINE PRINT It's very popular, so you'll need to get there early at lunch if you want to sit down.

17–19 Regency Street, SW1. ℭ **020 7821 6596.** Mains £3.50–£6.50. Mon–Fri 7am–2:30pm & 4–7pm, Sat 7am–midday. Tube: Pimlico, St James's Park. Tube/Train: Victoria.

Seafresh *FISH & CHIPS*   Just around the corner from Victoria Station, Seafresh occupies the middle ground between traditional chippies, and

Getting Battered

In a health-conscious climate, you might imagine that the fish and chip shop would have had its day. After all, deep frying runs contrary to the prevailing low-fat, cholesterol-free culinary ethos. But chippies continue to thrive for the reasons that first popularised them back in the 19th century—great-tasting, generously portioned food at spot-on prices. No one is suggesting you should eat it every day, but for a cheap treat, there's little that can top the crisp, yet light batter that breaks with a satisfying crunch to release a puff of steam from the flaky white fish within; the finger-sized chips covered in a haze of vinegar; and that radioactive slush of mushy peas—all for around £5 to £7.50. If you are worried about health implications, London also boasts a rash of upmarket eateries that provide a more refined take on the genre, offering grilled and steamed alternatives. Even at these top-end eateries you'll rarely pay more than £10 for your plateful. Try these capital chippies: **The Chippy**, p. 59; **The Fish Club**, p. 84; **Fryer's Delight**, p. 67; **Golden Fish Bar**, p. 72; **The Golden Hind**, p. 66; **Masters Super Fish**, p. 73; **Rock & Sole Plaice**, p. 70; **Seafresh**, p. 74.

the 'gastrochippies' that have become popular in recent years. Seafresh offers the standard fare—cod, haddock, rock, steak and kidney pies—plus a few unusual options (for a chippy, at least) such as fishermen's pie, calamari, and a seafood platter. You can either take away or enjoy with your own bottle of wine (it's BYO) in a long, canteen-esque dining room. It's hugely popular locally and at £10.75, the two-course set lunch is good value.

80 Wilton Road, SW1. ℂ **020 7828 0747.** Mains £6.25–£15. Mon–Fri midday–3pm & 5–10:30pm, Sat midday–10:30pm. Tube/Train: Victoria.

★ **The Vincent Rooms** *MODERN EUROPEAN/FINE DINING*   The gourmet creations of Gordon Ramsay, Jamie Oliver, and Alain Ducasse may be beyond most of our budgets, but what about their successors? Come to the Escoffier Room and Brasserie of Westminster Kingsway Cooking College (Jamie Oliver's alma mater) to find out. Here would-be kitchen colossi practise their trade by serving up fancy concoctions for a fraction of the price they'll charge in a few years.

Braised pork belly with truffle and sage for £5? Poached turbot with *cep* gnocchi for under £10? These are not prices usually associated with such quality of cooking. FINE PRINT The rooms are open for lunch in term-time only. Check ahead.

Vincent Square, SW1. ℂ **020 7802 8391.** www.thevincentrooms.com. Mains £6–£9.50. Mon–Fri midday–2pm term-time only. Tube: St. James's Park. Tube/Train: Victoria.

8 North London

From Japanese, Chinese, and Thai to Turkish, European, and even English, North London offers rich (so to speak) pickings for anyone looking to tour the world's cuisines on a budget.

CAMDEN, CHALK FARM & KENTISH TOWN

Satuma *JAPANESE*   Satuma is tiny and, as such, is perhaps best experienced with a group of friends. If you're going to be squashed up alongside a fellow diner, it might as well be someone you know. The food is mainly Japanese—sushi, sashimi, chicken teriyaki—with a few Korean specialities, including the famous *bibimbap* (Korean dish of white rice topped with vegetables, beef, a whole egg, and chile pepper paste), thrown in courtesy of super-friendly Korean owner, Moon Sang Park. If you want to know the correct way to eat sushi, just ask. It's BYO with a £2.50 charge for corkage.

8 Fortess Road, NW5. ℂ **020 7485 7078.** www.satuma.co.uk. Mains £4.50–£8. Mon–Fri midday–2:30pm & 5:30–10:30pm. Tube/Train: Kentish Town.

Yum Cha *CHINESE*   One of the capital's top choices for authentic, inexpensive dim sum (or *yum cha*, as they call it here, and indeed in Hong Kong). There are 16 steamed and 24 fried dim sum to choose from, most priced at £2.40 and none above £4. They also serve some interesting side dishes, including cold chicken feet for £2.40 and spicy duck tongue for £3.50.

28 Chalk Farm Road, NW1. ℂ **020 7482 2228.** www.silks-nspiceyumcha.co.uk. Mains £6.30–£7.50. Mon–Wed midday–11pm, Thurs–Sat midday–midnight, Sun midday–10:30pm. Tube: Camden Town, Chalk Farm.

HARLESDEN

Tong Kanom Thai *THAI*   This small, jauntily decorated place attracts a loyal following of local Thais—always a good sign. There's not a duff dish on the menu, but top picks include the *tom yum* soups (vegetable, chicken, or prawn) and the *som tam*, a hot and sour papaya salad. The BYO policy keeps prices (which are reasonable to begin with) down. There's an off-licence 50m down the road.

833 Harrow Road, NW10. ℭ **020 8964 5373.** Mains £4–£6.50. Mon–Fri midday–3pm & 6–10pm, Sat 6–10pm. Tube: Kensal Green. Tube/Train: Willesden Junction.

HIGHBURY

Tbilisi *GEORGIAN* The competition to be crowned 'best value Georgian restaurant in London' isn't, in truth, very fierce… but an award is an award, and Tbilisi is our clear and deserving winner. Victory comes courtesy of both the reasonably priced food (rich and intensely spiced) and some excellent, sweetish Georgian wines. Recommendations include the *chakhokhbili*, a tarragon-infused lamb casserole, the spicy beef soup and, by way of contrast, a number of fresh light salads. FINE PRINT You come for the food and the prices, but note that the decor is on the dowdy side, and the service can be a bit downbeat.

91 Holloway Road, N7. ℭ **020 7607 2536.** Mains £6.95–£9.95. Daily 6:30–11:30pm. Tube/Train: Highbury & Islington.

ISLINGTON

Alpino *CAFF* An archetypal caff at the heart of one of London's archetypal markets, Alpino offers a perfect distillation of the capital's caff culture. The interior is a real Formica, lino, and wood-panelled museum piece (with some great booth seating), and the menu is of equally antique vintage. The eggs, bacon, and slices are expertly flipped by the amiable chef, Steve. His full English is one of the best in town.

97 Chapel Market, N1. ℭ **020 7837 8330.** Mains £3.50–£6. Mon–Fri 7am–5pm, Sat 8am–2pm. Tube: Angel.

The Barnsbury *PUB* The Barnsbury is a great place to cheaply (-ish) sample the joys of gastropub cooking. Establishments of this ilk typically charge £12 or more for main courses—as The Barnsbury does in the evening—but at lunch during the week prices fall to a more reasonable £7 to £8.50. The range of choices is similarly reduced, but expect superior British pub fare—'gourmet' sausage and mash, and fish pie—among it.

209–211 Liverpool Road, N1. ℭ **020 7607 5519.** www.thebarnsbury.co.uk. Mains £11.50–£40. Mon–Fri midday–3pm & 6:30–10pm, Sat & Sun midday 4pm & 6:30–10pm. Tube: Angel.

KILBURN

★ **Little Bay** *EUROPEAN* Though Little Bay positions itself firmly at the bargain end of the restaurant market, it does so without compromising on food quality. The menu in each of the four London branches is short and focused—typically just half a dozen starters and the same number of mains—which helps the kitchen to maintain consistent standards. Recommended choices include a succulent breast of duck with leek and Grand Marnier sauce. Starters are £2.25 and mains £5.25 before 7pm, rising to £6.85 after (a bit more in other branches). You could easily spend twice as much on something three times as bad in another restaurant. FINE PRINT It markets itself as a fun 'occasion' restaurant, with decor reminiscent of a riot in a fabric factory, and you should expect plenty of parties and groups at the weekend.

228 Belsize Road, NW6. ℭ **020 7373 4699.** www.littlebay.co.uk. Mains £5.25–£6.85. Mon–Sat midday–midnight, Sun midday–11pm. Tube: Kilburn High Road. Other locations: *Farringdon*, 171 Farringdon Road, EC1. ℭ **020 7278 1234.** Tube/Train: Farringdon. *Battersea*, 228 York Road, SW11. ℭ **020 7223 4080.** Train: Wandsworth Town. *Croydon*, 32 Selsdon Road, CR2. ℭ **020 8649 9544.** Train: South Croydon.

STOKE NEWINGTON

The Best Turkish Kebab *TURKISH/KEBAB* These days the doner kebab is regarded as the poor relation to the shish, the sheikh, and the shami, conjuring up images of limp pitta filled with flaccid slices of indeterminate meat, whose greasy flavours are mercifully masked by lashings of chilli sauce. At this immodestly named establishment, they are attempting to restore the dish's reputation with their delicately spiced, flavourful meat, carefully cooked to retain its succulence and served in a fluffy pitta pocket for £4.

125 Stoke Newington Road, N16. ℭ **020 7254 7642.** Mains £3–£6. Sun–Thurs 7pm–2am, Fri–Sat 7pm–4am. Train: Rectory Road.

STROUD GREEN

Dotori *JAPANESE/KOREAN* At Dotori, a hybrid Japanese–Korean affair, they've achieved the perfect ratio between menu size and dish price: the former long, the latter so cheap you could potentially get away with paying less than a tenner for soup, starter, main, and green

Pub Grub Love

Pub grub has always been among the cheapest options for a meal out. Yet, until recently, it didn't always represent the best *value*. Food was usually cheap, but then it wasn't very good, so it should have been. Things have changed in recent years, as the smoking ban ate into traditional custom and publicans cottoned on to the pulling power of a decent menu. Also in the mix, the emergence of the 'gastropub' aimed to provide restaurant-quality food in the relaxed confines of a local boozer. Many gastropubs have set prices at or near restaurant levels, which does slightly undermine the concept of going for a pub meal. Thankfully, establishments at the middle and lower end have upped their game too: it's now fair to say that pub food standards have increased across the board. There are still some shocking spots out there, of course, but these days your chances of finding a pub serving honest fare—sausage and mash, lasagne, steak and kidney pie—and a decent pint at reasonable prices are greatly improved. Try any of these: **The Barnsbury,** p. 77; **The Churchill Arms,** p. 89; **The Gowlett Arms,** p. 86; **The Norfolk Arms,** p. 68; **Wetherspoons,** p. 87.

tea. Your main decision will be whether to opt for the fresh sushi flavours of the Japanese side of the menu or the spicy, *umami*-heavy Korean dishes, such as the iconic *dolsot bibimbap*, a super-hot sizzling dish of rice and vegetables on which a raw egg is cooked at your table. Dotori also offers a set Korean meal: £20 for two people.

3 Stroud Green Road, N4. © **020 7263 3562.** Mains £4–£6. Tue–Sun 5–11pm. Tube/Train: Finsbury Park.

★ **Jai Krishna** *INDIAN/VEGETARIAN* This veggie Indian doesn't look too promising from the outside, but once within the cooking (and prices) will make you forget its slightly shabby aesthetic. Lightly spiced southern Indian creations—from pumpkin, aubergine, and okra curries to the rich *dhosas* (flour, and lentil crêpes filled with a variety of tasty fillings)—are right on the money, and don't cost that much. Many dishes come in at under £3 and, just to keep costs as low as possible, drink works on a BYO policy.

61 Stroud Green Road, N4. ✆ **020 7272 1680.** Mains £3–£5. Mon–Sat midday–2pm & 5:30–11pm. Tube/Train: Finsbury Park. Train: Crouch Hill.

9 East London

The many communities of the East End produce a wonderful variety of budget eateries, encompassing everything from caffs to Vietnamese noodle bars and popular Pakistani places.

BETHNAL GREEN

★ **E. Pellici** *CAFF* This little piece of East End history has been in business since 1900, when it was a simple ice-cream parlour set up by Nevio Pellici, an immigrant from Tuscany. It's still owned and operated by the family, doling out great coffee, gurgled from a Ferrari logo-adorned machine, and simple caff fare—spag bol, full English breakfasts, bubble and squeak, steak pie and chips—to a horde of dedicated regulars. Its Art Nouveau wood-panelled interior was created by local carpenters in the 1940s, and saw the building awarded Grade II listed status in 2005—not every caff can boast that. A full English with chips (some of the best in London) comes to just £4.80.

332 Bethnal Green Road, E2. ✆ **020 7739 4873.** Mains £3.50–£8. Mon–Sat 6:15am–5pm. Tube/Train: Bethnal Green.

DOCKLANDS

China Palace *CHINESE* The menu here is a typically truncated Chinese affair, with only the 300-plus dishes to select from. Your best bet, as chosen by local Chinese families every weekend, is the dim sum (choose from just 60). Highlights include *siu mai* (pork dumplings), octopus in satay sauce, and whelks in black bean sauce, but they're all pretty good. And if you want to make a night of it, they have six private rooms for hire, each equipped with a karaoke system.

2 Western Gateway, Royal Victoria Dock North, E16. ✆ **020 7474 0808.** www.china-palaceexcel.com. Mon–Thurs midday–11pm, Fri & Sat midday–11:30pm, Sun 11am–11pm. DLR/Train: Custom House.

SHOREDITCH & HOXTON

Albion *CAFÉ/BRITISH* Albion is one of the capital's new breed of 'gastrocaffs', serving what on the surface looks like traditional greasy-spoon fare—bacon sarnies, full English breakfasts—but which on closer inspection is a cut above the norm. Passing through a small

Pie Trays in Motion

The numbers have been falling for decades, but there are probably around two dozen pie and mash shops still trading in the capital. Most are in the cuisine's heartland of East and South-East London, with a few lonely survivors out in West and South London. You'll find almost none, however, beyond the M25. The rest of the country seems strangely immune to the charms of a plateful of pastry, meat, mash, and parsley sauce. Many establishments also serve up that most London of fish specials—jellied eels, typically a container-full for around £2.90. Some of the best include: *Walworth*, **Arments,** 7–9 Westmoreland Road, SE17. ℂ **020 7703 4974.** Tues–Wed & Fri 10:30am–5pm, Thurs 10:30am–4:30pm, Sat 10:30am–6pm. Tube: Elephant & Castle. *Clerkenwell*, **Clarks,** 46 Exmouth Market, EC1. ℂ **020 7837 1974.** Mon–Thurs 10:30am–4pm, Fri–Sat 10:30am–5pm. Tube/Train: Farringdon. *Shepherd's Bush*, **A. Cooke's,** 48 Goldhawk Road, W12. ℂ **020 8743 7630.** Tues–Sat 10am–4pm. Tube: Goldhawk Road. *Upton Park*, **Duncan's,** 365 Green Street, E13. ℂ **020 8552 1288.** Tues–Sat 10:30am–4pm. Tube: Upton Park. *Poplar*, **Maureen's,** 6 Market Way, Chrisp Street Market, E1. ℂ **07956 381216.** Tues–Sat 10am–4pm. DLR: All Saints.

grocery shop and bakery, you enter a dining room whose decor could best be described as gastrodome-meets-austerity-Britain—stark white walls, stripped floors, and oak-topped tables garnished with HP Sauce bottles and teapots in cosies. For the standard of cooking, the menu is decently priced. Breakfast is served all day and there's a selection of British mains for dinner—shepherd's pie, fish and chips, steak—all for under a tenner.

2–4 Boundary Street, E2. ℂ **020 7729 1051.** www.albioncaff.co.uk. Mains £6–£9. Daily 8am–midnight. Tube/Train: Liverpool Street, Old Street.

Loong Kee *VIETNAMESE*   Amid a glut of Vietnamese cafés on a stretch of Kingsland Road known as 'Little Hanoi', Loong Kee does well to stand out from the crowd. Inside it's not much to look at, with basic furniture and minimal ornamentation, but whatever costs have been saved on decor have clearly been passed on to the kitchen.

Most dishes come in under a fiver, but could justifiably cost much more. The staff are friendly and happy to recommend different choices. Try the signature *pho*, a spicy soup of beef and rice noodles. The BYO policy (with no corkage) makes it even more of a bargain.

134G Kingsland Road, E2. ℂ **020 7729 8344**. Mains £4–£6. Mon & Wed–Sun midday–11pm. Tube/Train: Old Street.

The Shepherdess *CAFÉ*   Just around the corner from Jamie Oliver's 15, which offers cooking of a very different standard and price, The Shepherdess's old-school, no-frills charms have made it something of a local legend—hence the celebrity pictures that adorn the walls (including one of Mr Oliver). The food is resolutely proletarian caff fare, and never going to win any awards, but it will fill you up and leave you with change in your pocket to spend elsewhere: £4.50 gets you egg, beans, sausage, bacon, and chips.

21 City Road, EC1. ℂ **020 7253 2463**. Mains £4–£6. Mon–Fri 6.30am–4pm, Sat 7am–3pm. Tube/Train: Old Street.

Shish   *TURKISH/KEBAB*   The kebabs in this shiny Old Street favourite are definitely a cut above. They're also rather pricey, ranging from £7.90 (for chicken) to £9.70 (for prawn). However, Shish also offers a couple of good deals: a mezze and a shish for £6.95 or two mezze, a shish, and a drink for £8.45, midday to 7pm. ⌊FINE PRINT⌋ Note that the deals don't apply to the takeaway service.

313–319 Old Street, EC1. ℂ **020 7749 0999**. www.shish.com. Mains £7.70–£10.80. Mon–Sat midday–midnight, Sun midday–10:30pm. Tube/Train: Old Street. Other locations: *Willesden Green*, 2–6 Station Parade, NW2. ℂ **020 8208 9292**. Tube: Willesden Green.

Kebab Rehab

There are few foods as closely associated with alcohol intake as kebabs, the traditional British post-pub sponge. Indeed, it's the view of some that these Greek/Turkish staples should only be consumed when you're drunk and thus no longer in full command of your tastebuds. This isn't wholly unfair—there are some *very* shoddy kebab houses out there—but there are also some great ones that, because of the nation's booze-impaired palettes, don't get their due. Try our pick of the capital's delightful doners and super shishes: **The Best Turkish Kebab,** p. 78; **Marmaris,** p. 84; **Ranoush Juice,** p. 68; **The Real Greek,** p. 74; **Shish,** p. 82; **Tayyabs,** p. 83.

WHITECHAPEL

Lahore Kebab House *PAKISTANI*
In an area not exactly short of restaurants from the subcontinent, the Lahore still stands alone. The decor and seating are functional and drab, and it can get almost unpleasantly crowded on Fridays and Saturdays, but the quality of the cooking helps it to rise above such concerns. The cuisine is authentic Pakistani and very spicy: curries are served traditionally, with bread (roti, naan, paratha) rather than rice. Starters are £1 to £3 and include some greet *seekh* kebabs for just £1. They also do a mean Karahi chicken for £7.

2–10 Umberston Street, E1. ℂ **020 7481 9737.** www.lahore-kebabhouse.com. Mains £5.50–£7.50. Daily 11:30am–1am. Tube: Aldgate East.

★ **Tayyabs** *PAKISTANI* Tayyabs is a ferociously popular Pakistani restaurant, whose queues spill out onto the street every night. The hordes are drawn by a combination of top-grade, expertly spiced cuisine and ludicrously low prices. The prices start at around £1 for starters, which include *seekh* kebabs and Tandoori chicken pakora, and don't rise much for the mains.

83–89 Fieldgate Street, E1. **020 7247 6400.** www.tayyabs.co.uk. Mains £5–£10. Daily midday–11:30pm. Tube: Aldgate East.

Home Gourmet

Though the skills you acquire might ultimately save you money, cookery lessons in London can be costly (typically £100 a day or more). **The Kitchen** in Parsons Green offers a cheaper alternative. Rather than learning general kitchen skills, here a Michelin-starred chef will teach you how to prepare a gourmet-standard dish up to the point where it can be packaged up and finished off at home. Each dish costs £5, so over several lessons you could create a week's worth of Michelin-rated cuisine for less than £40. The Kitchen provides the ingredients (and does the washing up). Your role is simply to turn up and follow the instructions as best you can. Your dinner-party guests need never know.

The Kitchen, 275 New Kings Road, SW6. ℂ **020 7736 8067.** www.visitthekitchen.com. Tube: Parsons Green.

10 South London

The 'Sarf' is a loose agglomeration of areas—the maritime heritage of Greenwich, the tennis poshness of Wimbledon, the suburban shopping mall culture of Croydon below the reach of the furthest Tube—all united by one thing: the unwillingness of anyone in North London to cross the river and visit them. Well, they're missing out. From the Caribbean treats of **Brixton Market** (p. 91) to the spicy subcontinental cooking of Vauxhall, they do budget eating here as well (and more importantly as cheaply) as anywhere in the capital.

BALHAM

Marmaris *TURKISH/KEBAB* There are many among Marmaris' devoted local following who believe this to be the 'best kebab shop in London', and they may be on to something. It's certainly one of the top choices south of the river, turning out freshly prepared, generously portioned lamb and chicken shish for £3 to £5. There's a small seating area.

3 Bedford Hill, SW12. ✆ **020 8675 6556.** Mains £3–£6.50. Mon–Sat 6pm–2am, Sun 6am–11:30pm. Tube/Train: Balham.

BATTERSEA

Gourmet Burger Kitchen *BURGERS* There are two types of burger sold in London. The low-quality kind microwaved *en masse* in international fast-food chains usually sell for under £1 for a basic version. Alternatively, farm-sourced, stilton-topped gourmet affairs are served in the various high-end burger joints to have opened over the past decade. Unfortunately, there's not a great deal of in-between. The Gourmet Burger Kitchen, one chain largely responsible for the posh-burger movement, is among the more reasonably priced. Its classic burger is £5.95, rising to £7.95 if, for some reason, you'd like it with extra beetroot, egg, or pineapple. 'Small burgers' are just £3.95— great for a snack on the go. This is the chain's original branch, opened at the turn of the millennium.

44 Northcote Road, SW11. ✆ **020 7228 3309.** www.gbkinfo.com. Mains £5.95–£9.95. Mon–Fri midday–11pm, Sat 11am–11pm, Sun 11am–10pm. Train: Clapham Junction. Other locations: *Covent Garden*, 13–14 Maiden Lane, WC2. ✆ **020 7240 9617.** Tube: Covent Garden. *Fulham*, 49 Fulham Broadway, SW6. ✆ **020 7381 4242.** Tube: Fulham Broadway. *Greenwich*, 45 Greenwich Church Street, SE10. ✆ **020 8858 3920.** DLR: Cutty Sark. *Soho*, 15 Frith Street, W1. ✆ **020 7494 9533.** Tube: Tottenham Court Road. *The City*, Unit 4, Condor House, St Paul's. EC4. ✆ **020 7248 9199.** Tube: St Paul's.

CLAPHAM

The Fish Club *FISH & CHIPS* One of the capital's modern breed of 'gastrochippies', the Fish Club offers a refined take on a traditional eating experience. The choices are much wider than at your average chippy. There's a huge range of fish—including coley, skate, tuna, plaice, and mackerel—displayed at their fresh counter. Pick your favourite and then decide whether you want it battered and fried, steamed, or grilled. Your final choice is whether to go takeaway or eat in at their communal tables. Prices aren't rock bottom, but at £8.45 for cod (line caught, of course: they take sourcing seriously) and chips and a BYO booze policy, it makes for a reasonably priced meal.

189 St. John's Hill, SW11. ℂ **020 7978 7115.** www.thefishclub.com. Mains £4.95–£10.95. Tues–Sat midday–10pm, Sun midday–9pm. Tube/Train: Wandsworth Town/Clapham Junction.

CROYDON

Mirch Masala *INDIAN*   Mirch Masala ('Chilli and Spice') has hit on a winning formula to draw in the punters, eschewing the traditional Indian restaurant trappings of furry wallpaper, soft lighting, and piped subcontinental music—in fact, dispensing with that whole 'atmosphere' thing altogether. Instead, it offers circular Formica tables, bright (almost harsh) lighting, and sports showing on big flat-screen TVs. It's not the place to come on a first date, but for a meal with friends, it's just the ticket. Generous portions of well-cooked Indian dishes at cut-rate prices are supplemented by a money-saving BYO policy. It's popular with local Indian families.

40–42 Southend Road, CR0. ℂ **020 8680 3322.** www.mirchmasalarestaurant.co.uk. Mains £4–£7. Mon–Sat midday–midnight, Sun midday–11pm. Train: South Croydon. Other locations: *Norbury*, 1416 London Road, SW16. ℂ **020 8679 1828.** Train: Norbury. *Tooting*, 213 Upper Tooting Road, SW17. ℂ **020 8672 7500.** Tube: Tooting Broadway. *Whitechapel*, 111–113 Commercial Road, E1. ℂ **020 7377 0155.** Tube: Aldgate East.

EARLSFIELD

Amaranth *THAI*   This busy Thai right on the high street offers three bargain options in one: a bustling and extremely popular café/noodle bar; a takeaway service; and, just down the road, a Thai supermarket where you can pick up the ingredients and cookbooks to create your own Thai meals. The food here could perhaps best be described as 'Anglo-' rather than true Thai—expect the usual red, green, and *pad thai* combinations—but it's good value and operates a BYO policy.

FINE PRINT This is not the place for a lingering romantic dinner. It's basically decorated, and fairly noisy—plus you're expected to eat and hit the road pretty quickly.

346–348 Garratt Lane, SW18. ℭ **020 8874 9036.** Mains £6–£8. Mon–Sat 6:30–11:30pm. Train: Earlsfield.

GREENWICH & BLACKHEATH

Gambardella *CAFF*   Way out in the sticks, but worth seeking out if only for its glorious retro interior—all vitriolite, curvy table tops, and revolving chairs. It's like the 1960s never ended. The food also harks back to a previous era. You'll find no roasted vegetable paninis here: it's old-school caff fare—bacon butties, omelette, and chips, full English breakfasts—in generous portions.

47 Vanbrugh Park, SE3. ℭ **020 8858 0327.** Mains £4–£6. Mon–Fri 7am–5:30pm, Sat 7am–2:30pm. Train: Maze Hill, Westcombe Park.

Tai Won Mein *ASIAN*   Greenwich's restaurants are not, in the main, particularly good value; prices seem aimed more at the weekend hordes than hungry locals. The happy exception is Tai Won Mein, where huge portions at low prices buck the SE10 trend. All dishes come in at under £4 and the house wine is just £8 a bottle. The food is standard noodle house—soups, fried noodles, and fried rice with various combinations of chicken, duck, beef, and seafood—but it's all freshly prepared and served straight from the wok. You eat at communal eight-seater tables and are expected to get going pretty much as soon as you are done to make way for new arrivals. FINE PRINT It's cash only. The decor is a bit dingy, but so what… it's cheap.

39 Greenwich Church Street, SE10. ℭ **020 8858 1668.** Mains £3.40–£3.95. Daily 11:30am–11pm. DLR: Cutty Sark.

PECKHAM

The Gowlett Arms *PUB/PIZZA*   There are people who'll tell you that the Gowlett is a great Dulwich boozer, but don't you believe them… it's actually located in the much less fancy borough of Peckham. Either way, it's still a great place, and you should certainly listen to patrons who tell you it dishes up the best pizzas in London. There are nine stone-baked, thin-crust Italian-style offerings, including Fungi, Fiorentina, and Italian Hawaiian. A half and half is easily enough for two, and costs £8 to £9.

Dining with the Devil

For all the vehement criticism hurled at pubs owned by the JD Wetherspoon organisation—they've been called everything from 'chav palaces' to 'pub supermarkets'—there is one undeniable fact: an awful lot of people eat and drink in them. There are more than 70 Wetherspoonbranded pubs in London. Their success over the past decade can be put down to a number of factors—the lack of piped music, a wide range of cask ales, the fact that there are so many that it's quite difficult to avoid them—but the telling one is undoubtedly price. Wetherspoon pubs are the cheapest around for drinks and food (for drinking, p. 260). They serve a standard menu across their branches featuring simple mains (cottage pie, sausage, chips, and beans, etc.) for £2.99, or a burger and a pint for £4.50. They also run three 'clubs' (a curry club, a steak club, and a Sunday roast club) when you can get your food and drink for around £5 to £6. It's not outstanding food, of course, but it's cooked to a consistent quality and, whatever quibbles you have about corporate blandness, you can't knock the price. Consult their website to find your local: www.jdwetherspoon.co.uk.

62 Gowlett Road, SE15. ℂ **020 7635 7048.** www.thegowlett.com. Mains £8–£9. Mon–Fri 12:30–2:30pm & 6:30–10:30pm, Sat 12:30pm–10:30pm, Sun 12:30–9pm. Train: East Dulwich, Peckham Rye.

VAUXHALL

★ **Hot Stuff** *INDIAN*   Hot Stuff can seat 24 people, which is exactly the number that always seems to be here. This is a seriously popular place with a fervent following, and it's easy to see why. The cooking, which is Indian by way of East Africa, is from the top drawer, while the prices come straight out of the bottom— £4 for a fiery chilli chicken, £4.25 for their speciality, massala fish. No main costs more than £6. It's BYO, with no corkage, so pick up something at the off-licence next door, and get eating (and saving). Be sure to book in advance.

19 Wilcox Road, SW8. ℂ **020 7720 1480.** www.eathotstuff.com. Mains £4–£6. Mon–Fri midday–10pm, Sat 3–10pm. Tube/Train: Vauxhall.

11 West London

In addition to the places listed below, which includes some fine Japanese and Indian eating, also check out **Shepherd's Bush Market** (p. 198) for its eclectic array of (particularly Caribbean) food stalls.

EALING

★ **Sushi Hiro** *SUSHI/SASHIMI*   The strictness of this place is legendary. You'll need to know exactly what you want (the fact that they serve only sushi and sashimi makes this easier), have the money to pay for it (they don't accept credit cards), and get here early—they close the door on the dot at 1:30pm at the end of lunch and at 9pm after dinner, no exceptions. Thankfully, the same discipline is also clearly in evidence in the kitchen where dishes—all fantastically fresh tasting—are prepared as expertly as anywhere in the capital. With minimal overheads—the place is tiny and situated in unfashionable Ealing—Sushi Hiro can afford to charge absurdly low prices. An absolute steal.

1 Station Parade, Uxbridge Road, W5. ℂ **020 8896 3175.** Sushi pieces 60p–£2.40. Tues–Sun 11am–1:30pm & 4:30–9pm. Tube: Ealing Common.

HAMMERSMITH

Sagar *INDIAN/VEGETARIAN*   While generic Indian food is not exactly hard to find in London, this elegant eatery is one of just a handful to specialise in the vegetarian dishes of Karnataka in southern India. The cooking is light and comes in generous portions. Try a *dhosa*, a flour-and-lentil crêpe stuffed with a variety of fillings, for £3 to £4 – it's a meal in itself. This is the original branch of a three-strong chain.

157 King Street, W6. ℂ **020 8741 8563.** Mains £5–£13. Mon–Thurs midday–3pm & 5:30pm–11pm, Fri midday–3pm & 5:30–11:30pm, Sat midday–11pm. Tube: Hammersmith. Other locations: *Fitzrovia*, 17A Percy Street, W1. ℂ **020 7631 3319.** Tube: Goodge Street. *Twickenham*, 27 York Street, TW1. ℂ **020 8744 3868.** Train: Twickenham.

Shilpa *INDIAN*   As with many of the capital's restaurants, the best savings here are time specific—£3.99 will get you a set lunch of spicy Keralan cuisine, while for £2.99 you can take away a lunchbox with rice, a vegetable curry, rice, lamb, or chicken curry, naan bread, pickle, and a dessert.

206 King Street, W6. ℃ **020 8741 3127.** www.shilparestaurant.co.uk. Mains £3.95–£6.50. Sun–Wed midday–3pm & 6–11pm, Thurs–Sat midday–3pm & 6pm–midnight. Tube: Ravenscroft Park.

NOTTING HILL

The Churchill Arms *PUB/THAI*   Inside a traditional pub, which in summer seems so overwhelmed by flower boxes that it resembles a burst mattress, is a rather special little Thai restaurant. It's located at the back, through the main bar—where you can sit and have a pint if you're ordering a takeaway—in a greenhouse bedecked with plants. The menu offers around 20 main courses (no starters), a mixture of fried noodles, rice, and the usual curry dishes. FINE PRINT The quality and quantity are great, but service can be a bit hectic. They expect you to be done with your meal in under an hour, after which you'll have to retire to the bar.

119 Kensington Church Street, W8. ℃ **020 7727 4242.** Mains £6–£7. Mon–Sat 11am–11pm, Sun midday10:30pm. Tube: Notting Hill Gate.

PUTNEY

River Café *CAFF*   No, not *that* River Café… they don't do full English breakfasts, and if they did they'd cost a lot more than at this cheery little place next to Putney Bridge Tube station. For caff connoisseurs, however, this will tick all the boxes, from the Formica tables and nifty blue and white tiles to the friendly Italian owners and menu of simple fry-ups and sandwiches. It's located close to the offices of record company, BMG, so you may find yourself dining next to someone famous.

1A Station Approach, SW6. ℃ **020 7736 6296.** Mains £3–£5. Mon–Sat 12:30–2:30pm & 7–9:30pm. Tube: Putney Bridge.

Thirsty Thursday

International organic superstore chain **Wholefoods Market** trades on the quality and provenance of its produce rather than bargains, opting in the main for a 'reassuringly expensive' pricing policy. The exception comes every Thursday at its Kensington High Street branch, when you can sample five highly regarded wines and five gourmet food treats for £5.

The Barkers Building, W8. ℃ **020 7368 4500.** www.wholefoods market.com. Mon–Sat 8am–9:30pm, Sun 11am–5:45pm. Tube: High Street Kensington.

SHEPHERD'S BUSH

Blah Blah Blah *VEGETARIAN* One of the capital's top veggie choices, this charmingly cluttered place serves a changing menu of seasonal dishes that draws inspiration from around the world— Europe, the Middle East, Africa, India, and Southeast Asia. Expect a mixture of risottos, curries, tagines, and *lhaksas,* all fragrantly spiced and flamboyantly presented. It's not super cheap, but all the mains are under a tenner (which they wouldn't be if this were closer to the centre of town). A BYO policy (£1.50 corkage) helps keep down the overall bill. FINE PRINT Cash only.

78 Goldhawk Road, W12. ✆ **020 8746 1337.** Mains £9.95. Mon–Sat 12:30–2:30pm & 6:30–10:30pm. Tube: Goldhawk Road.

12 Street Market Food

Street food is not something London does particularly well. There may be people who have consumed a hot dog bought from a street vendor *and* lived to tell the tale, but I've yet to meet one. The exception to this rule is provided by the city's markets, many of which have stalls serving up tasty foil trays of grub to hungry shoppers and office workers at good prices, typically for under a fiver. All of the city's current favourite cuisines—Indian, Chinese, Thai, Italian and, increasingly of late, Mexican—are represented.

★ **Borough Market** London's pre-eminent foodie market, Borough is packed with stalls selling free-range meats, organic fruit and veg, homemade cheeses, and artisan produce from around the country. It's a real gourmet paradise. However, while much is clearly of a very high quality, little of it is exactly what you'd call cheap, at least first thing. You need to bide your time, stock up on all the free samples— little cubes of cheese, slices of sausage, brownie squares—and wait till near the end of trading, when overstocked stalls start to offer deals. Move in as prices tumble.

Borough High Street, SE1. ✆ **020 7407 1002.** www.boroughmarket.org.uk. Thurs 11am–5pm, Fri midday–6pm, Sat 9am–4pm. Tube/Train: London Bridge.

Brick Lane Sunday Up Market Every Sunday a huge former brewery building plays host to one of London's most fashion-conscious markets; around 140 stalls sell all manner of vintage clothes, recycled fashions, and painfully trendy designs. To keep the hungry hipsters' energy levels up there are also around 20 food stalls near the entrance, at the Brick Lane end, which offer a range of ethnic cuisines, including Japanese, Indian, Thai, Moroccan, Spanish, and even Ethiopian, usually for around £4 a trayful. Top picks include a two-chorizo sandwich for £2 and six spring rolls for just £1.

Ely's Yard, The Old Truman Brewery, E1. ℂ **020 7770 6028.** Sun 10am–5pm. Tube: Aldgate East. Tube/Train: Liverpool Street.

★ **Brixton Market**   Europe's largest source of Afro-Caribbean foodstuffs is supposed to confine itself to a purpose-built building on Electric Avenue (as in 'We gonna rock down to...'), but in practice spills out to fill surrounding streets. It's a real all-sorts place selling everything from cheap batteries to hair extensions, but the mainstay is food. It's filled with stalls selling value meat, fresh fish, tropical produce—plantains, sweet potato, cassava, yams, custard apples, mangos—and Caribbean street-food specialities such as patties, jerk chicken, and cassava cake.

Electric Avenue. ℂ **020 7926 2530.** www.brixtonmarket.net. Market arcade Mon–Sat 10am–6pm; street stalls Mon–Tues & Thurs–Sat 8am–6pm, Wed 8am–3pm. Tube: Brixton.

Goodge Street Market   It comes as something of a surprise to find such a selection of stalls on this otherwise unprepossessing turn-off from Tottenham Court Road. Select from Chinese, Thai, Middle Eastern, Mediterranean, and no less than three burrito places—the place has a touch of Little Mexico about it—including the outstanding Freebird's, which will whip you up a monster for £4.

Goodge Place, W1. Mon–Fri 10am–3pm. Tube: Goodge Street.

Greenwich Market   One end of Greenwich's well-to-do arts and crafts market is occupied by an equally aspirational food court. The food is varied market fare—sushi, tapas, *pad thai*, exotic salads, homemade bread and cookies—and not as pricey as you might expect, typically around £4 to £6.

King William Walk. ℂ **020 8293 3110.** www.greenwichmarket.net. Wed 11am–6pm, Thurs–Sun 10am–5:30pm. Train: Greenwich. DLR: Cutty Sark.

Leather Lane Market   Though it runs adjacent to the diamond mecca of Hatton Garden, there's nothing shiny or fancy about Leather Lane. This is an honest, down-to-earth London street market selling cheap fashions, luggage, homewares (toothpaste, batteries, and the like), a bit of fruit and veg, and lunches for local office workers. The range of cuisines is respectable—including Indian, Chinese, and Mexican—and typically goes for around £2.50 to £5 a tray. Look out for **Daddy Donkey,** which serves huge (almost too big) burritos and tacos packed with rice, beans, meat (chicken, beef, or pork), sour cream, and guacamole for £5.50.

Leather Lane, EC1. Mon–Fri 9am–3pm. Tube: Chancery Lane, Farringdon.

Whitecross Street Market   Recent years have seen this regular neighbourhood market joined by an increasing number of food stalls serving up value grub to the workers of nearby Clerkenwell and Hoxton. Food styles include Thai, Indian, Italian, and Mexican. **Mantra** does some of the best bargains, and consequently has some of the longest queues, offering two types of vegetarian curry, rice, and a samosa for just £3.50.

Whitecross Street, EC1. ℂ **020 7527 1761.** General market Mon–Fri 10am–5pm; speciality food market Thurs & Fri 11am–5pm. Tube/Train: Old Street.

Cuisine Directory

American

Gourmet Burger Kitchen, see p. 84

Maze Grill, see p. 66

Asian

Cha Cha Moon, see p. 58

Tai Won Mein, see p. 86

British

A. Cooke's, see p. 81

Albion, see p. 80

Alpino, see p. 77

Arments, see p. 81

The Barnsbury, see p. 77

Clarks, see p. 81

The Cock Tavern, see p. 70

Corrigans, see p. 64

Duncan's, see p. 81

E. Pellici, see p. 88

Frizzante, see p. 303

Fuzzy's Grub, see p. 72

Gambardella, see p. 86

Gordon Ramsay at Claridge's, see p. 64

Maureen's, see p. 81

M. Manze, see p. 73

Mother Mash, see p. 61

Porky's Pantry, see p. 69

Regency Café, see p. 74

The River Café, see p. 89

The Shepherdess, see p. 82

The Stockpot, see p. 62

Wetherspoon, see p. 87

Chinese

China Palace, see p. 80

Leong's Legend, see p. 59

Kay Mayfair, see p. 65

Wong Kei, see p. 62

Yum Cha, see p. 76

European

Arbutus, see p. 64

Little Bay, see p. 78

The Vincent Rooms, see p. 75

Fish & Chips

The Chippy, see p. 59

The Fish Club, see p. 84

Fryer's Delight, see p. 67

Golden Fish Bar, see p. 72

The Golden Hind, see p. 66

Masters Super Fish, see p. 73

Rock & Sole Plaice, see p. 70

Seafresh, see p. 74

French

Ambassade de l'Ile, see p. 64

L'Atelier de Joel Robuchon, see p. 65

Club Gascon, see p. 64

Pied à Terre, see p. 65

Pierre Victoire, see p. 61

Georgian

Tbilisi, see p. 77

Greek

The Real Greek, see p. 74

Indian

Hot Stuff, see p. 87

India Club, see p. 69

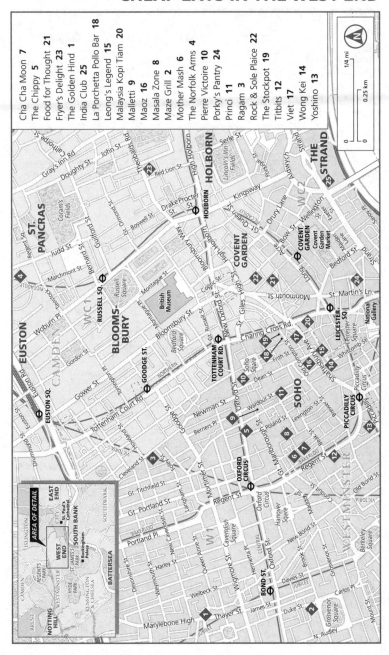

Cha Cha Moon **7**
The Chippy **5**
Food for Thought **21**
Fryer's Delight **23**
The Golden Hind **1**
India Club **25**
La Porchetta Pollo Bar **18**
Leong's Legend **15**
Malaysia Kopi Tiam **20**
Malletti **9**
Maoz **16**
Masala Zone **8**
Maze Grill **2**
Mother Mash **6**
The Norfolk Arms **4**
Pierre Victoire **10**
Porky's Pantry **24**
Princi **11**
Ragam **3**
Rock & Sole Plaice **22**
The Stockpot **19**
Titbits **12**
Viet **17**
Wong Kei **14**
Yoshino **13**

CHEAP EATS IN THE CITY

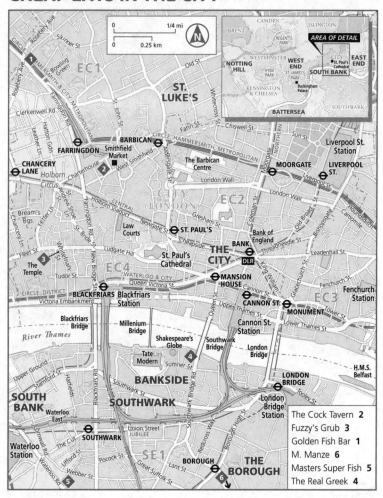

The Cock Tavern **2**
Fuzzy's Grub **3**
Golden Fish Bar **1**
M. Manze **6**
Masters Super Fish **5**
The Real Greek **4**

CHEAP EATS IN VICTORIA & WESTMINSTER

Regency Café **3**
Seafresh **1**
The Vincent Rooms **2**

A visitor strolls through the Cast Court in the Victoria & Albert Museum.

EXPLORING LONDON

4

O ne of the paradoxes of exploring London is that, while it can be infuriatingly expensive to travel between its attractions, the attractions themselves are often free. If London wasn't so enormous, the whole pricey travel situation wouldn't be such a problem. However, for certain trips, particularly out into Greater London, your only real option is to rely on public transport. Just be sure to do it at the cheapest time of day (p. 311). Thankfully, in the centre, there's much that's walkable, providing the rain holds off (no guarantee, of course), including a collection of museums and galleries to rival any world city. Plus the capital's many parks and gardens, which again measure up to anything the rest of the world can offer, provide a series of verdant stepping stones between urban hotspots.

1 The Collection Selection

FREE & LOW-COST MUSEUMS

Museums are a Londoner's conversational get-out-of-jail-free card. We may hang our heads and mumble our apologies when a visitor asks about hotel prices or transport costs, but when talk turns to cultural treasure houses we can puff out our chests and feel proud. All of London's major museums are free to visit, although many do ask (some more forcefully than others) for a 'suggested' donation of a few pounds. The priceless antiquities of ancient civilisations, modern medical curiosities, and scary animatronic dinosaurs are all displayed for your viewing pleasure. All you have to do is stump up the cost of getting to them. And, as if that wasn't enough, many museums also offer free guided tours of their collections and lay on free events—talks, concerts, film screenings, and the rest. Really, they're spoiling us.

ART & DESIGN MUSEUMS

Fashion & Textile Museum Gaudily painted with a bright pink top (a bit like its founder, designer Zandra Rhodes), the FTM was recently taken over by Newham College and is now primarily an educational centre running courses and workshops,

Free At Last

London's museums weren't always quite so altruistically minded. Until less than a decade ago most charged an admission fee, sometimes a hefty one. It was only in 2001 that the government took the decision to make all state-funded collections free to all. The ruling has not been universally popular. Museum-goers certainly don't complain, but several curators do, claiming that government funding falls well short of what they could earn from entrance fees. The ruling was challenged in the courts during 2007, but upheld. Who knows whether it would survive another challenge under another government, particularly if the economy is doing badly. In the meantime, get out there and start enjoying. This particularly applies to all those Londoners whose last museum visit was as part of a school trip.

although it does still hold a small collection of designs by its day-glo founder, and also hosts temporary exhibitions. The main attraction for bargain-hunters, however, is the shop which stocks interesting, and often well-priced, clothes by students and up-and-coming designers. FINE PRINT You don't have to pay the admission fee if you just want to visit the shop.

83 Bermondsey Street, SE1. ℂ **020 7407 8664.** www.ftmlondon.org. Admission £6.50. Wed–Sun 11am–6pm. Tube/Train: London Bridge.

Geffrye Museum FREE Like a giant 3D interior design magazine, the Geffrye is dedicated to showcasing the interiors—and particularly the living rooms—of Britain's historic homes, from stark 17th-century parlours through chintzy Victorian dining rooms to spacious, minimalist 1990s' loft conversions. Imagine heaven as designed by Laurence Llewelyn-Bowen, and you've got the general idea. The chronological theme is continued outside with a series of period gardens dating from the 17th to the 20th centuries.

Kingsland Road, E2. ℂ **020 7739 9893.** www.geffrye-museum.org.uk. May–Sept timed entry at 11am, midday, 2pm, 3pm, & 4pm; Oct–April timed entry at 11am, midday, 2pm, & 3pm. Tube/Train: Old Street.

★ **Sir John Soane's Museum** FREE Perhaps the finest small museum in London, the Soane is both a repository for a fascinating

> ## Heritage Nation
>
> Britain's architectural and garden heritage is among the richest in the world. Much of it is tended by two bodies: the member-funded **National Trust** (ℂ **0844 800 1895,** www.nationaltrust. org.uk) and part publicly funded, part member-funded **English Heritage** (ℂ **0870 333 1181,** www.english-heritage.org.uk). Between them, these two august bodies own and manage more than 500 properties across England and Wales—country houses, palaces, historic houses, landscaped parks, and more—including several dozen in and around London. Members of each organisation can visit its respective properties free of charge. Membership of the National Trust (NT) costs £47.50 a year, while English Heritage costs £43. Some overseas cultural organisations have reciprocal arrangements with the Trust, which allow their members free entry to any NT property. See the NT website for a list including Australia, Canada, New Zealand, Italy, and nine other countries.

collection of curios—Egyptian sarcophagi, Greek marbles and bronzes, Roman jewellery, medieval sculptures, Renaissance paintings—and an enchanting demonstration of architectural ingenuity. Both are the work of the eponymous Sir John (1753–1837), one of the country's foremost architects and collectors, who clearly saw no point in acquiring something if it couldn't be displayed, and so adorned every wall, every surface, and even the ceilings of his home with artefacts and artworks. He even designed fold-out cupboards and panels so as to show off as much art as possible. The result is a wonderfully stylish clutter. On the first Tuesday evening of every month, this most evocative of collections ups the ante by giving visitors the chance to explore its labyrinthine confines by candlelight.

13 Lincoln's Inn Fields, WC2. ℂ **020 7405 2107.** www.soane.org. Tues–Sat 10am–5pm. Tube: Holborn.

★ **Victoria & Albert Museum** `FREE` Though dedicated to design and the decorative arts, the V&A is perhaps the least show-offy and least designery of the big three Kensington museums. But then, with 145 galleries filled with treasures from all over the globe—African statues, Ancient Egyptian sculptures, Chinese ceramics, Islamic jewellery, Renaissance cartoons, and more—it probably feels its exhibitions don't need sexing up with touchscreen computers. Highlights include the Cast Collection, filled with plaster copies of some of the world's great stonemasonry (including Michelangelo's *David* and Trajan's column), the Jameel Islamic Art Gallery, and an eye-popping Jewellery Gallery. Free guided tours taking in selected highlights from the collection are given daily at hourly intervals 10:30am to 3:30pm.

Cromwell Road, SW7. ℂ **020 7942 2000.** www.vam.ac.uk. Mon–Thurs & Sat–Sun 10am–5:45pm, Fri 10am–10pm. Tube: South Kensington.

ASTRONOMY MUSEUMS

Hampstead Observatory `FREE` On a clear weekend night between October and April (by no means a given, I know, but go with me), should you find yourself gazing heavenwards and wishing you could get a closer glimpse of some celestial bodies, then head down to this observatory, set on the highest point in London, where the helpful staff will let you. There's no need to book, just turn up, wait your turn, and see what's up there. The least you can expect are the moon, planets, and stars, but your visit might coincide with a comet, a transit, a meteor shower, or other such unusual event.

Lower Terrace, NW3. ℂ **020 8346 1056.** www.hampsteadscience.ac.uk. Fri–Sat 8–10pm, Sun 11am–1pm. Tube: Hampstead.

Old Royal Observatory `FREE`   Designed by Sir Christopher Wren in the early 17th century, the observatory holds a small but interesting collection of astronomical gizmos and gadgets, including a few interactive exhibits. Effects-laden star shows at the newly revamped planetarium are £6. A cheaper thrill is available outside in the courtyard where a line marks the position of 0° longitude, allowing you to stand with one foot in the Earth's eastern hemisphere and one in the west— it's one of the capital's most enduring photo opps.

Blackheath Avenue, Greenwich, SE10. ℂ **020 8858 4422.** www.nmm.ac.uk/places/ royal-observatory. Daily 10am–5pm. DLR: Cutty Sark. Train: Greenwich.

CHILDHOOD & TOY MUSEUMS

Foundling Museum   In 1741, London's first home for abandoned children was set up by three of the great figures of the age: the philanthropist Thomas Coram; the satirical artist, Hogarth; and the composer, Handel. It continued caring for the discarded offspring of the city's underclass until relocated to the country in 1920. Today the old building tells the story of the three men's campaign, as well as the lives of those children rescued from a life of destitution. Some of what it has to relate is a bit grim, understandably, but it provides a fascinating record of London's first serious attempt to tackle the problem of childhood poverty. The museum organises plenty of stuff for families, including drop-in sessions and activity backpacks for 3 to 12 year olds, and on the first Sunday of each month there's a free gallery talk and classical concert at 3pm.

40 Brunswick Square, WC1. ℂ **020 7841 3600.** www.foundlingmuseum.org.uk. Tues–Sat 10am–5pm, Sun 11am–5pm. Admission £5. Tube: Russell Square.

Ragged School Museum `FREE`   A sort of mini-Victorian theme park, the museum was once part of London's largest free school, run by Dr Barnardo (these were also known as 'ragged schools', owing to the unkempt appearance of the pupils). The chief draw is the replica 1970s' classroom where, between 2pm and 5pm on the first Sunday of the month, children (and, if you're really missing your school days, adults) can have a lesson taught to them in a Victorian style using slate boards, dunce's hats, and plenty of discipline (£2). Free themed activities, such as Victorian parlour games and sweet-making classes, are laid on every Wednesday and Thursday during the school holidays. FINE PRINT Note: it's only open 3 days a week.

46–50 Copperfield Road, E3. ⓒ **020 8980 6405.** www.raggedschoolmuseum.org.uk. Wed & Thurs 10am–5pm, Sun 2–5pm. Tube: Mile End.

V&A Museum of Childhood FREE This offshoot of the capital's foremost design museum is dedicated to examining the creation, construction, and meaning behind the country's favourite children's playthings. It boasts a vast array of toys including board games, construction toys (like Lego and Meccano), rocking horses, teddy bears, more than 8,000 dolls, and, in pride of place, the country's largest publicly accessible collection of historic dolls houses. Of course, looking at toys, but not touching them, can prove frustrating for younger visitors. Thankfully, the museum also boasts a hands-on 'Creative Gallery' and organises free activities and workshops for children on weekends and during the school holidays.

Cambridge Heath Road, E2. ⓒ **020 8983 5200.** www.vam.ac.uk/moc. Daily 10am–7:45pm. Tube: Bethnal Green.

HISTORY, SOCIAL HISTORY & CULTURE MUSEUMS

Bank of England Museum FREE Located next to the 'Old Lady of Threadneedle Street', the museum does its best to explain the growth of banking and money over the past few hundred years without putting visitors to sleep. It's largely successful, perhaps because in these days of banking upheaval, people are more willing to pay attention. Displays range from the bizarre—a mock-up of an old bank stock office complete with bewigged cashiers—to the downright (and worryingly) confusing, notably the interactive exhibit on the Monetary Policy Committee. There are lots of interesting historic banknotes, but the highlight for both adults and children is always the plastic pyramid filled with gold bars.

Threadneedle Street, EC2. ⓒ **020 7601 5545.** www.bankofengland.co.uk/education/museum. Mon–Fri 10am–5pm. Tube: Bank.

★ **British Library** FREE Ignore the exterior of the building, which looks like a suburban supermarket, and head straight to the permanent exhibition gallery within, which displays choice selections from the country's greatest repository of books (more than 14 million), newspapers, and sound recordings, including *Magna Carta*, the *Lindisfarne Gospel*, and a copy of Gutenberg's *Bible*. There's also a gallery for temporary shows, such as a recent exhibition of 19th-century photographs of London. For gaining access to the collection, see p. 165.

96 Euston Road, NW1. ⓒ **0870 444 1500.** www.bl.uk. Mon, Wed–Fri 9:30am–6pm, Tues 9:30am–8pm, Sat 9:30am–5pm, Sun 11am–5pm. Tube/Train: Euston, King's Cross. Train: St. Pancras.

★ **British Museum** `FREE`   The votes are in and the British Museum has won again. The 6 million-plus people who explore its acres of galleries each year make it London's most popular tourist attraction. With 250 years of experience, it's had time to build quite a collection. Much of it was accumulated during the days of the Empire, when Britain regarded a large portion of the world as its personal closing-down sale, removing any treasures that weren't physically tied down (and quite a few that were) and shipping them back to its capital. Star exhibits include the Rosetta Stone, 2,000-year-old Lindow Man, the Sutton Hoo Treasure, and the Elgin Marbles/Parthenon friezes (depending on what side of the keep them/give them back debate you're on). The museum's Great Court, with its crazy-paving-style glass roof, is a lovely public space to sit and plan your route through the huge collection. Free half-hour 'Eye Opener Tours' to different sections of the museum (Ancient Greece, Africa, and so on) depart every 15 to 30 minutes from 11am to 3:45pm, and free in-depth drop-in gallery lectures by guest speakers are given at 1:15pm Tuesday to Saturday. Check with the front desk for the current programme.

Great Russell Street, WC1. ⓒ **020 7323 8000.** www.britishmuseum.org. Galleries: Mon–Wed & Sun 10am–5:30pm, Thurs & Fri 10am–8:30pm. Great Court: Mon–Wed & Sun 9am–6pm, Thurs–Sat 9am–11pm. Tube: Holborn, Tottenham Court Road, Russell Square.

The Charles Dickens Museum   Come on a Wednesday afternoon and your £5 not only gains you access to the great 19th-century novelist and chronicler's only surviving London home and its associated memorabilia, but also entitles you to handle some of his possessions, and even to write with his quill pen. Try to plan something suitably worthy to scribe. `FINE PRINT` Handling sessions are run by volunteers and so do not happen every week. Check ahead.

48 Doughty Street, WC1. ⓒ **020 7405 2127.** www.dickensmuseum.com. Admission £5. Mon–Sat 10am–5pm, Sun 11am–5pm. Tube: Russell Square.

★ **Museum of London** `FREE`   By the time this guide hits the streets, the capital's only museum dedicated to itself should have fully reopened following a £20 million revamp. Newly souped-up galleries on 'London Before London', 'Roman London', 'Medieval London', and the 'Great Fire' will augment the existing post-1666 displays to create an entire overview of the city's history. Free gallery tours are given daily at midday and 4pm, and free drop-in, historically themed children's activities are offered in the museum's Clore Learning Centre during school holidays.

London Wall, EC2. ✆ **020 7001 9844**. www.museumoflondon.org.uk. Mon–Fri 9:15am–6pm, Sat & Sun 10am–6pm. Tube: St. Paul's. Tube/Train: Barbican.

Museum of London: Docklands   It's £5 to enter the Museum of London's Thameside outpost, but since that ticket buys you unlimited visits for a year, it represents good value. The museum's focus is on the capital's river and, in particular, the growth and demise of the trading industry founded upon it. Housed in a relic of that industry, a Georgian warehouse, displays look at the history of the docks, focusing on both the local social aspects—you can walk through 'Sailor Town', a reconstructed Victorian community—and the global implications of London's rise as a major trading city. The more unsavoury aspects of the subject are examined in 'London: Sugar and Slavery'. Various London-themed family events, such as storytellings, drawing sessions, and drum-making workshops, many of them free, are staged during the school holidays. Free 'highlights' tours of the collection are given on Wednesdays and Saturdays at 3pm.

West India Quay, Canary Wharf, E14. ✆ **020 7001 9844**. www.museumindocklands. org.uk. Admission £5. Daily 10am–6pm. Tube: Canary Wharf. DLR: West India Quay.

National Archives FREE   If you fancy uncovering a government conspiracy, or just doing a bit of research into your own family history, this is the place to start your investigation. The Archives' vast vaults contain countless official government documents dating back to the 11th century—everything from parchment scrolls to e-mails. If you want to do a bit of general snooping into the past, there's also a museum featuring changing displays of historic documents—they'll probably have just a few low-key items like the *Domesday Book*, the original design for the Spinning Jenny, or a letter from Sir Francis Drake to Elizabeth I. FINE PRINT Much of the collection can be viewed on microfilm, although you'll have to apply for a reader's card to look at original documents. Take along two forms of ID.

Ruskin Avenue, Kew, Richmond, Surrey, TW9. ✆ **020 8876 3444.** www.national archives.gov.uk. Mon & Fri 9am–5pm, Tues & Thurs 9am–7pm, Wed 10am–5pm, Sat 9:30am–5pm. Tube: Kew Gardens.

★ **National Maritime Museum** `FREE` Three floors of exhibits trace the nation's long seafaring history. The first two cover all the serious stuff—exploration, navigation, trade, London's growth as a port, the environment—with lots of model ships, uniforms (including the one worn by Nelson at Trafalgar), and assorted nautical paraphernalia. The top floor is given over to interactive fun, with a ship simulator and hands-on gallery, and is aimed principally at children but always seems to attract a fair share of adults. Free guided tours of the collection are available most days, usually starting between midday and 3:30pm.

Romney Road, Greenwich, SE10. ✆ **020 8858 4422.** www.nmm.ac.uk. Daily 10am–5pm. DLR: Cutty Sark. Train: Greenwich.

★ **Petrie Museum of Egyptian Archaeology** `FREE` A personal favourite from my university days, this gloomy, dusty, and sparsely attended museum of Egyptian antiquities has an appropriately sepulchre-like ambience. You'll need to pick up a torch from the reception desk to explore the dimly lit confines (the low lighting is for conservation purposes, not to save money), which adds to the *Tomb Raider*-ish atmosphere and allows you to pretend to be Howard Carter on the hunt for 'wonderful things', which in this instance includes 7,000-year-old pieces of linen, a 5,000-year-old dress, papyrus documents, frescoes, carvings, burial goods, jewellery, and more.

University College London, Malet Place, WC1. ✆ **020 7679 2884.** www.petrie.ucl. ac.uk. Tues–Fri 1–5pm, Sat 11am–2pm. Tube: Euston Square, Warren Street. Tube/ Train: Euston.

The Reminiscence Centre `FREE` Most museums pitch themselves squarely at the younger generation, offering plenty of hands-on, brightly coloured doo-dahs for the benefit of short attention spans. At the Reminiscence Centre, visitors are encouraged to take their time. Aimed at those with experience rather than fresh faces, its purpose is to celebrate the lives and memories of the country's older generations—those born in the first half of the 20th century. It's part support group—where people can meet and reminisce—and part museum, filled with stuff to reminisce about, including a recreated 1930s' shop stocked with ancient produce, gramophone records, retro clothes, and wartime memorabilia.

11 Blackheath Village, SE3. ℂ **020 8318 9105.** www.age-exchange.org.uk. Mon–Fri 10am–5pm, Sat 10am–4pm. Train: Blackheath.

MEDICAL MUSEUMS

★ **Hunterian Museum** `FREE` The recently refurbished Hunterian, the museum of the Royal College of Surgeons, now looks slick and smart, its polished cases providing a gleaming contrast to the often grim and gruesome—if undoubtedly fascinating—exhibits within: human and animal skeletons (many 'interestingly' deformed), pickled organs (including Charles Babbage's brain), teaching models, and some archaic, scary- looking surgical equipment. Free guided tours of the collection take place every Wednesday at 1pm. Places are limited to 25, so you'll need to book in advance. Regular free 'talks of the day' are also given—check ahead for times and topics.

The Royal College of Surgeons of England, 35–43 Lincoln's Inn Fields, WC2. ℂ **020 7869 6560.** www.rcseng.ac.uk/museums. Tues–Sat 10am–5pm. Tube: Holborn, Chancery Lane.

Old Operating Theatre Museum & Herb Garret If you don't leave here with a new-found appreciation for the medical advances of the past 2 centuries, then you haven't really been paying attention. The theatre, the only one of its kind known to exist, was once part of St. Thomas's Hospital. Situated in the roof of the hospital church, beneath a herb garret, it was closed and forgotten for over a century when the hospital relocated in 1861. When rediscovered, following 100 years of medical progress, it provided a glimpse into a simpler and *much* more grisly medical age. Flanked by seating for the grim appreciation of medical students, the theatre was where the hospital's patients were taken for operations, which in those days meant amputations without the benefit of anaesthetic or antiseptic. Pain relief was provided by alcohol and the speed of the surgeon. It's absorbing, disquieting stuff, retold with ghoulish relish. Used for drying medicinal plants, the herb garret above, rediscovered at the same time, provides a peaceful, aromatic counterpoint.

9a St. Thomas's Street, SE1. ℂ **020 7188 2679.** www.thegarret.org.uk. Admission £5.60. Daily 10:30am–5pm. Tube/Train: London Bridge.

Royal London Hospital Museum `FREE` A collection of medical exhibits relating to the 3-century history of 'The London' housed in the spooky confines of the hospital's former crypt. The displays trace the evolution of patient care from the gory days of pre-antiseptic surgery through the development of nursing in the 19th century, the introduction of the NHS after World War II, to today's world of forensic care. There are plenty of interesting oddities to be found among the documents, uniforms, and frightful items of antique surgical equipment, including George Washington's false teeth and the hat and hood of Joseph Merrick, the 'Elephant Man', which forms part of a display on Victorian London's most famous 'freak show' performer and former resident of the hospital.

The Royal London Hospital, St. Augustine with St. Philip's Church, Newark Street, E1. ℭ **020 7377 7608.** www.bartsandthelondon.nhs.uk/aboutus/royallondonhospital museum.asp. Mon–Fri 10am–4:30pm. Tube: Whitechapel.

★ **The Wellcome Collection** `FREE` Sir Henry Wellcome (1853–1936) had a passion for all things medical. Not only did he found a pharmaceutical company which would eventually become part of GlaxoSmithKline; he also amassed a vast collection of historical medical artefacts. These form the basis of one of the museum's permanent collections, 'Medicine Man'. It's a delightfully eclectic bunch of stuff: ancient Egyptian canopic jars, Roman phallic amulets, Peruvian mummies, a 19th-century chastity belt, a phrenological skull, even a lock of George III's hair. The other exhibition, 'Medicine Now', brings things up to date with a look at modern medical advances, the discovery of DNA and combating malaria among them. These are augmented each year by temporary exhibitions and art installations. Free tours are given on Saturdays (11:30am and 2:30pm) and Sundays (2:30pm). At 1pm on the first Friday of each month visitors also have the chance to see behind the scenes of the Foundation on a free guided visit.

183 Euston Road, NW1. ℭ **020 7611 2222.** www.wellcomecollection.org. Tues–Wed & Fri–Sat 10am–6pm, Thurs 10am–10pm, Sun 11am–6pm. Tube: Euston Square, Warren Street. Tube/Train: Euston.

MILITARY MUSEUMS

★ **Imperial War Museum** `FREE` London's flagship military museum strikes a good balance between the sensational—all that dazzling hardware, including tanks, guns, submarines, and planes—and the sobering, in displays devoted to the devastating human cost of conflict, the most affecting of which is the Holocaust gallery. With lots of interactivity, including touchscreen computers, a walk-through World War I trench, and a World War II Blitz 'experience', it's hugely popular with children. Free talks and events for families, such as 'Make Do and Mend' sewing activities and 'Life in the Past' interactive talks, are laid on at the weekends and during the school holidays. The Tibetan peace garden outside provides a neat counterpoint.

Lambeth Road, SE1. ℰ **020 7416 5000.** http://london.iwm.org.uk. Daily 10am–6pm. Tube: Lambeth North, Elephant & Castle.

National Army Museum `FREE`   Next door to the Sir Christopher Wren-designed Royal Hospital, home of the capital's red-coated Chelsea pensioners (army veterans), the museum traces the development of the British Army and the British soldier from the Middle Ages to today—from the archers of Agincourt to tank commanders. Its appeal will depend on your interest in weapons, uniforms, and battle pictures—the mainstays of the collection. The 18th-century Indian toy soldiers are fun, though. The museum lays on plenty of activities—including 'meet soldiers from the past' events and family weekends—most of which are free. Check the website for details.

Royal Hospital Road, SW3. ℰ **020 7881 2455.** www.national-army-museum.ac.uk. Daily 10am–5:30pm. Tube: Sloane Square.

Royal Air Force Museum `FREE`   Offering everything the hardcore plane enthusiast could possibly want (plus a little bit more), the museum is located on the site of the former London Aerodrome where its huge hangers are home to more than 90 aircraft from throughout the history of flight—from biplanes to fighter jets. Specific exhibitions look at 'Milestones of Flight' and the Battle of Britain, but for many (particularly those whose love of planes isn't quite at the obsessive level), the highlight will be the interactive gallery where you can sit in a cockpit and try more than 40 aviation-related games and experiments.

Grahame Park Way, NW9. ℰ **020 8205 2266.** www.rafmuseum.org.uk. Daily 10am–6pm. Tube: Colindale.

Music Museums

The Musical Museum   In the days before recorded music, there were only two (rather expensive) ways to hear a favourite song in the comfort of your own home. The first was to hire musicians to play for you; the second was to buy an automatic instrument. These ranged in size and sophistication, from tiny pocket music boxes to self-playing pianos, organs, and violins, and were given strange portmanteau names—organettes, orchestrions, violano-virtuosos. A collection of these jerky, quavery creations is on display at this Brentford museum. Pride of place goes to a giant Wurlitzer cinema organ, the 'synthesiser of its day', which is often wheeled out and performed in all its hammy glory on the museum's regular event days.

399 High Street, Brentford, TW8. ℂ **020 8560 8108.** www.musicalmuseum.co.uk. Admission £7. Tues–Sun 11am–5:30pm. Train: Kew Bridge.

Royal Academy of Music Museum `FREE` The Academy's collection of musical instruments and historic manuscripts is as impressive as you'd expect, featuring a number of priceless Stradivarii. However, looking at musical instruments does seem to be rather a misuse of the senses. To get the full aural flavour of the collection, attend one of the regular free events, when the Academy's instruments are expertly demonstrated. These sometimes run in conjunction with the regular term-time 'Free on Fridays' concert series. (p. 242).

Marylebone Road, NW1. ℂ **020 7873 7373.** www.ram.ac.uk. Mon–Fri 11:30am–5:30pm, Sat & Sun midday–4pm. Tube: Baker Street, Regent's Park.

NATURE MUSEUMS

Grant Museum of Zoology `FREE` Primarily an educational resource for students at UCL, the Grant is also open to the public and is filled with a musty, dusty assortment of animal oddities—skeletons in antique cases, stuffed animals, strange pickled things in jars, thousands of pinned insects, and a remarkable collection of detailed 19th-century glass models of marine invertebrates. Pride of place, however, goes to the remains of three of the most well-known species to have become extinct in recent centuries—the dodo, the quagga, and the thylacine. It's based on the collection of Robert Grant, one of the early 19th-century's most renowned biologists and tutor to the young Charles Darwin (whatever happened to him?).

Malet Place, WC1. ℂ **020 7679 2647.** www.ucl.ac.uk/museums/zoology. Mon–Fri 1–5pm. Tube: Euston Square, Warren Street, Russell Square. Tube/Train: Euston.

★ **Natural History Museum** `FREE` From children staring wide-eyed at growling animatronic dinosaurs to scientists peering at pickled jars of crustaceans, everyone with even the slightest interest in the natural world will find something to intrigue them among the NHM's 70 million-plus specimens. Highlights are too numerous to mention. It's just a great place to wander and let the fossils, skeletons, models, and assorted bits of nature take you by surprise. By the time this guide is published a new eight-storey addition to the Darwin Centre should have opened, providing a gleaming steel and glass counterpoint to the cathedral-esque old building.

The museum offers plenty of free resources, including self-led 'Discover' tours and 'Explorer' backpacks for children, hands-on activities in the school holidays, and 'Nature Live' audiovisual talks given daily in the Attenborough Studio. Free tours of the Darwin Centre's 17 miles of shelves, 22 million specimens, and miscellany of scientists are also given Monday to Friday in term-time at 2:45pm and 4pm. Book at the information desk when you arrive.

Cromwell Road, SW7. ⓒ **020 7942 5000.** www.nhm.ac.uk. Daily 10am–5:50pm. Tube: South Kensington.

SCIENCE & TECHNOLOGY MUSEUMS

Clockmakers' Museum FREE   The museum is maintained by the Clockmakers' Livery Company of the City of London, an organisation founded in 1631 with the unusual remit of encouraging the 'art and mystery' of clock making. There's certainly a good deal of art on display (if not quite so much mystery) in this one-room collection of some of the world's oldest timepieces. Standout items include John Harrison's marine timekeeper (the 'longitude' clock), a gas-powered clock from the 19th century, the world's first electric clock, and the watch worn by Edmund Hillary for his ascent of Everest.

Guildhall Library, Guildhall Yard, off Gresham Street, EC2. ⓒ **020 7332 1868.** www. clockmakers.org. Mon–Sat 9:30am–5pm. Tube: St. Paul's, Bank, Moorgate.

Royal Institution FREE   Founded in 1799 with the intention of 'diffusing the knowledge… of useful mechanical inventions and improvements', the RI and its members have over the years come up with all manner of breakthroughs, theories, and ingenious devices, from the world-changing—electrical transformers, safety lamps—to the more mundane—thermos flasks. At the Institution's small museum you can find out about its achievements—14 members have won Nobel prizes—and see the preserved laboratory of Michael Faraday, the discoverer of electromagnetism. Opposite, as if to show the Institution's continued relevance, is an exhibition on nanotechnology. Somewhat incongruously the Institution is also home to a snazzy cocktail bar called Time & Space.

21 Albemarle Street, W1. ℂ **020 7409 2992.** www.rigb.org. Mon–Fri 9am–9pm. Tube: Green Park.

★ **Science Museum** `FREE` No potted description can do justice to the Science Museum; it's just jam-packed with fascinating sciencey stuff. The three main galleries, 'Making the Modern World', the 'Energy Hall', and 'Exploring Space', are filled with icons of technological progress: Stephenson's *Rocket,* Babbage's difference engine (the first automatic calculator), the Apollo 10 command module, still bearing the scorch marks from re-entry, and, of course, the world's first lawnmower. It's probably the most interactive of all London's museums, with games and experiments to absorb you while sneakily imparting a little scientific theory. At the ever-popular Launchpad there are over 50 hands-on experiments to try.

The museum also stages numerous free events, most of them aimed at children. Daily tours of the galleries are often led by costumed characters, and have names such as 'Roaring Rockets, Amazing Astronauts, and Smelly Space Poo'; child-orientated space shows are given daily in the

`FREE` South London's Bit of Everything

South London's modest collections always seem to be overshadowed by the shiny show-offs north of the river. The ★ **Horniman Museum,** in suburban Forest Hill, does its best to restore a bit of balance. It's not an easy collection to categorise, being made up of all sorts, and everything—South American tribal marks, stuffed animals, live animals (in a giant aquarium), musical instruments (it holds one of the country's most important collections), and more—much of it collected by 19th-century tea magnate Frederick Horniman. In total it holds more than 350,000 objects divided into three broad categories: natural history, music, and world cultures. Surrounded by lovely gardens, it's popular with families, dishing out free activity sheets (also available online) and organising free drop-in workshops for children (on subjects including puppets, toys, music, and bugs). 100 London Road, SE23. ℂ **020 8699 1872.** www.horniman.ac.uk. Museum: daily 10:30am–5:30pm. Gardens: Mon–Sat 7:30am–sunset, Sun 8am–sunset. Train: Forest Hill.

Launchpad, and storytelling workshops and themed days are put on during school holidays. To provide some adult respite, the museum offers the chance to explore the museum free of children at its 'Lates' evenings, held once a month. See p. 155 for information about events held at the adult-only Dana Centre. FINE PRINT Charges apply for some displays, including the simulator rides and Imax cinema.

Exhibition Road, SW7. ℂ **0870 870 4868.** www.sciencemuseum.org.uk. Daily 10am–6pm. Tube: South Kensington.

2 Landmarks & Monuments

London is a city with a great deal of history, and a lot of notable former residents to remember. Perhaps this explains our huge number of monuments, statues, sculptures, and memorials. Below are five worth making a detour to see.

Albert Memorial   A look-at-me monument if ever there was one, this was erected on the southern fringe of Hyde Park on the orders of Queen Victoria, in honour of her beloved late husband and Prince Consort. Constructed in a style known technically as 'mid-Victorian bonkers', the monument is a gaudy, gilded tribute both to Albert and to the glory of the British Empire. The Consort, some 4m (13ft) high, sits surrounded by more than 200 sculptures representing the nebulous concepts that supposedly underpinned our Empire—the arts, industry, moral virtue, and so on. Such is the Memorial's excess that during World War II it was painted black for fear that its kitschy glory would attract the attention of enemy bombers.

Hyde Park, W2. Tube: South Kensington, Gloucester Road.

Cleopatra's Needle   Worth seeking out if only for the contrast it highlights between the British and French way of receiving gifts. In 1819, the obelisk, taken from the Temple of the Sun God in Heliopolis, Egypt, was presented by the Egyptian ruler to the British government, who clearly had no idea what to do with it. It took nearly 60 years and several near sinkings for us to sail it home. Once finally here, the site originally allocated for it, near the Houses of Parliament, was deemed unsuitable, so it was quickly stuck in the gloomy surrounds of the Victoria Embankment, with the lions at its base erected the wrong way round. France's obelisk, presented at about the same time, was sailed with fanfare in a purpose-built boat back to Paris where it became the centrepiece of Place de la Concorde. Our version is, perhaps, best viewed from Hungerford footbridge, where you can stand and wonder what the 12 prettiest girls of 1878 looked like, portraits of whom were buried in a time capsule beneath the obelisk.

Victoria Embankment, WC2. Tube: Embankment.

Eros All those foreign tourists furiously snapping each other in front of the fountain statue on the south side of Piccadilly Circus (London's most bafflingly popular square) are not being pictured with Eros, as the statue is commonly but mistakenly known, but with his brother, Anteros, the Greek god of requited love. Erected in the late 19th century to commemorate the philanthropic life of Lord Shaftesbury, he of the avenue just to the north, it was the world's first statue cast in aluminium. It was also one of the first public memorials in Britain to feature nudity.

Piccadilly Circus, WC2. Tube: Piccadilly Circus.

The London Stone A shapeless lump of stone set behind a metal grill outside a disused shop on Cannon Street… the London Stone really isn't much to look at. However, at one time, the Stone was arguably the heart of the city, placed by the Romans, founders of Londinium, to mark the point from where all roads should radiate, and from where all distances should be measured. Its importance continued into the Middle Ages, when the Stone became a focus of superstition: people believed it had supernatural powers that protected anyone who touched it. Famously, Jack Cade, leader of the 1450 Kent Rebellion, struck the Stone with his sword as he entered the city en route to place demands before the king (not that it did him much good, he was killed shortly after). The legend faded in subsequent centuries, hence its current less-than-exalted home.

111 Cannon Street, EC4. Tube/Train: Cannon Street, Monument.

The Monument It's hardly a giant by modern standards, and indeed is rather obscured these days by the mid-sized buildings surrounding it, but at 61.5m (202ft) this is still the world's tallest free-standing stone column—a boast that probably has more to do with changing building materials than anything else. Designed by Sir Christopher Wren, it was erected in 1671–77 to commemorate the devastation of the Great Fire, hence the metallic burning urn at the top. If you pushed it over in the right direction, it would supposedly land on the exact spot where the fire started, in Pudding Lane. FINE PRINT It's £3 to climb the spiral staircase (311 steps) for views out over the rooftops (much cheaper than either St. Paul's or the London Eye). In 2008, the Monument underwent a £4.5 million renovation.

Junction of Monument Street and Fish Street Hill, EC3. ✆ **020 7626 2717.** www.the monument.info. Admission £3. Daily 9:30am–5:30pm. Tube: Monument. Tube/Train: London Bridge.

3 Free Galleries (plus a few others)

From the comforting Old Masters of the Renaissance to the provocative *enfants terribles* of the contemporary art world, London's gallery scene has them all covered, mostly for free. Do note, however, that while the permanent collections of the major galleries—the Tates, the National, the Wallace and more—are all gratis, temporary exhibitions usually incur a charge, often in excess of £10.

Camden Arts Centre FREE   As much a community meeting place as an arts venue, the Centre boasts three separate galleries that stage a succession of scrupulously contemporary shows by artists both new and established. The great café seems always to be filled with chattering locals, particularly on Wednesdays when the Centre stays open late and serves cheap beer (see also p. 155).

Arkwright Road, NW3. ✆ **020 7472 5500.** www.camdenartscentre.org. Tube: Finchley Road. Train: Finchley Road & Frognal.

The Cartoon Museum   While the number of galleries in the capital devoted to fine art is in the dozens, the number dedicated to the great British art of cartooning is just one. It's a strange disparity considering the wonderful range of material on display here. The ground floor is a chronological display of satirical and political cartoons, from Hogarth to Steve Bell, while the upstairs is given over to comic strip art—*The Beano, The Dandy, Dan Dare,* and other Comic Britannia favourites.

35 Little Russell Street, WC1. ✆ **020 7580 8155.** www.cartoonmuseum.org. Admission £5.50. Tues–Sat 10:30am–5:30pm, Sun midday–5:30pm. Tube: Tottenham Court Road, Holborn.

The Courtauld Gallery   Monday morning is the time to visit this small but outstanding collection—like a sort of mini National Gallery—when entry is free; if you stick around, there's also a free lecture about the collection at 1:15pm. The Gallery, one of three in **Somerset**

House (p. 126), covers the period from the Renaissance to the present day and is particularly strong on Impressionism and Post-Impressionism, with works by Monet, Renoir, Gaugin, Van Gogh (including his *Self-Portrait with Bandaged Ear*), and Manet (it holds his final painting *A Bar at the Folies-Bergère*).

Somerset House, Strand, WC2. ✆ **020 7848 2526.** www.courtauld.ac.uk. Admission £5; free Mon before 2pm. Daily 10am–6pm. Tube: Temple, Covent Garden. Tube/Train: Charing Cross.

Dulwich Picture Gallery   The entrance fee is a fiver, it's true, but that does gain you entry to the world's first purpose-built public art gallery. Indeed, the handsome neo-classical building with its cunningly positioned skylights, the work of the great Sir John Soane (p. 101), is almost as big a draw as the collection, which includes works by masters from Britain (Reynolds, Hogarth), Holland (Van Dyck, Rembrandt), and Italy (Raphael, Canaletto). Free guided tours of the collection are given at 3pm on Saturdays and Sundays.

Gallery Road, SE21. ✆ **020 8693 5254.** www.dulwichpicturegallery.org.uk. Admission £5. Tues–Sun 10am–5pm. Train: West Dulwich, North Dulwich.

Getty Images Gallery `FREE`   With some 40 million images to draw on from the vast Hutton Archive, this is London's largest independent photographic gallery. It's also a handy resource for restaurants and bars, offering a printing and framing service for its images.

46 Eastcastle Street, W1. ✆ **020 7291 5380.** www.gettyimagesgallery.com. Mon–Fri 10am–6:30pm, Sat midday–6pm. Tube: Oxford Circus.

Guildhall Art Gallery `FREE`   The gallery is housed in the city's medieval and much restored Guildhall, and displays a constantly rotating selection from the City of London Corporation's 4,000-plus works. Fridays are the best time to visit when you can join a free tour of the collection at 12:15pm, 1:15pm, 2:15pm, and 3:15pm. Beneath the gallery are the scanty remains of London's Roman amphitheatre, which dates from the a.d. 2nd century but remained undiscovered until 1988 (and didn't go on display until 2003).

Guildhall Yard, off Gresham Street, EC2V. ✆ **020 7332 3700.** www.cityoflondon.gov.uk. Mon–Sat 10am–5pm, Sun midday–4pm. Tube: Moorgate. Tube/Train/DLR: Bank.

Hogarth House `FREE`   Eighteenth-century London's greatest satirical painter may have spent his days gaining inspiration for his works among the society parties and gin palaces of central London but, in the evening, he retired to his country retreat in Chiswick. Today Chiswick has been subsumed into the Greater London sprawl and is more suburban than rural. But the great man's house remains much as he left it, full of memorabilia and examples of his work, including copies of some of Hogarth's most famous, and most earnestly moral, sequential pieces, such as *Marriage à la Mode* and *A Rake's Progress*.

Hogarth Lane, Great West Road, W4. ℭ **020 8994 6757.** www.hounslow.info/arts/ hogarthshouse. Tues–Fri 1–5pm, Sat & Sun 1–6pm. Tube: Turnham Green.

London International Gallery of Children's Art `FREE`   People often come out of galleries saying 'a child could have done that'—and in this instance they'd be dead right. The capital's only gallery dedicated to children's art recently moved to a new Highgate home, where it showcases work from around the world (in 2009 it hosted works from Cuba) and from youngsters on its doorstep. It also offers free art classes to local schools and community groups, plus drop-in Sunday workshops open to anyone aged 2 to 12, which cost £5.

Waterlow Park Centre, Dartmouth Park Hill, N19. ℭ **020 7281 1111.** www.ligca.org. Fri–Sun 10am–4pm. Tube: Archway.

★ **National Gallery** `FREE`   A real London heavyweight, the National could go toe to toe with any of the world's great collections—the Prado, the Uffizi, bring 'em on. It contains more than 2,300 paintings from the Middle Ages to 1900. If you were to look at each one for just 2 minutes, it would take you more than 3 days to see them all; in other words, it's a big collection. Its layout is colour-coded and confusing, but essentially runs chronologically as follows: Sainsbury Wing, West Wing, North Wing, East Wing.

The National is great at any time, but Friday evenings are definitely the pick when it stays open till 9pm and lays on a range of extra entertainment, including classical music recitals and themed tours of the collection, most of which are free. A range of free talks—lunchtime lectures, 'painting of the month'—are also staged, as are family events on Sundays and during the school holidays. These include storytellings for under 5s, art workshops for 5 to 11s, and teen workshops for 12 to17 year olds. All are free.

Trafalgar Square, WC2. ℭ **020 7747 2885.** www.nationalgallery.org.uk. Mon–Thurs & Sat–Sun 10am–6pm, Fri 10am–9pm. Tube: Embankment, Leicester Square. Tube/ Train: Charing Cross.

National Portrait Gallery `FREE` Like a gossip magazine version of the National, the NPG's works are chosen on the basis of the celebrity of the sitter rather than the ability of the painter. The collection runs chronologically from top to bottom, from the forgotten heroes of the Middle Ages to the stars of today—by far the most popular section. Free 'portrait of the day' talks are given every Saturday at midday, and 'highlights' talks at 3pm on a Sunday. The gallery stays open late on Thursdays and Fridays when music—typically classical, jazz, or blues—is laid on. The fancy top-floor restaurant offers a great view of Trafalgar Square (and a two-course set menu from 5:30–6:30pm for £16.95). FINE PRINT The first- and second-floor galleries don't open till 11am on Mondays. Last admission is 45 minutes before closing.

St. Martin's Place, WC2. ✆ **020 7306 0055.** www.npg.org.uk. Mon–Wed & Sat–Sun 10am–6pm, Thurs & Fri 10am–9pm. Tube: Embankment, Leicester Square. Tube/ Train: London Bridge.

The Photographers' Gallery `FREE` There's something a bit 'Plat-form 9¾' about tiny Ramillies Street, a barely noticed alley off the thrumming commercial highway of Oxford Street. Venturing down it to find the new location of London's largest public photography gal-lery feels like entering a secret society. The four-storey building's high ceilings and light-filled rooms play elegant host to a small permanent collection plus various themed temporary exhibitions, such as the annual 'Fresh and Wild' graduate show in June to July. Free events, including evening 'photosocials' and book signings, are often staged (check the website) and there's a good art bookshop on the first floor. FINE PRINT It's due to close in the next couple of years for a major refurb; check ahead.

16–18 Ramillies Street, W1. ✆ **0845 262 1618.** www.photonet.org.uk. Tues–Wed & Sat–Sun 11am–6pm, Thurs–Fri 11am–8pm. Tube: Oxford Circus.

Royal Academy of Arts `FREE` Famed for its annual summer exhibi-tion and blockbuster shows—'Aztecs', 'Turks', and 'Monet in the 20th Century' have been some of the biggest hits—which tend to cost £9 to £12, this venerable institution also has something to offer penny-pinchers in the form of the John Madejski Fine Rooms, home to the Academy's ever-changing 'Highlights from the Academy Collection' display. Free guided tours relating the history of the building, the Royal Academy, and the collection (which will probably feature works by illustrious former members like Reynolds, Turner, Millais, and Hockney) are given at 1pm Tuesday to Friday (repeated at 3pm on a Wednesday) and 11:30am Saturday.

Burlington House, Piccadilly, W1. ℂ **020 7300 8000.** www.royalacademy.org.uk. Tues–Fri 1–4:30pm, Sat & Sun 10am–6pm. Tube: Green Park, Piccadilly Circus.

Saatchi Gallery `FREE`   If British contemporary art is a balloon, then the Saatchi Gallery is the hot air that's been keeping it aloft for the past 20 years. The advertising mogul's collection recently pitched up in the grand and spacious surrounds of the Duke of York's HQ Building in Chelsea and now offers free admission to all its shows, a welcome rarity for a non-publicly funded collection. It hosts a constantly changing series of temporary exhibitions drawn from across the modern art world. Expect plenty of controversy—at least one big one a year or it's not really doing its job.

Duke of York's HQ, King's Road, SW3. ℂ **020 7823 2332.** www.saatchi-gallery.co.uk. Daily 10am–6pm. Tube: Sloane Square.

Serpentine Gallery `FREE`   If August showers curtail your sunbathing or boating in Hyde Park, head to Serpentine Gallery to check out the contemporary art show. In summer the gallery is adjoined by a temporary pavilion deliberately designed by a big- name architect (we're talking Daniel Libeskind or Frank Gehry league here) to be as 'provocative' and 'challenging' as possible. Check out the past years' structures on the website. On Fridays, the Serp hosts its 'Park Nights', a series of changing entertainment—concerts, talks, film screenings, all terribly arty, of course—for which tickets are £5 (see p. 242 for details).

Kensington Gardens, W2. ℂ **020 7402 6075.** www.serpentinegallery.org. Daily 10am–6pm. Tube: Lancaster Gate, South Kensington.

> **Tate à Tate**
>
> With all the money you're going to save in viewing the collections, you may consider splashing out on a trip between the two Tates aboard the **Tate Boat,** a 220-seat catamaran with livery designed by Damien Hirst; it shuttles backwards and forwards on the Thames 10am to 5:30pm. Services depart every 20 minutes. A single ticket is £5, or £3.35 for a Travelcard holder; £12 (£8 with a Travelcard) will get you a multiple use hop-on, hop-off ticket which can also be used to whizz downriver to the Tower of London.

Tate Britain `FREE`   Tate Britain's generosity does not merely extend to providing free access to its galleries of British paintings since 1500—featuring pieces by anybody who was anybody as well as the world's largest collection of Turners. It also offers free short 'Art in Focus' tours, usually on Tuesdays and Saturdays and concentrating on a particular artist or work. On the first Friday of each month are 'Late at Tate' nights, with free events such as talks, film screenings, and/or live music (p. 242). FINE PRINT There are charges for some temporary exhibitions, including the annual 'is-it-art?' outrage-fest known as the Turner Prize.

Millbank, SW1. ℂ **020 7887 8888.** www.tate.org.uk/britain. Daily 10am–5:50pm. Tube: Pimlico, Vauxhall.

★ **Tate Modern** FREE Tate Britain's groovier younger brother, this converted Thameside power station is, just a decade after it opened, established as one of the world's leading contemporary art galleries. Its Turbine Hall is quite simply one of art's greatest spaces. True, the permanent collection may not be quite up to New York's MoMA mark, but then neither are entry prices. Temporary exhibitions aside, everything here is free. Free 10-minute talks on an aspect of the collection are given every Saturday at 1pm. Free events are also often staged on Fridays and Saturdays, when the gallery stays open till 10pm.

Bankside, SE1. ℂ **020 7887 8888.** www.tate.org.uk/modern. Mon–Thurs & Sun 10am–6pm, Fri & Sat 10am–10pm. Tube/Train: London Bridge.

Wallace Collection FREE One of the free guided tours given at 1pm Monday to Friday, 11:30am Saturday, and 3pm Sunday is the best

First Thursdays

On the first Thursday of the month, many of the myriad private galleries of the East End, particularly those along Vyner Street, keep their doors open till around 9pm for free night-time viewings. Some galleries use the occasion to launch new exhibitions, which may mean free nibbles and wine. Sometimes, these may be 'private views', supposedly by invite only, but there's often no one guarding the door, so it's quite easy to gain entry as long as you look interested in the art—get practising your 'this is fascinating' face. In truth, many galleries do little business outside of art fairs and are more than happy to welcome anyone who might turn up. Hand a business card to a member of staff and next time you'll probably get a proper invitation.

FREE I'm Forever Blowing Bottles

Like blacksmiths or cutlers or chandlers, I'd always assumed that glassblowers were a largely extinct breed, their skills no longer required in a mechanised world. Well, thanks to Peter Leyton's London Glassblowing Workshop, I now know different. True, the pieces he creates via 'free-blowing' (the technical term, apparently) are very much art pieces rather than for practical home use, but there is still considerable craft on display. You can watch Peter and his team at work fashioning their delicate, multicoloured creations from molten sand for free. If you like what you see you can also browse the contents of the next door gallery, also for free. However, if you want to buy something, you're going to have to come packed with cash (at least several hundred pounds).

London Glassblowing Workshop, 7 The Leather Market, Weston Street, SE1. ℂ **020 7403 2800.** www.londonglassblowing.co.uk. Mon–Fri 10am–1pm & 2–5pm. Tube: Borough. Tube/Train: London Bridge.

way to get your head round this vast and disparate collection of poshness built up over 2 centuries by one of London's leading aristocratic families. Their London HQ, Hertford House, is a real hi-falutin mish-mash, including paintings by Titian, Rembrandt, Velázquez, and Hals (*The Laughing Cavalier*), Sèvres porcelain, Limoges enamels, as well as a large assortment of armour and weapons.

Hertford House, Manchester Square, W1. ℂ **020 7563 9500.** www.wallacecollection.org. Daily 10am–5pm. Tube: Bond Street.

★ **Whitechapel Art Gallery** FREE One of the capital's most prestigious local galleries, the Whitechapel was established in 1901 with the intention of both bringing art to, and showcasing the art of, the people of the East End. In the decades that followed, its remit and ambition widened to the point where it often found itself playing a leading role in the development of artistic trends: the Whitechapel introduced the capital to Picasso's *Guernica* in the 1930s, Pollock's abstracts in the 1950s, and Pop Art in the 1960s. It shows little sign of mellowing in old age and, following a major revamp and expansion for 2009, is now better placed than ever to promote its series of cutting-edge exhibitions. It also offers regular free talks, as well as cheap film screenings and concerts; check the website.

77–82 Whitechapel High Street, E1. ℂ 020 7522 7888. www.whitechapelgallery.org. Tues 11am–5pm, Wed 11am–4pm, Thurs 11am–9pm, Fri–Sun 11am–6pm. Tube: Aldgate East.

William Morris Art Gallery FREE   The former home of the influential 19th-century designer—perhaps one of the most influential of all time—contains plenty of his pre-Raphaelite, flowery, twirly designs for book covers, fabrics, furniture, and wallpaper, many of which are still popular today, plus hordes of memorabilia.

Lloyd Park, Forest Road, E17. ℂ **020 8496 4390**. www.walthamforest.gov.uk/william-morris. Wed–Sun 10am–5pm. Tube/Train: Walthamstow Central.

4 Cool Buildings: Religious & Other

London can be justifiably proud of its architectural heritage. Its skyline—a mixture of old buildings, new buildings, and cranes constructing the buildings of the future—is an endlessly fascinating jumble of mansions, terraces, palaces, high-rise blocks, offices, homes, government buildings, and churches. The last is a particularly well-represented category. London is blessed with hundreds of churches that showcase some of the capital's finest architecture. Most, aside from the very grandest, are happy to let you wander around their confines for free. Some even actively entice people inside with free classical music recitals (p. 240). In September members of the public can visit hundreds of otherwise closed buildings during **London Open House Weekend** (p. 21).

Inns of Court's Hidden Gardens FREE   London's four inns of court— **Gray's Inn, Lincoln's Inn, Inner Temple,** and **Middle Temple**—are self-contained legal colleges to which every barrister in the country must belong. Though most people don't seem to realise it, their 'magnificent ample squares' and 'classic green recesses', as Charles Lamb put it in the 19th century, are open to the public, and well worth a wander, in among all the bewigged lawyers, Gothic/Tudor buildings, and gas lamps. It's so *ye olde*, it could easily pass for a set in a period drama—and has done on several occasions, including for one of the *Harry Potter* films. FINE PRINT You can only visit the inns' grand interiors by prior appointment.

FREE See Democracy in Action (& See Where You Live) at City Hall

Like a giant glass paperweight holding down the riverbank, the Norman-Foster designed City Hall is a distinctive, if not universally admired, London landmark, a bit like the mayor himself. Members of the public can watch Boris being grilled at Mayor's Question Time once a month, as well as general meetings of the London Assembly. If politics isn't your thing (or not much is going on when you visit), head to the visitor centre on the lower ground floor for one of the best—albeit artificial—views of London found anywhere in the capital: the **London Photomat,** a walk-on aerial photograph of the entire city. See if you can find your house (and then demand that the mayor does something about your neighbour's Leylandii). The building's ninth-floor viewing gallery, known as **London's Living Room,** offers great vistas north across the river and is open some weekends. Call in advance for details.

City Hall, Queen's Walk, SE1. ✆ **020 7983 4100.** www.london.gov.uk. Mon–Thurs 8:30am–6pm, Fri 8:30am–5:30pm. Tube/Train: London Bridge.

Lincoln's Inn, Serle Street, WC2. ✆ **020 7405 1393.** Gray's Inn, High Holborn, WC1. ✆ **020 7458 7800.** Middle Temple, Middle Temple Lane, EC4. ✆ **020 7427 4800.** Inner Temple, Crown Office Row, EC4. ✆ **020 7797 8250.** www.barcouncil.org.uk. Tube: Holborn, Chancery Lane, Temple. Tube/Train: Blackfriars.

Kenwood House FREE This is a great place to come at the end of a hard day's frisbee on the Heath, particularly if the House is staging one of its outdoor classical concerts. Though you have to pay to enter the grounds at these times, you can hear what's going on very well from just outside, and if it comes accompanied by a firework finale, there's no way they can cordon off the sky. The house itself, a fine example of Georgian neo-classicism with a facade by Robert Adam, is free to enter and contains a notable painting collection, with works by Turner, Reynolds, and Gainsborough.

Hampstead Heath, NW3. ✆ **020 8348 1286.** www.english-heritage.org.uk. Daily 11:30am–4pm. Tube: Archway, Golders Green. Train: Gospel Oak, Hampstead Heath.

London Central Mosque FREE The mosque, with its gleaming dome and 40m (131ft) minaret, was born out of a wartime cultural exchange. In 1944, George VI donated the land in Regent's Park on which the mosque and adjoining Muslim Cultural Centre were built in return for a similar plot in Cairo that could be used as the site for an Anglican cathedral. The mosque is free to visit, though you must dress respectfully—legs covered below the knee, and women to wear headscarves, which can be borrowed from the bookshop. The main hall has room for more than 1,000 worshippers.

146 Park Road, NW8. ℂ **020 7725 2213.** ww.iccuk.org. Mon–Fri 9am–5pm. Tube: St. John's Wood.

Oxo Tower FREE This Thameside landmark is the capital's foremost monument to commercial chutzpah. When the famous stock cube company first commissioned the tower in the 1920s, it wanted its name spelt out in lights at the top. Advertising laws of the time forbade it, so Oxo top-brass ordered that its name be cunningly incorporated into the design of the windows instead. The Oxo company is long gone, though its windows remain, and today the Tower is home to smart shops, arts and crafts studios, a restaurant, and, best of all, a free viewing platform on the eighth floor with a great vantage point over the river.

Oxo Tower Wharf, Bargehouse Street, South Bank, SE1. ℂ **020 7021 1600.** www.coinstreet.org/oxotower_wharf.aspx. Daily 11am–6pm. Tube: Southwark. Tube/Train: Waterloo, Waterloo East.

St. Etheldreda FREE Though one of the capital's lesser- known churches, St. Etheldreda enjoys an illustrious pedigree. Built in the 13th century, it's London's oldest Catholic church and one of only two buildings to survive from the reign of Edward I. It's also mentioned in two Shakespeare plays (*Richard II* and *Richard III*). Inside it's a typically Gothic affair with some good stained glass and a renowned choir. In June, the square outside plays host to a traditional 'Strawberry Fayre', a sort of village fête with added strawberries.

4 Ely Place, EC1. ℂ **020 7405 1061.** www.stetheldreda.com. Daily 8am–6pm. Tube: Chancery Lane. Tube/Train: Farringdon.

St. Martin-in-the-Fields FREE Following a £36 million makeover, this grand 18th-century church now looks as good as it did when it did in fact stand amid fields, rather than at the centre of today's concrete jungle. It's particularly fine when spot-lit at night. The interior boasts sumptuous Italian plasterwork and a royal box for its most illustrious parishioners, from down the road at Buck House. Free lunchtime classical concerts are given on Mondays, Tuesdays, and Fridays (a £3.50 donation is 'suggested'). The café down in the crypt enjoys one of the most atmospheric lunchtime locations in London.

Trafalgar Square, WC2. ✆ **020 7766 1100.** www2.stmartin-in-the-fields.org. Daily 8am–6pm. Tube: Embankment, Leicester Square. Tube/Train: Charing Cross.

St. Paul's Church FREE Not to be confused with the great domed cathedral in the City, which is far from being free or dirt cheap, this more modest church sits next to Covent Garden. It's known as the 'actors' church' because of its long association with the West End's theatrical community, and its walls commemorate the lives of notable thespians, including Charlie Chaplin, Boris Karloff, and Noel Coward. Fittingly, the portico at the church's eastern end provides an impromptu stage for street performers on Covent Garden's piazza (p. 249). The church boasts a lovely (and strangely overlooked) garden with benches, perfect for stepping out from the West End hurly-burly for a few minutes.

Bedford Street, WC2. ✆ **020 7836 5221.** www.actorschurch.org. Mon–Sat 8:30am–5:30pm, Sun 9am–1pm. Tube: Covent Garden.

Shri Swaminarayan Mandir FREE The construction of this Hindu temple, the largest outside India, seems to have been almost comically impractical. The stone to make its soaring white turrets was quarried in Bulgaria and Italy, sent to India to be shaped, and then shipped all the way to England to be assembled. The results, however, are clearly worth it. Non-Hindus can visit the temple to tour the interior and visit an exhibition on the history of Hinduism (£2), but must dress appropriately— clothing must be below the knee (ask to borrow a sarong). FINE PRINT Shoes must be removed at the entrance.

105–119 Brentfield Road, Neasden, NW10. ✆ **020 8965 2651.** www.mandir.org. Daily 9am–6pm. Tube: Neasden.

Somerset House FREE Visit the exhibition on the history of this 18th-century mansion for free to learn about the various homes it has provided over the centuries: to an aristocratic family, the Navy Board, the Inland Revenue, and even the Register of Births, Marriages, and Deaths. Today it houses a number of galleries, one of which, the Courtauld, can be visited for free, if you come on a Monday before

2pm (p. 116). The architectural highlight is undoubtedly the courtyard, where in summer children play among the water jets and in winter skaters topple and slide on a temporary (and pricey) ice rink.

Strand, WC2. © **020 7845 4600.** www.somersethouse.org.uk. Daily 10am–6pm. Tube: Temple, Covent Garden. Tube/Train: Charing Cross.

Thames Barrier `FREE` London has a competent defence against tidal flooding, the Thames Barrier, comprising 10 20m- (65.5ft-) high, 3,300-tonne gates that can be raised to block the 520m span of the river in just 10 minutes. It's an astounding piece of 1980s' engineering. Most of the time, you can't see the gates themselves, which rest on the riverbed, but the piers that raise and lower them are always visible, strung across the river like a row of giant space helmets. Gate tests occur regularly—call the Visitor Centre to find out when. The best views are from the Thames Barrier Park on the north side of the river and the Woolwich Ferry (p. 140). It's £3.50 to go inside the Visitor Centre.

Unity Way, Woolwich, SE18. © **020 8305 4188.** www.environment-agency.gov.uk. DLR: Pontoon Dock.

Tower Bridge `FREE` This icon of London was surprisingly unpopular when first unveiled in 1895. It's a hit with the crowds now, all right, particularly when its enormous decks (known as 'bascules') raise up to let a tall ship through—check the website calendar to find out when this happens. The best views are from much more dowdy London Bridge, to the west. If you're desperate to find out more, you

> ## Justice Seen To Be Done
>
> It is one of the tenets of the English legal system that, except in exceptional circumstances, all criminal trials are open to public viewing. The most serious crimes are tried at the Central Criminal Court, more commonly known as the **Old Bailey,** a domed building topped by a gilded statue of Lady Justice holding a pair of scales. If you want to attend a cross-examination, details of current trials are posted at the front door and online at www.hmcourts-service.gov.uk/xhibit/centralcriminalcourt.htm. Civil cases are tried at the Royal Courts of Justice on the Strand. Central Criminal Court, Old Bailey, EC4. © **020 7248 3277.** www.cityoflondon.gov.uk. Mon–Fri 10am–1pm & 2–5pm. Tube: St. Paul's.

Open House Weekend

On the third weekend of September, Londoners (and anyone else in town) get the chance to have a look behind the scenes of their city when more than 700 buildings—everything from private houses, historic buildings, and modern offices to artist's studios, banks, and schools—open up their doors to the public for free. Check the website to find out about this year's crop, which usually includes several major landmarks such as the Lloyds Building and Camden's Roundhouse.

ⓒ **020 3006 7008.** www.london openhouse.org.

can visit the bridge's exhibition, which will allow you to see the lifting mechanism and span the walkway at the top of the bridge, but will set you back £7.

Tower Bridge Road, SE1. ⓒ **020 7403 3761.** www.towerbridge.org.uk. Bridge open 24 hours; exhibition: Apr–Sep 10am–6:30pm, Oct–Mar 9:30am–6pm. Tube: Tower Hill. Tube/Train: London Bridge.

Westminster Cathedral FREE
The views from the top of the cathedral's tower, 85m up, are some of the best in the city and, at £5, considerably cheaper than the London Eye. Entry to the main body of the building, London's main Catholic place of worship, is free. It was built in 1902 in a retro-Byzantine style. To get the look just right, builders used green stone hewn from the same quarries used for the great 6th-century basilica of St. Sophia in Istanbul. The cathedral's renowned choir usually performs daily at 5:30pm.

Victoria Street, SW1. ⓒ **020 7798 9055.** www.westminstercathedral.org.uk. Mon–Fri & Sun 7am–7pm, Sat 8am–7pm. Tube/Train: Victoria.

5 Park Life

London is a surprisingly green city, home to rolling lawns, colourful flowerbeds, and shady trees in parks that provide a welcome counterpoint to the congestion and big-city hustle out on the streets. Most of the great central London parks—including St. James's Park, Green Park, and Hyde Park, which together form an almost unbroken 730 acres in the heart of the city—owe their existence to royal patronage. Entrance to all parks is free. In addition to their natural charms, many parks also offer various entertainment—walks, bandstand concerts, talks—often for free.

Alexandra Palace Park   Set around 'Ally Pally', the former home of BBC TV and now an all-purpose exhibition and events venue, the park's upper reaches offer glorious views out across the suburban terraces to the high rises of the City beyond. Other than that, the park's 196-acre confines have plenty to offer the cash-strapped visitor with grassy lawns, meadows, acres of woodland, rose gardens, a lake, and, most Sundays, a farmers' market. See p. 181 for details of the park's pitch 'n' putt course.

Alexandra Palace Way, Wood Green, N22. ℂ **020 8365 2121.** www.alexandrapalace. com. Open 24 hours. Tube: Wood Green.

Battersea Park   Though perhaps less well known than many other central parks, Battersea has attractions to rival any of them, most of which are free: a great riverside location, a lake that various wildfowl call home, rolling grassy lawns, formal gardens, London's largest adventure playground (free), an art gallery, the Pump House, which hosts free temporary shows, statues by Henry Moore and Barbara Hepworth, and (slightly incongruously), a Buddhist peace pagoda. FINE PRINT You'll have to put your hand in your pocket if you want to visit the Children's Zoo (£6.50) or go boating on the lake (£4 per half-hour).

Battersea Park, SW11. ℂ **020 8871 7530.** www.batterseapark.org. Dawn till dusk. Train: Battersea Park, Queenstown Road.

Camley Street Natural Park   A 2-acre nature reserve with a pond, meadows, and woodland providing a home for birds, bats, amphibians, and plants is not what you expect to find amid the urban density of King's Cross. But here it is, sandwiched between Regent's Canal and the St. Pancras Eurostar terminal. It has a genuinely wild feel to it, making a great city escape or stop-off en route to Paris. Various events—dawn chorus walks, bat walks—occur throughout the year, some of them free.

12 Camley Street, NW1. ℂ **020 7833 2311.** www.wildlondon.org.uk. Daily 10am–5pm. Tube/Train: King's Cross.

Coram's Fields   If you want to spend some time amid Coram's Fields' well-equipped 7 acres, you'll need to have a child with you: adults are only admitted in the company of a member of the younger generation. Established in the 1930s, this was London's first public children's park and is still one of the best, with lawns, sandpits, a paddling pool, sports pitches, a supervised playground with slides, and a pets' corner (home to sheep, goats, and ducks).

93 Guildford Street, WC1. ℂ **020 7837 6138**. www.coramsfields.org. Summer daily 9am–7pm, winter daily 9am–dusk. Tube: Russell Square.

★ **Crystal Palace Park**   There be monsters lurking amid the manicured suburban shrubbery of Sydenham, for it was here in 1854 that
the world's first life-sized dinosaur models were erected. These
charming antique creatures are still standing, even if subsequent
research has revealed the reconstructions to be less than wholly accu-
rate. The other great draw of the mid-19th century, the Crystal Palace,
re-erected here following the Hyde Park Great Exhibition of 1851,
burned down in the 1930s. Today, just the foundations remain. The
park, which also boasts a free maze, stages numerous events and concerts throughout the year, many of which are free.

Sydenham, SE19. ℂ **020 8778 9496.** www.crystalpalacepark.org. Daily 7:30am–
dusk. Train: Crystal Palace.

★ **Epping Forest**   On the outskirts of the capital, but still accessible
by Tube, this is one of the few parts of London to feel properly wild.
In Epping's inner depths, the city can suddenly seem *very* far away. At
almost 6,000 acres it's the largest public open space in London,
encompassing a variety of habitats, including swaths of oak, beech,
and hornbeam forest, which provide an important refuge for the
region's wildlife. Near Chingford stands the forest's most famous feature, Queen Elizabeth's Hunting Lodge, built in 1543 to provide the
royals with elevated views of their hunt. It contains a free exhibition
on Tudor domestic life and offers great views over the forest. Details
of nature-themed forest walks organised once or twice a month by the
Friends of Epping Forest (ℂ **020 8418 0730,** www.friendsofepping-
forest.org.uk) can be picked up at the Visitor Centre in High Beach.

Epping Forest Visitor Centre, High Beach, IG10. ℂ **020 8529 6681.** www.cityoflon-
don.gov.uk. Daily 10am–3pm. Tube: Epping.

Green Park   Visually, it's got a lot less going on than most other London parks, consisting of little more than trees and lawns (hence the
name) plus hordes of daffodils in spring. But it makes a welcome oasis
of calm close to the West End, despite its lack of facilities or water
features. It's just a nice spot to picnic and natter.

Piccadilly, W1. ℂ **020 7930 1793.** www.royalparks.org.uk. Open 24 hours. Tube:
Green Park, Hyde Park Corner.

Greenwich Park   Part of the Greenwich World Heritage Site, the
park has plenty of free entertainment to offer, starting at the top of the
hill with the galleries of the Old Royal Observatory and the line of the
Prime Meridian (p. 103), not to mention views out towards Canary

Wharf (p. 139). Down in the park itself, there are picnic-friendly lawns, a deer enclosure, a children's playground, a teahouse, and a bandstand where free concerts are held (check the website for details). Free guided walks of the park's flower gardens are given in summer, leaving from the Park Office by Blackheath Gate. Again, the website is the place to head for up-to-date specifics.

Greenwich Park Office, Blackheath Gate, Charlton Way, SE10. ℂ **020 8858 2608.** www.royalparks.org.uk. Daily 6am–dusk. DLR: Cutty Sark. DLR/Train: Greenwich.

Hampstead Heath   Encompassing 800 acres of grassland, meadows, ponds, and woods, the Heath is so vast it almost feels as if you're in the countryside. Provided you look north, that is. Turn your head southwards to admire the sweeping views and it soon becomes apparent just how close to the city centre you are. The Heath's attractions are many and nearly all are free or very cheap: flower gardens, masses of birdlife, playgrounds, kite-flyers, ponds and a lido for swimmers (p. 185), a bandstand where concerts are given, and a stately home, Kenwood House, with a renowned art collection (free, p. 124.).

Hampstead, NW3. ℂ **020 7482 7073.** www.cityoflondon.gov.uk. Open 24 hours. Tube: Belsize Park, Hampstead. Train: Hampstead Heath, Gospel Oak.

Highgate Wood   At one time nearly all of North London was cloaked in primeval forest. Today these 70 acres just north of Archway represent the last remaining outpost. Despite its reduced dimensions, the wood is still home to a remarkable array of flora and fauna—seven species of bats, more than 30 species of birds, more than 200 species of butterflies and moths, and more than 50 species of trees. The Woodland Centre provides a free booklet to help you tell what's what, and also organises free regular nature-themed activities, such as bird of prey displays, fungi walks, and the popular twilight bat walks, for which you'll need to book well in advance.

Muswell Hill Road, N6. ℂ **020 8444 6129.** www.cityoflondon.gov.uk. Daily 7:30am–dusk. Tube: Highgate.

Holland Park   The former estate of Holland House, a Jacobean mansion, Holland Park has (as you might expect) some grand formal gardens. These provide a home to aristocratic peacocks, who patrol the lawns during the day before retiring to the trees to squawk at each other come nightfall. Perhaps more surprisingly it also has an area of dense woodland at its northern end. The Ecology Centre gives regular free talks in summer about the resident wildlife. See p. 40 for details of the park's YHA hostel.

Kensington High Street, W8. ⓒ **020 7471 9813.** www.rbkc.gov.uk. Daily dawn–dusk. Tube: Holland Park, High Street Kensington.

★ **Hyde Park & Kensington Gardens**   It has two names, and often commands two separate entries in guidebooks, but this is really just one big park split down the middle by the Serpentine. To the east, Hyde Park's 344 acres of former hunting ground contain formal gardens, woodland, a lido, and the Princess of Wales Memorial Fountain. To the west, Kensington Gardens' 275 acres boast the Serpentine Gallery (p. 120), a model boating pond, a celebrated statue of Peter Pan (erected by J.M. Barrie in the middle of the night), a bandstand where free concerts are staged, and the Princess Diana Memorial Playground. Free themed walks—bat walks, 'Summer in Hyde Park', 'Hidden River', and so on—are offered in summer. Check the website for a timetable.

> **FREE Speaker's Corner**
>
> If you feel like hearing a passionate speech in praise of Marxism, or Buddhism, or the decline of moral standards (or even fancy orating one), then head down to the north-east corner of Hyde Park where for more than 150 years members of the public have been allowed to offer their heartfelt (and often decidedly odd) opinions on whatever topic they choose. Arguments between speakers and spectators, who rarely amount to more than a straggle, are frequent and usually highly entertaining.

Hyde Park, W2. ⓒ **020 7298 2100.** www.royalparks.org.uk/parks/hyde_park. Open 24 hours. Tube: Hyde Park Corner, Marble Arch, Lancaster Gate.

Lee Valley Regional Park   In theory, Lee Valley Regional Park follows the River Lea for 26 miles from the Thames north into Hertfordshire. In reality, there are only isolated patches of greenery until you leave the city. Still, it's possible to walk or cycle the entire length on the towpath, notwithstanding the temporary closure of some stretches owing to Olympic Park construction work. It boasts a huge number of attractions: ecology parks, marinas, camping grounds (p. 45), leisure complexes, golf courses, and more. There's also a dragonfly sanctuary at Cornmill Meadows, where you can see 23 different species between May and September. The Lee Valley Walk is a 50-mile route taking you past some of the highlights. You can download details of the many free activities—pond dipping, dragonfly searches, and the rest—from the website.

Lee Valley Regional Park Authority, Myddelton House, Bulls Cross, Enfield, EN2. ℂ **0845 677 0600.** www.leevalleypark.org.uk. Train: (for Authority offices) Turkey Street.

Postman's Park   This unremarkable park surrounded by offices, with lawns, benches, a fountain, and a statue of a minotaur, boasts one of the capital's most curious memorials. A wall lined with Art Nouveau-style Doulton tiles commemorates doomed acts of public bravery that ended badly for the would-be heroes.

King Edward Street, EC1. Daily 8am–dusk. Tube: St. Paul's, Barbican.

Richmond Park   This is London's best park for exploring by car (or, if you're more health-conscious, by bike). Richmond Park is home to around 450 red and fallow deer, whose presence dates back to the reign of Charles I when the park was first set aside as a royal hunting ground. Now a national reserve, the park's 2,500 acres contain grasslands, woodlands, plantations, gardens, a road network, and ponds plus one of the capital's most celebrated vistas—the 'Long View' all the way to St. Paul's Cathedral. Free walks on the lookout for deer, butterflies, bats, and owls are organised by the Friends of Richmond Park (ℂ **020 8549 897,** www.frp.org.uk) in summer.

Richmond Park, Surrey, TW10. ℂ **020 8948 3209.** www.royalparks.org.uk/parks/ richmond_park. Summer 7am–dusk, winter 7:30am–dusk. Tube/Train: Richmond.

Ruislip Woods   Within Ruislip Woods' 726 acres lies the 250-acre Park Wood, the capital's largest stretch of unbroken woodland. The Visitor Centre, located next to the lido, has displays on the local fauna, which include badgers, stoats, grass snakes, woodpeckers, and bats, and can provide details of three colour-coded walks through the reserve. Maps can also be downloaded from the website.

Woodland Centre, Reservoir Road, HA4. ℂ **01895 250 635.** www.hillingdon.gov.uk. Sun 10am–3pm. Tube: Ruislip.

St. James's Park   The 'bird park', as I used to call it when I was a child, is the best place in the centre of town to watch wildfowl. Its central pond provides a home to more than 20 species, including ducks, geese, and even pelicans—all fed daily at 2:30pm. Guided walks to Duck Island in the centre of the pond, on the hunt for the park's bats, and following the course of the River Tyburn (which flows beneath the park) are all offered by the park office; see website for details of times and frequencies. Brass and military combos play on the bandstand throughout the summer.

St. James's Park, SW1. ⓒ **020 7930 1793.** www.royalparks.org.uk/parks/st_james_ park. Daily dawn–dusk. Tube: St. James's Park.

Victoria Park   When it opened in 1865, this was the city's first public park, and it's still East London's largest open space. Divided in half by Grove Road, it covers an area of just under 220 acres and contains two lakes, a number of formal gardens, sports facilities, and a bandstand. In summer it hosts open-air music events of the Madstock/ Lovebox ilk. The Victoria Steam Boat Club, the world's oldest, held its first meet here in 1904 and still hosts regular regattas, including on the first Sunday in July. Other notable features include a Grade II listed 1862 drinking fountain and an arch from the pre-1831 London Bridge. See p. 160 for details of free summer fishing lessons.

Grove Road, E3. Daily 6am–dusk. Tube: Mile End. Train: Hackney Wick, Homerton.

Wimbledon Common   Animals that can be seen on this large stretch of heath and woodland include bats (seven species), hedgehogs, shrews, voles, rabbits, stoats, weasels, muntjac, adders, and horses (from nearby Wimbledon Stables), but unfortunately not Wombles. At the centre of the common is a windmill with an attached museum (about windmills) for which there is a £2 entrance fee. Free events, including the Wimbledon Village Fair, are staged in summer.

The Ranger's Office, Manor Cottage, Windmill Road, Wimbledon Common, SW19. ⓒ **020 8788 7655.** www.wpcc.org.uk. Open 24 hours. Tube/Train: Wimbledon.

6 City Farms

If you love animal encounters, you have several options: you could pay £18.50 for a ticket to London Zoo; you could sign up for one of the free nature walks offered by many of the capital's parks and hope that the animals play their part and put in appearances; or you could pay a visit to one of London's numerous city farms, which exist mainly to give urban children a taste (and, alas, smell) of the countryside, all within the local community. True, you won't see anything especially exotic—mainly sheep, goats, chicken, cattle, and perhaps the odd alpaca or llama—but the animals are at least guaranteed to be there, you're usually allowed to stroke and pet them, and the visit will be free—notwithstanding a 'voluntary' donation. Most farms offer variations on this standard theme.

Deen City Farm `FREE` Animals: Chickens, cows, geese, horses, peacocks, pigs, ponies, sheep, turkeys. Activities: Pony rides (£1 per child), horse riding, farm tours (for groups). Extras: Horse-riding school (lessons £14 per half-hour), vegetable garden, café, shop.

39 Windsor Avenue, Merton Abbey, SW19. ℂ **020 8543 5300.** www.deencityfarm. co.uk. Tues–Sun 10:30am–4:30pm. Tube: Colliers Wood, South Wimbledon. Tram: Phipps Bridge.

Freightliners City Farm `FREE` Animals: Bees, chickens, cows, ducks, geese, goats, pigeons, pigs, quail, rabbits. Activities: Farm tours (for groups), spinning and weaving classes (£5). Extras: Café, shop, Saturday market.

Freightliners Farm, Sheringham Road, N7. ℂ **020 7609 0467.** www.freightliners farm.org.uk. Tues–Sun 10am–5pm. Tube: Caledonian Road. Tube/Train: Highbury & Islington.

Hackney City Farm `FREE` Animals: Chickens, chinchillas, cows, donkeys, goats, guinea pigs, pigs, rabbits. Activities: Courses on vegetable gardening, bee keeping, straw bale building, and more. Extras: Garden, café.

Hackney City Farm, 1a Goldsmiths Row, E2. ℂ **020 7729 6381.** www.hackneycity farm.co.uk. Tues–Sun 10am–4:30pm. Tube: Bethnal Green. Train: Cambridge Heath.

Kentish Town City Farm `FREE` Animals: Chickens, cows, ducks, geese, goats, horses, pigs, sheep. Activities: Drop-in activities for under 5s, pony rides (£1). Extras: Garden, horse-riding lessons (£60 for four).

1 Cressfield Close, off Grafton Road, NW5. ℂ **020 7916 5421.** www.ktcityfarm.org. uk. Suggested donation £1. Tues–Sun 9:30am–5:30pm. Tube/Train: Kentish Town. Train: Gospel Oak.

Mudchute Park & Farm `FREE` Animals: Canaries, chickens, cows, donkeys, ducks, geese, ferrets, goats, guinea pigs, llamas, pigs, sheep, turkeys. Activities: Animal encounter sessions. Extras: Equestrian centre, café, picnic areas.

Pier Street, Isle of Dogs, E14. ℂ **020 7515 5901.** www.mudchute.org. Daily 9:30am–4:30pm. DLR: Mudchute.

Spitalfields City Farm `FREE` Animals: Chickens, donkeys, goats, pigs, ponies, rabbits (mostly rare breeds). Activities: Young farmers' club, animal encounter sessions, workshops on dairying and sustainability. Extras: Café, gardens.

Buxton Street, E1. ℂ **020 7247 8762.** www.spitalfieldscityfarm.org. Tues–Sun 10am–4:30pm. Tube: Whitechapel.

Surrey Docks Farm FREE Animals: Bees, chickens, cows, donkeys, ducks, geese, goats, sheep, turkeys. Activities: Young farmers' club for 8 to 13 year olds. Extras: Herb garden, dairy, orchard, forge, café, shop.

South Warf, Rotherhithe Street, SE16. ℂ **020 7231 1010**. www.surreydocksfarm.org. uk. Tues–Sun 10am–5pm. Tube: Canada Water.

Vauxhall City Farm FREE Animals: Alpacas, chickens, cows, ferrets, goats, guinea pigs, horses, rabbits. Activities: Talk tours, young farmers' club. Extras: Dye garden, ecology garden, riding therapy centre.

165 Tyers Street, SE11. ℂ **020 7582 4204**. www.vauxhallcityfarm.org. Tues–Thurs & Sat–Sun 10am–5pm. Tube/Train: Vauxhall.

7 Walks & Tours

Walking is one of London's great free attractions—perhaps the greatest. The city's crazy, jumbled layout, which adheres to no grid or plan, makes for wonderful adventures with surprises and architectural treats around almost every corner. This haphazard layout also makes it easy to get lost: never go off-piste without a map. Several companies offer themed guided walks around the capital, including ghost walks, royal walks, *Harry Potter* walks, and the inexplicably popular Jack the Ripper walks. Some are pretty expensive. **London Walks** (ℂ **020 7624 3978**. www.walks.com), one of the best companies, offers its services and a huge list of options for a reasonable £7.

Bike Tours for under £20 Cycle hire is just not that cheap in London, starting at around £15 a day for a bike and around £20 for a guided tour. The London Bicycle Company does a reasonable deal on a 6-mile tour of central London for £15.95, with an extra day's cycling for £4.

London Bicycle Tour Company, 1a Gabriel's Wharf, 56 Upper Ground, SE1. ℂ **020 7928 6838**. www.londonbicycle.com. Daily 10am–6pm. Tube/Train: Waterloo. Train: Waterloo East.

Jubilee Walkway This 14-mile-long route, created for the Queen's Silver Jubilee in 1977, takes you past many of the headline sights of central London—Tate Modern, the London Eye, and Big Ben among them—as well as occasional hidden corners. More than 300 silver discs point the way, panoramic panels interpret the views; and gold discs, added for the Golden Jubilee in 2002, mark significant events. Download a map at www.jubileewalkway.org.uk.

DIY London—Bus Tours

An official open-top sightseeing bus tour around tourist London will set you back something in the region of £25. However, with a £3.80 1-day bus pass in hand, it' s possible to DIY (although you will also have to provide your own running commentary). London's double-decker buses, as well as being efficient means to get from A(ldgate) to B(rockley), are perfect for sightseeing, particularly if you snaffle yourself a front seat on the top deck. From here you can peer down at the scurrying mass of humanity and up at the ever-changing skyline (and pretend to drive the bus, of course). Some of the capital's most interesting and scenic routes include:

RV1: Along the South Bank taking in Tower Bridge, County Hall, Tate Modern, the South Bank, and the London Eye.

3: Oxford Circus to Crystal Palace via Piccadilly, Westminster, Kensington, and Brixton.

9: This heritage route from Kensington to Aldwych, via Knightsbridge, Hyde Park, Green Park, Piccadilly Circus, and Trafalgar Square, is run with a limited service by London's traditional, iconic Routemaster buses.

11: West to East, Fulham to Liverpool Street by way of Chelsea, Westminster, and St. Paul's.

15: Another 'heritage route' from Tower Hill to Trafalgar Square, via Cannon Street, aboard a Routemaster.

24: Hampstead Heath to Pimlico via Camden, Tottenham Court Road, and Westminster.

X26: London's longest bus route (but not so long on classic sights), from Heathrow to West Croydon via Kingston.

73: My old favourite, Stoke Newington to Victoria via King's Cross, and Marble Arch.

You can download routes from the Transport for London website, www.tfl.gov.uk.

Regent's Canal Towpath   The canal-side path follows a 9-mile course from Little Venice down to Docklands, weaving its way under the bridges and between the back gardens of North and East London. The most scenic, and most popular, section links Little Venice with Camden Lock via

DIY London—Blue Plaque Tours

Ticking off the commemorative plates mounted on the former homes of illustrious residents makes for a good impromptu walk. More than 500 blue plaques adorn London's streets, all erected and maintained by English Heritage (www.english-heritage.org. uk). The website has a complete list, which you can use to devise your own tour. Some notables to look for in central London include:

John Logie Baird, the inventor of television, 22 Frith Street, W1.

George Frideric Handel, 18th-century composer, 25 Brook Street, W1.

Jimi Hendrix, rock star, next door to Handel at 23 Brook Street, W1.

Karl Marx, radical political philosopher, 28 Dean Street, W1.

Keith Moon, drummer with The Who, 90 Wardour Street, W1.

William Pitt the Younger, 18th-century prime minister, 120 Baker Street, W1.

Regent's Park and London Zoo. If you fancy splashing out, to take it easy, the London Waterbus Company offers narrowboat trips along this stretch for £6.50, one way. Download a map of the canal's route from www.waterscape.com.

London Waterbus Company. ✆ **020 7482 2660.** www.londonwaterbus.com.

Walk London Transport for London's (p. 311) perambulatory offshoot, this dedicated walking website provides free information, section-by-section maps, and audioguides for half a dozen major London walking routes. These include the 14-mile Jubilee Walkway around central London (see above), the 13-mile Lee Valley route from the Thames to the countryside (p. 132), the Thames Path (four sections covering the 36-mile London stretch of the river), and the London Loop, 150 miles around the circumference of Greater London, split into 24 sections of 8–17 miles long.

Walk London. ✆ **0870 240 6094.** www. walklondon.org.uk.

8 London's Best Complimentary Vistas

To catch a lift to the top of Westminster Cathedral costs £5 (p. 128), to clamber to the highest gallery of St. Paul's £11, while a spin above the skyline aboard the London Eye is a whopping £17. They all offer great views, no question, with the city assembled before you like a giant, intricate Lego set. But there are free alternatives.

Canonbie Road This little-known viewpoint is one of the best, the steep climb to the top of a South London street revealing Battersea Power Station, the London Eye, the BT Tower, Canary Wharf, and the Millennium Dome—practically the whole set. Train: Honor Oak Park.

Greenwich Park One of London's loveliest views, encompassing the park, the Inigo Jones-designed Queen's House, Sir Christopher Wren's Old Royal Naval College, and across the river to a Canary Wharf backdrop (p. 130). DLR/Train: Greenwich.

London Bridge For more than 1,500 years, this was central London's only permanent river crossing. The current bridge, opened in 1973, is so featureless and nondescript as to seem almost like an ironic comment on the fascinating, riotous medieval version, which was once lined with shops and houses. However, London Bridge does serve up great views of the capital's current most photogenic span, Tower Bridge just downriver, as it raises and lowers its decks (p. 127). Tube/Train: London Bridge.

The Long View This is the appropriate name given to the uninterrupted vista stretching for 10 miles from King Henry's Mound in Richmond Park to St. Paul's Cathedral. There are strict laws preventing the erection of any building that might obscure this view, so it's not going anywhere anytime soon. Tube/Train: Richmond.

Parliament Hill, Hampstead Heath From the bucolic heights

Going Underground

South-east London has two foot tunnels that burrow directly under the Thames, one at Greenwich and one at Woolwich. There's not a great deal to them—they're just tunnels—but children (and, if we're honest, a few adults) always get a kick out of walking *beneath* the river. There's something wonderfully impossible about it. Greenwich opened in 1902 and runs for 371m between Cutty Sark Gardens and Island Gardens on the Isle of Dogs; Woolwich opened in 1912 and runs for 504m from Woolwich to North Woolwich. Greenwich Foot Tunnel, Cutty Sark Gardens, SE10. www.greenwich.gov.uk. Open 24 hours, lift operates Mon–Sat 7am–7pm, Sun 10am–5:30pm. DLR: Cutty Sark.

Woolwich Foot Tunnel, SE18. www.greenwich.gov.uk. Open 24 hours, lift operates Mon–Sat 7:30am–6pm, Sun 9am–4:30pm. Train: Woolwich Arsenal.

of the Heath, sit yourself on a bench and see how many London landmarks you can tick off: the Gherkin, Tower 42, St. Paul's, and Canary
Wharf are just a handful of them. Tube/Train: Hampstead Heath.

Primrose Hill   A plaque at the summit of this terribly pretty (and terribly posh) park identifies all the buildings you can see punctuating
the middle distance, including the BT Tower, the London Eye, and
Centre Point. Tube: Chalk Farm, Camden.

Shooters Hill   South London's highest point, 132m up, was named
after either archers, who used to practise here in the Middle Ages, or
highwaymen who used to rob here, depending on which story you
believe. It offers grand views out across the low-rise South London
skyline to the high rises of the city centre. Train: Blackheath.

Westminster Bridge   Stand in the centre and you can see, to the
north, the fussy neo-Gothic bulk of the Houses of Parliament, and to
the south, County Hall and the London Eye. The views are particularly lovely at night when the spotlights come on. Tube: Westminster.

Woolwich Free Ferry   The only free boat trip available on the
Thames, the ferry crosses a fairly wide stretch of river with views
upstream to the O2 and Canary Wharf and downstream to the Thames
Barrier (p. 140). The journey takes 10 to 15 minutes. Woolwich Ferry,
SE18. & **020 8853 9400.** www.greenwich.gov.uk. Operates Mon–Sat
6:10am–8pm, Sun 11:30am–7pm. Train: Woolwich Arsenal.

   See also **Alexandra Palace Park** (p. 128), the **Monument** (p. 115),
the **Oxo Tower** (p. 125), and the **Photomat** and **London's Living
Room** inside City Hall (p. 124).

Free Museum Talks

Monday
Victoria & Albert Museum (10:30am, 11:30am, 3:30pm; British Galleries 12:30pm, 2:30pm)
British Museum (Japan 11am; Roman Britain 11:15am; Ancient Greece 11:30am; Ancient Iraq 11:45am; Africa midday; China 12:15pm; The Enlightenment 12:30pm; North America 1pm; Middle East 2pm; Money 2:15pm; Ancient Egypt 2:30pm; Medieval Europe 2:45pm; Ancient Rome 3:15pm; Assyria 3:45pm)
Museum of London (midday, 4pm)
Wallace Collection (1pm)
Natural History Museum (Darwin Centre 2:45pm, 3pm, 4pm)
Science Museum (Challenge of Materials 2pm; Making the Modern World 3pm)

Tuesday

Victoria & Albert Museum (10:30am, 11:30am, 3:30pm; British Galleries 12:30pm, 2:30pm)

British Museum (Japan 11am; Roman Britain 11:15am; Ancient Greece 11:30am; Ancient Iraq 11:45am; Africa midday; China 12:15pm; The Enlightenment 12:30pm; North America 1pm; Themed Gallery Talk 1:15pm; Middle East 2pm; Money 2:15pm; Ancient Egypt 2:30pm; Medieval Europe 2:45pm; Ancient Rome 3:15pm; Assyria 3:45pm)

Museum of London (midday, 4pm)

Wallace Collection (1pm)

Natural History Museum (Darwin Centre 2:45pm, 3pm, 4pm)

Science Museum (Challenge of Materials 2pm; Making the Modern World 3pm)

Wednesday

Victoria & Albert Museum (10:30am, 11:30am, 3:30pm; British Galleries 12:30pm, 2:30pm)

British Museum (Japan 11am; Roman Britain 11:15am; Ancient Greece 11:30am; Ancient Iraq 11:45am; Africa midday; China 12:15pm; The Enlightenment 12:30pm; North America 1pm; Themed Gallery Talk 1:15pm; Middle East 2pm; Money 2:15pm; Ancient Egypt 2:30pm; Medieval Europe 2:45pm; Ancient Rome 3:15pm; Assyria 3:45pm)

Museum of London (midday, 4pm; Docklands 3pm)

Wallace Collection (11:30am)

Hunterian Museum (1pm)

Natural History Museum (Darwin Centre 2:45pm, 3pm, 4pm)

Science Museum (Challenge of Materials 2pm; Making the Modern World 3pm)

Royal Academy of Arts (3pm)

Thursday

Victoria & Albert Museum (10:30am, 11:30am, 3:30pm; British Galleries 12:30pm, 2:30pm)

British Museum (Japan 11am; Roman Britain 11:15am; Ancient Greece 11:30am; Ancient Iraq 11:45am; Africa midday; China 12:15pm; The Enlightenment 12:30pm; North America 1pm; Themed Gallery Talk 1:15pm; Middle East 2pm; Money 2:15pm; Ancient Egypt 2:30pm; Medieval Europe 2:45pm; Ancient Rome 3:15pm; Assyria 3:45pm)

Museum of London (midday, 4pm)

Wallace Collection (1pm)

Natural History Museum (Darwin Centre 2:45pm, 3pm, 4pm)

Science Museum (Challenge of Materials 2pm; Making the Modern World 3pm)

Friday

Victoria & Albert Museum (10:30am, 11:30am, 3:30pm; British Galleries 12:30pm, 2:30pm)

British Museum (Japan 11am; Roman Britain 11:15am; Ancient Greece 11:30am; Ancient Iraq 11:45am; Africa midday; China 12:15pm; The Enlightenment 12:30pm; North America 1pm; Themed Gallery Talk 1:15pm; Middle East 2pm; Money 2:15pm; Ancient Egypt 2:30pm; Medieval Europe 2:45pm; Ancient Rome 3:15pm; Assyria 3:45pm)

Museum of London (midday, 4pm)

Guidhall Gallery (12:15pm, 2:15pm, 3:15pm)

Wallace Collection (1pm)

Wellcome Collection (1pm final Friday of month)

Natural History Museum (Darwin Centre 2:45pm, 3pm, 4pm)

Science Museum (Challenge of Materials 2pm; Making the Modern World 3pm)

Saturday

Victoria & Albert Museum (10:30am, 11:30am, 3:30pm; British Galleries 12:30pm, 2:30pm)

V&A Museum of Childhood (Moving Toys 11am; Creativity Gallery midday)

British Museum (Japan 11am; Roman Britain 11:15am; Ancient Greece 11:30am; Ancient Iraq 11:45am; Africa midday; China 12:15pm; The Enlightenment 12:30pm; North America 1pm; Themed Gallery Talk 1:15pm; Middle East 2pm; Money 2:15pm; Ancient Egypt 2:30pm; Medieval Europe 2:45pm; Ancient Rome 3:15pm; Assyria 3:45pm)

Wallace Collection (11:30am, 3pm)

Wellcome Collection (11:30am, 2:30pm)

Natural History Museum (Darwin Centre 11:30am, 1:30pm, 3pm, 4pm)

Science Museum (Exploring Space 11:30am, 1:30pm; Challenge of Materials 2pm)

Museum of London (midday, 4pm; Docklands 3pm)

National Portrait Gallery (3pm)

Sunday

Victoria & Albert Museum (10:30am, 11:30am, 3:30pm; British Galleries 12:30pm, 2:30pm)

V&A Museum of Childhood (Moving Toys 11am; Creativity Gallery midday)

British Museum (Japan 11am; Roman Britain 11:15am; Ancient Greece 11:30am; Ancient Iraq 11:45am; Africa midday; China 12:15pm; The Enlightenment 12:30pm; North America 1pm; Middle East 2pm; Money 2:15pm; Ancient Egypt 2:30pm; Medieval Europe 2:45pm; Ancient Rome 3:15pm; Assyria 3:45pm)

Wallace Collection (11:30am, 3pm)

Wellcome Collection (2:30pm)

Natural History Museum (3pm; Darwin Centre 11:30am, 1:30pm, 4pm)

Science Museum (Exploring Space 11:30am, 1:30pm, 3:30pm)

Museum of London (midday, 4pm)

Foundling Museum (2:30pm free talk with £5 admission)

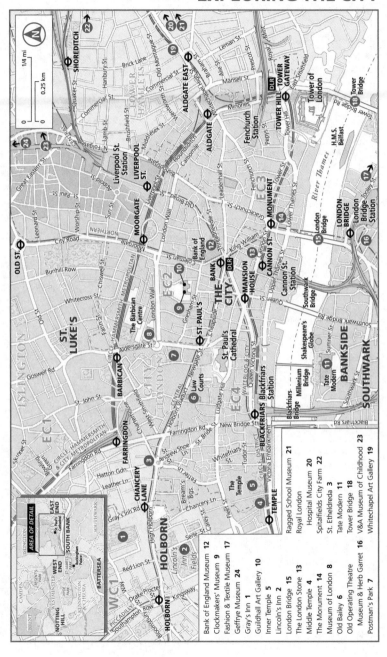

Bank of England Museum **12**
Clockmakers' Museum **9**
Fashion & Textile Museum **17**
Geffrye Museum **24**
Gray's Inn **1**
Guildhall Art Gallery **10**
Inner Temple **5**
Lincoln's Inn **2**
London Bridge **15**
The London Stone **13**
Middle Temple **4**
The Monument **14**
Museum of London **8**
Old Bailey **6**
Old Operating Theatre,
Museum & Herb Garret **16**
Postman's Park **7**

Ragged School Museum **21**
Royal London
Hospital Museum **20**
Spitalfields City Farm **22**
St. Etheldreda **3**
Tate Modern **11**
Tower Bridge **18**
V&A Museum of Childhood **23**
Whitechapel Art Gallery **19**

EXPLORING GREATER LONDON

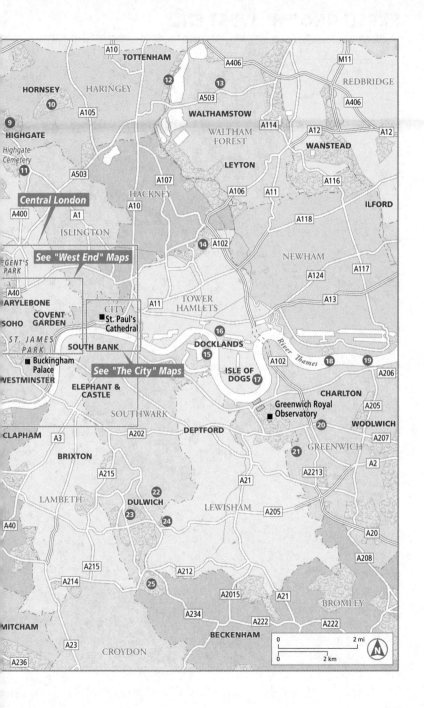

EXPLORING THE WEST END

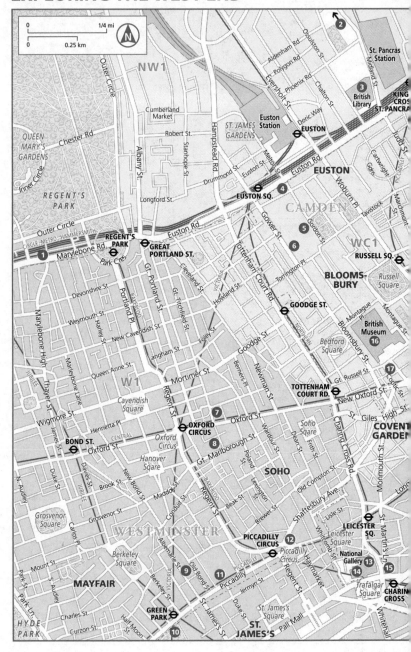

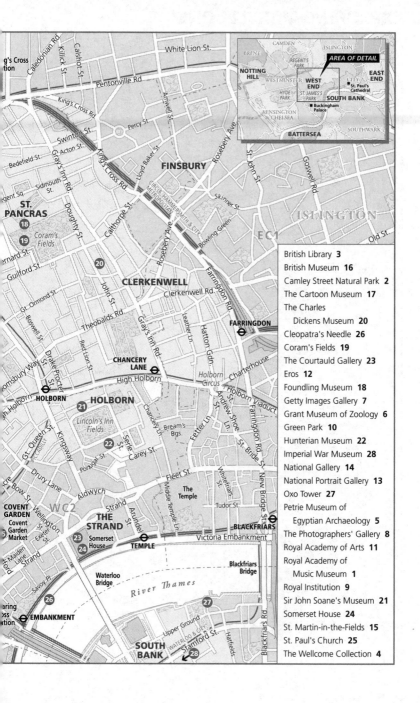

EXPLORING MARYLEBONE

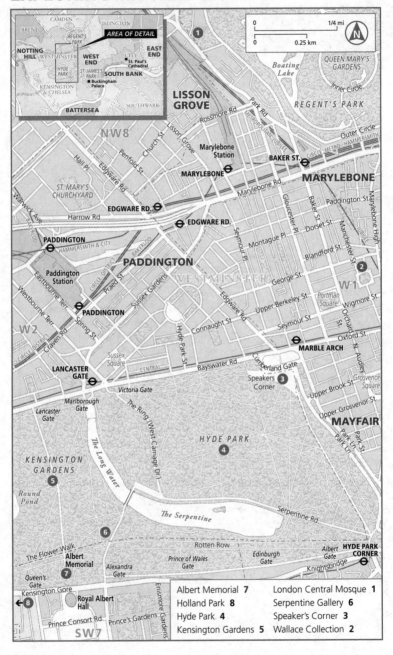

Albert Memorial 7	London Central Mosque 1
Holland Park 8	Serpentine Gallery 6
Hyde Park 4	Speaker's Corner 3
Kensington Gardens 5	Wallace Collection 2

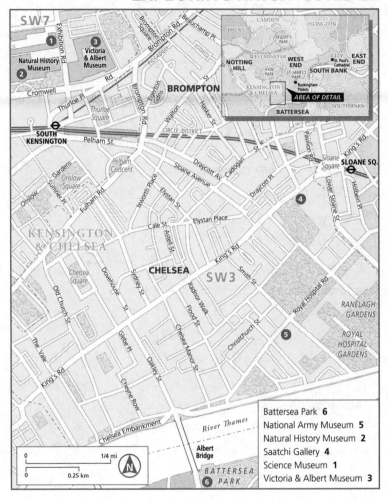

Battersea Park **6**
National Army Museum **5**
Natural History Museum **2**
Saatchi Gallery **4**
Science Museum **1**
Victoria & Albert Museum **3**

EXPLORING VICTORIA

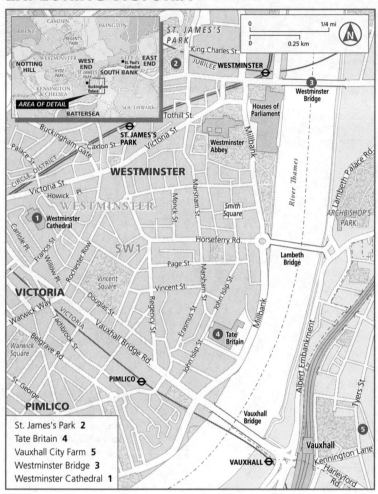

St. James's Park **2**
Tate Britain **4**
Vauxhall City Farm **5**
Westminster Bridge **3**
Westminster Cathedral **1**

EXPLORING GREENWICH

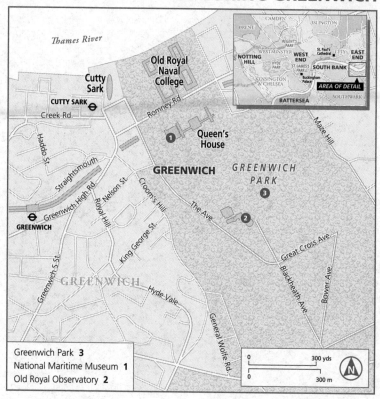

Greenwich Park **3**
National Maritime Museum **1**
Old Royal Observatory **2**

All ages can enjoy the Parliament Hill Lido pool at Hampstead Heath.

LOCAL LIVING

Until recently, whenever someone published a survey listing the world's most expensive cities, we could be confident that London would be right up there in the top five. A credit-busting combination of high rents, exorbitant transport fares, and pricey brand-name goods put us in the top tier of metropolises for the monied. We were expensive, we knew that; in a way our bad value and empty pockets gave us some impoverished pride.

Then, in 2008, something bizarre happened—London fell out of the top 10. US consultants Mercer published a chart of the most expensive cities for American expats to inhabit, and London came a mere 16th. Falling rents, coupled with a tumbling exchange rate, against both dollar and euro, had transformed the city's status from *ridiculously* expensive to merely *very*. It's a start, but we need to build on it. London can be as pricey a place as your purse will allow, but there are resources out there that help cut your cost of living—free lectures and classes, public libraries, cheap haircuts and beauty treatments, cut-priced sports, and more—and it's time we started taking advantage. Let's see if next year we can't drop out of the top 20 altogether. (Oh, and don't feel too sorry for London . . . we're still the world's third-most expensive city in which to buy a home.)

1 Talk Is Cheap: Lectures, Talks & Readings

Education has never been so expensive. In these days of tuition fees and student loans, learning seems to command an ever higher premium. Yet, as long as you don't have a specific course to complete or an exam to pass, it's possible to educate yourself here for free. Gratis lectures, talks, and discussions are staged almost nightly in the capital by a range of august bodies. Given time and dedication, you could learn about everything from nanotechnology to the world's financial crisis in a single week. In addition, many of the capital's museums and galleries also offer talks, usually about some aspect of their collection—and usually for free. See Chapter 4 on 'Exploring London' (p. 99) for more details. The Lecture List, **www.lecturelist.org,** provides a searchable calendar of public talks taking place in London and across the UK.

British Academy `FREE`   Our national 'Academy for the Humanities and Social Sciences' has been laying on lectures and talks on the issues of the day ever since its foundation in 1902. Most are completely free. Recent events have focused on such diverse subjects as 'Classical Music and the Subject of Modernity', 'Toleration Past and Present', and 'Reassessing the 1970s'. Talks normally begin at 7pm, with doors opening about half an hour prior. No tickets are issued. Instead, the first 100 people get a seat in the lecture hall, the next 50 watch the lecture remotely next door, while the 151st person has to retire to the pub and wait for someone to emerge and fill her in on what she missed.

10 Carlton House Terrace, SW1. ℂ **020 7969 5200.** www.britac.ac.uk. Tube/Train: Charing Cross. Tube: Piccadilly Circus.

Camden Arts Centre FREE This contemporary art gallery, which specialises in showcasing the work of new artists, hosts 'Wednesday Late' evenings when it stays open till 9pm, usually laying on a free talk by a featured artist about their work followed by a round-table discussion. For these occasions the beer in the café is reduced to just £2 a pint, a price presumably designed to make the conversation flow easily (if not a bit slurrily).

Arkwright Road, NW3. ℂ **020 7472 5500.** www.camdenartscentre.org. Tube: Finchley Road.

Dana Centre FREE While most of the Science Museum is about entertaining the children with hands-on displays and whizz-bang games, the Dana Centre is more concerned with engaging the minds of grown-ups—or, more accurately, confusing them with a range of high-brow talks, performances, and stand-up shows about science. These often feature collaborations between scientists and artists. For instance, a doctor and a writer might talk about the different applications of nanotechnology. Or a choreographer might arrange a dance sequence followed by a scientific talk on how movement affects the human mind. Many of the events are 'dialogues' with members of the audience invited to contribute to the discussion (or nod thoughtfully, if you prefer). FINE PRINT Events are normally free, but must be booked in advance.

The Science Museum's Dana Centre, 165 Queen's Gate, SW7. ℂ **020 7942 4040.** www.danacentre.org.uk. Tube: South Kensington.

The Ethical Society FREE A kind of 'church of ethics', albeit one that admits the existence of no deity, the Ethical Society was set up

---

Bookshop Talks

Bookshop talks and signings take place regularly throughout the capital. The biggest celebrity events are usually held at the chains' flagship stores: **Borders** (www.borders.co.uk), **Foyles** (www.foyles.co.uk), and the current book-selling daddy, **Waterstones** (www.waterstones.com). All list upcoming events on their websites. Obviously these occasions are laid on as a way of promoting and selling books, which means you'll normally have to buy the relevant volume to gain access to the celebrity. Most are free but if there is a charge (typically of around £3) it's usually redeemable against the cost of the featured book. For more on free in-store events, see p. 257.

more than 200 years ago to promote the discussion and debate of ethical matters and to expound living in accordance with ethical principles. To this end it provides a range of worthy free talks and debates, the most notable of which is its free Sunday morning lecture, given at 11am by a guest speaker on a particularly thorny issue of the day, such as 'Intellectually Respectable Creationism' or 'Public Order Policing'.

Conway Hall, Red Lion Square, WC1. ✆ **020 7242 8037.** www.ethicalsoc.org.uk. Tube: Holborn.

Gresham College `FREE`   The 16th-century merchant and financier, Thomas Gresham, had two great ideas in his life; one, the establishment of a Royal Exchange, was about making lots of money. But it was balanced out by the other, which was about giving it away again, or at least setting aside funds in his will for the foundation of a college to provide free lectures to the public. Some 400-plus years later and Gresham College, which does not enrol students, teach courses, or award degrees, is still delivering the free aural goods with a year-round programme of lectures and talks by its eight resident professors. Subjects tend to cover a range of different disciplines, as a selection of past talk titles show: 'The Ascent of Money: An Evolutionary Approach to Financial History', 'Our Changing Bodies: The Lessons of Anthropometric History', and (my favourite) 'Sisters-in-Law: The Irresistible Rise of Women in Wigs'.

Barnard's Inn Hall, EC1N. ✆ **020 7831 0575.** www.gresham.ac.uk. Tube: Chancery Lane.

London School of Economics `FREE`   Countless illustrious speakers have addressed the LSE's lectern, Bill Clinton among them. Most of the series of lectures and discussions is free to attend, although any featuring well-known public figures usually require pre-booking. During term-time you'll choose from a huge range of events, many timetabled simultaneously. On one night there might be a round-table discussion on 'Rising Asia in the World Crisis' at the same time as a lecture on 'Reflections on the Revolution in Europe: Can Europe be the Same with Different People in It?' Which to attend is almost too tough a call to make. As you might expect given the host, most talks tackle weighty economic and political issues. FINE PRINT Events usually start at 6:30pm and typically last till 8pm.

London Conference and Events Office, London School of Economics and Political Science, Houghton Street, WC2. ✆ **020 7955 6043.** www.lse.ac.uk/collections/LSE PublicLecturesAndEvents. Tube: Temple, Holborn.

Royal Institution of Great Britain `FREE` Although the famous Christmas lectures, in which earnest scientists with wilfully academic hair try to explain the wonders of the universe to an audience of young people, do incur a hefty admission fee of £23 (£13 for RI members), the institution also organises plenty of cheap and free talks and events. These include Fiction Lab, a free monthly book club based on works of fiction that deal with scientific issues, and Cafe Scientifique, a series of informal talks and debates on the latest scientific and technological developments. See p. 112 for details of the Royal Institution's Faraday Museum. `FINE PRINT` Tickets are free but must be booked in advance.

21 Albemarle Street, W1. © **020 7409 2992**. www.rigb.org. Tube: Piccadilly Circus.

Royal Society of Arts `FREE` If you're expecting a cosy society dedicated to the promotion of watercolours, you're going to be disappointed. Founded in 1754, the body's full name, 'The Society of Arts, Manufactures, and Commerce', gives a clearer indication of its remit. It's primarily concerned with political, social, and economic matters and likes to see itself, rather immodestly, as 'a cradle of enlightenment thinking and a force for social progress'. To this end, the Society offers a generous programme of free events featuring talks by leading politicians, scientists, and economists (Alain de Botton, George Osborne, and Al Gore have spoken recently). Free lunchtime talks are given most Thursdays at 1pm, usually with only-this-talk-can-save-the-world titles: 'Freedom for Sale: How We Made Money and Lost Our Liberty'; 'The Crisis of Islamic Civilisation'; and 'God, Globalisation, and the End of the War on Terror'. You can also watch live videocasts of the talks on its website and access an archive of past lectures and discussions.

8 John Adam Street, WC2. © **020 7930 5115**. www.thersa.org. Tube/Train: Charing Cross.

★ **University College London** `FREE` A little thought with your takeaway? My alma mater has been staging lunch-hour lectures since 1942. These typically take place at 1:15pm on Tuesdays and Thursdays during term-time with speakers drawn from across the university's many academic departments, who deliver 40-minute talks that often focus on emerging areas of research. Recent subjects have included the 'Biology of Ageing', 'M.K. Gandhi and his Opponents',

'Observing the Dark Side of the Universe', and 'The Right to Obscene Thoughts'. Speakers provide the ideas, but you supply your own lunch. FINE PRINT There's no need to book. It's first come, first seated. If you're unable to attend, videos of the lectures are available on the UCL website for 7 days after the event.

Darwin Lecture Theatre, UCL, Gower Street (entrance via Malet Place), WC1. ℭ **020 7679 7675.** www.ucl.ac.uk/lhl. Tube: Goodge Street.

2 Cut-Price Classes: Learn How To . . .

It's nice to know there are still generous souls out there willing to take us through the rudiments of Brazilian dance, or knitting, or gamelan playing, for no reason other than a love for their craft and a desire to spread its joy, rather than any financial considerations—beyond perhaps asking you to drink in their bar or buy a computer from their shop.

Skills for Life

LearnDirect is a government-run e-teaching organisation offering accredited courses in a range of 'skills for life', including basic maths and English, IT (for both home and office), business, and management. Courses are taught via internet tutorials that can be completed either at home or, if you don't have access to a computer, in a LearnDirect centre. Most English and maths courses are free, while e-courses in other disciplines start at just £19.99 (or free to the registered unemployed). See www.learndirect.co. uk for more details and to find your nearest LearnDirect centre.

BREAKDANCE

Basement Dance Studio Or, if breakdancing sounds a little too energetic, jazz dance, or Latin Jazz dance, or street jazz dance, or salsa, or if you really want to bring back that 1980s' Electric Boogaloo vibe, 'locking and popping'. You can choose to sample one (and just one) of the aforementioned styles for free at the Basement Dance Studio, so choose carefully. If you like the way you move, classes are £15 each or £65 per month (if you book for a full year). If you have ever thought about taking up a particular dance style, they probably offer it here—from ballet to belly, and pole dancing to tap, although not the foxtrot unfortunately.

400 York Way, N7. ℭ **020 7700 7722.** www.jumpanddance.com. Tube: Caledonian Road.

DRAW NAKED (OR NEARLY NAKED) PEOPLE

Beach Blanket Babylon Shoreditch `FREE`   Most of the time this is a too-cool-for-school (and terribly expensive) hipsters' bar-restaurant, but every Tuesday it offers free life-drawing classes. Each consists of two 40-minute sessions—the first at 6:30pm, the second at 7:30pm—with a teacher on hand to give tips, advice, and encouragement. There's no need to book, but every would-be artist must bring their own materials—paper, pencils, drawing board, or whatever you want to use to create your masterpiece. `FINE PRINT` Although you can order food and drink while you draw, it'll cost you: the cheapest plates are £6.50, wine starts at £16, and cocktails at £8.90. Concentrate on your drawing and retire elsewhere for refreshment.

Beach Blanket Babylon East, 19–23 Bethnal Green Road, E1. ℂ **020 7749 3540.** www.beachblanket.co.uk. Tube: Old Street, Bethnal Green.

Prince's Drawing School `FREE` The school was founded in 2000 by the Prince of Wales to teach drawing skills. It offers a range of life drawing, etching, and painting classes for around £150 to £300 a term, as well as free 'Create! Don't Consume!' drop-in life-drawing classes on the first Thursday of the month during term-time.

19–22 Charlotte Road, EC2. ℂ **020 7613 8599.** www.princesdrawingschool.org. Tube: Old Street.

Cabaret Art School

A life-drawing class can set you back around £25 to £30, an evening of burlesque cabaret about the same. At Dr Sketchy's monthly events you can enjoy both for just £8.50 (if booked in advance; it's £10 on the door). It's perhaps not the most obvious of unions, but they work well together. After all, burlesque is all about the artful removal of clothes, while life drawing is the artful rendering of the unclothed. Evenings usually begin with a performance by the burlesque artists (male and female), who then strike a few provocative poses for the audience-artists to capture, before continuing with their act. Each song is punctuated by a bit more art and a whole lot more drinking as the evening builds to its climax. Events are held at different venues, which have included the Old Queens Head in Islington, the Royal Vauxhall Tavern, and The Paradise By Way of Kensal Green. `FINE PRINT` Bring your own materials. www.drsketchy london.co.uk.

FISH

Victoria Park FREE The Victoria Park Anglers Alliance, set up in 2003 to improve fishing conditions in Hackney park's two lakes, offers two free coaching events a year. Equipment and bait are supplied; you just need to turn up in suitable clothing—fishermen are hardy souls and the lessons, which typically take place between 10am and 2pm, go ahead whatever the weather. Fish that can potentially be caught (and released, of course) in the lakes include tench, rudd, roach, carp, and perch. Check the website for details of the next free course.

Grove Road, E3. www.victoria-park-lakes.co.uk. Tube: Mile End.

FREE RUNNING (OR PARKOUR)

Urban Freeflow Despite the name, classes for the French sport of jumping up walls, hopping over bollards, and swinging round lampposts cost £8 per person—a pretty good deal for being taught how to 'unleash your inner monkey'. These are group classes, held around central London, which last around an hour and a half and teach some of the basic moves—the cat, the crane moonstep, the flat… you know, the classics—and major things to avoid, such as falling on your head. Private tuition starts at £30 per hour. FINE PRINT Classes must be booked online. www.urbanfreeflow.com.

GET FIT

British Military Fitness FREE If you fancy getting really fit, as in being ready-to-invade fit, then pop along to one of 19 London park locations (including Battersea Park, Hampstead Heath, and Hyde Park), where British Military Fitness instructors will offer you a free trial lesson. And if that doesn't put you off, you can then join for £50 and pay £35 a time for the privilege of being put through your paces by military professionals. Although it sounds daunting, the instructors tailor their classes to varying abilities and levels of fitness, with lessons for beginners (fun and gentle), intermediates (challenging), and advanced level (really quite scary) offered.

Unit 7B and C3/11 Imperial Studios, Imperial Road, SW6. ℂ **020 7751 9742.** www.britmilfit.com.

The Scoop FREE Every Wednesday morning between May and August (7:30–8:30am) a free fitness class is held at this multi-purpose 'amphitheatre' next to City Hall. The focus is on simple cardiovascular routines—often with a topical theme, such as the Gym Tennis routines held during Wimbledon—designed to give early risers a full-body workout on their way to work. Classes are aimed at all fitness levels, but you'll need to turn up early to ensure a place, and to fill in the necessary fitness questionnaire (and legal waiver). For more relaxing entertainment offered at the venue, see p. 234 and p. 253.

Queen's Walk, SE1. © **020 7403 4866.** www.morelondon.co.uk/scoop.html. Tube/ Train: London Bridge.

Sweaty Betty `FREE`   The evocatively named ladies sportswear chain offers free classes to female customers at branches across the capital. These include running clubs, which operate out of the Battersea, City, Fulham, Hampstead, and Richmond branches (the actual running happens in nearby parks), pilates clubs from its Canary Wharf and Richmond branches, a body blast (circuit training) club at the Notting Hill Branch, and yoga clubs at the City, Chelsea, Kingston, and Soho branches. Not only are the classes free but you're given an added incentive to turn up. Make it five times and you'll receive a free T-shirt; make it 10 and bag a pair of SB trainers at half-price. All clubs last an hour.

www.sweatybetty.com. Locations: *Battersea*, 136 Northcote Road, SW11. © **020 7978 5444.** Running Tues 6:30–7:30pm. Train: Clapham Junction. *Canary Wharf*, Unit R1, 360 Cabot Place East, E14. © **020 7513 0666.** Pilates Wed 7:15pm. Tube/DLR: Canary Wharf. *Chelsea*, 281 Kings Road, SW3. © **020 7751 4350.** Yoga Wed 6pm. Tube: Sloane Square. *City*, 5 Rood Lane, EC3. © **020 7929 1790.** Running Mon 6–7pm, yoga Thurs 6:30–7:30pm. Tube: Monument. *Fulham*, 833 Fulham Road, SW6. © **020 7610 8390.** Running Mon 6:30pm. Tube: Parsons Green. *Hampstead*, 35 Heath Street, NW3. © **020 7794 2914.** Running Wed 6:30pm. Tube: Hampstead. *Kingston*, 37 Market Place, KT1. © **020 8541 4101.** Yoga Tues 6:30pm. Train: Kingston. *Notting Hill*, 2a Chepstow Road, W2. © **020 7727 8646.** Body blast Wed 6:15pm. Tube: Notting Hill Gate. *Richmond*, 4 Red Lion Street, TW9. © **020 8948 8459.** Running Mon 6pm, pilates Thurs 6pm. Tube/Train: Richmond. *Soho*, 21 Beak Street, W1. © **020 7287 5128.** Yoga Tues 9:30pm. Tube: Oxford Circus.

KICK SOMEONE IN THE FACE (IN A MARTIAL ARTS STYLE)

Many of London's large number of martial arts centres offer inducements to would-be Bruce Lees in the form of free taster trials. Of course, face kicking is but a small part of what it's all about. Kung fu, for instance, is concerned with developing 'physical intelligence' and 'mastering space through movement' in order to improve your 'self-awareness' allowing you to realise your 'full potential as a human being'. And if you learn all that, you'll be able to kick really hard.

The London Wing Chun Academy FREE   Hosts free demonstration days and kung fu sessions for prospective martial arters.

Unit C (2nd Floor), Cypress House, 2 Coburg Road, Wood Green, N22. ℭ **07976 855259.** www.londonwingchun.co.uk. Tube: Wood Green.

The Martial Arts Place FREE   Offers free taster kickboxing classes (so you can find out what being kicked in the face really tastes like).

88 Avenue Road, NW3. ℭ **020 7586 1222.** www.themartialartsplace.com. Tube: Swiss Cottage.

Tokei Martial Arts & Fitness Centre   The Tokei provides training in a whole range of disciplines, including Aki Ju Jitsu, Wu Shan Kwan (Chinese kickboxing), judo, karate, and Thai kickboxing, as well as the slightly less antagonistic pursuits of yoga and pilates. Deals are usually available for newbies.

28 Magdalen Street, just off Tooley Street, SE1. ℭ **020 7403 5979.** www.tokeicentre. org. Tube/Train: London Bridge.

Weng Chun Kung Fu Academy FREE   This East London kung fu academy offers one free trial lesson to all new students.

82 Hanbury Street, E1. ℭ **07515 868532.** www.wengchun.co.uk. Tube: Aldgate East, Whitechapel.

Willesden Judo Club   The adult beginner classes on Wednesdays from 7:30 to 9pm are a very reasonable £4. And, as an incentive to progress, the Tuesday and Friday advanced sessions are just £3.

Willesden Sports Centre, Donnington Road, NW10. ℭ **07702 322464.** www.willesden judo.com. Tube: Willesden Green.

KNIT

★ **Stitch & Bitch London** FREE   This free knitting group for anyone who wants to turn up is held in a different central London venue 1 night each week. All ages and abilities are welcome, even novices who will be taught the basics of casting off and pearling by one of the Stitchettes, the five women who founded the group. Bring your own needles (recommended size 5.5mm to 7mm) and yarn (not black as you won't be able to see the stitches). The Stitchettes also promise to 'laugh till it hurts', although hopefully not at your knitting. Join the website mailing list to receive details of forthcoming venues and events. www.stitchandbitchlondon.co.uk/join.html.

MASTER THE DOWNWARD FACING DOG

Iyengar Yoga Institute `FREE`   Learn how to tie yourself in eastern knots at the Iyengar Yoga Institute in Maida Vale. There are free taster classes for the yogically curious, and if you like the way you bend, a 6-week beginner's course is £60. `FINE PRINT` Classes must be booked in advance.

223a Randolph Avenue, W9. ✆ **020 7624 3080.** www.iyi.org.uk. Tube: Maida Vale.

PLAY BALINESE PERCUSSION

LSO St. Luke's `FREE`   Members of the public are invited to join the London' Symphony Orchestra's Community Gamelan Group, which meets every Monday at St. Luke's Church. There's a beginners' session from 5:45pm to 7:15pm during which newbies are taught the basic techniques of this Balinese percussion instrument. The first session is free, after which it's £5 a lesson. Should you improve enough, you can progress to intermediate/advanced sessions (7:30–8:45pm) and perhaps even perform at a concert. `FINE PRINT` Pre-booking is essential.

161 Old Street, EC1. ✆ **020 7382 2539.** http://lso.co.uk/lsostlukes. Tube: Old Street.

RING THE CHANGES

Middlesex County Association & London Diocesan Guild `FREE` Ringing the changes is the technical name given to church bell-ringing, a musical craft developed in the 16th century. Bells are tuned to different notes and rung in a series of changing patterns—hence 'ringing the changes'. As a hobby, it has a lot going for it: it's musical, technical, physical, and above all social—you can't ring a change on your own. The guild can put you in touch with your nearest bell-ringing parish. No prior experience or musical knowledge is required, although it would help if you had a sense of rhythm. Lessons are provided free in return for weekly loyalty to the cause.

✆ **01264 366 620.** www.mcaldg.org.uk.

SAMBA

Guanabara `FREE`   This Brazilian bar in Covent Garden is so keen to get everyone involved, it offers free dance lessons most week nights:

learn the basic steps of the samba as well as the less well-known *forró* and *gafieira*. Classes usually start around 8pm, and by the end of the lesson you can expect several Brazilians to have turned up to show you how it's really done. If it all starts to become a bit too energetic and your hips are beginning to flag, feel free to retire to a table with a drink and some Brazilian nibbles. Live music is laid on most nights. FINE PRINT If you want to loosen up a little beforehand, beers are just £2 and some cocktails just £3.20 during the 'Sunset Session', Monday to Saturday 5pm to 7pm. Don't go mad though. You want to be loose, not staggering.

Parker Street, WC2. ℂ **020 7242 8600.** www.guanabara.co.uk. Tube: Covent Garden, Holborn.

SCUBA DIVE

London Scuba   This scuba school offers 2-hour 'Discover' sessions on Thursday evenings for £10. If you like the experience of exploring the centre's pool, you can move on to an open-water course, which will cost around £100. Note that the same introductory course on a Saturday morning costs a less-than-bargain £25. Over 10s only. FINE PRINT Despite its name, the centre is located outside Greater London near Gatwick Airport, around 45 minutes from London Victoria.

Raby's Barn, Newchapel Road, Lingfield, Surrey, RH7. ℂ **07834 772225.** www.london scuba.com. Train: Lingfield.

USE A COMPUTER

Apple Store FREE   Every day Apple's flagship store on Regent Street offers a range of free workshops to help you make the most of your Mac. The pitch varies from beginners' courses, which show you the on switch and highlight some differences between PCs and Macs, to in-depth looks at how to use apps like iPhoto and Garageband. FINE PRINT Places must be booked via the website.

235 Regent Street, W1. ℂ **020 7153 9000.** www.apple.com/uk/retail/regentstreet. Mon–Sat 9am–9pm, Sun midday–6pm. Tube: Oxford Street.

3 Libraries

When the internet was set to conquer the world in the late 1990s, commentators were lining up to declare the end of the library. With so much information available online, who in the coming century was going to do something as last millennium as borrowing a book? In fact, what would be the point of books now that all information could be sent in bits and bytes down a phone line? As it turned out, it was the arrival of these new technologies that saved the library. Far from conforming to their dusty, old-fashioned image, libraries began embracing modern formats, offering DVDs and CDs for loan, uploading their databases to computers (which made browsing easier), and providing internet access, often for free. Suddenly, from being consigned to the scrapheap of history, libraries were reborn as the community centres of the future. They are perhaps the greatest free resource of all, a comforting reminder that in an ever-inflating world you can still get some things for absolutely nothing.

PUBLIC LIBRARIES

Each of the following allows anyone to borrow items as long as they can provide valid ID and proof of a permanent address, unless otherwise stated.

British Library `FREE` If you can't find the book you want here, there's nowhere left to look. The British Library receives a copy of

Your Local Library

London boasts one of the world's finest collections of public libraries. Many of our 360-plus repositories of learning were founded at the height of the British Empire, growth fuelled by a Victorian obsession with self-improvement. Pretty much every town and suburb in Greater London boasts its own library. The new millennium has seen an expansion of the capital's infrastructure, with a number of cutting-edge places opening and several old favourites refurbished. Membership is up, and it's easy to understand why. My local library card entitles me to take out nine books without charge, borrow nine CDs for around £1 each and six DVDs for around £2 for up to 4 weeks, and unlimited free Wi-Fi access.

That's value that even the internet struggles to match (at least legally). To pinpoint your local, visit www.londonlibraries.org.uk, which not only provides a comprehensive list of all the capital's libraries but also allows you to search their catalogues.

every single title published in the UK, each then stored on its 400 miles of shelves. Principally a research institute rather than a lending library, the collection can be accessed for free by British citizens, although the application process is by no means straightforward. First, you need to obtain a reader pass, for which you'll need valid ID, a list of items you wish to see (you cannot browse the collection; items are brought from storage to order), and most importantly a valid reason for wanting to examine them. That reason better be good—of the researching a book, completing your PhD variety—if you're to guarantee admission. The building also exhibits some of the Library's illustrious treasures, open to all (p. 104).

96 Euston Road, NW1. ℰ **0870 444 1500.** www.bl.uk. Mon, Wed–Fri 9:30am–6pm, Tues 9:30am–8pm, Sat 9:30am–5pm, Sun 11am–5pm. Tube/Train: Euston, King's Cross. Train: St. Pancras.

The Ideas Store `FREE` When is a library not a library? When it's had a zany makeover and been rebranded an 'Ideas Store', perhaps. This giant steel and glass cube provides a 21st-century setting for all the usual library services: books, CDs, DVDs, newspapers, free internet access, plus more modern offerings including legal advice clinics and spaces for teaching dance and complementary therapies.

321 Whitechapel Road, E1. ℰ **020 7364 4332.** www.ideastore.co.uk. Mon–Thurs 9am–9pm, Fri 9am–6pm, Sat 9am–5pm, Sun 11am–5pm. Tube: Whitechapel.

★ **Peckham Library** `FREE` Worth visiting as much for the building as what it contains, this ultra-modern resource set the template for the libraries of the new century—dusty wooden Victoriana was out, replaced by lots of glass, lots of colour, and 'reading pods'. Shaped a bit like a giant glass 'L' laying on its side, the library was awarded the prestigious Stirling Prize for Architecture as 2000's best new building by an RIBA member. However, for all its new-fangledness, what it offers is comfortingly familiar: books, CDs, and DVDs for loan, free Wi-Fi access, and plenty of study space. It also lays on a range of events, including regular book groups. The upper floors have great views over the city.

122 Peckham Hill Street, SE1. ℰ **020 7525 2000.** www.southwark.gov.uk. Mon–Tues & Thurs–Fri 9am–8pm, Wed 10am–8pm, Sat 10am–5pm, Sun midday–4pm. Tube: Peckham Rye.

SPECIALIST LIBRARIES

GARDENING

Lindley Library `FREE` The Royal Horticultural Society's largest library is arguably the finest in the world dedicated to gardening and horticulture, with more than 50,000 books and 22,000 botanical drawings dating from the early 16th century. It's open to all for reference purposes, provided you can produce two forms of ID showing proof of address. Only RHS members can borrow items.

Royal Horticultural Society, 80 Vincent Square, SW1. ✆ **020 7821 3050.** www.rhs. org.uk. Mon & Wed–Fri 10am–5pm, Tues 10am–7pm. Tube/Train: Victoria.

LONDON
Guildhall Library FREE   When London's multi-time mayor and pantomime inspiration, Sir Richard Whittington, died childless in the early 15th century, he left his £7,000 fortune to various noble causes. These included St. Bart's Hospital, the rebuilding of Newgate Prison, and establishing a library in the Guildhall. Today's successor to the medieval collection is the capital's largest dedicated to the history of London, containing sections on local history, English law, parliament, wine and food, marine history, and clocks (see p. 112 for details of the Clockmaker's Museum). FINE PRINT The collection is open to the public, but you'll need to provide ID if you want to look at some of its more precious items.

Guildhall Yard, off Gresham Street, EC2. ✆ **020 7332 1868.** www.clockmakers.org. Mon–Sat 9:30am–5pm. Aldermanbury, EC2. ✆ **020 7332 1868.** www.cityoflondon. gov.uk. Mon–Sat 9:30am–5pm. Tube: St. Paul's, Bank, Moorgate.

MEDICINE
Wellcome Library FREE   If you fancy a bit of blood and guts, you'll find it at this vast (2½ million things) and growing collection of books, films, drawings, and paintings relating to the history of medicine from ancient times. The library provides plenty of resources to help you find your way around, including two themed 'Insights' sessions a month when museum staff guide visitors through the collection and provide a closer look at selected highlights. The library also stages a range of free workshops once or twice a month, usually at 2pm, which provide advice about using the collection, such as how to hunt for information relating to your family history. For details of the Wellcome Collection itself, see p. 109. FINE PRINT The collection, including its images, can be searched online.

183 Euston Road, NW1. ✆ **020 7611 8722.** http://library.wellcome.ac.uk. Mon–Wed & Fri 10am–6pm, Tues 10am–8pm, Sat 10am–4pm. Tube: Euston Square. Tube/Train: Euston.

MUSIC

Barbican Library `FREE`   The City of London's principal lending library has a dedicated Music Library where you can browse and borrow thousands of CDs, DVDs, and scores. The website has a browsable index of more than 62,000 pieces of sheet music, and members can hear sound recordings dating from the 1930s at listening booths. Additional facilities include internet access, free 'starting out on the internet' courses, and reading groups. `FINE PRINT` Anyone can join, although if you don't live in the square mile, you'll need to prove that you are a student, have a job, or are a member of a local library.

Level 2, Barbican Centre, Silk Street, EC2. ✆ **020 7638 0569.** www.cityoflondon.gov. uk & www.barbican.org.uk/visitor-information/barbican-library. Mon & Wed 9:30am–5:30pm, Tues & Thurs 9:30am–7:30pm, Fri 9:30am–2pm, Sat 9:30am–4pm. Tube: Barbican, Moorgate.

PHILOSOPHY & PSYCHOLOGY

Swiss Cottage Library `FREE`   Whenever a newspaper or magazine publishes a feature on libraries, it nearly always comes accompanied by a picture of Swiss Cottage's famed establishment. The library's elegant, modernist building seems to capture perfectly that combination of ancient learning and modern living that libraries are supposed to embody. It offers a wide range of services, including free internet use for library members, and has a particular specialisation in philosophy and psychology—it holds the largest accessible collection of such titles in London.

88 Avenue Road, NW3. ✆ **020 7974 6522.** www.camden.gov.uk. Mon–Fri 10am–8pm, Sat 10am–5pm, Sun 11am–4pm. Tube: Swiss Cottage.

POETRY

Poetry Library `FREE`   The South Bank's collection dedicated to modern verse contains more than 100,000 items representing pretty much every book of poetry published in the UK since 1912. There are also CDs, DVDs, and, if you like your modern poetry in an old-fashioned format, cassettes. There's also a searchable poetry magazine archive available on the website, a children's section, and an exhibition space displaying poetry-inspired artworks.

Level 5, Royal Festival Hall, SE1. ✆ **020 7921 0943.** www.poetrylibrary.org.uk. Tues–Sun 11am–8pm. Tube/Train: Waterloo.

WOMEN

Women's Library `FREE` Established in 1926, this is the country's largest collection of works relating to British women's history and the women's movement, with sections covering women's rights, suffrage, sexuality, health, education, employment, reproductive rights, the family, and the home.

London Metropolitan University, 25 Old Castle Street, E1. ℂ **020 7320 2222.** www. londonmet.ac.uk/thewomenslibrary. Tues–Fri 9:30am–5pm. Tube: Aldgate East.

4 Beauty & Wellness

ALTERNATIVE THERAPIES

Our glorious NHS may be free to all at the point of use, but the sheer number of sick people out there means that it can sometimes take quite a while to get to that point. There are, however, alternative paths to health and happiness to explore whilst waiting to be at the top of your patient list.

ACUPUNCTURE & CHINESE MEDICINE

The Institute of Chinese Medicine `FREE` The Institute offers various health freebies, including seminars on the Chinese approach to nutrition, lifestyle, and exercise, plus occasional free acupuncture 'experiences' (and I imagine it would be quite an experience). It's also a well-respected dispenser of traditional Chinese medicines.

44–46 Chandos Place, WC2N. ℂ **020 7836 5220.** www.instituteofchinesemedicine. org. Tube/Train: Charing Cross.

ALEXANDER TECHNIQUE

The Alexander Studio This Mayfair centre devoted to the famous posture-improving exercises normally charges £30 a session, but its students also need to practise on live human flesh. These sessions cost just £15. There's also usually one annual open day when the public can

Rest & Relaxation

Such is the popularity of the spa break that budget-hunting travel website www.lastminute.com now has a dedicated section listing all the current reductions available at the country's otherwise extraordinarily expensive retreats. Two-for-one deals are the most common form of discount. There's often something going cheap(ish) in or around London.

Laugh Yourself Better

Here's the theory: whenever you laugh your body releases endorphins which help to lower stress levels, giving you an increased feeling of well-being, which in turn boosts your immune system. Taking yourself to a stand-up gig every night may be impractical (although see p. 254), but that doesn't matter because, according to **Laughing Matters,** a 'laughter therapy' coaching group, the body can't tell the difference between real and fake laughter. Its response and the effect are the same. In summer the company runs sessions in Lincoln's Inn Park near the bandstand, teaching people how to laugh, guffaw, giggle, and generally achieve a state of happy elation without anything funny having happened first—nobody is going to tell you a joke or trip on a banana skin. Instead, the process involves lying on the grass and entering a state of 'meditative laughter'. These sessions cost £8, but they also run regular free 'Laughter Workouts', for you to find out what's so funny before handing over your cash. 📞 **07789 954972.** www.laughingmatters.co.uk.

learn about the technique and enjoy (if that's the right word) a free 30-minute session, subject to availability.

16 Balderton Street, W1K 6TN. 📞 **020 7629 1808.** www.alexander-technique-london.co.uk. Tube: Bond Street.

MEDITATION

Inner Space FREE The prime goal of this meditation and self-improvement centre is to help you relax. It doesn't promise to give out the answers to your problems, but it will try and help you calm down so you're in a better state of mind to solve them for yourself, offering half-hour lunchtime courses in creative meditation, relaxation strategies, time management, and other forms of relaxing self-improvement. And, once you're suitably relaxed, your irritation levels won't peak when you see the bill—all the courses are free. At other times you can pop in to use the 'quiet room' and sit in comfortable chairs while soothing music plays, or browse the bookshop for a tome on home meditation.

36 Shorts Gardens, WC2. 📞 **020 7836 6688.** http://innerspace.org.uk. Tube: Covent Garden, Tottenham Court Road.

The London Buddhist Centre A £1 donation is all you need to learn how to meditate during a lunchtime drop-in session at the

London Buddhist Centre. No booking is necessary. Evening and weekend classes are £3 to £7. Sessions aim to teach two basic practices: 'The Mindfulness of Breathing' and 'The Development of Loving Kindness'. It's certainly much calmer than what went on during the building's former incarnation, as a fire station.

51 Roman Road, E2. ℂ **0845 458 4716.** www.lbc.org.uk. Tube: Bethnal Green.

Reflexology

Maurice James Reflexology   A free half-hour consultation with Mr James, a member of the Association of Reflexologists, will tell you if the ancient practice of healing and promoting well-being via the manipulation of the feet is for you. Not for the super-ticklish.

Helios Healthy Living Centre, 116 Judd Street, WC1. ℂ **020 7713 7122.** www. mauricejamesreflexology.co.uk. Tube/Train: King's Cross. Train: St. Pancras.

TURKISH BATHING

Ironmonger Row Baths   Now that York Hall's Victorian baths have been transformed into a spa, the 1930s' Ironmonger Row Baths are London's last remaining outpost of cheap Turkish bathing. Unlike modern competitors, Ironmonger Row is a simple setup with minimal branding, and no wellness-speak involving purification, deep cleansing, or detoxing. The bathing ritual proceeds according to set stages. First, relax in a warm steam room to get a sweat going. Next, enter into a much less relaxing set of three hot rooms which are endured (for as long as you can) rather then enjoyed, followed by a reviving plunge into an icy pool. The session is topped off by a full body wash and massage on a traditional marble slab. Arrive before midday during the week and a session costs just £8, rising to £13.20 at other times.

Ironmonger Row, EC1. ℂ **020 7253 4011.** www.aquaterra.org/ironmonger-row-baths. Mon 2–9:30pm, Tues–Sat 9am–9:30pm, Sun 10am–6:30pm. Mixed bathing Mon, men only Tues, Thurs, Sat, women only Wed, Fri, Sun. Tube: Old Street.

BUDGET BEAUTY

There's one word that sums up your best chance of finding a bargain beauty treatment: students. Once qualified and in possession of that diploma, hairdressers, beauticians, and nail technicians can start charging big money for their transformative services. Until then, they need to keep honing their craft and passing their exams, and for that they need people to practise on. Which is where you come in. If

you're willing to place yourself in the hands of the soon-to-be qualified, though nearly always overseen by the already qualified, then a
range of beauty services—haircuts, facials, and manicures included—
can be yours for a fraction of the market rate, and sometimes even for
free.

TREATMENTS ON THE CHEAP

Cucumba   Cucumba markets itself as an 'urban pit stop' for stressed-
out office workers. Pop in for a 10-minute head massage (£9.50), a
10-minute foot and leg massage (£12.50), or a 20-minute neck, back,
and shoulder massage (£20), before returning, rejuvenated and
refreshed, to your daily grind.

12 Poland Street, W1. ℘ **020 7734 2020.** www.cucumba.co.uk. Mon–Fri 10am–8pm,
Sat 11am–7pm. Tube: Oxford Circus.

London College of Beauty Therapy   The College's salon is one of
the best sources of low-cost beauty treatments for both men and
women. All procedures are carried out by students 'trained in the latest industry techniques'. Prices start at £5 for a mini-manicure at the
nail bar, and rise from there: eyelash shape £6.50; bikini wax £9;
1-hour deep cleansing facial £20; 75-minute full body massage £25.
For the more adventurous, a half-hour Faradic body treatment is just
£15—this involves the electrical stimulation of the nerves and is
named after Michael Faraday, father of modern electrical science; he
would have been proud. FINE PRINT Advance booking is essential.

47 Great Marlborough Street, W1. ℘ **020 7208 1302.** www.lcbt.co.uk. Tube: Oxford
Circus.

London School of Beauty & Make-Up   Frugal facials and bargain
bikini waxes are available at the school's Esthetique Student Salon:
eyebrow shape £5, bikini wax £7, Indian head massage £12, deep-
cleansing facial £15, Swedish massage £22, aromatherapy massage
£25. All procedures are performed by students, but overseen by
professionals.

First Floor, 47–50 Margaret Street, W1. ℘ **020 7580 0355.** www.lond-est.com. Tube:
Oxford Circus.

HALF-PRICE HAIRCUTS

Model cuts can be a risk. A dodgy manicure can be covered up with
the judicious use of false nails, badly applied make-up can be washed

off, but short of spending the next 6 weeks wearing a hat, there's no disguising a botched haircut. It just sits there, looking uneven and unflattering, until it grows out. With that in mind, you're best off getting a free or cheap 'model haircut' at one of the bigger hairdressing names. There you'll be in the hands of experienced students trying to improve their skills and practise their techniques, rather than a beginner learning the basics on your precious locks.

Alan D   This snazzy salon offers a limited number of appointments each day for student cuts, which take place in a downstairs education salon away from prying eyes. Prices range from £8 for cutting long hair or a dye job, to absolutely nothing for a short haircut.

61–62 Eastcastle Street, W1. ℂ **020 7580 1911.** www.aland.co.uk. Mon–Fri 10am–7pm, Sat 10am–6pm. Tube: Oxford Circus, Tottenham Court Road.

Toni & Guy Academy   If you're precious about your hair and want it done just so, then it's probably not a good idea to book a student haircut. It may finish up exactly as you'd hoped—or it may come out as that crazy new asymmetric cut your student stylist has spent the past few weeks mastering. If you're open to the idea of change and a new style, however, then Toni & Guy is the place to go. Trainees provide free and low-cost haircuts (£5) during the week with a teacher on hand to check each of the steps—although that is no guarantee against disaster. The cut takes about 3 hours, by the end of which you'll probably have forgotten what your hair originally looked like anyway.

71–75 New Oxford Street, WC1. ℂ **020 7836 0606.** www.toniandguy.com. Tube: Tottenham Court Road.

Vidal Sassoon Academy   You can't be in a rush if you're to take advantage of the low-cost haircuts (typically £5 but sometimes free with promotional offers) performed by the students at the Sassoon Academy. You're asked to set aside 3 hours for a haircut, and up to 5 if you want it coloured. Essentially this is because you're having your hair cut at the same time as 15 other people, one student per client, and each step of the process has to be approved and signed off by the tutor to 'ensure the best possible results' (i.e. to make sure that they haven't mucked it up). Bring a supply of your best anecdotes and be prepared for in-depth discussion of your future holiday plans.

58 Davies Mews, W1. ℂ **020 7318 5205.** www.sassoon.com. Tube: Bond Street.

5 Low Rent: Housing Resources

Finding somewhere affordable to live is London's ultimate challenge. In the end, you may have to concede that, no matter what sacrifices you're prepared to make regarding locality, the amount of space you can squeeze into, or your personal safety, living in one of the world's most vibrant cities comes at a price. Advice on buying a property lies beyond the remit of this book, but if you're thinking of renting in the capital there are measures you can take to reduce the financial pain slightly (I stress *slightly*).

As with (almost) anything, the more central your postcode, the more you can expect to pay. So, you might be shelling out £1,200 a month for a one-bed flat in NW1 but just £600 in SE16. However, be aware that there are enclaves of exclusivity even on the outskirts, in places such as Wimbledon (SW19) and Greenwich (SE10). The key points are to give yourself as much time as possible to make your search—do not rush into any decision—to be as flexible about your potential new neighbourhood as possible (safety concerns notwithstanding), and to have patience. Lots and lots of patience. A bottomless vat of coffee wouldn't hurt either.

Social Housing

Another rental option for anyone on a low income is to apply to live in a council or housing association property. The former are owned and managed by the local borough; the latter by housing associations (or 'registered social landlords' as they're technically known), privately funded, not-for-profit organisations who provide most of London's new low-rent accommodation. Both operate in the same way: applicants are asked to join a waiting list for vacant properties. Priority is given to those in greatest need, such as single mothers and low-income families. You can apply for housing in any borough, but will start further down the list than anyone already living there. To find out more about the National Housing Federation, the body representing the UK's housing associations, go to www.housing.org.uk. You can register for a council property via www.direct.gov.uk.

ESTATE AGENTS

Property professionals are your obvious first point of call. The benefits are, of course, their access to a range of properties from the entire financial spectrum. The downsides are the relentless sales patter, constant attempts to get you to up your maximum affordable price (so as to increase their commission: *be firm*), and fees charged for credit checks or unspecific 'administration costs'—anything from £50 to over £300. Still, if time is short, having an agent do the hunting for you can be the painless option. London's leading property agents include the following:

Black Katz, www.blackkatz.com, the capital's largest lettings-only agency.

Felicity J Lord, www.fjlord.co.uk

Foxtons, www.foxtons.co.uk, the snazziest offices and high admin costs.

Hamptons, www.hamptons.co.uk

Winkworth, www.winkworth.co.uk

GOING IT ALONE

Flat-hunting solo is much more time-consuming than using an agent. It obliges you to spend hours scouring newspapers and websites, and to place call after call on the hunt for that elusive, perfectly located, astoundingly low-priced flat. However, you're more likely to uncover a bargain going it alone, particularly if you can deal with a landlord direct. Many property owners choose not to use agents and instead advertise directly, usually on the major listings websites: Loot, Gumtree, and the like. Dealing direct will usually mean avoiding that administration fee. However, it also means that if you get into a dispute with your landlord, there's no recourse to a third party, although you can always contact the Citizens Advice Bureau (see www.citizens advice.org.uk). Some less-than-upstanding landlords deal direct with tenants because estate agents refuse to deal with them, and not the other way round. The main property hunting websites include:

www.findaproperty.com

www.gumtree.com

www.loot.com

www.propertyfinder.com

www.rightmove.co.uk

BARGAIN FLAT-HUNTING (& LIVING) TIPS

- Use as many different sources of information as possible, such as estate agents and listings websites.

- Pick a price range you can afford and stick to it. Don't be persuaded to upgrade by an agent's slick patter.

- Make a thorough inspection of the property during a viewing. Don't just glance around. Check it has the requisite amenities—cooker,

Squatting

Squatting is not illegal, but neither is it to be condoned. However, should you find yourself making free use of a vacant property for a while, you need to bear the following in mind:

- Squatting is a civil offence (i.e. a disagreement between an individual and an individual and/or an organisation), not a criminal one. The police can't arrest a squatter or remove them from a squat without a court judgement, unless there is evidence of forced entry.

- In order to qualify for 'squatters' rights', the squatter must own and be in control of the locks to the property and make no use of utilities paid for by somebody else.

- To have a squatter removed, landlords must prove in court that they are the genuine owners of the property.

- However, unless there are extreme mitigating circumstances, once a landlord discovers your existence and wants you out, it's probably best to get out ASAP. The law is not on your side. Technically, squatters who have lived in a property continuously for 12 years can claim ownership, but in practice this almost never happens, since the process can be derailed by a single objection from the landlord.

For more information, you could visit the **Advisory Service for Squatters** in Whitechapel, although, rather ironically, they advise ringing first to 'make sure someone's in'.

Angel Alley, 84b Whitechapel High Street, E1. ℂ **020 3216 0099.** www.squatter.org.uk.

washing machine, freezer, central heating. Any omissions, plus any patches of damp or tatty decor, can be used to negotiate a discount.

- Always haggle about the price, even if it seems cheap. Use any telling data picked up during your viewing (low water pressure, say) to back up your argument. It may not always work, but with a glut of buy-to-let properties having come onto the market in recent years, many landlords are willing to accept a lower monthly rent just to get someone into their property.

- Remember council tax. It's an oft-overlooked criterion, but council tax can add a hefty chunk to your monthly outgoings. The tax is levied according to the value of the property, with eight bands rated from A (lowest) to H (highest). This means that the more people there are sharing a property, the lower the tax per head. At press time, the borough with the lowest council tax was Wandsworth (£451–£1,397 annually) while the highest was Kingston (£1,014–£3,044).

Live for Free

Tired of living in the same old flats with the same basic amenities? How about living on a demolition site instead, or in a church, or a school? These are just some of the options offered on occasion by Camelot, a specialist in vacant property protection. Their role is to provide low-level security for empty properties, which they do by finding people to live in them—rent free. London properties regularly come onto their books. Prospective tenants must be over 18, gainfully employed, and quick on the draw—places are almost always snapped up quickly. Unsurprisingly, there's no shortage of volunteers. Unit 4 Pegaso, 20 Westland Place, N1. ℂ **0845 262 2002.** http://uk.cameloteurope.com.

- Be prepared to argue with the estate agent about their fees, but be sure to do this *before* you've signed your rental contract. A credit reference check should cost no more than £50. If an argument ensues, threaten to take your business elsewhere.

- Check the inventory thoroughly and raise discrepancies (in writing) right at the start, so that you cannot be held accountable later for any damage that was already there when you moved in.

- Don't be shy about getting things fixed. There are few benefits to renting, but one of them is having maintenance problems sorted gratis.

- Remember, since 2007, deposits have to be kept in a Tenancy Deposit Scheme. This should make it harder for landlords to keep hold of your money once the tenancy is up, without a valid, provable reason.

6 Sport & Recreation

BASKETBALL

Visit **www.rangirobinson.com/london_basketball_courts.php,** which features a map locating many of the capital's outdoor courts, most of which are free. The site also lists indoor courts located in sports centres, for which a fee is usually payable, typically of around £45 an hour. It also offers plenty of wise advice, such as this pearl for the courts on Walford Road, Hackney: 'small kids usually use it for football, they can be easily kicked off'.

BOWLING (TEN-PIN)

Bloomsbury Lanes   Bloomsbury Lanes not only gives you the chance to bowl for less than a fiver—the walk-up fee is £3 per game Mon to Wed before 4pm, £4.50 Thurs to Fri, £5.50 at other times—as opposed to the £7 or more that it usually costs, but also lets you do it somewhere other than a suburban shopping mall. But then, unlike most of the country's lanes, Bloomsbury is not part of a chain. The solo enterprise is decked out in full '1950s' America' style with a bar made from old lanes, a genuine 1950s' carpet, and their proudest boast, 'the only vintage above lane ball return outside the US'. The jukebox is pretty retro too and they have karaoke rooms for hire. FINE PRINT No under 18s after 4pm on a Friday.

Basement of Tavistock Hotel, Bedford Way, WC1. ℭ **020 7183 1979.** www.blooms burylanes.co.uk. Mon–Thurs 2pm–midnight, Fri & Sat midday–3am, Sun 1pm–midnight. Tube: Russell Square.

CANOEING

Lee Valley Canoe Cycle   Beginners and novices can hire cockpit kayaks for self-guided trips up the River Lea for £8 an hour or £30 for the whole day. Anyone wanting to take out one of the more advanced

Eskimo Kayaks will have to show proof of proficiency, such as a BCU star certificate. The company also hires out bikes from £4 an hour, £15 for the whole day.

London Valley Canoe Cycle, The Watersedge, Stonebridge Lock, Tottenham Marshes, N17. © **07747 873831.** www.lvcc.biz. Wed–Fri midday–4:30pm, Sat & Sun 11am–5:30pm. Tube: Tottenham Hale.

CARROM

Carrom Café FREE   To sit down here, you have to buy a drink (coffee, tea, milkshakes, and lassis) for around £2 to £2.50. That meagre amount entitles you to an afternoon of carrom at this Sunday Up Market favourite. The game is like a cross between Subbuteo and pool, in which you flick flat round counters onto each other and (hopefully) into the corner pockets of a board. See p. 90 for more on the Sunday Up Market.

Sunday Up Market, Ely's Yard, The Old Truman Brewery, E1. © **07944 303749.** http://carromcafe.com. Sun 10am–5pm. Tube: Aldgate East.

GYMS & FITNESS

Getting fit can be expensive, particularly if you opt to do it in a private gym. Many oblige customers to take out a full year's membership, all too aware that most people stop attending after a month. This is particularly evident every January, when fierce

Fair Trade Footie

Part of the appeal of a game of football is that it can happen almost anywhere. All you need is a ball, a vaguely flat surface, and a couple of objects to act as goalposts—a traditionalist will always opt for the jumpers. It you fancy a kickabout on a proper pitch, however, things are more tricky. Some parks, and recreation grounds have five-a-side pitches where you can play for free, either legally (because there's no charge) or when the park-keeper isn't looking. However, these are often poorly maintained and/or occupied by local children, and eventually the parkie will turn up. To guarantee a pitch, you'll have to book at a leisure centre (5-, 7-, and 11-a-side pitches available, both indoor astroturf and natural grass). These can be pricey—typically £40 an hour off-peak, rising to over £70 at peak times—but remember this cost will be spread between all the players, so make sure everyone turns up. Visit www.londonpitches.com to find your closest.

'this-is-the-year-I-get-fit' resolutions soon fade to vague 'I'll-start-again-when-the-weather-turns-nicer' aspirations.

There are alternatives. One is not to join a gym at all, but exercise in your local park or with a fitness DVD. (See also 'Get Fit', p. 160.) However, if you crave the facilities but don't want to commit the cash, you could become a serial trialist. Many gyms offer free trials for potential members. When you've exhausted these and need to commit, be sure to haggle. Terms are not written in stone: it's possible to bring down both the price and the contract length with a bit of negotiation. Many gyms incentivise their staff on a commission basis, so employees will go the extra yard to close a sale. If you can guarantee to go at off-peak times only, this could entitle you to cheaper membership. Alternatively, check out facilities at your local leisure centre. They may not be as shiny as an Esporta, but they're probably a lot cheaper, especially as paying by the session (typically around £5) is the usual format.

If you're spending a lot of time in the gym, then the **London Fitness Network** membership card gives you access to more than 80 gyms and swimming pools across town for a monthly fee of £48.95, www.londonfitnessnetwork.org.

★ **Green Gym** `FREE` This isn't really a gym, but it does involve a good deal of exercise. The British Trust for Conservation Volunteers (BTCV) has hit on a crafty wheeze to get people to help out with its conservation projects by marketing them as keep-fit programmes. Volunteers are invited to help with a variety of physical projects—digging, clearing weeds, building pathways—and rewarded with the chance to burn off unwanted calories while they help the environment. Each session begins with a gentle warm-up and some instruction on the day's task. After that, unlike a proper exercise class, you're largely left to get on with it with plenty of time for chatting (and not a bit of Lycra in sight).

80 York Way, N1. ℭ **020 7278 4294.** www.btcv.org.uk. Tube/Train: King's Cross.

ICE SKATING

Shepherd's Bush Green Ice Fair Each winter the number of temporary outdoor rinks in the capital grows. Somerset House, the Natural History Museum, Kew Gardens, and even the Tower of London are now in on the act. The cheapest option for having your fingers sliced

Putt Your Money Where Your Mouth Is

Eighteen holes at one of the championship golf courses that ring the capital will set you back from £45 at a suburban lightweight like Selsdon Park to more than £285 at Wentworth, the home of the World Matchplay Championship. That's for a single round of 18 holes. That's presuming you're qualified to play in the first place, and can get a tee time. Pitch and putt courses are a cheaper alternative, typically under a fiver for nine holes. They're also much more accessible, with neither membership requirements nor dress codes, and players generally take themselves far less seriously. You're unlikely to find anyone breaking their clubs over their knees. Check out www.pitchnputt.co.uk for locations.

Alexandra Palace Pitch & Putt   Ten holes £5, clubs 50p each, balls 50p. Muswell Hill, N22. ☏ **020 8365 2121.** Mon–Fri 9:30am–dusk, Sat & Sun 9am–dusk. Train: Alexandra Palace.

Hangar Lane Pitch & Putt Centre   Nine holes £4.50, clubs 75p each. Hillcrest Road, E5. ☏ **01245 257682.** Mon–Fri 9:30am–dusk, Sat & Sun 8am–dusk. Tube: Hangar Lane.

Oakwood Park Pitch & Putt Centre   Nine holes £4.50, 18 for £6.50, clubs 75p each, balls 50p.
Prince George Avenue, Enfield N14. ☏ **07990 665845.** Mar–Oct Mon–Fri 9:30am–dusk, Sat & Sun 9am–dusk; Nov–Feb Sat & Sun 9am–dusk. Tube: Oakwood.

Palewell Park Pitch & Putt Golf Course   Set in delightful surrounds next to Richmond Park, close to Roehampton Golf Course and the National Tennis Centre, albeit considerably tattier than all of them. Offers nine holes for £4.20, club hire for 50p, and balls for £1 (40p refund if returned).
Palewell Park, SW14. ☏ **020 8876 3357.** Mar–Oct Mon–Fri 10am–dusk, Sat & Sun 9am–dusk. Train: Barnes, Mortlake.

off by a fellow Londoner comes out west, where a 1-hour session between Monday and Thursday costs just £8 (rising to £10 Friday to Sunday). It's well over a tenner at the central London venues.

Shepherd's Bush Green, W12. ☏ **020 8893 8993.** www.shepherdsbushfestival.com. Tube: Shepherd's Bush.

POKER

Poker, and particularly Texas Hold 'Em, has taken over the world. The internet is awash with gambling sites, big-stakes poker tournaments seem to happen every week, and there's even been a desperate attempt to turn it into a TV spectator sport—with cameras mounted under the table so you can see players' cards. If you want to see what all the fuss is about, but don't fancy losing your shirt, then check out the Bubble Poker League. It organises games in pubs around the capital, mostly out west, from Monday to Thursday and on Sundays. The emphasis is on fun and sociability rather than making a killing; the maximum you can win/lose in an evening is set at £5. You'll also have to stump up £2 for 'admin costs'.

Locations: *City*, The Samuel Pepys, Stew Lane, 48 Upper Thames Street, EC4. ℂ **020 7489 1871.** www.thesamuelpepys.co.uk. Games Tues from 8pm. Tube: Mansion House. *Earls Court*, The Pembroke, 261 Old Brompton Road, SW5. ℂ **020 7373 8337.** Games Thurs from 8pm. Tube: Earls Court. *Holland Park*, The Mitre, 40 Holland Park Avenue, W11. ℂ **020 7727 6332.** Games Wed from 8pm. Tube: Holland Park. *Kensal Town*, 170 Kensal Road, W10. ℂ **020 8960 4222.** www.cobdenclub.co.uk. Games Mon from 8pm. Tube: Westbourne Park. *Limehouse*, 5b Urban Bar, 27 Three Colt Street, E14. ℂ **020 7537 1601.** Games Sun from 3pm. DLR: Westferry. *Westbourne Park*, The Metropolitan, 60 Great Western Road, W11. ℂ **020 7229 9254.** Games Tues from 7:30pm. Tube: Westbourne Park. *Whitechapel*. 76 Whitechapel Road, E1. ℂ **020 7247 8978.** Games Mon from 8pm. Tube: Whitechapel.

RUNNING

Wimbledon Common Park Run `FREE` Every Saturday at 9am, a whole gaggle (if that's the collective noun) of runners, from beginners to proper athletes, gather to take part in a 5km time trial on Wimbledon Common. It's free, although prospective participants are asked to register online by 6pm the day before. The course starts in the centre of the common, around 100 yards from the windmill, and is largely flat. After the times are in, runners can retire for refreshments at the Windmill café. For information on other Park Run events, check the website.

Wimbledon Common, SW19. www.parkrun.org.uk/wimbledon/Home.aspx. Tube/Train/Tram: Wimbledon.

SKATEBOARDING

Skateboarders are as much a part of the South Bank experience as the London Eye or Tate Modern. You hear them before you see them—the clack, clack, clack as they practise their tricks in a graffiti-covered overhang below the concrete Southbank Centre. Of course, this is not an official skate venue; architects thought they were creating the last word in 1960s' functional brutalism. It's just that all those ramps and steps have proved perfect for boarding. There are better, custom-built facilities elsewhere, equipped with half-pipes, bowls, tombstones, hips, grindboxes, and various other terms I've just looked up. Many are free, including the following:

Alexandra Palace Skatepark FREE This is located between the ice rink and the children's playground, should you still feel like skating having made it all the way up the hill. It boasts two funboxes, two grindboxes, and a half-pipe.

Muswell Hill, N22. Daily 24 hours. Train: Alexandra Palace.

Cantelowes Skatepark FREE Built in 2006, this is one of the more recent additions to the London skate scene.

Cantelowes Gardens, Camden Road, NW1. www.cantelowesskatepark.co.uk. Daily 11am–9pm. Train: Camden Road.

Meanwhile FREE The oddly named venue occupies the site of London's very first skatepark, which opened in 1976 next to Regent's Canal. It features a couple of large 1980s-style bowls. Smaller ramps are available nearby at its sibling park, Meanwhile two, under the Westway.

Meanwhile Gardens, Great Western Road, W9. Daily dawn–dusk. Tube: Westbourne Park.

Stockwell Skatepark FREE An ever present on the skate scene since the 1970s. It was resurfaced a couple of years ago. The local area is a bit rough.

Stockwell Road, SW9. Daily 24 hours. Tube: Brixton.

Friday Night Skate

Every Friday at 8pm at Wellington Arch, Hyde Park Corner, a rolling sea of humanity embarks on a 10 to15-mile route through the capital. Made up of hundreds of rollerskaters of all ages, the Friday Night Skate has become a major event since its inception in 2001. If a night skate sounds a bit intense (and there are plenty of people here that skate hard), then try their daylight 'Sunday Stroll' instead. These leave at 2pm from Serpentine Road in Hyde Park and follow a shorter (8 mile) route. www.lfns.co.uk.

SNOOKER & POOL

There's nothing quite like the studied hush of a snooker hall, the gentle plock of ball on ball, the silent exasperation of another shot missed, the faint whiff of dodginess. These temples of quiet concentration are not as common as they once were, but there are still a good number to be found, often in down-at-heel areas. Membership tends to cost around £10 annually, plus £2.50 to £5 an hour for table hire. With many clubs open 24 hours, they're great places to meet fellow insomniacs. The more anti-social your hours, the less you'll pay. Many clubs also have pool tables for hire, although do remember that pool is to snooker as a chimpanzee is to a human—they're ostensibly similar but one's a whole lot more complicated.

London's cheapest snooker deals are listed below. For other venues, check out www.londonsnooker.co.uk.

Locations: *Acton*, 3 East Acton Arcade, Old Oak Common Lane, W3. ℂ **020 8743 8284.** Best snooker/pool rates: £2.50 per hour Mon–Fri 10am–6pm, £4.20 an hour at other times. Daily 24 hours. Tube: East Acton. *Manor Park*, 501 High Street North, E12. ℂ **020 8478 5087.** Best snooker rates: £2.50 per hour Mon–Thurs midnight–6pm, £3.10 an hour at other times. Daily 24 hours. Train: Woodgrange Park. *Stepney*, 137 Whitehorse Road, E1. ℂ **020 7790 9569.** Best snooker rates: £2.50 an hour Mon–Fri 10am–6pm, £3.80 per hour at other times. Daily 24 hours. Tube: Stepney Green. Train/DLR: Limehouse.

SWIMMING

Splashing about in water is one of your cheapest active options, typically around £3 to £5 for unlimited swimming time, sometimes less, even during peak hours. The pools recommended below all charge less than £5 for a session.

INDOOR SWIMMING POOLS

Britannia Leisure Centre This beach-style pool starts at zero depth and gets gradually deeper, making it great for nervous little ones.

40 Hyde Road, N1. ℂ **020 7729 4485.** www.gll.org/centre/britannia-leisure-centre. asp. Member/non-member rates £2.85/£4.10. Mon–Fri 7am–10pm, Sat & Sun 8am–8pm. Tube: Old Street.

Crystal Palace National Sports Centre Until it's superseded by a 2012 aquatic centre, this remains the country's pre-eminent swimming venue—and one of just two in London to boast a 50m Olympic pool and competition diving boards (scary).

Ledrington Road, SE19. ✆ **020 8778 0131.** www.gll.org/centre/crystal-palace-national-sports-centre.asp. Peak/off-peak rates £3.95/£2.25. Mon–Thurs 7am–9:30pm, Fri 9am–9pm, Sat & Sun 9am–5pm. Train: Crystal Palace.

Fulham Pools   A 25m pool, a smaller teaching pool, and a fun club for children.

Normand Park, Lillie Road, SW6. ✆ **020 7471 0450.** www.lbhf.gov.uk. Member/non-member rates £2.20/£3.20. Mon–Thurs 6:30am–10pm, Fri 6:30am–9pm, Sat & Sun 8am–8:30pm. Tube: West Brompton.

Outdoor Swimming Pools

★ **Hampstead Ponds & Lido**   Hampstead boasts three lovely wooded ponds (former reservoirs dug in the mid-19th century) where you can take refreshing dips. There's a men's pond, a ladies' pond, and a mixed pond, which gets particularly busy in summer. All cost £2. There's also a slightly more expensive lido.

Hampstead Heath, NW5. ✆ 020 7332 3511. www.cityoflondon.gov.uk/hampstead. Lido £4.30; ponds £2. **Lido** open May-mid Sep daily 7-9.30am, 10am-6.30pm (Mon, Thurs, Fri only 6.45-8.30pm). Mid Sep–May daily 7am-12.30pm. **Single-sex ponds** open mid-May–mid-Sept 7am–7:30/8:30pm (for winter times call or consult the website); **mixed ponds** open May–Sept 7am–6:30pm; lido open May–Sept 7am–8pm, Oct–Apr 7am–midday. Train: Hampstead Heath.

London Fields Lido   For those who like the idea of swimming outside, but not the cold, this is London's only heated outdoor pool.

London Fields Park, E8. ✆ **020 7254 9038.** www.hackney.gov.uk/c-londonfields-lido.htm. Rates £4. Mon–Fri 6:30am–8pm (Tues 7–8pm women only), Sat & Sun 8am–6pm. Train: London Fields.

Serpentine Lido   This sectioned-off part of Hyde Park's lake has been a designated lido for more than a century. There's a paddling pool for the children and a sunbathing area with deckchairs for hire.

Hyde Park, South Kensington, W2. ✆ **020 7706 3422.** www.serpentinelido.com. Rates £4. May Sat & Sun and June–mid-Sept daily 10am–6pm. Tube: Lancaster Gate.

TENNIS

A lack of cheap, accessible public courts, particularly compared with countries like Spain, is one reason we haven't produced a Wimbledon champion since Fred Perry. However, although a typical tennis club charges several hundred pounds for a year's membership, there

A Christmas Dip

If you're the direct descendant from a long line of polar bears, consider joining the Serpentine Swimming Club on its annual Christmas morning outing. The plunge into the icy waters of Hyde Park goes by the deceptive name of the 'Peter Pan Cup'. If you fancy it, it will cost you a £20 membership fee plus a few months' hard graft acclimatising yourself to winter conditions—the club doesn't admit newbies without suitable preparation. However, it's free to watch—and what better way to put the disappointment of those presents behind you than by watching grown men and women willingly submit themselves to some sub-4°C (39.2°F) water. www.serpentineswimmingclub.com.

are better-priced alternatives. Many local parks have (sometimes poorly maintained) courts, available for a few pounds an hour or even for free. To find your nearest, check with **Tennis for Free,** www.tennisforfree.com, a pressure group dedicated to making 'all publicly managed tennis courts in the UK available for use by all for free'. Their website details all of London's free courts. If you need someone to hit with (tennis is one sport you can't play on your own), try registering with www.londontennis.co.uk; enter your details and tennis standard, no payment is requested. The site also lists London's cheap and free courts, and provides details of registered players and their (claimed) abilities, so you can match up for cheap or free games.

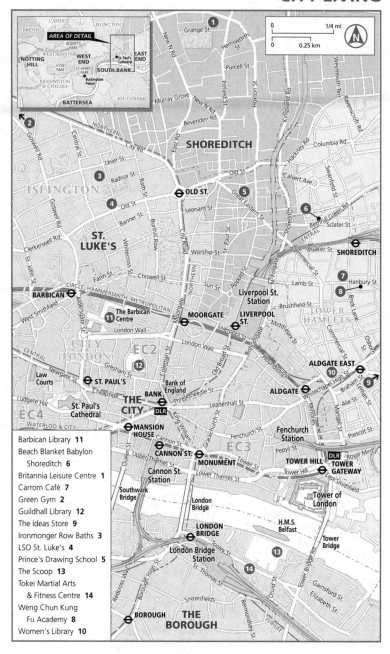

Barbican Library **11**

Beach Blanket Babylon
Shoreditch **6**

Britannia Leisure Centre **1**

Carrom Café **7**

Green Gym **2**

Guildhall Library **12**

The Ideas Store **9**

Ironmonger Row Baths **3**

LSO St. Luke's **4**

Prince's Drawing School **5**

The Scoop **13**

Tokei Martial Arts
& Fitness Centre **14**

Weng Chun Kung
Fu Academy **8**

Women's Library **10**

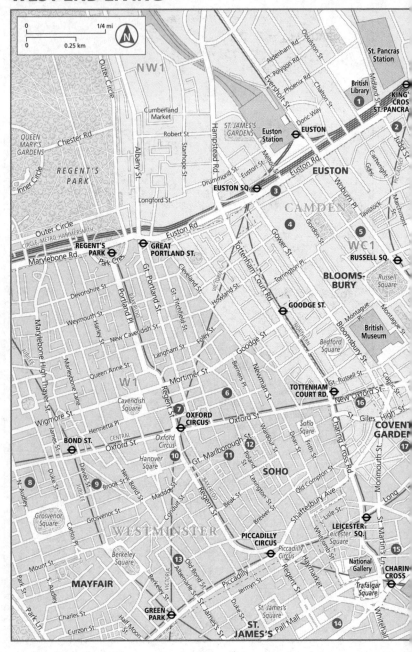

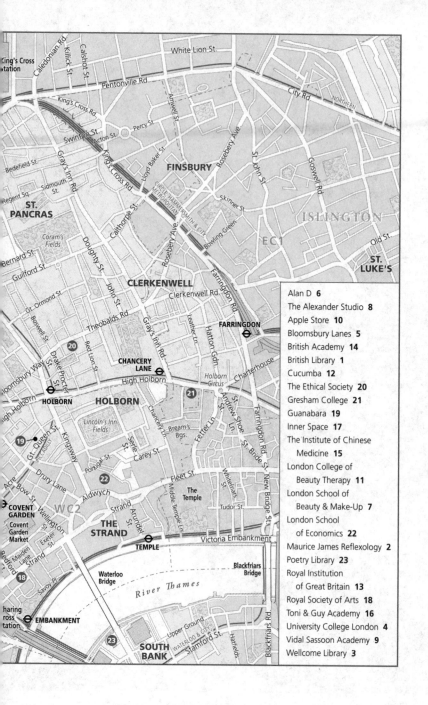

Browsing for bargains at Alice's art prints shop at Portobello Market.

SHOPPING

When the pound was riding high on the Forex markets, shopping in London must have seemed to overseas visitors about as expensive an experience as you could indulge in this side of flying around the world in a gold-plated private jet. Brand-name goods often commanded eye-watering prices compared with other countries. However, the recent global economic downturn, and the pound's plunge against the dollar and euro, has driven UK prices down to competitive levels. For the first time in over a decade—since the pound's last dramatic fall, in fact—the capital is welcoming bargain-hunters from abroad. And, for them, long may the UK's economic misery continue.

Sale Away

London has two main sale seasons a year, one in January, which often starts the day after Christmas (you can often spot the poor sales staff setting out the new lines late on Christmas Eve), and one in summer, usually beginning in July. However, since the 'credit crunch', sales have become much more common, and are almost a year-round thing now. Whenever you go, somewhere on the high street is probably offering some sort of deal. Sales at the big department stores, such as Harrods and Selfridges, can be manic events attracting thousands of shoppers, who queue from dawn and charge en masse into the store to claim their bargains.

Of course, there are money-saving opportunities for us Londoners too, if you know where to look. In general, the further from the centre you go, the cheaper prices become; but bargains can turn up anywhere, even in the overpriced West End, at the clothes chains of Oxford Street, the electrical outfitters of Tottenham Court Road, and the quirky fashion stores of Covent Garden. Perhaps the greatest source of shopping savings, however, are London's many and munificent markets, dotted throughout the capital, which sell cut-price versions of everything from fresh food, clothes, and household goods to antiques, antiquarian books, and vintage fashions.

1 Haggle Time: London's Markets

London may have a justified reputation for being expensive, but it's not as if you can rip off 7½ million people all of the time (just some of the time). There's plenty of cheap shopping around, a good deal of which is to be found at the plethora of markets. These offer all manner of bargains, from antiques (Bermondsey, Portobello), clothes (Petticoat Lane), and arts and crafts (Greenwich, Spitalfields) to fish (Billingsgate), meat (Smithfield), flowers (Columbia Road), and much more. Camden is now so popular with visitors that it's rated as one of London's top five most popular tourist attractions. See also p. 90 for lunchtime food markets and p. 198 for antique markets.

THE THREE FS: FOOD, FARMERS' & FLOWER MARKETS

London is home to a number of good fresh food markets selling fruit and veg at prices well below what you'd pay in a supermarket. These unpretentious neighbourhood standbys are augmented by a growing band of gourmet food and farmers' markets, which showcase the best in organic, free-range, artisan fare from around the country. Prices tend to be higher at these than at local markets—and even most supermarkets—but it's still possible to pick up bargains, particularly late in the day when overstocked stalls begin to offer deals. Most farmers' markets set up just once or twice a week; visit www.lfm.org. uk to locate your nearest.

Berwick Street   Berwick Street always makes the list of London's favourite markets, not so much for what it is, which in all honesty isn't that much, but more for where it is and what it represents: the last traditional, down-to-earth, daily street market trading in the West End. It's been doing its thing since the late 18th century and, though it has seemed on its last legs for decades, it keeps staggering on like a boxer too tired even to collapse. Despite its problems, it's still regarded with much fondness and its few stalls are great places to pick up a bit of cheap fruit and veg on your way home. The street itself offers a very Soho mix of fancy cafés, second-hand vinyl emporiums, and sex shops.

Berwick Street, W1. ℂ **020 7641 7813.** Tube: Oxford Circus, Tottenham Court Road.

Broadway Market   One of the capital's oldest markets, Broadway looked like going under a few years ago, but has enjoyed a revival of late by turning itself into a 'hip urban hangout'. The street is lined with trendy restaurants, galleries, and shops selling arts and crafts and vintage clothes, plus a couple of decent pubs. These are joined on Saturdays by a fancy foodie market filled with great produce: organic meats, fish, and veg, homemade cheeses, fair trade coffee, all at reasonable—if not exactly bargain basement—prices. Still, there are deals to be had if you're willing to haggle.

Broadway Market, E8. www.broadwaymarket.co.uk. Train: London Fields.

★ **Columbia Road Flower Market**   Worth coming if only for the views and the smells, which are among the prettiest and headiest of any London market. On Sundays this East End street fills with blooms, foliage, and flowers, providing a burst of colour and fragrance that can't help but bring a smile to your face, so long as you ignore the crowds. The stalls sell a huge range of stock, from humble bedding plants to giant tropical fancies, and there are plenty of discounts and bargains to be had, particularly from midday onwards when stallholders begin selling in bulk—listen out for cries of 'three bunches for a fiver'. You'll need to shop around, however. Prices aren't universally cheap and the road's current hip status with slouchy Shoreditch fashionistas does seem to be driving prices upwards a little.

Columbia Road, E2. ℭ **020 7364 1717.** http://columbiaroad.info. Tube: Old Street. Train: Cambridge Heath.

Marylebone Market London's largest farmers' market takes place on a Sunday right in the centre of town, in a car park off Marylebone High Street. Despite its big-city location, this has a rather villagey feel to it with plenty of organic meat and unsprayed veg, most of it sourced from the home counties, as well as organic bread, homemade biscuits, and other delicious treats. Prices aren't dirt cheap, so you're best off going with a fixed budget and targeting killer items you can't buy in your local supermarket—giant beef tomatoes, strong goat's cheese, and buffalo sausages are among the best finds.

Cramer Street Car Park, W1. ℭ **020 7704 9659.** www.lfm.org.uk/mary.asp. Tube: Bond Street.

THE WHOLESALE EXPERIENCE

If you want to make real savings on fresh food, and are prepared to buy in bulk, then make your way to one of London's three great wholesale markets. Between them, Billingsgate, New Covent Garden, and Smithfield supply the capital's restaurants, and smaller markets with much of their produce. Trading typically starts around 4am, and most of the best stuff is snapped up within a couple of hours. These markets can be fairly intimidating, staffed and frequented principally by food professionals—not members of the public—with their own impenetrable language, who do their business quickly and with a minimum of fuss. Expect little in the way of customer service. To find the best deals (and good deals are definitely on offer), you'll need to know your stuff, so start researching.

Billingsgate You're going to need a big freezer; London's wholesale fish and seafood market deals only in bulk. The dozens of stalls here sell pretty much every type of seafood you can think of: salmon, mackerel, halibut, swordfish, lobster, the list goes on, with around 40% of the stock flown in daily from exotic climes. Aim to arrive here early—too late and all the fish will be gone—but don't dive straight in. Wait a couple of hours and watch prices start to come down. Of course, if you've never bought wholesale before, it can be difficult to know what constitutes a good deal: expect to pay around third to a half of supermarket prices, say £15 for a kilo of prawns, £5 a kilo for red snapper, and £2 a kilo for fresh sardines. The market also offers courses that teach members of the public how to prepare fish.

Trafalgar Way, E14. ℂ **020 7987 1118.** www.billingsgate-market.org.uk. Tube: Canary Wharf. DLR: Blackwall.

New Covent Garden   Nearly 3,000 people work at the UK's largest fresh produce market, which supplies most of London's markets and high-end restaurants with their fruit and veg, not to mention florists with their flowers. The 56-acre site is somewhat industrial looking—it's a business not a tourist attraction, after all—but inside it's sheer gourmet heaven. The food is displayed under neon on long aisles, known as 'buyer's walks'. Prices change daily according to supply and demand, and buyers are expected to touch, smell, and feel the produce. The market also sells a range of top-end oils, pickles, and smoked fish, also in wholesale quantities. The car park outside hosts a huge general market on Sundays, FINE PRINT The market is due to be redeveloped and expanded over the next few years. Check its status before setting your alarm for a 3am wake-up.

Nine Elms Lane, SW8. ℂ **020 7720 2211.** www.newcoventgardenmarket.com. Tube/Train: Vauxhall.

Smithfield Market   One of London's oldest markets, Smithfield has been satisfying the capital's carnivorous cravings for over 800 years. It's estimated that more than 120,000 tonnes of dead flesh pass through its Victorian Grade II-listed confines each year. The sheer volume of carcasses on display can make for an intense and slightly macabre sight (and smell), although it's presumably not as extreme as it was up until the 19th century when animals were also slaughtered here. Fresh meat and poultry are the market mainstays, but the stalls also sell deli produce, such as pies, specialist sausages, and cheeses. As with all the wholesale giants, things kick off at 4am and all the best stuff is usually gone soon after. Still, if you can't find what you want, you could always sample a selection of the market's produce at a nearby café or pub.

Charterhouse Street, EC1. ℭ **020 7248 3151.** www.cityoflondon.gov.uk. Tube/Train: Barbican.

LOCAL MARKETS

Local markets do exactly what their name implies, offering a range of produce catering for the interests of their local community. This can include food, particularly the specialities and favourite ingredients of immigrant populations, but also clothing and household essentials— no local market worth its salt is without a stall selling cheap batteries. Food and clothes aside, much of the produce is not particularly exotic, but it is often very cheap, and can save you pounds on equivalent items bought at a supermarket. We can't recommend you indulge, of course, but local markets are also prime sources of knock-off designer gear and pirate CDs and DVDs. But, above all, local markets are places where apostrophes are given free rein, no longer constrained by normal grammatical rules. In addition to the below, see also Brixton Market (p. 91).

★ **Brick Lane Market**   Lying at the centre of the local Bengali community, Brick Lane and its surrounding streets are home every Sunday morning to a vast and sprawling market: part general household goods market, part jumble sale, part fruit and veg market, part flea market, part vintage fashions and crafts market (specifically at the Sunday Up Market; p. 90), and part all-purpose dodgy market for shadily acquired DVDs, mobile phones, and bikes. Strolling its vast array of bric-a-brac, books, clothing, electrical goods, and second-hand furniture is a great way to spend a morning, particularly as you can fortify yourself afterwards at one of the area's famous Bangladeshi restaurants or at the legendary 24-hour bagel shop at no. 159.

Brick Lane, E1. ℭ **020 7364 1717.** Sun 8am–3pm. Tube: Aldgate East.

Chapel Market   Almost the archetypal London market, this narrow street lined with stalls sells pretty much everything the average Islingtonite could possibly want: fruit and veg, household goods, cheap clothes, leatherwear, jewellery, and more. Prices are cheap; you can buy premium fruit (such as blueberries) for about one-third the price you'd pay in a nearby supermarket, and you'll find a good range of lunch food stalls selling jacket potatoes, jerk chicken, burgers, and the like; the Naked Sausage stall proffers giant burgers and sausages in buns for £3 to £4. There's also a decent café, a pie and mash shop, a couple of record shops, and an army surplus store where you can pick up ex-issue boots, combat trousers, and camouflage jackets.

Chapel Market, N1. Tues–Wed & Fri–Sat 9am–3:30pm, Thurs & Sun 9am–1pm. Tube: Angel.

East Street Market The 'Lane', as it's known locally, has been servicing the budget needs of South Londoners since the 1880s. Today it stocks everything from bargain meat, fish, fruit, and veg—giant bowls of tomatoes, carrots, garlic, and green beans sell for £1—to clothes, trainers, fabrics, perfumes, bags, and CDs. It's particularly strong on Afro-Caribbean produce, such as red snapper, cassava, and sweet potato. East Street is also dotted with food stalls and cafés where you can fortify yourself with a quick cup of tea—or, if you're feeling brave, a bowl of jellied eels.

East Street, SE17. *©* **020 7525 6000.** Tues–Fri 8am–5pm, Sat 8am–6:30pm, Sun 8am–2pm. Tube: Elephant & Castle.

Petticoat Lane Market Petticoat Lane can be an overwhelming place on a busy Sunday: over 1,000 stalls and several times that number of people fill its narrow confines. But for cheap clothes, this is the place (especially for women's fashions). The quality can be a bit up and down but the prices are always way lower than you'd pay on the high street. Just don't expect the items to last a lifetime (or even many months). Almost everything here retails for less than £20. You can pick up T-shirts for £1, trousers for £3, and even suits and coats for around £10 to £15. Asian fabrics, jewellery, Middle Eastern rugs, bedding, leather jackets (particularly around the Aldgate East end), and household goods are also sold.

Wentworth Street, E1. *©* **020 7377 8963.** Mon–Fri 10am–2pm, Sun 9am–2pm.

Ridley Road Market Ridley Road, also known as Dalston Market, is just as a local market should be—superbly cheap, a bit rough around the edges, and proudly ungentrified. It's great for African, Asian, Jewish, Turkish, Eastern European, and particularly Caribbean food. You'll find lots of cheap fruit and veg (including tropical produce like papaya, durian, plantain, yams, green coconut), classic Caribbean meats (goat, pig's feet, and turkey gizzards by the bucket), and fish (look out for dirt cheap red snapper). Lots of the fruit sells for £1 a bowl, and stallholders don't mind haggling if you want to bag it even cheaper. There are also stalls selling cosmetics, clothes, and an array of household goods. FINE PRINT Saturday morning is the busiest time when the entire community seems to descend en masse. Try to go during the week.

Ridley Road, E8. ℭ **0844 3574634.** Mon–Wed 9am–3pm, Thurs 9am–midday, Fri–Sat 9am–5pm. Tube: Dalston Kingsland.

Shepherd's Bush Market   By a railway viaduct off the Goldhawk Road, this has an almost casbah-like vibe with its narrow walkways weaving through tightly packed stalls piled high with colourful, fragrant produce. It offers a truly multicultural experience, with stalls hawking Caribbean, African, Indian, Polish, and even American delicacies (the last in the shape of a fresh popcorn stall). It also does a particularly mean line in falafel. Elsewhere you'll find fabrics, aimed mainly at Asian residents, as well as all the usual mass of budget-priced cleaning products, bedding, cosmetics, bags, socks, tea towels, costume jewellery, and shoes.

Railway Approach, W12. ℭ **020 8743 5089.** Mon–Sat 9am–6pm. Tube: Goldhawk Road, Shepherd's Bush.

Wembley Market   On days when there aren't any football matches or concerts scheduled at the stadium, there's still plenty of entertainment on offer in the shape of Wembley Market, the UK's largest Sunday market; every weekend 500-plus stalls set up for business in the stadium car park (where there's also parking for 1,000 cars). It's hugely popular: coachloads of people turn up every week to browse the high-street fashions (much of it hooky), sportswear (appropriately), jeans (a vast array), shoes, accessories, electrical items, household goods, and fruit and veg, all of it offered at a significant discount. There's also a decent array of food stalls to keep you fortified while you explore. FINE PRINT Avoid the back-of-a-lorry scams selling dodgy (and often non-existent) electrical equipment.

Stadium Car Park, Wembley, HA9. ℭ **01895 632221.** www.wembleymarket.co.uk. Sun 9am–4pm. Tube: Wembley Park.

CRAFT, ART & ANTIQUE MARKETS

While local markets are primarily utilitarian affairs, providing day-to-day necessities for local communities, arts and craft markets are all about frippery and decoration, shiny fancies and treats to brighten up your home. Their potential for bargains depends on how much you're prepared to pay for something you don't really need. There's certainly plenty of choice: as you'd expect, London is home to some of the UK's major players. Camden, Greenwich, and Portobello markets are among the biggest of their type in the country—and tourist attractions in their own right. Although they can be (extraordinarily) crowded, particularly on weekends, the general experience at craft markets is much more genteel, and middle class, than at their down-to-earth local siblings.

Bayswater Road Market   Not really a market in the traditional sense, this bills itself as the 'longest art exhibition in the world' and consists of around a mile of paintings, sculptures, and handmade jewellery lined up against the railings of Kensington Gardens. More than 250 artists display their work here. Prices vary but are generally much less than in a commercial gallery, and can always be brought down a little further with some judicious haggling. There are also various jobbing artists who'll paint your picture, or do a caricature, for around £10 (and it may even look a bit like you).

Bayswater Road, from Clarendon Place to Queensway, W2. Sun 10am–6pm. Tube: Bayswater Road.

Bermondsey Market   As if from nowhere, Bermondsey Market appears Brigadoon-like every week in the early hours of a Friday morning. Comprising dozens of stalls in the centre of Bermondsey Square, it is undoubtedly one of the best places for bargain antiques—particularly silver—in the capital. To benefit from the most competitive prices, however, you'll have to set your alarm clock, as trading begins at 4am. Things begin winding down by about 10am, and by midday all the stalls are closed again for another week. FINE PRINT The square is currently undergoing a good deal of redevelopment, which may in time affect the market's viability.

Bermondsey Square, SE1. © **020 7351 5353.** www.bermondseysquare.co.uk/antiques.html. Fri 4am–1pm. Tube/Train: London Bridge.

Camden Market   You can find almost anything at this sprawling market made up of five interconnected areas: arts and crafts, rugs, jewellery, ethnic art, musical instruments (Camden Lock Market); vintage clothes, antiques, food and drink (The Stables, under the railway arches); 'club wear' fashions (the Electric Ballroom); and fruit and veg (Buck Street and Inverness Street). Finding a bargain, however, is a bit trickier. At the weekend, when business is booming, the stallholders here have no real incentive to slash prices. There's a lot more haggle room during the week, particularly in poor weather, when sellers are more willing to cut you a deal.

Chalk Farm Road, NW1. ⓒ **020 7485 7963.** www.camdenlockmarket.com. Camden Lock Market, The Stables, Buck Street, Inverness Street daily 10am–6pm; Electric Ballroom Fri–Sat 10am–3pm. Tube: Camden Town, Chalk Farm.

Camden Passage Not to be confused with the above, the Passage is a covered walkway in Islington High Street lined with shops and stalls selling antiques, collectibles, bric-a-brac, and, for want of a better word, junk. It's a good place to pick up reasonably priced silverware, an antique watch or, in the Georgian Village indoor market, antique fabrics. Every Thursday there's a small book fair. Early morning Wednesdays and Saturdays, when new stock comes in, are the best times for bargains.

Camden Passage, N1. www.camdenpassageislington.co.uk. Wed 10am–2pm, Sat 10am–5pm. Tube: Angel.

Greenwich Market Greenwich's weekend market scene is pretty much the dictionary definition of sprawling, its various areas selling everything from antiques, arts and crafts, bric-a-brac, and books to clothes, toys, and food. There are four main areas to explore: an antiques market, a food market, a village market, and the covered market. The latter is housed inside the original 19th-century market building and now sells well-to-do arts and crafts and also has a good selection of hot food stalls (p. 91). Weekends can be fiercely crowded. You'll find it a more pleasant experience during the week, particularly on Thursdays and Fridays, which are the best days for antiques, vintage clothing, and collectibles, and for rooting out bargains.

College Approach, SE10. ⓒ **020 8293 3110.** www.greenwichmarket.net. Antiques Market Mon–Tues & Thurs–Sun 10am–5:30pm, Wed 11am–6pm; Village & Food Market Sat–Sun 8am–5pm; Arts & Crafts Market Sat–Sun 9:30am–5:30pm. Train: Greenwich. DLR: Cutty Sark.

★ **Portobello Market** Portobello is one of those anything-and-everything affairs that could be filed under any category, but since it's principally known for its antiques market—the world's largest—we've decided to house it here. Collectible relics from the past dominate the southern end between Chepstow Villas and Elgin Crescent. Beyond this are stalls selling hot food, fruit and veg, flowers, plenty of vintage clothes (particularly denim and leather), handmade garments by new designers, and, at the north end, records, books, and general bric-a-brac as well as household items. A few decades ago, when it was still a local secret, the market was *the* place for antique bargains. Things are a lot pricier these days. You'll need to come early on Saturday to see the best stuff (and know what you're looking for). But even if you're not buying, this is one of the great free sights in London. Wandering the mile-long stretch fills a fascinating morning, rummaging through the stalls, watching the multicultural swell of humanity surging along the street, admiring the stuccoed Notting Hill houses, and popping in and out of the various pubs and cafés.

Portobello Road, W10. www.portobellomarket.org. General Market Mon–Wed & Fri–Sat 8am–6:30pm, Thurs 8am–1pm; Antique Market Sat 8am–6:30pm. Tube: Notting Hill.

Spitalfields Market This venerable institution has undergone various renovations and rebirths over its 350-year history. Today it's home to the epitome of the genteel, artsy market—think stalls selling homemade candles, decorated picture frames, mobiles made of spoons, and ethnic sculptures, much of it rather overpriced. It's got a good reputation for clothes, particularly vintage fashions, and many independent designers test out reaction to their latest creations here. There are also plenty of food stalls (falafel alert), as well as upmarket delis selling organic cheese, artisan bread, free-range sausages, and so on. It's hugely popular on Sundays, when an estimated 10,000 people visit. Things are much quieter, and there's much more chance of turning up a bargain, during the week.

Commercial Street, E1. ✆ **020 7377 1496.** www.spitalfields.co.uk. Tues–Fri 10am–4pm, Sun 9am–5pm. Tube/Train: Liverpool Street.

2 Car Boot Sales

Even prior to the invention of eBay, there was a way for us to sell the unwanted contents of our attics, or buy the unwanted contents of other people's: a car boot sale. For the uninitiated, a car boot sale is like a giant jumble sale or rummage sale held in a large open space, such as a field, car park, or school playground. People arrive early, usually from around 6 to 7am, to sell their stuff, either direct from the boot of their car (hence the name) or from a stall. Despite the growth of internet trading, they're still hugely popular; indeed, even more so since the 'credit crunch'. A seller's pitch is typically around £10 to £15, while buyers may be charged an entrance fee of around 50p–£2, although many are free. For details of sales in your area check out any of these websites: www.yourbooty.co.uk; www.carbootcalendar.com; www.carbootjunction.com.

Battersea

Where: Battersea Technology College car park, Battersea Park Road, SW11. ℭ **07941 383588.** Tube/Train: Battersea Park/Queenstown Road.

When: Sunday 1:30–5pm (sellers from 11:45am), except 2 weeks over Christmas and New Year excepted.

How much: Sellers £10 per car, plus £3 for a table; buyers 50p, or £3 early entrance.

Buyer Beware

People will sell almost anything at a car boot sale—old clothes, unwanted Christmas presents, souvenirs of forgotten holidays, vacuum cleaners, bits of vacuum cleaners, old games with the instructions missing, broken watches, plugless and bulbless lamps, bits of rope. But the truly amazing thing is that people will buy almost anything at a car boot sale, no matter how old or broken or useless. By the end of a sale most boots have been picked clean. The vast majority of items sell for under a couple of quid. Do note, however, that your purchases will come with no guarantees and you will probably not be able to test any electrical equipment on site. *Caveat emptor.*

Epsom

Where: Hook Road Arena, junction of Hook Road and Chessington Road, KT19. Tube/Train: Ewell West.

When: April to September every Bank Holiday and some Sundays, 7:30am onwards.

How much: Sellers £10 per car; buyers 50p, £1 before 8am.

Kilburn

Where: St Augustine's School, Kilburn Park Road, NW6. Tube: Kilburn Park.

When: Saturday 11am–3pm (sellers from 7:30am).

How much: Sellers £11 per car; buyers 50p, £3 before 11am.

Walthamstow

Where: William Morris School, Folly Lane, Billet Road, E17.

℗ **07932 919707.** Tube/Train: Blackhorse Road.

When: Sunday 7am–midday.

How much: Sellers £9 per car; buyers 50p, £2 before 8am.

Wimbledon Stadium

Where: Plough Lane, Wimbledon, SW19. ℗ **020 7240 7405.** Tube/Train: Haydens Road.

When: Saturday 7:30am–1pm.

How much: Sellers £10 per car; buyers 50p, £2 before 8am.

3 Charity Shops

Like bad-taste time capsules, filled with (usually deservedly) forgotten fashions, board games that never found an audience, dolls missing several limbs, and trashy, yellowing novels, charity shops can nonetheless be

Sellers & Buyers

Sellers at car boot sales range from professional traders to first-timers, plenty trying to clear some space and raise a little cash following or preceding a house move. Buyers can be a similarly varied bunch. Most are enthusiastic amateurs out for a quick rummage, but most sales also attract a hardcore of hawk-eyed experts on the hunt for an under-valued heirloom. Be warned that a promising-looking carload will attract a vulture-like mass of potential buyers, often before the goods have even been taken out for display, which can be slightly unnerving for inexperienced car booters.

strangely addictive. As the name implies, these are not-for-profit institutions that sell their stock—all donated for free by the public—to raise money for a nominated charity. Oxfam operates the largest number of branches in the capital.

Barnardo's Good for: High-street fashions, designer clothes, shoes, club wear, books, and records. Your bargain hunting supports: Providing support and care to vulnerable and disadvantaged children and young people.

Brixton, 414 Brixton Road, SW9. ℗ **020 7274 4165.** Tube: Brixton. *Golders Green*, 18 Golders Green Road, NW11. ℗ **020 8455 5390.** Tube: Golders Green. *Marylebone*, 7 George Street, W1. ℗ **020 7935 2946.** Tube: Bond Street. www.barnardos.org.uk. Mon–Sat 9am–5pm, Sun 10am–5pm.

British Red Cross Good for: Postcode bargains, designer fashions, bags, hats and *objets d'art*. Your bargain hunting supports: Providing humanitarian aid to those in crisis around the world.

Chelsea, 67 Old Church Street, SW3. ℂ **020 7352 8550.** Mon–Wed & Fri 10am–5:30pm, Thurs 10am–7pm, Sun 1–6pm. Tube: Sloane Square. *Victoria*, 85 Ebury Street, SW1. ℂ **020 7730 2235.** Tube/Train: Victoria. www.redcross.org.uk. Mon–Fri 10am–5:30pm, Sat 10am–4pm.

Cancer Research   Good for: Pretty much everything, including fashions, books, and games. Your bargain hunting supports: Take a guess.

Chelsea, 393 King's Road, SW10. ℂ **020 7352 4769.** Tube: Fulham Broadway. *Fulham*, 350 North End Road, SW6. ℂ **020 7381 8458.** Tube: Fulham Broadway. *Islington*, 34 Upper Street, N1. ℂ **020 7226 8951.** Tube: Angel. *Marylebone*, 24 Marylebone High Street, W1. ℂ **020 7487 4986.** Tube: Baker Street. *West Hampstead*, 234 West End Lane, NW6. ℂ **020 7433 1962.** Tube/Train: West Hampstead. www.cancerresearchuk.org. Mon–Sat 9am–5pm, Sun 11am–5pm.

Postcode Bargains

Though the tat always outweighs the gold, charity shops are still great places to find discarded treasures—a retro tweed suit, a natty bowler hat, or a game of Boggle. To improve your gold-panning odds, your best bet is to head to charity shops located in swankier neighbourhoods: Fulham, Chelsea, Kensington, St John's Wood, etc. The better the postcode, the better the standard of cast-offs, and the better your chances of finding a proper bargain.

Crusaid   Good for: The 'Harvey Nichols of charity shops' nearly always has a good selection of designer fashions, books, art and bric-a-brac. Your bargain hunting supports: Supplying aid to people living with HIV and Aids in poverty across the world.

19 Churton Street, SW1. ℂ **020 7233 8736.** www.crusaid.org.uk. Mon–Sat 10am–6pm, Sun 11am–3pm. Tube: Pimlico.

Octavia Foundation Having recently taken over the running of several establishments formerly under the control of the Notting Hill Housing Trust, the Octavia Foundation now operates 21 shops, many in prime locations. Those listed below are particularly good for postcode bargains, designer fashions, vintage books and furniture. Your bargain hunting supports: Providing low-cost accommodation to those in need in central London.

Brompton, 211 Brompton Road, SW3. ℂ **020 7581 7987.** Tube: South Kensington. *Chelsea*, 303 King's Road, SW3. ℂ **020 7352 8606.** Tube: Sloane Square. *Fulham*, 309 Fulham Road, SW10. ℂ **020 7352 7986.** Tube: Fulham Broadway. *Hampstead*, 33 South End Road, NW3. ℂ **020 7435 3453.** Tube: Hampstead Heath. *Kensington*, 266

Kensington High Street, W8. ℂ **020 7602 6043.** Tube: High Street Kensington. *Richmond*, 394 Richmond Road, TW1. ℂ **020 8891 6819.** Train: St Margaret's. *South Kensington*, 3 Bute Street, SW7. ℂ **020 7582 9458.** Tube: South Kensington. www.octaviafoundation.org.uk. Mon–Sat 10am–6pm, Sun midday–5pm.

Oxfam Good for: The Chelsea, Pimlico and South Kensington branches are good for cast-off designer fashions, while the Bloomsbury branch, a dedicated bookshop (see p. 210), has more than 12,000 titles (Oxfam is the country's largest second-hand bookseller). Other branches are good for vintage clothes, homewares, CDs and greetings cards (custom created for the charity). Your bargain hunting supports: Overcoming poverty, starvation, and suffering via famine relief, humanitarian aid, and funding development projects.

Bloomsbury, 12 Bloomsbury Street, WC1. ℂ **020 7637 4610.** Tube: Tottenham Court Road. *Chelsea*, 123a Shawfield Street, SW3. ℂ **020 7351 7979.** Tube: Sloane Square. *Covent Garden*, 23 Drury Lane, WC2. ℂ **020 7240 3769.** Tube: Covent Garden. *Marylebone*, 91 Marylebone High Street, W1. ℂ **020 7487 3570.** Tube: Baker Street. *Pimlico*, 15 Warwick Way, SW1V. ℂ **020 7821 1952.** Tube/Train: Victoria. *St John's Wood*, 61 St John's Wood High Street, NW8. ℂ **020 7722 5969.** Tube: St John's Wood. *South Kensington*, 46 Gloucester Road, SW7. ℂ **020 7591 0469.** Tube: Gloucester Road. *Victoria*, 34 Strutton Ground, SW1. ℂ **020 7233 3908.** Tube: St James's Park. .Mon–Sat 9:30am–6pm, Sun midday–4pm.

The Salvation Army Good for: Large, two-floor store filled with high-street fashions, shoes, vintage clothes, and old paperbacks. Your bargain hunting supports: Social welfare provision—building, and running homeless shelters, drug rehabilitation centres, schools, and hospitals in the UK, and around the world.

9 Princes Street, W1. ℂ **020 7495 3958.** Tube: Oxford Circus. Mon–Sat 10am–6pm. www1.salvationarmy.org.uk.

4 Dirt Cheap Shopping A to Z

ANTIQUES
See also 'Craft, Art & Antique Markets', p. 198.

Alfie's Antiques This former three-floor department store is home to more than 100 antique dealers, who fill almost every inch of a maze-like space. Between them they stock pretty much anything that could possible be labelled antique, from art deco tea sets and 1960s' lampshades to 1970s' jigsaws and Disney memorabilia. It's a great place to pick up something cheap and vintage for a special occasion, such as

Antique Auction Houses

At the top end, these should really come under the heading of window shopping rather than bargain hunting, unless you're a real expert in the field. The capital's big three auction houses, Bonhams, Christie's, and Sotheby's, which between them sell millions of pounds worth of antiques and fine art each year, allow members of the public to tour their showrooms before most sales. Only the biggest mega-sales—when a Picasso comes on the market, say—see them restrict that access. And, if you've got a valuable heirloom, they'll be more than happy to give you a free verbal valuation. On a more realistic note, the capital does also have a number of smaller auction houses specialising in antiques and collectibles where you're much more likely to pick up something old and tasteful for a song—just remember not to scratch your nose when the bidding starts (this is a myth, by the way, you have to register in order to bid).

Bonhams

101 New Bond Street, W1. ℃ **020 7629 6602.** www.bonhams.com. Tube: Bond Street.

Chiswick Auctions

1 Colville Road, W3. ℃ **020 8992 4442.** www.chiswickauctions.co.uk. Tube: South Acton.

Christie's

8 King Street, SW1. ℃ **020 7839 9060.** www.christies.co.uk. Tube: Green Park.

Criterion Auction Rooms

53 Essex Road, N1. ℃ **020 7359 5707.** www.criterion-auctioneers.co.uk. Tube: Angel.

Lots Road Auctions

71-73 Lots Road, SW10. ℃ **020 7376 6800.** www.lotsroad.com. Tube: Fulham Broadway.

Sotheby's

34–35 New Bond Street, W1. ℃ **020 7293 5000.** ww.sothebys.com. Tube: Bond Street.

a wedding. And once you've made your purchases, you can retire to the rooftop for some coffee and a view. Open Tuesday to Saturday 10am–6pm.

Church Street, NW8. Tube: Edgware Road. Tube/Train: Marylebone.

Gray's Antique Market This pair of grand Edwardian buildings are full of hidden treasures, not the least of which is the river, a tributary of the Thames, which flows through the basement. Above are 200 stalls piled high with collectible relics—jewellery, books (it's particularly good for books, see p. 208), vintage clothes, and furniture—many of them extremely pricey, but with affordable items dotted here and there. Dealers are (mostly) friendly and knowledgeable. Hours are Monday to Friday 10am–6pm.

1–7 Davies Mews, 58 Davies Street, W1. ℂ **020 7629 7034.** www.graysantiques.com. Tube: Bond Street.

> ## Misery Misers: Repo Sales
>
> It's not a nice thing to admit, but one person's financial pain can often be another's bargain gain. There are several London auction houses dedicated to selling goods made available as a result of liquidations, repossessions, and bankruptcies. Items coming up for resale can range from office equipment, clothing, and household goods to motor vehicles and even houses. Bargains are plentiful, if touched with a tinge of sadness. Check out www.infolondon.ukf.net/auctions, which provides comprehensive details of auction houses specialising in liquidated and bankrupt stock.

London Silver Vaults According to its own publicity, this boasts the world's largest retail collection of antique silver, amounting to many millions of pounds worth. Like an East End Aladdin's cave, the subterranean vaults are home to around 40 shops filled with shiny, sparkly items from the small—jewellery, tea sets, snuff boxes—to the large—a solid silver armchair (how comfy). Prices are similarly varied. You could quite easily empty a bank vault's worth of cash here, but you can also pick up trinkets for under £5.

Chancery Lane, WC2. ℂ **020 7242 3844.** www.thesilvervaults.com. Tube: Chancery Lane.

BOOKS

With more than seven million inhabitants, countless schools, 20-odd universities and an ingrained respect for the written word, London reads a lot of books. Many of these eventually find their way onto the discounted shelves of our myriad second-hand dealers. Charing Cross Road and Museum Street are two of the prime browsing areas.

Any Amount of Books   On Charing Cross Road, London's second-hand book mecca, this charmingly cluttered place stocks plenty of expensive titles aimed at collectors—first editions, leather-bound sets, antiquarian treasures—but you can also pick up your holiday reading for as little as £1.

56 Charing Cross Road, WC2. ✆ **020 7836 3697.** www.anyamountofbooks. com. Tube: Leicester Square.

Biblion   Taking up a large swath of Gray's Antique Market (see p. 207), this is one of the capital's largest and best-stocked second-hand emporiums, comprising 100 dealers and more than 20,000 books covering pretty much every topic imaginable, including children's books and art. Even more choice, and more saving potential, is offered on the website. It has a searchable UK-wide database and will connect you directly with the relevant bookshop or dealer without taking a commission.

Gray's Antique Market, 1–7 Davies Mews, W1. ✆ **020 7629 1374.** http://biblion. co.uk. Tube: Bond Street.

Book & Comic Exchange   This grungy little place is a great source of second-hand comics and graphic novels. The high turnover of stock means that prices are constantly cut to clear shelf space—which in turn means patience is rewarded with some real steals.

4 Pembridge Road, W11. ℂ **020 7229 8420.** Tube: Notting Hill Gate.

Books for Amnesty International   There are book and vinyl bargains aplenty—and all for a good cause—at this well-stocked Hammersmith charity shop. Most fiction titles are £1 to £3.50.

139b King Street, W6. ℂ **020 8746 3172.** www.amnesty.org.uk. Tube: Hammersmith.

British Heart Foundation Bookshop   The BHF's cosy little shop offers some of the most competitively priced second-hand books going. Prices start at 50p and they regularly offer three-for-£2 deals. They also have a selection of equally keenly priced used CDs and DVDs.

94 Streatham High Road, SW16. ℂ **020 8664 7490.** www.bhf.org.uk. Train: Streatham Hill.

British Red Cross Bookshop   These days it's difficult for second-hand bookshops to compete with the discounts being offered online at websites such as Amazon. Still, even if the prices here aren't startling cheap, at least you know your money is going to a worthy home. The shop has a wide range of titles, including sections devoted to children's books, history, and art, as well as well-stocked English literature and poetry shelves. Paperback novels start at £1, hardbacks at £5.

385 Green Lanes, N13. ℂ **020 8886 8364.** www.redcross.org.uk. Train: Palmer's Green.

Copperfields   This looks just how a second-hand bookshop should: a tatty sign, overflowing bookcases on the pavement outside, and somewhat chaotic arrangement, with books packing every interior space from floor to ceiling. Its over-packed appearance is hardly surprising when you consider that the shop contains something like 30,000 books, and has another 20,000 in storage. That's a lot of choice, covering everything from art to zoology. Rare and antiquarian books are fairly pricey, but there are plenty of modern books for sale too, including recent bestsellers that you can pick up for around a third of what you'll pay new.

37 Hartfield Road, SW19. ℂ **020 8542 0113.** Tube/Train: Wimbledon.

Foyles   Not quite the crazily cluttered, counter-intuitive, almost anti-commercial place it was when Christina Foyle, the daughter of the original owner, was in charge up until the late 1990s. Thankfully customers no longer have to queue up at three different points to buy a book, but this is still a very singular bookstore. Its five floors and 50 miles of shelves hold books on pretty much every subject imaginable. There are 56 separate sections in all—that's a lot of browsing. If you can't find it here, it probably hasn't been published. It also operates two smaller branches, on the South Bank and at St Pancras station.

113–119 Charing Cross Road, WC2. ✆ **020 7437 5660.** www.foyles.co.uk. Tube: Tottenham Court Road. Other locations: *South Bank*, Southbank Centre, Riverside, SE1. ✆ **020 7440 3212.** Tube/Train: Waterloo. *St Pancras Station*, Euston Road, N1. ✆ **020 3206 2650.** Tube/Train: King's Cross. Train: St Pancras.

Judd Books   Its 50,000-plus new and used titles, spread over two floors, make this a top contender for the best-stocked second-hand academic bookstore in London. Books are displayed floor to ceiling—ladders are provided to reach the topmost shelves—and touch all bases from fiction, film, cookery, and travel (it's particularly good for relatively recently published travel guidebooks) to heavyweight subjects like history, philosophy, and economics. Students receive a 10% discount. Prices start low, from 50p for the books in boxes out front.

82 Marchmont Street, WC1. ✆ **020 7387 5333.** www.juddbooks.com. Tube: Russell Square.

My Back Pages   Its location, opposite Balham station, doesn't seem promising but this is a great repository of second-hand books (and a few new titles), which are packed tightly onto shelves and piled high on tables. There are sections devoted to history, geography, travel, classics, politics, and psychology, among others, as well as a whole room of fiction. Incidentally, the name is a reference to a Dylan song.

8–10 Balham Station Road. ✆ **020 8675 9346.** Tube/Train: Balham.

★ **Oxfam Bookshop**   Taken as a whole, Oxfam's 700 UK shops make them the country's largest vendor of second-hand books. Some 12,000 can be found lining the shelves of the company's flagship bookstore which is fittingly located in the heart of bookish Bloomsbury. Titles are generally low priced and the profit contributes towards a good cause, so you can feel good about yourself while bargain hunting. The store also hosts regular events, such as author readings and book signings, often by well-known literary names.

12 Bloomsbury Street, WC1. ℂ **020 7637 4610.** http://oxfambloomsburybooks. wordpress.com. Tube: Tottenham Court Road.

Skoob   Skoob is Judd's only real rival in the world of second-hand academic bookselling. They certainly believe they are the biggest, and with a claimed stock of 60,000 titles, covering everything from literature, languages, and art to history, politics, maths, and science, the numbers seem to back them up. Incredibly, Skoob also has a further 65,000 books stored in an Oxfordshire warehouse, all catalogued on their website (what a Sisyphean task that must have been) and which can be sent to the shop, free of charge, on request. A generous complement of chairs helps the browsing process, and there's even a piano where you can give the sheet music a quick run-through.

66 The Brunswick Centre, off Marchmont Street, WC1. ℂ **020 7278 8760.** www. skoob.com. Tube: Russell Square.

South Bank Book Market   This small outdoor book market sensibly situated beneath the protective arches of Waterloo Bridge makes for a great browsing intermission during a walk along the South Bank. It comprises four long rows of tables filled with all manner of books, from biographies, and cookbooks to Snoopy books, autobiographies, and novels, as well as magazines and old prints, all displayed together with no real ordering system. It's not quite as cheap as some charity bookshops, but it's not too expensive either—most titles sell for a few pounds.

Thameside Walkway, beneath Waterloo Bridge, SE1. Tube/Train: Waterloo.

The Travel Bookshop   Few books date as quickly as travel guides. However, as the years pass and the information within them grows increasingly redundant, so the books can be judged on their own merits rather than as functional holiday companions. Guidebooks from previous decades, particularly those dating back to the early days of mass vacationing in the 1950s and 1960s, provide fascinating historical snapshots, not just of destinations but of contemporary social attitudes. This charming shop just off Portobello Market stocks a great range of both new and second-hand guidebooks and travel writing.

13–15 Blenheim Crescent, W11. ℂ **020 7229 5260.** www.thetravelbookshop.com. Tube: Ladbroke Grove.

Book Swaps

As cheap as many of the country's second-hand bookshops are, there's an even cheaper way of acquiring new reading material—swapping. Of course, you're expected to contribute something to the transaction, but in the form of your old books rather than money. There are now several dedicated book-swapping websites, most of which work in the same way. First you upload a list of which of your old books you're willing to swap. Then, you find something on the site you'd like to read and send a request to the owner. Finally, they take a look at your list to see if there's anything they want and then confirm or reject the request.

Read It Swap It, http://readit swapit.co.uk

BookMooch, www.bookmooch.com

Vintage Magazine Shop The upper floor of this decades-old Soho institution is full of retro tat—greetings cards, key-rings, T-shirts, mouse pads, and so on. It's downstairs where the shop really comes into its own. Here you'll find rack after rack filled with magazines and periodicals dating to the 1930s. Prices start at about £1, but you'll have to shell out a little more for that perfect kitschy birthday present. A 1982 *Doctor Who* annual is £7.50, a 1977 *Jackie* is £15, while a mint 1966 copy of *Playboy* will set you back £30 (retro... the acceptable face of pornography).

39–43 Brewer Street, W1. ℂ **020 7439 8525.** www.vinmag.com. Tube: Leicester Square.

CLOTHES

See also 'Charity Shops', p. 203.

Absolute Vintage Just around the corner from Brick Lane, this is one of the largest retro stores in the capital offering a huge selection of vintage and vintage-like (i.e. modern retro-looking) clothes, covering fashions from the 1930s to the 1980s. The range of shoes is enormous. Prices across the board aren't rock bottom, but they are competitive, with most shoes £15–£20 and dresses £20–£30. You can also buy online.

15 Hanbury Street, E1. ℂ **020 7247 3883.** www.absolutevintage.co.uk. Tube: Aldgate East. Tube/Train: Liverpool Street.

Beyond Retro If you want to uncover the genuine bargains at this Brick Lane branch of the Swedish chain you're going to have put the time in, sifting through the racks to find that perfect glam dress amongst all the tat. It's an enormous place, filled with more than 10,000 items. But look carefully, as not everything here is true vintage. They also sell plenty of recent second-hand stuff, as well as retro-'looking' items, and it's store policy not to offer refunds (only exchanges). Most importantly, watch out for the store cat weaving its way through the customers' legs. American fashions dominate the collection and prices are decent: scarves and jewellery from £1, T-shirts from £5, coats and dresses from £15, and even vintage wedding dresses from £50. There's a smaller branch in Soho.

110–112 Cheshire Street, E2. 𝄯 **020 7613 3636.** www.beyondretro.com. Tube: Whitechapel. Other locations: *Soho*, 58–59 Great Marlborough Street, W1. 𝄯 **020 7434 1406.** Tube: Oxford Circus.

★ **The East End Thrift Store** Thrift is to vintage as 'junk' is to 'antique'. Vintage implies clothes of a certain quality, a recognised provenance and in good condition. Thrift just implies old. That's not to say that there aren't plenty of great clothes in this warehouse-like space in the depths of the East End, but they're on sale alongside a lot of ordinary ones, which means you're going to have to put in a bit of browsing time. However, even if you get it wrong, it won't be too costly a mistake—most items retail for under £10. Unlike most vintage shops, this place doesn't make a kitschy song and dance about its stock. Items are displayed simply, almost starkly beneath strip lighting. It's particularly good for men's clothing, that oft-ignored other half of the vintage world.

Unit 1A, Watermans Building Assembly Passage, E1. 𝄯 **020 7423 9700.** www.theeastendthriftstore.com. Tube: Stepney Green, Whitechapel.

Fashion & Textile Museum Shop Or Shop@FTM, to give it its more GenY-friendly moniker. The shop is free to enter (unlike

> ## A Cheap Sample
>
> Homewares and fashion retailers often dump excess stock and old catwalk or showroom samples at 'sample sales'. There are various websites listing upcoming London happenings, of which http://samplesal.es is one of the most comprehensive. It lists sales of accessories and homewares, as well as men's and women's fashion, and is also one of the few sites that doesn't require you to register to access the information. You can also follow on Twitter: @londonsales.

the museum itself) and stocks, in addition to books on fashion, clothes and accessories made by up-and-coming London designers, many of them very reasonably priced.

The Fashion and Textile Museum, 83 Bermondsey Street, SE1. ✆ **020 7407 8664.** www.ftmlondon.org. Tube/Train: London Bridge.

H&M   H&M is like a slightly grander, slightly less youth-orientated, slightly more expensive (but only slightly) version of Top Shop. Its stock changes regularly, but prices always remain low: T-shirts for less than a fiver, cardigans for less than a tenner, and even thick winter coats for around £40. It's corporate, sure, but it provides a slick, well-oiled service and the clothes are generally of a quality that won't fall apart after a couple of washes, The Regent Street store is probably the biggest and best stocked in the capital. It's certainly superior to the Oxford Street branch just down the road, yet is always less crowded. As always, womenswear dominates the collection, but men are catered for too, on the top floor.

234 Regent Street, W1. ✆ **020 7758 3990.** www.hm.com. Tube: Oxford Street.

The Outdoors   If military chic is your thing, then The Outdoors, a specialist in surplus from Britain's Army, Navy and Royal Air Force, has the outfit for you. You can kit yourself out from head to toe for under £50 by buying a soldier suit—camouflage trousers, shirt, and jacket—for £22, a pair of army boots for £20, and topping the ensemble off with either an RAF peaked cap (£6) or a desert bush hat (£7.50). And if you want to take your new look on the road, the stores also stocks camping supplies (sleeping bag for £20, kit bags for £5). Its two branches are way out east in Dagenham and Rainham, but the full collection, which also includes ex-police and firefighter equipment, is also offered online.

66 Whalebone Lane South, RM8. ✆ **020 8596 9845.** www.the-outdoor.co.uk. Train: Chadwell Heath. Other location: Rainham, 26 Upminster Road South, RM13. ✆ **01708 524915.** Train: Rainham.

Primark   Primark has proved a major hit with British consumers in recent years for one simple reason: bargains. It consistently offers the lowest prices on the high street for staples like T-shirts (from £1), shirts (from £3), and jeans (from £7). You could argue that Primark has introduced a whole new high-street concept, disposable fashion. It may not be the place to buy a winter coat to last a lifetime, but for something shiny and new for the weekend that's going to be worn a few times and then tossed aside, it can't be beaten. The Oxford Street store is enormous, but no matter how much space there is, every square inch is filled with shoppers come the weekend. For more peaceful browsing, go during the week. Womenswear is on the ground floor, menswear above.

499 Oxford Street, W1. ✆ **020 7495 0420.** www.primark.co.uk. Tube: Marble Arch. Other locations: *Hammersmith*, 1 King's Mall, King Street, W6. ✆ **020 8748 7119.** Tube: Hammersmith. *Hackney*, 365 Mare Street, E8. ✆ **020 8985 2689.** Train: Hackney Central.

TK Maxx   One of the few central London branches of this suburban shopping mall stalwart conforms to the classic TK Maxx template, offering well-known brands including designerware by the likes of Versace and Tommy Hilfiger at discounts of up to 60%. Savings seem to be maintained by cutting down on floor staff—don't look for assistance, you're essentially on your own to wade through the three floors of bargains in the search for those hidden gems (or, more often, shoes that actually fit). Whether you find anything or not is down to luck, but stock is replenished every day, so it's worth making repeat visits.

26–40 Kensington High Street, W8. ✆ **020 7937 8701.** www.tkmaxx.com. Tube: High Street Kensington.

TopShop   A London institution, TopShop's bargain takes on the latest designer fashions have proved as popular with celebrities as with average high-street shoppers. The flagship Oxford Street branch takes up four floors, and boasts a blow-dry bar, nail salon, café, and pick and mix counter. Oh, and clothes. Lots and lots of clothes. New lines hit the racks here first before being rolled out nationwide, but prices are no more expensive. There's also a basement with vintage clothes

Your Coup

A camouflage jacket and a pair of desert boots is all very well but if your attempted coup is ultimately to be successful, you'll need to have some more serious hardware. Your best route is to log on to the website of the Disposals Services Agency, the body charged with selling the Ministry of Defence's old and obsolete gear: everything from uniforms (£20), water bottles (just £8), and mobile hydration systems (£22.50) to vans (from £2,250), cranes (£29,500), and even occasionally planes and ships (£300,000-plus). No guns or bombs though. www.edisposals.com.

Tea for You

A red bus moneybox? A Big Ben paperweight? A postcard of a grey, overcast sky? It can be difficult picking that perfect souvenir of London. For something a little more refined, you could try a gift selection of teas (after all, what's more British than tea—you can hardly wrap up an orderly queue?). The city's oldest tea shop was founded here in 1706 by Thomas Twining, who took a gamble on the growing popularity of an exotic new drink from Asia. It proved an inspired punt. Londoners' love of tea grew so great that the shop has now been in operation for over 300 years, making it the oldest shop in the capital still occupying its original location. The shop also stocks range of souvenirs—teapots, tea cups, and mugs among them, of course—and has a small museum detailing the history of tea drinking and the Twinings family. 216 Strand, WC2. ℭ **020 7353 3511.** www.twinings.co.uk. Mon–Fri 9am–5pm, Sat 10am–4pm. Tube: Temple.

plus a few in-store concessions. It can be scarily crowded on weekends, particularly on the ground floor, as hordes of teenagers crowd around the accessories. 214 Oxford Street, W1. ℭ **020 7636 7700.** www.topshop.com. Tube: Oxford Circus.

Wow Retro   These two shops, one for men and one for women, stock vintage gear from the 1940s to the 1980s, from zoot suits, drape jackets, and tea dresses to mini-skirts, mohair jumpers, and frilly New Romantic tops. Prices tend to be just below what the average vintage emporium would charge. 10 & 14 Mercer Street, WC2. ℭ **020 7379 5334.** Tube: Covent Garden.

ELECTRONICS

Ask   The stretch of Tottenham Court Road just north of Oxford Street is the place to go for electronic bargains, where a cluster of stores compete to undercut each other on the latest HD, Blu-ray, DAB, and MP4 gear. There's not a great deal to choose between them, in all honesty, but Ask is one of the big players with three stores along this stretch—Kamla, Harp, and the four-storey flagship Ask store—packed with every brand of laptop, digital camera, printer, sat nav, or TV you can think of. The staff are knowledgeable and sometimes even friendly. You can also order via their website.

248 Tottenham Court Road, W1T. ℭ **020 7637 0353.** www.askdirect.co.uk. Tube: Tottenham Court Road.

FOOD
See 'Haggle Time: London's Markets', p. 192.

RECORDS & CDS
Record shops are never going to be able to compete for price with downloads. The rise of the iTunes generation has been largely responsible for the closure of around a quarter of London's independent music stores over the last half-decade, including Beano's, once Europe's largest indie. Those that survive do so by appealing to a certain type of hardcore fan who desires the physical object as much as the music it carries. It is this hardcore who have been responsible for the revival of 7-inch vinyl singles, which are now selling around five times the numbers they were a decade ago. The following all offer comparative bargains—i.e. well priced compared to what you'll find in any other store, but still more than a download.

Harold Moores Records   Second-hand classical music specialist.

2 Great Marlborough Street, W1. ℭ **020 7437 1576.** www.hmrecords.co.uk. Tube: Oxford Circus.

Intoxica! Specialists in 60s beat, ska, reggae, soul, and 70s funk. They also sell a wide range of second-hand posters and magazines, both from their shop and online.

231 Portobello Road, W11. ℭ **020 7229 8010.** www.intoxica.co.uk. Tube: Ladbroke Grove.

Record Fairs

Though not held in the numbers they once were, record fairs still occur regularly in the capital. These days they often cater to niche tastes—such as dancehall, northern soul, or breaks 'n' beats—that are difficult (if not impossible) to track down online. Some of the best include the **Spitalfields Fair** (www.visitspitalfields.com), held in the market building on the first and third Wednesday of the month, the **Soundbite Fairs** staged at various venues across the capital, including Wimbledon and Shepherd's Bush (http://freespace.virgin.net/infora.spin), and **MusicMania**, the biggest fair of the year which takes place over a November weekend at Olympia (www.vip-24.com).

Window Shopping

Treating shopping as a sightseeing rather than a purchasing experience remains upmarket retail's most painless option. Places such as the Harrods Food Hall, fashion displays at Harvey Nics, toy demonstrations at Hamleys, and the rare jewels of Bond Street are sights in themselves, regardless of whether you pull out your wallet or not. Here are my favourite London window-shopping areas:

Brompton Cross   For high fashions: the intersection of the Brompton Road and the Fulham Road is home to one of the capital's highest concentration of designer chains; Gucci, Prada, Armani, and Paul Smith included.

Charing Cross Road   For second-hand and antiquarian books.

Knightsbridge   For the grand department stores of Harrods and Harvey Nichols.

Old & New Bond Street   For expensive designer clothes, shoes, and jewellery: Nicole Farhi, MaxMara, Jimmy Choo, Rolex, Cartier, Bulgari.

Oxford Street   For big-name chains: any multiple worth its salt has a flagship on the nation's favourite retail thoroughfare. The street's 17-million-plus annual visitors often make it somewhere to be endured rather than enjoyed, particularly on weekends and pre-Christmas.

Piccadilly   For the Ritz, Waterstones (Europe's largest bookshop), the Burlington Arcade (an elegant 19th-century covered shopping walkway patrolled by top-hatted beadles), and the mechanical clock, inventive window displays, and stylish food counters of Fortnum & Mason, grocers to The Queen.

Regent Street   For the graceful John Nash 19th-century architecture, the toys of Hamleys, the Apple Store, the fancy fabrics and homewares of Liberty, and (usually) the best central Christmas lights.

Savile Row & Jermyn Street   For tailored suits (Oswald Boateng, Gieves & Hawkes) and shirts (Thomas Pink, Turnball & Asser).

Sloane Street   For fancy fashions, perfumes, and stationery—Gucci, Louis Vuitton, Dior, Mont Blanc.

Revival Records   One of the few survivors from the recent purge of Berwick Street's record shops. All kinds of music sold.

30 Berwick Street, W1. © **020 7437 4271.** www.revivalrecords.uk.com. Tube: Oxford Circus, Tottenham Court Road.

Sounds of the Universe These vinyl purists also operate their own label, Soul Jazz Records, and sell dance music from around the world: dubstep, grime, Balearic, Italo-disco, hip hop, Turkish beats, Afrobeat, and more.

7 Broadwick Street, W1. © **020 7734 3430.** www.soundsoftheuniverse.com. Tube: Oxford Circus, Tottenham Court Road.

SHOES

Clarks Factory Shop Cheap shoes by the thousand are sold at this outlet of the famous footwear chain. There's a particularly good selection for little feet, but then putting on your first pair of Clarks shoes—and having your feet measured in one of those slidey devices—has long been a rite of passage for British children. Parents are well cared for, too. In addition to their traditional specialisms of 'sturdy' and 'comfortable', Clarks have branched out into 'stylish' with nifty shoes and boots for as little as £15.

67–83 Seven Sisters Road, N7. © **020 7281 9364.** www.clarks.co.uk. Tube: Holloway Road. Other locations: *Peckham*, 61–63 Rye Lane, SE15. © **020 7732 2530.** Train: Peckham Rye.

Swap Shopping

Swapping has grown hugely popular as a recycling, eco-friendly alternative to traditional shopping. There are now several websites dedicated to putting people and their unwanted goods in touch with each other. List the items you are prepared to swap and you're awarded a number of points based on their value, which you redeem for other people's listed goods.

If that sounds rather cold and impersonal, you could try Swishing, a face-to-face, designer alternative to swapping. Aimed at ladies looking to liven up their wardrobes, Swishing organises regular events where participants are invited to exchange old clothes with like-minded souls. Each lady must bring 'at least one good quality, clean item of clothing, or an accessory, that she'd feel proud to hand on'.

SwapItShop, www.swapitshop.com

SwapShop, www.swapshop.co.uk

Swishing, www.swishing.org

SHOPPING IN THE WEST END

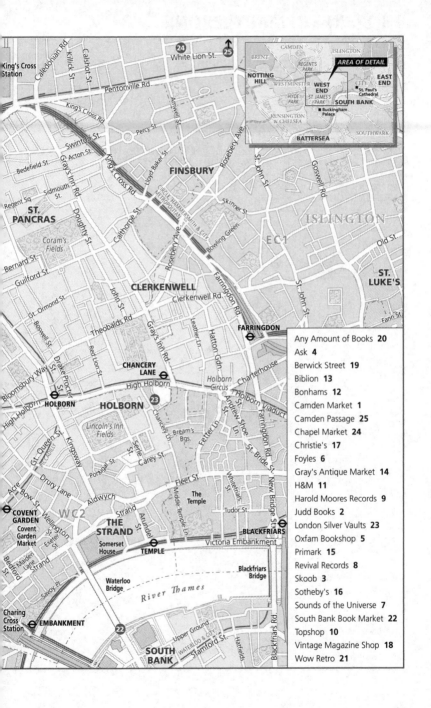

SHOPPING IN MARYLEBONE

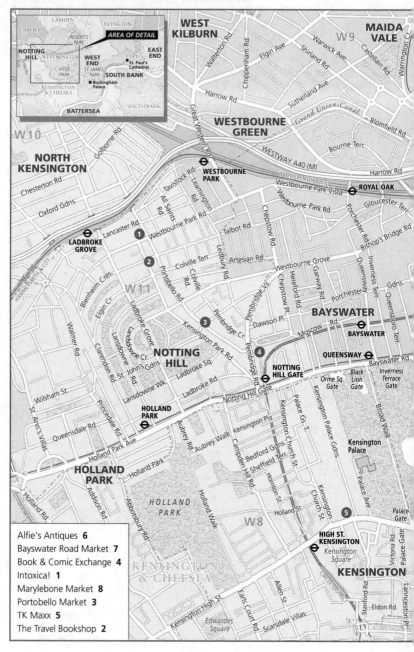

Alfie's Antiques **6**
Bayswater Road Market **7**
Book & Comic Exchange **4**
Intoxica! **1**
Marylebone Market **8**
Portobello Market **3**
TK Maxx **5**
The Travel Bookshop **2**

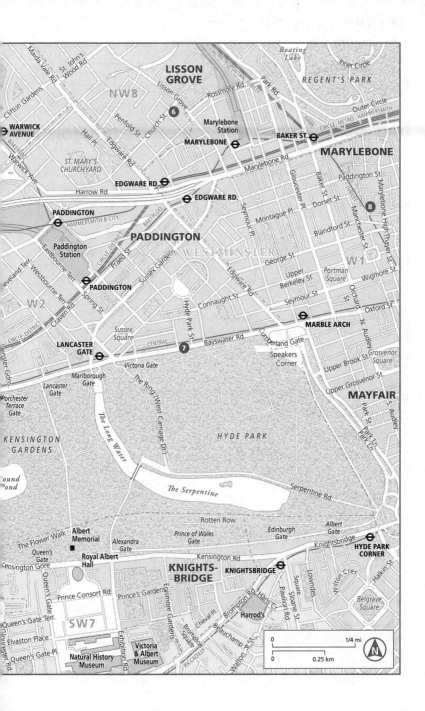

SHOPPING IN THE CITY

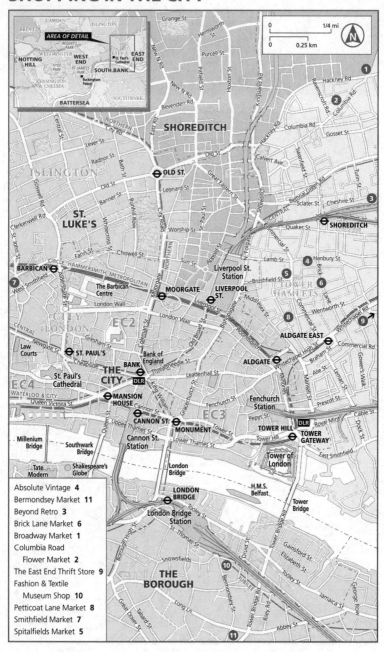

Absolute Vintage **4**
Bermondsey Market **11**
Beyond Retro **3**
Brick Lane Market **6**
Broadway Market **1**
Columbia Road
  Flower Market **2**
The East End Thrift Store **9**
Fashion & Textile
  Museum Shop **10**
Petticoat Lane Market **8**
Smithfield Market **7**
Spitalfields Market **5**

Be part of the world's biggest classical music festival, the Proms take place annually at the Royal Albert Hall.

ENTERTAINMENT & NIGHTLIFE

With weekend cinema prices over £12 a pop, face-value theatre seats starting at £20 (and not for a good seat), and a concert by a 'big name' performer at Wembley or the O2 upwards of £50, it's all too easy to break the bank on entertainment. And yet, with a little forward planning, huge savings are out there—you just have to be a little open-minded about your evenings. Hit West End musicals, first-run Hollywood releases, and opening nights at the opera are out. In their place come free TV and radio programme tapings, half-price theatre tickets (for less celebrated offerings), and £5 berths for Shakespeare. Free events and cut-price entertainment are staged throughout the year. Can't afford front row for the London Symphony Orchestra? Enjoy the free pre-performance gig in the Barbican foyer instead. Missed out on the latest *Hamlet* revival? Try a lunchtime play and a sandwich for £5 at the Southwark Playhouse. Need a cut-price opera fix? Head down to Covent Garden and wait for the Royal Opera House buskers to warble. In fact so many and varied are the choices that you could, with a flexible attitude and enough money-saving dedication, go 12 months without paying for a single event.

1 Live Music

On any given night, London's clubs, pubs, and concert halls reverberate to the sound of a staggering array of live music. Whatever your tastes, be it for lo-fi guitar fuzzouts, clean-cut classical, bleeptastic beats, bluesy folk, folky blues, earnest electronica, or jazz noodling, you'll find somewhere prepared to serve you a cut-price version.

POP, ROCK & INDIE VENUES

Even in these days of remotely accessed music, bedroom recording, file sharing, and iPods, clubs and pubs still provide a fertile compost in which new musical scenes grow. Setting up a MySpace page is all very well, but doing your thing live is still the best way to build a following for your band—or to provide confirmation that it's never going to happen for you. The capital has numerous venues willing to offer slots to up-and-comers. The usual approach is to put several new acts on a single bill and charge a minimal admission fee, say £5. Open-mic nights, when anyone can stroll in off the street with a guitar and give it some, are usually free.

The Bedford `FREE`   Displaying a commendably dedicated attitude towards live music, this large Balham pub puts on gigs 4 nights a week, 50 weeks a year, usually with three to five acts a night—that's something like 800 acts a year. Each and every one is free. Singer-songwriters are the mainstays: James Morrison and KT Tunstall played here in their early days, which should give you an idea of the edginess of the performers. In general, the music is as safe and cosy as its semi-suburban setting. Don't expect Throbbing Gristle-style audience confrontations.

72 Bedford Hill, SW12. ℂ **020 8682 8940**. www.thebedford.co.uk. Tube/Train: Balham.

The Cavendish   This plush place, decked out with leather sofas and velvet curtains, is one of the capital's most supportive venues for new bands. Those acts who can guarantee to bring in at least 20 people can play a prestigious Saturday night slot and receive a cut from the £5 per person entry money. Bands from outside London (or whose long-suffering friends have deserted them, or who nobody likes) play the free nights which take place on the first Friday of the month, alternate Mondays, the last Thursday of the month, and alternate Sundays—the last featuring acoustic sets only. The venue has an equally nurturing comedy policy, running a free 'Comedy Virgins' open-mic spot every Tuesday.

128 Hartington Road, SW8. 𝄢 **020 7627 0698.** www.thecavendisharmsstockwell. co.uk. Tube: Stockwell.

Dublin Castle   As its promotional blurb helpfully points out, this is not a castle and it's not in Dublin. Rather, it's an Irish pub with a tiny corner stage that plays host to some very Camden acts—each a random assortment of skinny jeans, choppy haircuts, punky riffs, and indie angst. Some good, some dross, but all very sweaty and entertainingly earnest. Occasionally acts have gone onto greater things, as Madness did in 1978–79 and... no doubt somebody will follow in their footsteps eventually. When no acts are on, you can choose your own entertainment from the punk and indie classics on the juke-box—£1 buys you five plays.

94 Parkway, NW1. 𝄢 **020 7485 1773.** www.bugbearbookings.com. Tube: Camden Town.

Half Moon, Herne Hill   Everyone has to start somewhere, and for many bands, including The Police, Van Morrison, U2 (and, on one ill-advised occasion, your author), that place was here, one of the vertebrae in the backbone of London's amateur live circuit. This Victorian affair still opens its large function room to new bands on Tuesday, Friday, and Saturday nights. While every one of them hopes this will be the springboard to greater things (and for roughly 0.001% of them, it might be), all of them are studiously ignored by the locals in the front bar.

10 Half Moon Lane, SE24. 𝄢 **020 7274 2733.** www.halfmoonpub.co.uk. Train: Herne Hill.

Halfmoon, Putney   This semi-legendary riverside venue has welcomed an impeccable roll-call of acts over the past 40 years, including Kate Bush, The Yardbirds, The Rolling Stones, The Who, Elvis

Costello, and Van Morrison. Gigs are held Tuesday to Sunday at 8pm and feature a mixture of new acts, established acts, and famous faces (looking to keep it real, yeah?). Prices range from £2.50 for an unplugged night to £10 for a big name. It's five songs for a £1 at the well-stocked jukebox.

93 Lower Richmond Road, SW15. ℂ **020 8780 9383**. www.halfmoon.co.uk. Tube: Putney Bridge. Train: Putney.

HMV Oxford Street `FREE`   The in-store appearance has become a vital marketing tool for new bands—particularly talent-show winners (and runners-up) being groomed by major labels. HMV Oxford Street is the Wembley of such venues, and attracts the biggest names, and the most screaming fans. Events are usually free, but typically involve a great deal of waiting around. Check the website for details.

150 Oxford Street, W1. ℂ **020 7631 3423**. http://hmv.com. Tube: Oxford Circus.

The Lock Tavern `FREE`   This renovated pub stages a number of free gigs each month, covering a broad range of musical bases, including indie, electronica, rock, and country—the last showcased at the regular Thursday night 'Countrier Than Thou' events. Some big names have entertained the nonchalant indie crowds here—Alex Turner (from Arctic Monkeys), Basement Jaxx, and the Dandy Warhols among them (see also p. 267).

35 Chalk Farm Road, NW1. ℂ **020 7482 7163**. www.lock-tavern.co.uk. Tube: Chalk Farm.

★ **Notting Hill Arts Club** `FREE`   For over a decade the Notting Hill Arts Club has been giving up-and-coming bands both a place to perform and—thanks to cheap drinks deals and comfy sofas—a ready-made audience. The Saturday afternoon ROTA sessions (4–6pm) offer happy hour drink prices and are sponsored by the legendary Rough Trade shop, so expect plenty of indie and angst.

21 Notting Hill Gate, W11. ℂ **020 7460 4459**. www.nottinghillartsclub.com & www.myspace.com/rotaclub. Tube: Notting Hill Gate.

Old Blue Last `FREE`   From the outside this is a typical East End boozer, but inside it's been given the full Shoreditch treatment. The ironically dingy downstairs bar attracts a lively crowd, particularly at weekends. Upstairs is a small music venue (capacity 100) which entices the hippest of local hipsters with its diet of DJ sets and live bands, who have included Foals, Kate Nash, Amy Winehouse, and the Arctic Monkeys. Most events are free, although there's occasionally a door charge of around £6.

38 Great Eastern Street, EC2. ℂ **020 7739 7033.** www.theoldbluelast.com. Tube: Old Street.

Pure Groove FREE If you like the idea of hearing a few sounds while you tuck into a midday meal, then head down to this record shop cum gallery space which invites acts to perform lunchtime sets on its purpose-built stage two to three times a week. There are also evening shows (Mon–Fri), typically starting at 6:30pm (7:30pm Fridays). Acts come firmly under the new and experimental category: lo-fi fuzz masters, laptop heroes, singer-songwriters, art school crazies, and the like. A fiendish, music-themed quiz is held on intermittent Thursdays.

6–7 West Smithfield, EC1. ℂ **020 7778 9278.** www.puregroove.co.uk. Tube/Train: Farringdon.

Rough Trade East FREE The eastern outpost of the legendary indie music shop hosts live bands from 7pm several nights a week—expect underground, punk, singer-songwriters, and quirky pop. The gigs are free, but for the most popular acts, you'll need to head down an hour early to pick up a wristband. It's first come, first served. Regular DJ nights are also staged at next door's **Big Chill Bar.**

Dray Walk, Old Truman Brewery, 91 Brick Lane, E1. ℂ **020 7392 7788.** www.rough trade.com. Tube: Aldgate East.

The Slaughtered Lamb The refined upstairs bar of this trendy boozer—all stripped wood and leather stools—leads down to a dingy subterranean area where, from Monday to Wednesday, the 'Electro-acoustic Club' lays on live music . The booking policy seems to encompass anything that could be described as either 'electro' or 'acoustic'—from folk and blues to experimental electronic bleeping. Tickets are generally in the £5 region for live acts and free for DJ nights. The pub also hosts a twice-monthly music-themed pub quiz.

34–35 Great Sutton Street, EC1. ℂ **020 7253 1516.** www.theslaughteredlambpub. com. Tube/Train: Farringdon, Barbican.

12 Bar Club This tiny Tin Pan Alley venue gets through a lot of musicians, playing host to around four acts a night, every night of the week. The sheer volume of bands makes for a necessarily eclectic music policy. There's plenty of blues, as the club's name would imply, but also folk, antifolk (just for a bit of balance), soul, funk, metal, and indie. All the acts are terribly keen—and all have their own MySpace pages. Over the years several famous names have played here before making it big, including the Libertines, Joanna Newsome, and Jeff Buckley. There are two ticket options: you can pay £5 every time you visit, or take the time to fill in a membership form, after which your £5 entitles you to free membership (and free gigs) for life—that's a pretty good deal. The venue also has a generously stocked jukebox.

26 Denmark Place, WC2. ✆ **020 7240 2066.** www.12barclub.com. Tube: Tottenham Court Road.

FOLK

The Betsey Trotwood   Folk for purists. The pub's upstairs acoustic room plays host every Tuesday to the 'Snake Mountain Review', a showcase for folk and 'Americana', which often as not means English people singing in fake US accents. Twice monthly it's the Lantern Society, which bills itself as 'folk… around the camp fire (but without the fire)'. Both evenings cost £3 and offer opportunities for 'floor spots' from folkily-inclined members of the audience, before the main action gets going at 8pm.

56 Farringdon Road, EC1. ✆ **020 7253 4285.** www.thebetsey.com. Tube/Train: Farringdon.

Cellar Upstairs Folk Club   Every Saturday this Euston pub lays on an evening of full-on, old-school beardy folk; performers indulge in earnest acoustic polemicising that would make Pete Seeger proud. Tickets are £6 or £5 for members (£2 secures you a 1-year membership). Shows start at 8:15pm.

Exmouth Arms, Starcross Street, NW1. ✆ **020 7281 7700.** www.cellarupstairs.org.uk. Tube: Euston Square. Tube/Train: Euston.

The Grove   The new management are trying to turn this pub opposite South Wimbledon tube into a serious live venue and a hub of music in the community offering not just gigs (any pub can do that), but also music tuition for local people. When not filled with the sound of music—principally folk—the pub also stages free comedy nights on Mondays that feature four new acts, and a 'Bottle It' open-mic spot.

2 Morden Road, SW19. ✆ **020 8543 9064.** www.thegrovewimbledon.com. Tube: South Wimbledon.

Walthamstow Folk Club Putting the folksy in folk, this friendly North London club takes place every Sunday. The programme consists of main shows by resident performers, showcases by guests, and, if you've brought an instrument (and some nerve), 'floor spots' for members of the audience. In between the songs expect lots of intense folky discussion and sharing of CDs. Things get underway at 7:15pm and finish at 10:30pm. Tickets are £6.

The Plough Inn, 173 Wood Street, E17. *℃* **07740 612607.** www.walthamstow-folk.co.uk. Train: Wood Street.

JAZZ

The Crypt This atmospheric church crypt is the venue for 'Jazz Live' on Fridays, a serious night for jazz aficionados who can tell their hard bop from their cubop, and their Latin from their township. Doors open at 8pm, and the music kicks off at 9:30pm. Tickets are £6 and you can eat a three-course meal for an extra £10.

St. Giles Centre, 81 Camberwell Church Street, SE5. *℃* **020 7701 1016.** www.jazzlive.co.uk. Train: Loughborough Junction.

The Haggerston FREE This cooler-than-cool Hackney late-licence bar plays host on Sundays

Open-Mic Nights

You've practised the chords in your bedroom till your fingers ache, you've mapped out a future of multi-million pound advances, global tours, and record-breaking album sales, but you've yet to actually perform in front of anyone. This is where the open-mic nights of the capital's pubs and clubs come in. These regular amateur evenings give wannabe singers the chance to dip their first tentative toes into the waters of public performance. Most venues supply a PA only, so attract acoustic guitar-wielding singer-songwriters and their sensitive ditties; a few places, such as the **12 Bar Club,** provide a full back line (drums, amps, and microphones), allowing bands to rock out to the max, so long as they bring their instruments. Experienced musicians can also sit in on open jam nights, including Mondays at the **Blues Bar** (www.aintnothinbut.co.uk) and Wednesdays at **Ronnie Scott's.** Do note, however, if you want to get involved, these are showcases for people who really know what they're doing, not chancers.

to Uncle Sam's Jazz and Blues night, a free jazz fest served up by main man Alan Weekes' expert quintet—guitar, double bass, sax, drums, and vocals. Things keep going till 1pm, after which you'll have to track down a night bus to get home.

438 Kingsland Road, E8. ℭ **020 7923 3206.** www.myspace.com/jazzunclesams. Tube: Dalston Kingsland.

Lord Rockwood Home on Tuesdays to the East Side Jazz Club, when singers, pianists, bassists, guitarists, trumpeters, and saxophonists arrive to join the only constant fixture, drummer and host Chris Fenner, for an evening of jazzy improv. Tickets £4 to £6.

314 Cann Hall Road, E11. ℭ **020 8519 0785.** http://eastsidejazzclub.blogspot.com. Tube: Leyton. Train: Leytonstone High Road.

Marathon Kebab Being drunk can make the world seem a very different place: utter nonsense sounds deep and meaningful; level surfaces become strangely difficult to negotiate; and a dingy kebab house in Camden transforms into a hip London hangout. There's something of the speakeasy about Marathon, which only really comes to life in the early hours of Saturday and Sunday. Pass the front counter where the slumped hordes are ordering doners to the small room at the back, where revellers fan the embers of the party that's begun to die down everywhere else. Here, in this greasy wonderland, live bands play (from jazz and swing to Elvis impersonators), DJs revolve, and the crowd dances—or sways semi-rhythmically—oblivious to the passing hours.

87 Chalk Farm Road, NW1. ℭ **020 7485 3814.** Tube: Chalk Farm.

Ronnie Scott's All the greats have played this legendary venue since it opened its doors in 1959. Seats for the main stage are pretty expensive—a restricted view

---

FREE More Music at the Scoop

The **More London Free Festival,** which takes place for 3 weeks each July, sees a surfeit of free musical performances at the Scoop amphitheatre next to City Hall. Every Wednesday, Thursday, and Friday at lunchtime, 12:30 to 2pm, and in the evenings 6:30 to 9:30pm, catch jazz (probably more jazz than anything else), funk, or singer-songwriters. As with all Scoop events, there's no booking; just turn up and claim a seat.

ℭ **020 7403 4866.** www.more london.co.uk/scoop.html.

starts at £20. Tickets for the upstairs bar, however, for smaller gigs and sessions, are just £5. Wednesday jam nights are free if you arrive before 8pm (or are a musician with a valid MU card), although you have to wait till 10:30pm for the music to start.

47 Frith Street, W1. *C* **020 7439 0747.** www.ronniescotts.co.uk. Tube: Leicester Square, Tottenham Court Road.

WORLD MUSIC

★ **Club Skaaville** The fancy Paradise by Way of Kensal Green pub plays host every other Sunday to Club Skaaville, a live showcase for some of the capital's best old-school Caribbean sounds. Ska, rock steady, and reggae dominate, but, depending on who the guest musicians are, you may also hear soul, R&B, calypso, funk, latin, salsa, or afrobeat. The one constant is that you'll be expected to show your appreciation by dancing—regular host and saxman Ray Carless is no fan of wallflowers. Admission is £5; £3 for members.

19 Kilburn Lane, NW10. *C* **07851 221230.** www.clubskaaville.co.uk. Tube: Kensal Green.

Hootananny Brixton Prices for gigs and club nights at this old-fashioned knees-up venue range from around £12 for well-known acts (usually on Sundays and midweek) to nothing for many Friday (ska and reggae) and Saturday (world music) gigs. Free karaoke

Busking on the Tube

For many people, busking is a free entertainment too far—something to be avoided rather than actively sought out. Every Londoner has experienced that spirit-sinking moment when you realise that the guy who just strolled into your carriage *is holding a guitar*. But, as a busker might rather flatly put it, the times they are a-changing. These days busking is a competitive enterprise—performers have to up their game if they're to secure one of the capital's prime patches. Transport for London has banned performing on Tube carriages (although determined souls persist). Instead, would-be performers are allocated specific pitches in the access tunnels and, to ensure quality (or to check they're at least moderately competent), each must pass an audition. The general standard has, as a result, been raised, and today you're just as likely to hear some adept jazz or classical players as you are scratchy versions of *You're Beautiful*—although there are still too many of the latter kind for my tastes.

sessions are also staged on the first Wednesday of each month, when you can indulge your rock-star fantasies by belting out some favourite tunes accompanied by a live band. The pub's beer garden is one of the largest in the capital.

95 Effra Road, SW2. ✆ **020 7737 7273.** www.hootanannybrixton.co.uk. Tube: Brixton.

Pangea Project   The Pangea Project is very typical of this area: a combined bar, live venue, and recording studio opened with the intention of showcasing local acts and then streaming their performances over the interweb. Everyone is a bit cool and artfully dishevelled, at least early in the evening. As time passes and beer flows it gets much more friendly. The venue lays on live music covering several different genres: jazz, blues, afrobeat, Belarussian gypsy punk, and so on. On Wednesdays (6–7pm) you can even listen to a choir singing close four-part harmony arrangements of folk, gospel, and pop standards. All events are free before 9pm, £5 after. Free 'new faces' comedy nights are on Mondays.

72 Stamford Hill, N16. ✆ **07853 725476.** www.pangeaproject.co.uk. Train: Stoke Newington.

★ SOAS FREE   Probably the best (and certainly the cheapest) venue for world music in the capital, SOAS (School of Oriental and African Studies) runs a fantastically eclectic concert series, encompassing Chinese opera, Ghanese drumming, Malinese ngoni recitals, Indian folk songs, Argentine tango, Orisha ritual music from Cuba, and countless other genres. One or two events are normally staged a month, usually on Tuesdays. All events start at 7pm and are free.

University of London, Thornhaugh Street, Russell Square, WC1. ✆ **020 7637 2388.** www.soas.ac.uk. Tube: Goodge Street, Russell Square.

2 Classical Music

It may be the 21st century, when everyone is supposed to be listening to computerised beats made by robots in laboratories, but traditional classical music is still a major draw. The capital boasts two opera houses (the Royal Opera House and the Coliseum), four major orchestras (the London Symphony, the Philharmonia, the London Philharmonic, and the Royal Philharmonic), and one of the world's greatest classical music festivals—the Proms. But these are merely the tip of one melodious iceberg. Classical music is everywhere: in churches, in museums, in galleries. Indeed, lunch hour in the capital may as well be renamed 'classical hour', such is the number of concerts available. Classical prices run the full gamut, from more than £200 for a seat at the Royal Opera House to absolutely nothing for recitals held in many arts venues.

MAJOR SAVINGS AT MAJOR VENUES

Barbican Centre **FREE** Here's a tip: doll yourself up as if you were going to attend a concert at the Barbican, one of London's most prestigious (if not most beautiful) classical arts venues. However, rather than going to the main event, turn up a little bit early and enjoy the free gig given before the performance on the aptly named Freestage in the foyer instead. Then, as the paying audience files into the auditorium, you can simply slip out the exit (and no one need ever know what a cheapskate you are). The Barbican, which is the home of the London Symphony Orchestra and the BBC Symphony Orchestra, sometimes also allows members of the public to attend open rehearsals for forthcoming performances for free, although tickets must be booked in advance through the box office.

Barbican Centre, EC2. ☎ **020 7638 4141.** www.barbican.org.uk. Tube/Train: Barbican.

FREE Summer Screens (Make Me Feel Fine)

Free opera may sound like an oxymoron, but it is a reality, albeit experienced at a distance. Every summer BP sponsors free screenings of three Royal Opera House performances (usually two operas and a ballet) on big screens erected at Trafalgar Square and Canary Wharf. These are non-bookable events: just turn up and claim a seat. Performances tend to start at 7 to 7:30pm with pre-performance entertainment beginning around an hour earlier.
www.roh.org.uk/whatson/bpbigscreens/index.aspx

London Coliseum From Monday to Thursday the English National Opera, London's second-most prestigious opera company (after the Royal), makes 60 tickets available for its operas and ballets for just £10, a fraction of the normal cost (stall tickets are in excess of £80). Just be aware that your seat will be towards the back, so bring some opera glasses. All performances, even of foreign operas, are sung in English. FINE PRINT Feed and water yourself before arriving, because a meal here will easily cancel out any savings you've made on the tickets.

St. Martin's Lane, WC2. ℭ **0871 911 0200.** www.eno.org. Tube: Leicester Square. Tube/Train: Charing Cross.

★ **LSO St. Luke's** FREE In addition to the Barbican, the London Symphony Orchestra also regularly performs at this 18th-century converted Anglican church on Old Street. Free 'Discovery Friday' lunchtime concerts are staged throughout the year, and see the orchestra tackle occasionally challenging pieces of 20th-century music. These usually start at 12:30pm. More user-friendly, easy-listening 'Family Lunchtime' concerts are also put on for £1.50. Sometimes the LSO also allows the public to attend open rehearsals for forthcoming performances, usually by up-and-coming composers, typically for little more than £4 and often for free. Tickets for some evening performances start at £5.

161 Old Street, EC1. ℭ **020 7588 1116.** http://lso.co.uk/lsostlukes. Tube: Old Street.

★ **Royal Festival Hall** FREE From the outside it's the last word in concrete brutalism, but inside it's a world-class music venue and one of the best sources of free live performances in the capital. In fact, the RFH puts on so much free stuff, it's a wonder anyone actually bothers to pay for anything. From Friday lunchtimes onwards various small bands—classical quintets, jazz groups, gamelan orchestras, choirs, cabaret acts, folk musicians—pitch up

The BBC Proms

Since its inception in 1895, the BBC Proms has grown into one of the largest classical music festivals in the world. From July to September around 70 concerts are staged at the Royal Albert Hall, and roughly another 30 at Cadogan Hall, covering all aspects of the classical universe from traditional big-hitters, such as Mozart and Beethoven, to obscure and crazily atonal contemporary works. Apart from the patriotic blow-out of the 'Last Night', when a heaving, bouncing crowd indulges in lusty versions of *Rule Britannia* and *Jerusalem*, you can pick up standing tickets for any of the concerts for just £5. The viewing areas are located in a gallery at the back of the auditorium and in the pit in front of the stage (where concert-goers used to 'promenade' during performances, hence the series' name). Tickets go on sale half an hour before the start of each performance.
www.bbc.co.uk/proms

at a number of locations to entertain the weekend crowds. Events typically start at 1 to 1:30pm at the Foyer Bar on Level 2, at 5:30pm in the Front Room, and at 7:30pm in the Clore Ballroom. Free concerts are also usually staged in the Front Room and the Foyer on Saturday lunchtimes, in the Foyer most Sunday lunchtimes, and occasionally in the Queen Elizabeth Hall (and sometimes even on the roof). And, as if that wasn't enough, you also have the chance every now and then to hear the full Philharmonia Orchestra perform a new work by a contemporary composer for free as part of the RFH's 'Music of Today' programme.

Southbank Centre, Belvedere Road, SE1. ℂ 0871 663 2501. www.southbankcentre. co.uk. Tube/Train: Waterloo.

Royal Opera House Ticket prices for performances at Covent Garden's temple to high-calibre warbling range from around £220 to just £10, and I know which I'd rather opt for. Going down the bargain route means making a few sacrifices, such as a view. The cheapest seats are a long way from the action and usually have 'restricted' (sometimes severely) sight-lines, but as opera singers tend towards the well built, you should be able to pick out something. Just close your eyes and let the mighty sound wash over you. But for the ballet, be sure to bring your opera glasses. The ROH also stages free lunchtime classical concerts, usually held in either the

Open Rehearsal Weekend

If you've ever wondered how a West End cast or a classical orchestra prepares itself for a big show, this event is your best chance of finding out. On the final weekend in September more than 300 venues open their doors a little earlier than normal to let the public observe their preparations. Participants change every year, but in the past have featured a number of prestigious theatres, including the Bubble and the Unicorn, and several of the city's most celebrated orchestras, including the London Philharmonic performing at the Royal Festival Hall. Bear in mind that, though this may be a rehearsal for the musicians and artists involved, you should treat it as a performance. Don't talk, don't eat, switch off your mobile phone, and don't leave your seat (particularly if the musicians have stopped mid-number—they'll start again soon enough).

www.openrehearsal.co.uk

Crush Room or the Linbury Studio, and in September plays host to 'Ignite', a free 3-day arts festival featuring dance performances, video installations, and comedy shows.

Covent Garden, WC2. ℂ **020 7240 1200.** www.roh.org.uk. Tube: Covent Garden.

Sadler's Wells All too aware that ballet and contemporary dance are not always the most accessible or cheap art forms, London's premiere dance outfit now offers 'Sampled' weekends every January. These are essentially 2-hour, reasonably priced taster sessions designed to give dance novices a brief introduction to a variety of forms—from ballet and flamenco to hip hop. All seats are £10, and standing tickets are just £5. If you like what you see and want to return for one of the regular scheduled performances, restricted view seats start at £10. Otherwise the cheapest circle seats are £18, rising to £49 for the stalls.

Rosebery Avenue, EC1. ℂ **020 7863 8198.** www.sadlerswells.com. Tube: Angel.

CHURCH RECITALS

Many of the capital's churches soothe harassed office workers with quality classical recitals. In fact, you'll find more classical music being performed during the lunch hour than at any other time of day. Entry is nominally free to most performances, although you are usually expected to cough up a 'voluntary' donation.

St. Anne's Lutheran Church Concerts held at 1:10pm on Mondays and Fridays. Donation at your discretion.

Gresham Street, EC2. ℂ **020 7606 4986.** www.stanneslutheranchurch.org. Tube: St. Paul's.

St. Giles-in-the-Fields Concerts on Fridays 1 to 1:50pm. Donation at your discretion.

60 St Giles High Street, WC2. ℂ **020 7240 2532.** www.stgilesonline.org. Tube: Tottenham Court Road.

St. James's, Piccadilly Fifty-minute concerts held Monday, Wednesday, and Friday at 1:10 pm. Suggested donation £3.

197 Piccadilly London W1J. ℂ **020 7734 4511.** www.st-james-piccadilly.org. Tube: Piccadilly Circus.

St. Martin-in-The-Fields Concerts held Monday, Tuesday, and Friday at 1pm. Suggested donation £3.50.

Trafalgar Square, WC2. ℂ **020 7766 1100.** www2.stmartin-in-the-fields.org. Tube/Train: Charing Cross.

St. Paul's Church   The 'actors' church' hosts one or two recitals a month, usually on a Thursday or Friday. Check the calendar on the website for details. Donation at your discretion.

Bedford Street, WC2. ✆ **020 7836 5221.** www.actorschurch.org. Tube: Covent Garden.

Southwark Cathedral   Organ recitals given on Mondays at 1pm. Donation at your discretion.

London Bridge, SE1. ✆ **020 7367 6700.** www.southwark.anglican.org. Tube/Train: London Bridge.

FREE MUSEUM & GALLERY CONCERTS

For many museums looking to give visitors a little extra, classical concerts are the free entertainment of choice. This is probably because they require the least amount of effort to stage—just book the musicians and let them get on with it, with no need for fiddly amps or light shows.

Foundling Museum   Classical concerts are staged in the museum's picture gallery on the 1st and 2nd Thursday of the month, the 1st and 'middle' Sunday of the month, and on the final Friday by performers including the New London Orchestra, and the Beethoven Piano Society of Europe. The first Sunday concert is preceded by a gallery talk. All these concerts are technically free, although you do have to stump up the £5 museum admission first. If you like what you hear, the best-value option is to buy a Foundling Pass for £15, which entitles you to free admission, and free concerts, for a year (see p. 103).

40 Brunswick Square, WC1. ✆ **020 7841 3600.** www.foundlingmuseum.org.uk. Tube: Russell Square.

National Gallery FREE   Every Friday the National stays open till 9pm, using those few extra hours to lay on a number of free events, including talks, guided tours, and often classical concerts. Once a month, on the third Friday, the gallery does its best to combine the worlds of art and music by offering a talk and a 45-minute concert themed on, and performed in front of, a particular painting from the collection.

Trafalgar Square, WC2. ✆ **020 7747 2885.** www.nationalgallery.org.uk. Tube/Train: Charing Cross.

National Portrait Gallery FREE   Like its sister collection next door, the NPG stays open late at the end of the working week for free

Park Nights

Every year a big-name architect is invited to create a temporary pavilion next to the Serpentine Gallery in Kensington Gardens, the more avant garde and quirky the better. This provides the venue for the gallery's annual 'Park Nights', a series of arty parties that take place on Friday nights and can feature anything from films and talks to performance art and music (sometimes all at once). The 2009 programme featured solo drumming concerts, a documentary about Lake Victoria, and a 1970s' French 'classic' film about middle-aged men trying to gorge themselves to death on rich food. Tickets are £5.
Kensington Gardens, W2. ℭ 020 7402 6075. www.serpentine gallery.org/park_nights. Daily 10am–6pm. Tube: Lancaster Gate, South Kensington.

'Friday Night Music' events. The concert starts at 6:30pm, with a repertoire around 75% classical, but there's a bit of jazz, blues, or folk thrown in from time to time.
St. Martin's Place, WC2. ℭ 020 7306 0055. www.npg.org.uk. Tube/Train: Charing Cross.

National Theatre FREE Free concerts are staged at the National's Djanogly Concert Pitch at 5:45pm Monday to Friday, and on Saturdays at 1pm and 5:45pm. The acts are as eclectic as you would expect, everything from classical recitals and a capella groups to cool jazz and 'upbeat ethnic'.
South Bank, SE1. ℭ 020 7452 3000. www.nationaltheatre.org.uk. Tube/Train: Waterloo.

Royal Academy of Music FREE Let the precociously talented students of the Academy entertain you during term-time with their regular 'Free on Fridays' concerts. There are usually four held each term in the Duke's Hall, at 11am in winter and 1:05pm in summer. Most are classical, but the odd jazz or percussion showcase does finds its way into the repertoire.
Marylebone Road, NW1. ℭ 020 7873 7373. www.ram.ac.uk. Tube: Baker Street, Regent's Park.

Tate Britain FREE   Britain's premier collection of British art keeps it doors open till 10pm on the first Friday of each month to entertain visitors with a variety of talks, films, and musical performances. Acts booked for these 'Late at Tate' happenings tend towards the avant-garde end of the artistic spectrum: sound artists, human beatboxes, experimental electronica, solo guitar recitals, Balkan folk music, Georgian choirs, and the like (see p. 120).

Millbank, SW1. ℗ **020 7887 8888.** www.tate.org.uk/britain/eventseducation/lateat-tatebritain. Tube: Pimlico, Vauxhall.

3 Theatre

Tickets for the best West End theatre seats can cost in excess of £70, but there's no reason why you should pay anything like that. London is one of the world's leading cities for staged drama, with more than 30 theatres in the West End alone plus dozens of fringe establishments. That's a lot of competition. And wherever there's competition, there are bargains.

On any given night, the theatrical equation is pretty much the same: too many seats, too few punters. For all but the most successful productions, theatres expect a large proportion of their audience to have picked up their tickets from a cut-price booth. Government-subsidised theatres, such as the National, are obliged to offer incentives to the less well-off to attend, with tickets starting at £10. Fringe theatres outside of the centre are usually less expensive than their West End counterparts, typically around £10 to £15. Many now offer pay-what-you-can nights, when ticket prices are left to your conscience. Some brass necks boldly hand over 50p; more charitable souls pay the full price (or more). A donation of £5 seems reasonable, allowing you to save money without taking the mick.

Arcola   Housed in a former carpet factory at the heart of London's largest Turkish community, the Arcola Theatre is one of the stalwarts of the fringe scene. It operates almost like a finishing school for the business, making a point of using untried writers, directors, and actors. Its director, Mehmet Ergen, is a prominent voice in the local community and the instigator of many worthy projects, including trying to make the theatre carbon neutral and providing workshops and theatre time to schools and community groups. The plays are usually issues based—sometimes a bit worthily so—but everything is done with great commitment and passion. Every Tuesday the theatre operates a pay-what-you-can policy: purchase tickets at the box office after 7pm on the day. Two tickets per person—first come, first served.

23–27 Arcola Street, E8. ℗ **020 7503 1646.** www.arcolatheatre.com. Train: Dalston Kingsland.

Half-Price tkts

The small hut in the centre of Leicester Square used to go by the straightforward, say-what-you-see name of the 'Half Price Tickets Booth'. Today it bears some modern textspeak instead: **tkts.** It still does the same job, however—offloading unsold tickets to West End shows at a discount, usually of around 50%. The nature of the beast means that tickets are for shows struggling to fill their seats, so don't go expecting to rustle up a cut-price *Phantom* deal. However, with so many shows in production, if you're willing to lower your expectations, you should find something to tickle your fancy. And with prices starting at around £9, if you do pick a dud, at least it'll be a fairly cheap dud. Currently discounted shows are displayed on a board next to the booth and on the tkts website. The £3 booking fee is covered in the quoted price, not something that can always be said for the booth's unofficial competitors operating on the margins of the Square.
Leicester Square, WC2H. ℭ **020 7557 6700.** www.tkts.co.uk. Tube: Leicester Square.

Battersea Arts Centre Housed in Battersea's former town hall, the BAC is one of the capital's main proponents of experimental fringe theatre: plays, spoken-word pieces, performance art, and puppetry (it has its own puppetry centre). The centre specialises in showcasing new works, often by first-time writers, at its main stage and two smaller studios. Tickets are generally in the £8 to £12 range, but the centre also operates an occasional pay-what-you-can policy, usually on Tuesdays, when, magically, almost no one can afford the full price. It also runs several festivals, including its yearly N20 Comedy festival, when Edinburgh previews and work-in-progress tickets can be bought for as little as £3, and its autumn Scratch festival when audiences are invited to give feedback on a series of new pieces (£5).

176 Lavender Hill, SW11. ℭ **020 7434 7584.** www.bac.org.uk. Train: Clapham Junction.

Bridewell Spending the morning working in the office, popping out to see a bit of theatre at lunch, and then returning to your desk in the afternoon can make for a slightly disorientating day. But it's one that's becoming increasingly popular, with several London theatres now offering lunchtime shows. The

Bridewell, a small venue inside a former Victorian swimming pool, stages, in addition to its main repertoire of evening performances (plenty of Shakespeare and Greek drama), lighter lunchbox events at 1pm Monday to Friday. These usually take the form of reduced 45-minute classics by the likes of Shakespeare, Oscar Wilde, and Shaw. Tickets are £5 and you can bring your own food.

4 Bride Lane, EC4. ✆ **020 7353 3331.** www.stbridefoundation.org/bridewell theatre/index.html. Tube/Train: Blackfriars.

Donmar Warehouse One of theatreland's most prestigious venues, the Donmar's repertoire is a mixture of classics—Shakespeare, Ibsen, Tennessee Williams—and new works, often starring big names from the screen (Nicole Kidman, Kenneth Branagh, Jude Law, and Dame Judi Dench have featured). As such, tickets are not dirt cheap, although they're hardly outrageous either, typically £13 to £24, and £12 standbys become available 30 minutes before each performance. However, cheapest of the lot are £7.50 standing tickets that go on sale on the day for sold-out performances.

41 Earlham Street, WC2. ✆ **0870 060 6624.** www.donmarwarehouse.com. Tube: Covent Garden.

Youthful Discounts

As if they didn't have enough going for them, Londoners under the age of 26 are also entitled to free theatre tickets at a variety of venues across the capital. These are offered as part of the Arts Council's 'A Night Less Ordinary' scheme, which will run till at least March 2011. To claim your youthful allocation you need to go to the scheme's website, find out what theatres are participating, pick your show, and note down the relevant theatre's phone number. In most instances you'll have to call the theatre on the day of the performance to buy the tickets. Most theatres allow you to book more than one ticket, rules state that you, and everyone in your party, must be no older than 25 on the date of the performance. Theatre-goers must show some form of photo ID (passport, driving licence) when collecting. Participating theatres in London include the Almeida, the Barbican, the Battersea Arts Centre, the Donmar Warehouse, the National Theatre, the Roundhouse, and the Royal Court.

www.anightlessordinary.org.uk

Gate Theatre   This tiny 70-seater above a Notting Hill pub is, despite its reduced dimensions, one of the capital's most respected playhouses for works by international writers. Productions tend to be bold and experimental (or obscure and pretentious depending on your view) and cost £16 full price. However, if you're lucky enough to be under 30 you can apply for one of the 500 £5 preview tickets made available for the first three performances of each new show. The box office also makes a limited number of pay-what-you-can tickets available on Mondays from 6:30pm, which must be bought at the door, one per person.

11 Pembridge Road, W11. ℭ **020 7229 0706**. www.gatetheatre.co.uk. Tube: Notting Hill Gate.

King's Head   London's very first pub theatre is still one of the best, staging a range of events including plays, cabaret revues, character monologues, comedy shows, and live music. For a good- value sampler, head along to one of its regular lunchtime performances. These cost £5 and may feature an abridged classic, or a 45-minute work by a new author, or three 20-minute pieces by different writers. The theatre also puts on occasional free shows on Sundays at 7:30pm. Check the website.

115 Upper Street, N1. ℭ **020 7226 1916**. www.kingsheadtheatre.org. Tube: Angel.

FREE Watch This (Outside) Space

The National Theatre's bargains aren't restricted to its indoor auditoriums. Between June and September the complex offers alfresco savings as part of its 'Watch This Space' programme. This series of short, playful, and, most importantly, free events— short plays, comedy, juggling, music, films—is staged on an astroturfed square between the theatre and the river and aimed at capturing the attention of people strolling the South Bank.

National Theatre   The capital's main publicly funded theatre may be a bit of a concrete shocker from the outside, but within it's world class. Three stages—the Olivier, the Cottlesloe, and the Lyttelton—put on an internationally recognised programme of drama, staging everything from classics to commissioned works by major modern writers. The theatre's reliance on state sponsorship obliges it to operate an accessible ticketing policy. To this end, the National makes a certain number of tickets available for just £10. Otherwise, they are £15 to £30. Once all the seats have been sold, standing tickets then go on sale for £5. As an added bonus, the theatre's foyer often stages free events and exhibitions, such as the annual Press Photographer's Year show (www.theppy.com).

South Bank, SE1. ✆ **020 7452 3000**. www.nationaltheatre.org.uk. Tube/Train: Waterloo.

Riverside Studios This lively Hammersmith complex puts on an almost bewildering array of shows and events at its three studio spaces and cinema: theatre, comedy, music, dance, film (p. 252), art exhibitions, even TV, as well as its annual 'Split Your Riversides' season of comedy preview for the Edinburgh Festival. Ticket prices are similarly varied, ranging from £6 to £18. They also offer regular pay-what-you-can nights, a limited number of £10 'recession tickets' for all shows, and Téte à Téte deals which allow you to attend three shows in one evening for £15.

Crisp Road, W6. ✆ **020 8237 1000**. www.riversidestudios.co.uk. Tube: Hammersmith.

★ **Royal Court Theatre** Twenty-five pounds or 10p, that's the choice between sitting in one of the best seats or standing for a performance at the Royal Court's Downstairs Jerwood Theatre. These standing tickets are the standout, cast-iron bargain in theatreland, and must be bought in person at the box office from 1 hour before the performance. One per person only: there are just eight available each night. The best sitting deal is on Mondays, when all seats are £10—they're £12 to £25 for the rest of the week. Tickets at the smaller Jerwood Upstairs studio are £15, or £10 on a Monday. The theatre has long specialised in showcasing new, often avowedly political works. This was where *Look Back in Anger* debuted, a performance that defined the template for the Royal Court's subsequent approach.

50–51 Sloane Square, SW1. ✆ **020 7565 5000**. www.royalcourttheatre.com. Tube: Sloane Square.

Shakespeare's Globe 'Groundling' was the term for the theatrical bargain-hunters of Shakespeare's day. Back then people saved money by forgoing comfortable seats in favour of watching a play standing up in a special area in front of the stage. It's a practice that's been revived at London's Globe Theatre, a venue so dedicated to providing an authentic Shakespearean experience that it could almost be regarded as a Bardic theme park. Today groundling tickets are just £5, compared to £15 to £35 for a seat, which is quite a saving—although be aware that you may be on your feet for over 3 hours, with just one 15-minute break.

21 New Globe Walk, Bankside, SE1. ℂ **020 7902 1400.** www.shakespeares-globe. org. Tube/Train: London Bridge.

Southwark Playhouse   This atmospheric venue in the cellars below London Bridge station stages both large, respected productions on its main stage and a season of innovative 'Secrets' in its bar. Each Secret is different: it may be comedy, theatre, storytelling, music, or various combinations thereof, but is usually experimental in nature. To give you some idea, previous Secrets have featured spoken-word performances of traditional Indian folklore, belly dancing, and exhibitions of minimalist dance. They take place at 10pm on Thursdays and Saturdays and cost just £3. The lunchtime shows at 1pm on Tuesdays and Thursday are slightly more expensive at £5, but that includes a free sandwich.

Shipwright Yard, corner of Tooley Street and Bermondsey Street, SE1. ℂ **020 7620 3494.** www.southwarkplayhouse. co.uk. Tube/Train: London Bridge.

Tricycle   Perhaps more than any other theatre, the Tricycle tries to immerse itself in the community, often staging overtly political works that reflect the experiences of local Irish, Jewish, Afro-Caribbean, and Asian populations. Think 'topical' and 'hard-hitting', as exemplified by the recent spate of productions based on public inquiries (including the Hutton Inquiry into the Iraq War and the Saville Inquiry into Bloody Sunday). As part of this neighbourhood commitment, the Tricycle makes its tickets as accessible as possible: £15 to £20 for evening performances Tuesday

---

FREE West End Live

A bit like the closing stages of *Children in Need* when they start padding it out with performances by the casts of West End musicals, but spread out over an entire June weekend… West End Live offers potential theatregoers the chance to watch free samples from the warbly mainstays of theatreland performed on a purpose-built stage in Leicester Square. In 2009 participants included *Jersey Boys*, *Wicked*, *We Will Rock You*, *Dirty Dancing*, *Avenue Q*, *Thriller*, *Stomp*, *Priscilla Queen of the Desert,* and *Sister Act*.

Leicester Square, WC2. ℂ **020 7641 5370.** www.westendlive. co.uk. Tube: Leicester Square.

to Saturday, and £10 for matinees. They also offer £8 'early bird' tickets for the first 80 seats of certain performances, plus pay-what-you-can deals for the 8pm Tuesday and 4pm Saturday performances for the first 20 people to turn up at the box office.

69 Kilburn High Road, NW6. (C) **020 7328 1000.** www.tricycle.co.uk. Tube: Kilburn.

Tristan Bates Theatre The theatre's mission statement is to promote 'new work, works in progress, and groundbreaking experiments', so don't go expecting any cosy revivals of *The Importance of Being Earnest*. Productions are typically £12, although there are low-cost exceptions, including the annual Edinburgh previews (£7.50–£10) and the infamous Midnight Matinees. These hugely popular shows take place, as advertised, at midnight on the third (or some-

> **FREE** Street Theatre at the Garden
>
> For the very best in impromptu street performance, your top tip is still to head to Covent Garden. Here, the Piazza outside the portico of the 'actors' church' has long provided an alfresco stage for some of the capital's best street performers. Expect jugglers, unicylists, unicyling-jugglers, mime artists, comedians, fire-eaters, and those painted guys who stand still. On weekends, large crowds gather both around the Piazza and on the first-floor balcony of the Punch & Judy pub to offer encouragement, applause, and raucous, beer-fuelled criticism. A pound is considered a fair donation if you've liked what you've seen.

times the second) Saturday of the month. Three companies perform new work-in-progress material to an often well-oiled (and thus highly engaged) West End crowd, before retiring for some post-show discussion, and a bit more oiling, at the late bar. They cost £5.

1A Tower Street, WC2. (C) **020 7240 6283.** www.tristanbatestheatre.co.uk. Tube: Leicester Square, Covent Garden.

4 Cinema

Forget those multiplexes in Leicester Square. Their screens may be the biggest in town, but so are their prices: weekend tickets for big Hollywood releases exceed £15. You can save a few pounds if you go on Monday or before 5pm Tuesday to Friday, but once you've factored in popcorn and drinks, it will still be an expensive experience. Anyway, who wants to watch a film in the middle of the day?

For genuine bargains you'll have to explore the varied (and cheaper) world of foreign and arthouse flicks. London is home to a good number of independent cinemas specialising in the old, the obscure, and the subtitled, as well as arts centres that lay on film-related events, often double bills or talk-and-film combos that represent great value for money. For the following recommendations we've settled on a maximum ticket price of £7.50.

★ **BFI Mediatheque** `FREE`   This film-library-cum-viewing room is a fantastic resource for all cine- and TV-philes. The archive covers the entire history of British film and television production, featuring classic British films from back in the days when the country still produced such things (*The 39 Steps*, *Brief Encounter*, *Peeping Tom*); hard-hitting documentaries (*7 Up*, *The Family*); and groundbreaking plays (*84 Charing Cross Road*, *Brimstone and Treacle*). Accessing the archive couldn't be easier. Just turn up, check in at the front desk, log into a 'viewing station', and get watching. If you want to sample some of the archive's more horrific or saucier offerings, you will be expected to provide proof of age. You can check the currently available viewing list at the website.

BFI Southbank, Belvedere Road, SE1. ✆ **020 7928 3535.** www.bfi.org.uk. Tube/Train: Waterloo.

Boleyn Cinema   This is the UK's second-largest cinema devoted solely to Bollywood. Show times are 4pm, 7pm, and 10pm daily and tickets are just £5.

7–11 Barking Road, E6. ✆ **020 8471 4884.** www.boleyncinema.co.uk. Tube: Upton Park.

Café 1001 `FREE`   Every Monday at 7:30pm this coffee shop in Brick Lane's Old Truman Brewery plays host to 'Short and Sweet', a free celebration of diminutive cinema: stories, documentaries, music videos, art pieces, animations, whatever, so long as they have a running time of under 20 minutes.

1 Dray Walk, 91 Brick Lane, E1. ✆ **020 7247 9679.** www.shortandsweet.tv. Tube: Aldgate East.

Ciné Lumière   Housed in the Institut Français and named after the Gallic inventors of moving pictures, this couldn't be any more French if it were wearing a stripey jersey and eating a baguette. Though opened with the intention of showcasing French cinema, the Lumière has grown into one of the capital's leading foreign language cinemas, also showcasing films from Eastern Europe, South Africa, South America, and even (gasp) the USA. Its first love remains, however, the cinema of France: every Sunday is dedicated to Gallic classics, when you can enjoy plenty of black and white smoky coolness from the likes of Goddard and Truffaut. Tickets are £7. FINE PRINT Being authentically French, the cinema obviously shuts for the whole of August.

Institut Français, 7 Queensberry Place, SW7. ✆ 020 7073 1350. www.institut-francais.org.uk. Tube: South Kensington.

The Exhibit Seated in comfy leather sofas sipping drinks bought at the bar, or perhaps even enjoying a bit of pudding brought in from the adjoining restaurant... this is the way to enjoy a film. The little Balham screening room seats around 24 and shows films on Tuesday and Wednesday evenings at 8:45pm. Tickets are £5, or you can book a two-course 'meal and film deal' for £15.95.

12 Balham Station Road, SW12. ✆ 020 8772 6556. www.theexhibit.co.uk. Tube/Train: Balham.

Inspiral Lounge FREE Fancy a little film criticism with your cous cous? This vegetarian/vegan restaurant hosts free Monday evening 'Cinema Libre' events, which feature Camden-esque selections of short arthouse films and documentaries shown from 7pm to 10pm. Attendees are invited to hang around afterwards to discuss any issues raised.

Picture Houses

The Picture House chain operates five London cinemas, including Brixton's Ritzy, all of which offer a range of time- and age-specific deals. Each has a kids' club where prices are set at £3 per film and each screens budget shows for over 60s at (typically) £4 per ticket, including tea and biscuits. Otherwise the best deals are: Clapham, £6.50 all day Monday and before 5pm Tuesday to Friday; Gate, £6 all day Monday; Greenwich, £6 Mondays before 5pm.

Clapham Picture House, 76 Venn Street, SW4. ✆ 0871 704 2055. Tube: Clapham Common. Gate Picture House, 87 Notting Hill Gate, W11. ✆ 0871 704 2058. Tube: Notting Hill Gate. Greenwich Picture House, 180 Greenwich High Road, SE10. ✆ 0871 704 2059. Train/DLR: Greenwich.

Camden Lock, 250 Camden High Street, NW1. ☏ **020 7428 5875.** www.inspiralled. net. Tube: Camden Town.

Ritzy   This Brixton favourite offers up new releases, plus the odd cult classic, for £6.50 before 5pm and late shows. In between the price rises to £8.50, but that also gives you the chance to sample the live music—jazz, blues, folk, or DJ sets—laid on for free in the café from 8pm onwards (Wednesday to Sunday). Despite its youthful ambience, the Ritzy is particularly accommodating to senior citizens: 'Silver Screen' performances for over 60s on Thursdays before 5pm are just £4 (including refreshments).

Brixton Oval, Coldharbour Lane, SW2. ☏ **0871 704 2065.** www.picturehouses.co.uk. Tube: Brixton.

★ Prince Charles Cinema   To every rule there's an exception. Rigidly obeying the injunction to avoid the cinemas of Leicester Square would mean missing out on this cut-price gem. The West End's only independent cinema has two screens which show very different fare: the 'Upstairs' screen specialises in new releases, for which it charges a competitive but hardly bargain £9.50. The fun 'Downstairs' shows films that are off general release, retro classics, and themed seasons (horror, singalonga musicals, 'Polish gems') for £4 on weekday afternoons and £5 in the evening and at weekends. If you become a member (£12 per year), the cost drops to £1.50 and £3.50.

Leicester Place, WC2. ☏ **0870 811 2559.** www.princecharlescinema.com. Tube: Leicester Square.

Riverside Studios   The Riverside screens double-bill features, usually themed around an actor (say a couple of Bette Davis pictures), a series (perhaps *Jean de Florette & Manon des Sources*), or a director (*Blue Velvet* and *Mulholland Drive* for David Lynch or *Riff-Raff* and *Looking for Eric* for Ken Loach). It's £7.50, or £3.75 per film.

Crisp Road, W6. ☏ **020 8237 1000.** www.riversidestudios.co.uk. Tube: Hammersmith.

Roxy Bar & Screen   The Roxy offers a civilised approach to film appreciation. From Sunday to Wednesday it shows a selection of modern classics (both features and documentaries) either for free or, if it's a recent release, for £3 on a screen at the back of the restaurant. You can order food and drink throughout each performance. The bar also stages regular events, such as film-themed quizzes or poker nights. FINE PRINT Although the films are free, the food most definitely is not—expect to pay around £8.50 for sausage and mash, £9.50 for a Sunday roast. A £20 membership buys you free entry to all screenings, plus 10% off your food bill.

128–132 Borough High Street, SE1. ℂ **020 7407 4057.** www.roxybarand screen.com. Tube: Borough.

Sands Film Club FREE . The Sands is a serious film club dedicated to increasing general knowledge about the history of world cinema, which is no mean ambition. To this end it shows films, from silent classics to present-day masterpieces, every Tuesday at 9pm, with each season themed around a different year—summer 2009 was '1928'. Admission is free (donations encouraged) although to attend you must first send your contact details to the club. Capacity is limited to 30 so you'll need to confirm in double-quick time.

www.sandsfilms.co.uk/Cinemaclub.html.

FREE Cinema at the Scoop

The **Scoop** is a swirly, sunken concrete amphitheatre next to City Hall, within sight of Tower Bridge, with seating for around 800 people—so long as everyone breathes in. Throughout the summer it lays on free events, including concerts, plays, and film screenings, on temporary big screens. Films are usually shown at 7pm Wednesday to Friday during the last 2 weeks of September, and feature a range of modern (and not so modern) classics. The 2009 season included *Slumdog Millionaire*, *Mamma Mia*, *The Usual Suspects*, and *The Wizard of Oz*. Arrive early to claim your spot.

www.morelondon.co.uk/scoop.html

Whitechapel Art Gallery This respected East End gallery screens appropriately arty fair most Thursday evenings—difficult documentaries, nonlinear narratives, bleak character studies. Tickets are £6. Once a month it also hosts a night of free open screenings, when budding film-makers are invited to show and discuss their work with their peers (and you). The gallery also stages regular talks, lectures, and discussions about artists' work, usually for free (see also p. 122).

77–82 Whitechapel High Street, E1. ℂ **020 7522 7888.** www.whitechapelgallery.org. Tube: Aldgate East.

5 Comedy

These days 'the new rock 'n' roll' (© every comedy journalist since 1980) is just as big a business as the old one was. Thirty years ago the number of places offering stand-up in the capital could be counted on one hand. Today it numbers in the hundreds, encompassing everything from pubs laying on once-a-week laugh-fests to shiny corporate clubs, such as Jongleurs and the Comedy Café, which stage highly professional nightly shows. Choice, standards, and the quality of the venues have increased across the board—as have prices. Tickets for a night of comedy at a dedicated venue are typically £8 to £12. However, like music, comedy is an art form that's never short of people willing to give it a go. Most comedy venues offer open-mic nights for would-be gagsmiths—often free of charge. Some newer venues offer free nights starring more established names to try and build up following, while in summer comedy clubland is awash with star-laden Edinburgh previews.

Open-Mic Nights

All careers start somewhere, and for the majority of comedians that somewhere is an open-mic night. This must surely be one of the most terrifying first days it's possible to imagine—the sweaty palms, the fluffed opening line, the predatory audience. No other art form judges its newcomers so harshly. Ballet dancers don't expect to have insults hurled at them when they mess up a *plié*. But would-be comedians who forget to include any good jokes in their act will be vociferously heckled, often to the point where they can no longer continue. It is this element of judgement and retribution at a modern open-mic night that makes it the closest thing to legal bear-baiting. See who thrives and who wilts at the clubs listed below, as well as the **Amersham Arms** (see p. 266), the **Cavendish** (see p. 229), the **Grove** (see p. 232), and the **Pangea Project** (see p. 236).

Banana Cabaret at the Bedford Friday comedy at this huge Balham pub costs £13; Saturday's version is an even steeper £16. However, Thursday's new-act night at the 'Banana Cabaret' is just £3. This is one of the best South London venues for live entertainment (see also p. 228).

72 Bedford Hill, SW12. ✆ **020 8682 8940.** www.thebedford.co.uk. Tube/Train: Balham.

Comedy Café FREE Wednesday's free 'New-Act Night' at this famous comedy venue will provide you with ringside seats for eight new acts. Which means a good amount of gratis comedy, provided they all make it through their sets. FINE PRINT Doors open at 7pm; the show starts at 9pm.

6 Rivington Street, EC2. ℭ **020 7739 5706.** www.comedycafe.co.uk. Tube: Old Street.

Downstairs at the King's Head Sunday night comedy at this long-established venue features well-known (in comedy circles at least) acts from 8pm onwards, and is a pretty reasonable £7. However, if you can't stretch to that, you could try the Thursday night comedy try-outs instead, when you'll be exposed to the would-be comic musings of up to 16 acts for just £4—which calculating pence per punchline is excellent comedy value. Edinburgh previews are in July, with tickets in the £7 region.

2 Crouch End Hill, N8. **020 8340 1028.** www.downstairsatthekingshead.com. Tube: Finsbury Park, then W7 bus.

Lower Ground Bar 'West Hampstead's premier nightspot' can be tricky to find; you're after the door next to the dental surgery. This leads down to an intimate underground venue that attracts circuit regulars of the 'ooh, aren't they on that thing on the telly?' level. Every Wednesday you can see five acts for just £3. There's also a £5 jazz club on Tuesdays. The rest of the time it is primarily known as the latest closing spot around here, typically till 2am, where people head to carry on drinking once all other avenues have closed.

FREE **London Bridge Festival**

A sort of free mini-Edinburgh Festival held a month before the real thing, this celebration of the fringe sees 175 acts—drama, comedy, film, music, and the arts—perform over 2 weeks in mid- July. Events are staged at a variety of often unusual venues near London Bridge, including the *Golden Hinde*, the Rose Theatre, and the Old Operating Theatre (p. 108). Awards are handed out for the best music, short films, photographs, and short fiction. However, as with the main event in Scotland, the most prestigious is the new comedy award, which sees acts compete for laughs over 3 days to win the coveted title of London's Best New Comedian. All performances are free of charge.

Edinburgh Previews

If Edinburgh in August is the site of the world's largest arts festival, then London in July could lay claim to host the world's biggest rehearsal. Comedians, theatre productions, dance troupes, and performance artists road test their Scotland shows at venues across town. As with the Festival itself, comedy dominates the preview season; the capital's comedy clubs are booked solid for the month, often with big-name stars and former Perrier award winners. These shows are works in progress, with comedians trying out new gags and as such are either free or much cheaper than would normally be the case. Venues that feature Edinburgh comedy previews include:

Amersham Arms, see p. 266.

Battersea Arts Centre, see p. 244.

Downstairs at the King's Head, see p. 255.

Phoenix Bar, see p. 256.

Riverside Studios, see p. 247.

Royal Vauxhall Tavern, see p. 270.

Theatre Royal Stratford East, see p. 256.

Up the Creek, see p. 257.

269 West End Lane, NW6. ℂ **020 7431 2211.** www.lowerground.co.uk. Train: West Hampstead.

Phoenix Bar This central bar, just off Oxford Street, offers a compelling mixture of old and new comedy. At its Monday 'Old Rope' events, established acts are invited to come and try out new material. Tickets are just £5, presumably because the jokes haven't been fully road tested, so the laughs aren't 100% guaranteed. In summer Edinburgh previews are £7.

37 Cavendish Square, W1. ℂ **020 7493 8003.** www.phoenixcavendishsquare. co.uk. Tube: Oxford Circus.

★ **Theatre Royal Stratford East** FREE The theatre's long, elegant bar is a great source of free entertainment, laying on events 7 days a week, the pick of which, for comedy fans, are the Monday comedy nights, the 'Comedy Extras' on the last Sunday of each month, and the annual Edinburgh previews during the last 2 weeks of July. It's a well-established venue that attracts big names as well as up-and-comers. Free poetry nights are held every second Sunday of the month.

Theatre Square, E15. ℂ **020 8534 0310.** www.stratfordeast.com. Tube/Train/DLR: Stratford.

Up the Creek   Sunday night prices at this Greenwich venue, the brainchild of legendary late comedian and compere Malcolm Hardee, are just £6, compared to £10 during the rest of the week. The line-up isn't usually announced in advance, but features a mixture of new acts and up-and-comers with the occasional very well-known face popping along to try out some new jokes. Performers to have braved the heckles have included Jimmy Carr, Al Murray, Harry Hill, Jo Brand, and Frank Skinner.

302 Creek Road, SE10. ℂ **020 8858 4581.** www.up-the-creek.com. DLR: Cutty Sark.

6 Spoken Word: Readings & Recitals

There's certainly a market in the capital for comedy's more serious, more softly spoken sibling, but it's not a particularly crowded one. Still, those few venues that specialise in readings and recitals tend to be intensely committed to the cause. Prices are not usually high, and there are plenty of free options, such as the Poetry Café's near-legend-ary 'Poetry Unplugged' events on Tuesday nights. Book signings, again usually put on for free, often draw the crowds, particularly when a famous author is making an appearance. Waterstones, the country's leading bookselling chain, offers the greatest number of events. See also the **Theatre Royal Stratford East** (p. 256) and the **Royal Vauxhall Tavern** (p. 257).

Calder Bookshop   This cheery little shop opposite the Young Vic has been in business for around a decade, in which time it has estab-lished a reputation as one of London's most literary-minded book-stores, hosting a year-round programme of prose, poetry, and drama events: discussions, talks, readings, comedy shows, film screenings, concerts, theatrical performances, and so on. These usually take place on Tuesdays and Thursdays at 7pm. Tickets are £8, which is slightly steep, but worth it to support such a great little independent.

51 The Cut, SE1. ℂ **020 7620 2900.** www.calderpublications.com/shop. Tube: Southwark.

Coffee Concept   Fancy listening to some earnest Saturday morning philosophising? In French? Well, you may be in luck. The Institut Français' philosophy club meets every week to debate the hot topic *du jour*—one week in French, the next in English. The argumentative balloon starts rolling at 10:30am and attendees are welcome to pitch in and contribute to the debate or sit back and listen with Gallic insouciance, a coffee, and a croissant if they prefer. Admission is £2.

Institut Français, 7 Queensberry Place, SW7. ℂ 020 7073 1350. www.institut-francais. org.uk. Tube: South Kensington.

★ **Poetry Café** FREE   During the day this peaceful vegetarian café makes the perfect place to sit with a coffee and a slice of quiche whilst putting the finishing touches to your poem about the state of the country/how much you love your cat/belly button fluff. Hang around till the evening on a Tuesday and you'll have the chance to perform it live at 'Poetry Unplugged'. Those who put their name down between 6 and 7pm are given a slot to perform and guaranteed some audience feedback on the quality of their rhymes. Poems can be about anything—no subjects are taboo and nothing is vetted in advance. It's free both to perform and to attend. As one of London's premier spoken word venues, the café stages events most nights, except Sunday. You can find out more from the café noticeboard, which is covered with flyers listing events across the capital.

22 Betterton Street, WC2. ℂ **020 7420 9888.** www.poetrysociety.org.uk. Tube: Covent Garden.

> **Book Slam**
>
> A spoken word event with real literary muscle. The monthly book-fest, usually held at 12 Aklam Road, in Kensington just off the Westway (or sometimes at the Tabernacle Bar), is one of the circuit's most prestigious events. It comprises a mixture of readings, talks, and discussions, often featuring big-name authors and screenwriters like Zadie Smith, Yasmin Alibhai-Brown, Will Self, and David Simon, as well as live music (again, often a marquee name). Tickets are £8 on the door, but just £6 reserved online (it's popular, so get in early).
> www.bookslam.com

Waterstones Piccadilly   People may rail against Waterstones' corporate ubiquity and the effect its market dominance (supposedly) has on independent book retailers, but there's no doubt that this dominance helps to attract the biggest names to signings and talks. Its flagship store on Piccadilly, the largest bookshop in Europe, is the prime venue. In the recent past Jon Ronson, Blake Morrison, J.K. Rowling, and Michael Palin have put in appearances. Obviously these events are aimed primarily at shifting books, and so usually also include a signing session. Most are free, but if there is a charge (typically around £3) it's usually redeemable against the cost of the featured book.

203–205 Piccadilly, W1J. ℰ **020 7851 2400.** www.waterstones.com. Tube: Piccadilly Circus.

7 Pubs & Bars

When people start tightening their belts, the pub is one of the first haunts to be cut from a social schedule. The country's most popular social activity can empty your pockets in double-quick time. Obviously, this is down to our love for an alcoholic tipple. If we all sat at the bar nursing a soda water, we'd be fine. Instead we gulp our way through pint after pint of beer, glass after glass of wine, and measure after measure of spirits, all of which cost around £3 in London's outskirts and closer to £4 in central London. Here are a few bargain(-ish) alternatives.

CHEAP CHAINS

SAM SMITH'S

Yorkshire brewery Samuel Smith's runs a number of pubs in London, all of which offer cheap drink prices—less than £3 for lagers and under £2 for some bitters. Prices are kept low by a number of factors, primarily that the pubs serve only Samuel Smith's drinks (including own-brand mixers). Prices are therefore fixed in line with government alcohol duties and rise with inflation, but are not affected by markups insisted on by the drinks mega-corps. A few years ago the chain also decided to silence its background music, thereby dodging the Performing Rights Levy. In general, Sam Smith's pubs are much nicer than their cheap-beer rival, Wetherspoon, and often housed in buildings with antique features rather than the one-style-fits-all venues favoured by Wetherpoons.

Angel in the Fields   With its narrow windows, dark wood panelling, and picnic-style outside benches, this has a traditional feel to it—and also charges traditional prices. A minute or so's walk north of Oxford Street, it spreads over two floors so despite its popularity, particularly with local students (the keenest of all bargain-hunters), it rarely gets too crowded.

37 Thayer Street, W1. ℰ **020 7486 7763.** Tube: Bond Street.

The Chandos   Just off Trafalgar Square, the clutter of sofas, seats, and stools in the upstairs bar is the place to head. It can be crowded, sometimes startlingly so at weekends, but it makes an atmospheric and mercifully cheap mid-city pit stop.

29 St. Martin's Lane, WC2. ℭ **020 7836 1401.** Tube/Train: Charing Cross.

The Lyceum   This largely undiscovered gem on the Strand near Waterloo Bridge is a welcome oasis of West End calm and quiet. Even on weekends it never seems to be too full. Downstairs there's some charming booth seating and a tiny smoking garden, while upstairs there's a larger seating area. The food isn't up to much, but it's a relaxing place to read the paper with a pint.

354 Strand, WC2. ℭ **020 7836 7155.** Tube: Covent Garden. Tube/Train: Charing Cross.

Ye Olde Cheshire Cheese   The name makes it sound like an Old Englandey tourist trap, but this is a genuine City relic that provides an intriguing glimpse into the pub life of centuries past. Built in the 16th century, the pub burnt down in the Great Fire of 1666 and was rebuilt shortly after in a charmingly higgledy-piggledy fashion with clusters of small, gloomy rooms. Many of the original features remain. Dickens was a regular here in the 19th century and even wrote about the pub in *A Tale of Two Cities*.

45 Fleet Street, EC4. ℭ **020 7353 6170.** Train: City Thameslink.

Wetherspoon

If you were to enquire about the latest happening bar in town, nobody, *absolutely* nobody, would recommend a Wetherspoon. They're regarded as dull, faceless, and ubiquitous chain pubs... which is exactly what they are. But they're also very cheap, so we're bound to recommend them. In a city where a round of drinks for five can leave you with little change from £20, it's good to know that there remain some oases of budgetary constraint. Most drinks in a Wetherspoon branch are considerably cheaper than in other pubs, and the chain runs promotions that sometimes bring prices down to under £1 a pint—cheap and potentially deadly.

Which brings us to the chain's other main problem—some people think Wetherspoon's drinks are too cheap. Britain's problems with binge drinking and public rowdiness—which have been ever present since at least the 18th century and show no sign of abating—mean that the government is trying to crack down on the sale of cheap booze. What can we say? Enjoy your bargains responsibly. Go to the website to find your nearest local branch. See p. 87 for information on Wetherspoon's food. FINE PRINT Note that the typical Wetherspoon crowd tends to be quite age specific, comprising a mixture of old folk trying to eke out their pensions and youngsters on low wages. www.jdwetherspoon.co.uk

HAPPY HOURS

This is a phrase that needs some explaining. 'Happy', in this context, means 'drunk'. Throughout the capital several otherwise pricey establishments offer cut-price incentives at certain times of the day/week to bring customers through the door, no doubt in the hope that, once their senses have been suitably impaired by the cheap booze, they'll stick around and pay full whack. 'Hour' is similarly euphemistic, being more of a concept than a specific measure of time, and often lasting several hours.

Browns All cocktails at the brasserie chain's six London branches are £3.50 (as opposed to the normal £5-plus) from 4pm to 11pm Sunday to Wednesday.

82–84 St. Martin's Lane, WC2. ℂ **020 7497 5050.** www.browns-restaurants.co.uk. Tube: Leicester Square. Other locations: *Butler's Wharf*, Shad Thames, SE1. ℂ **020 7378 1700.** Tube/Train: London Bridge. *City*, 8 Old Jewry, EC2. ℂ **020 7606 6677.** Tube/DLR: Bank. *Islington*, 9 Islington Green, N1. ℂ **020 7226 2555.** Tube: Angel. *Mayfair*, 47 Maddox Street, W1. ℂ **020 7491 4565.** Tube: Bond Street, Oxford Circus. *West India Quay*, Hertsmere Road, E14. ℂ **020 7987 9777.** DLR: West India Quay.

Dirty Martini Don't know about 'dirty', but the martinis are certainly cheap if you come at the right times. These are 5 to 9pm and 10:30 to 11:30pm Monday to Thursday (which, if you're making a night of it, means drinking slowly for the intervening hour and a half or popping out for a bite) and 5 to 8pm Friday and Saturday; all martinis are £4 and bottles of wine half-price. It's probably not worth it at any other time: the venue is rather small and a bit of a tourist trap.

11–12 Russell Street, WC2. ℂ **020 7257 8622.** www.dirtymartini.uk.com. Tube: Covent Garden.

The Lost Society Housed in what was originally a 16th-century barn, albeit updated in an 'Art Deco' style, the vibe of this restaurant-bar is very much 1980s (not so much a 'lost' society as deliberately thrown away). This is particularly evident on Thursday's 'fondue'

nights when 1980s' cocktails are £4.25 all night. It's free entry and DJs play from 9pm. All cocktails are £4.25 on Tuesdays and Wednesdays from 6 to 8pm.

697 Wandsworth Road, SW8. ℭ **020 7652 6526.** www.lostsociety.co.uk. Train: Wandsworth Road.

HAVE A DRINK &...

There is a term for the 50p to £1 mark-up that seems to apply to all drinks in the centre of town: 'London prices'. Outside of happy hours, and unless you frequent the few chain pubs that specialise in low-cost drinks (see above), the only way to get value for money is to go somewhere that offers additional free entertainment.

ANSWER QUESTIONS CORRECTLY
TO WIN POTS OF MONEY

Obviously for this to work, you'll need a brain packed with general knowledge, or at least have friends who do. Pub quizzes are one of the great British nights out, usually starting amid an air of casual jollity that grows ever more serious as the rounds pass and the stakes rise. You can see why pubs put them on. Quizzes typically last a couple of hours, often with a mid-session interval—which from a landlord's perspective means a captive audience making repeat visits to the bar. Many quizzes offer cash prizes (usually participants' entrance money, around £1–£2 per person), although a few cheapskate places offer vouchers for food or bottles of wine instead. Most quizzes are general knowledge based, but some are themed. The **Slaughtered Lamb** (p. 231) and **Pure Groove** (p. 231) run music quizzes, while the **Roxy Bar & Screen** (p. 252) hosts a film quiz. For an online guide to London's quizzes, point your browser at www.pubquizhelp.com/quiz/london.html.

DANCE

Bar Salsa `FREE` Buying a drink at Bar Salsa entitles you to a free dance lesson from 6 to 7pm on Sundays and 6:30 to 8:30pm on Fridays. For the particularly loose-limbed there are also free samba classes from 7:30pm on Tuesdays. Otherwise it's £5 for an hour-long class, or £8 for two.

96 Charing Cross Road, WC2. ℭ **020 7379 3277.** www.barsalsa.eu. Tube: Tottenham Court Road, Leicester Square.

A Game Of Pétanque

Balls Brothers `FREE`   The Hay's Galleria branch of Balls Brothers' wine bars maintains its own sandy *pétanque* (also known as 'French boules') pitch. It's outside in the roofed galleria, making it an all-weather option. Games, which involve throwing heavy metal balls as close as possible to a light wooden one (known as a *cochonnet* or '*piglet*'), are free but need to be booked in advance—it's a popular choice for office parties.

Unit 22, Hay's Galleria, Counter Street, SE1. ℭ **020 7407 4301.** www.ballsbrothers. co.uk. Tube/Train: London Bridge.

Play Board Games

Many pubs keep board games that you can use free of charge. It's a clever strategy: games can take a long time to complete. And once you get involved in a contest, you could be thirsty for several hours. Games stocked usually include the classics—Monopoly, Scrabble, Risk, Cluedo, chess, draughts, backgammon, dominoes—plus, on occasion, an unusual offering, such as giant Jenga. If you're a real aficionado, or feel like spending an evening in the company of hard-core board game enthusiasts, then head down to the **Shipwrights Arms,** a traditional pub opposite the shiny More London riverside development. It plays host every Wednesday to the Swiggers Games Club. Here regulars compete intently across a range of bewilderingly obscure games, including Escape from Colditz, Family Business, Agricola, and Race for the Galaxy. It's free to play (or watch).

Cargo

83 Rivington Street, EC2. ℭ **020 7749 7844.** www.cargo-london.com. Tube: Old Street.

The Dove

24–28 Broadway Market, E8. ℭ **020 7275 7617.** www.dovepubs.com. Train: London Fields.

Shipwrights Arms

88 Tooley Street, SE1. ℭ **020 7378 1486.** www.pevans.co.uk/Swiggers. Tube/Train: London Bridge.

Some Free Nibbles

Viva Verdi `FREE`   This fancy 'prosciutto and wine' bar next to the Tate Modern offers a huge range of Italian wines, and delicacies: cheeses, cured meats, olives, and pasta dishes. The drinks aren't particularly cheap (the lowest-priced wine is £3.95, while pints start at £3.50), but between 5:30 and 7:30pm they do come with a selection of free nibbles. Parma ham, slices of salami, and the like are offered in the hope that you'll be so bowled over that you'll order something pricey from the menu. Be strong and stick to the freebies. The bar also lays on free jazz most Fridays, as well as the occasional free opera performance.

6 Canvey Street, SE1. ℭ **020 7928 6867.** www.vivaverdiwinebar.com. Tube: Southwark.

STICK ON SOME OF YOUR OWN TUNES

The Gowlett Arms   The Gowlett, a rather lovely pub and pizzeria in Peckham/East Dulwich, has a wide-ranging music policy that utilises the skills of both professionals and amateurs. DJs play the first three Sundays of the month and there's live jazz on the final Sunday. Thursday is 'Lucky 7s' night when the lunatics briefly play with the asylum keys. Pick three favourite 7-inches from your collection and head down in the early evening to chalk your name on the blackboard. You will eventually be called upon to show what you've got. For the restaurant, see p. 86.

62 Gowlett Road, SE15. ℭ **020 7635 7048.** www.thegowlett.com. Train: East Dulwich, Peckham Rye.

THROW A CHEESE

Freemasons Arms   A cheese, in this instance, being the name given to a 4.5kg (10lb) disc of wood used during a traditional game of London skittles; the basement of the Freemasons Arms in Hampstead is one of just two London venues where the game is still played. London skittles shares characteristics with ten-pin bowling, but with certain crucial differences. There are just nine pins, the 'cheese' is thrown rather than rolled, and you don't have to put on two-tone shoes. Best of all, it's free on Tuesday (and some Saturday) club nights, when the experts will show you what's what.

32 Downshire Hill, NW3. ℭ **020 7433 6811.** www.londonskittles.co.uk. Tube/Train: Hampstead Heath.

WORTH A SPLURGE

FOR THE VIEW

Trafalgar Hotel   The Trafalgar Roof Garden is not cheap (£9 a cocktail), only open in the warm months, and then only intermittently owing to the meteorological ironies inherent in the phrase 'British summer'. But when it is, it's well worth popping along for a drink (just

DIY Music

A well-stocked jukebox was once a basic requirement for most London boozers. In these days of corporate homogenisation, however, where 'choice' means variations on the same half-dozen lagers (such as Fosters, Stella, Kronenbourg), music policy is often directed from head office and chain pubs mostly play the same middle of the road rotations. Thankfully, there are a few places still operating a democratic music policy. The following all have music machines packed with classics and obscurities from every era. A pound is the usual charge which, depending on the pub, will buy you anything from three to seven choices. See also the **Dublin Castle** (p. 229), the **Half Moon** (p. 229), **The Social** (p. 268), and the **12 Bar Club** (p. 231).

Boogaloo   312 Archway Road, N6. ℭ **020 8340 2928.** www.theboogaloo.org. Tube: Highgate.

Endurance   90 Berwick Street, W1F. ℭ **020 7437 2944.** Tube: Oxford Street, Tottenham Court Road.

The Reliance   336 Old Street, EC1. ℭ **020 7729 6888.** Tube: Old Street.

Three Kings of Clerkenwell   7 Clerkenwell Close, EC1. ℭ **020 7253 0483.** Tube/Train: Farringdon.

the one) and the cracking views from seven floors up. You're practically eye level with Nelson (and the pigeons) atop his column.

2 Spring Gardens, Trafalgar Square, SW1. ℭ **020 7870 2900.** www.thetrafalgar.com/roof_garden.shtml. Tube/Train: Charing Cross.

WATCH LIVE DOODLING

★ **ICA (Institute of Contemporary Arts)**   Not just any doodling of course. This monthly event held in the ICA bar sees renowned artists and cartoonists drawing live to a musical/DJ accompaniment, with the latter (in theory) inspiring the former. Results are projected onto the venue's walls as they are created, for the appreciation (or otherwise) of those propping up the bar. The event has no fixed date, but is usually held on a Thursday or Friday early in the month. Check the website for details.

12 Carlton House Terrace, SW1. ℭ **020 7930 3647.** www.ica.org.uk. Tube/Train: Charing Cross.

8 Clubs

Clubbing is a cyclical affair. One year it's all about spontaneous(-ish) warehouse parties and free underground raves, the next it's dominated by high-priced superclubs as the moneymen move in to co-opt, market, and sell a scene. Following the financial meltdown, London's nightclubs have entered a sort of in-between zone. Major venues are doing their best to survive the hard times by offering plenty of cut-price incentives—free nights, happy hours, 2-for-1 deals to stop the dancing masses from gyrating off and doing their own thing.

Amersham Arms   One of London's prime live music venues, the Amersham Arms (run by the same management behind Camden's Lock Tavern; p. 230) is perhaps even better known as a top-grade (but low-priced) dance mecca attracting many of the capital's top DJs. Friday's 'Whip It' sessions feature indie, rock, retro, and pop from 10pm to 3:30am and cost just £2, while Saturday's 'Disco' (same hours) is free till 11pm, then just £1 after that. The latter tries to subvert the cult of the omnipotent DJ by letting the audience choose the music. Anyone can sign up to hit the decks and play five records of their choice (and be judged accordingly), and will receive a free drink for their trouble. Things are taken down a notch on Sundays, when cracking roasts are served to an accompaniment of low-key grooves and acoustic acts. Comedy gigs are also performed here, including annual Edinburgh previews.

388 New Cross Road, SE14. ℭ **020 8469 1499.** www.amersham-arms.co.uk. Tube/ Train: New Cross.

Cargo FREE   Fridays are free at Cargo—expect live acts and DJs exploring various genres you've never heard of (and probably never will again): donk, booty, and the rest. The sultry, renovated garden is the place to be on a summer's night.

83 Rivington Street, EC2. ℭ **020 7739 3440.** www.cargo-london.com. Tube: Old Street.

Catch FREE   A venue for these more straitened times, Catch is all about basic partying with no fancy add-ons. There are two rather grungily decorated floors: a downstairs bar where DJs play, and an upstairs live venue and club. Both are free and attract a varied money-saving crowd: businessmen looking to cut loose, hipsters, and students.

22 Kingsland Road, E2. ℭ **020 7729 6097.** www.thecatchbar.com. Tube: Old Street.

★ **The Dogstar** FREE This legendary venue is a lot cosier and more user-friendly than its edgy, scene-setting reputation would suggest. Looked at objectively this is actually a rather pleasant three-storey converted pub with a good range of beers, a pool table, and decent food (including Sunday roasts). In fact it's somewhere you wouldn't mind taking your parents, at least in the late afternoon before the music kicks in. Obviously things get livelier as the evening progresses and people hit the dance floor. It's free entry most nights and till 10pm on Friday and Saturday when you can expect a right melange of styles: funk, drum and bass, punk, soul, disco, electronica, indie, global beats, Latin, and more.

389 Coldharbour Lane, SW9. ✆ **020 7733 7515.** www.antic-ltd.com/dogstar. Tube: Brixton.

The Eagle FREE The new air-conditioning hasn't cooled down this venue, one of London's most celebrated gay clubs. Its Friday 'Tonker' evenings promise the 'Hottest Guys, the Coldest Beers, and the Best Tunes'—and free entry. Free entry is also offered on other evenings to guys who dress according to a predetermined style: military, leather, whatever.

349 Kennington Lane, SE11. ✆ **020 7793 0903.** www.eaglelondon.com. Tube/Train: Vauxhall.

East Village If you get to this surprisingly friendly and attitude-free Shoreditch club before 10pm, it's free. Some evenings it stays that way all night, but events usually cost £5 to £8. The basement dance space is about as utilitarian as you can imagine: a DJ booth, a bar, a floor to dance on, a single sofa (you'll have to take turns recuperating), and that's it. A couple of caveats: the music policy is overwhelmingly house dominated—house, disco techno, hard house, dubstep, DnB, and so on—and drinks, as in all London clubs, are expensive.

89 Great Eastern Street, EC2. ✆ **020 7739 5173.** www.eastvillageclub.com. Tube: Old Street.

The Lock Tavern FREE If there's no gig (p. 230) or private party on a Friday or Saturday night, then the Small Disco upstairs at the Lock Tavern lets cheapskate clubbers get down (in necessarily close proximity) for free; 8:30pm to 1am.

35 Chalk Farm Road, NW1. ✆ **020 7482 7163.** www.lock-tavern.co.uk. Tube: Chalk Farm.

Queen of Hoxton   This cooler-than-a-penguin-sandwich East End haunt is free on Wednesdays, when it's quiz night (the first team to register gets a free round of drinks) and till 10pm Fridays (£5 after that), when there's live music and DJs at the downstairs bar and dance floor. The music touches all bases, from inaccessible arty bleeping to big pop ballads.

1 Curtain Road, EC2. ℂ **020 7422 0958.** www.thequeenofhoxton.co.uk. Tube: Old Street.

The Social FREE   Not only is this one of clubland's cheapest venues for drinks, but the Social also lays on DJ-led dance parties in its bijou basement 7pm to 12am Monday to Wednesday and 7pm to 1am Thursday to Saturday, mostly for free. Wine and beer prices hover just above the £3 mark, which may not sound that cheap, but for a London club that's practically giving it away. Occasional live bands play, for which there may be a small entrance charge. The music policy covers hip hop (check out the regular 'Hip Hop Karaoke' nights) drum and bass, R&B, funk, house, electro, pop, and disco, albeit usually not all on the same night. And, if that wasn't enough, the bar also boasts a killer jukebox.

5 Little Portland Street, W1. ℂ **020 7636 4992.** www.thesocial.com. Tube: Oxford Circus.

★ **The Star of Bethnal Green** FREE   Part local East End boozer, part hipsters' hangout, this grungy little venue always has something of value going on. Monday's 'recession sessions' offer discounted drinks and cheap food, Tuesdays see the popular quiz night with a top prize of £50 and free pasta for all, while Wednesdays usually mean a gig, which could be anything from indie and punk to jazz and soul (tickets are around £5). DJs take over at the weekend playing a mix of hi-tech house, pop, punk, disco, and northern soul to get the crowds moving. Fridays are free all night; Saturdays free till 9pm and then £5.

359 Bethnal Green Road, E2. ℂ **020 7769 0167.** www.starofbethnalgreen.com. Tube: Bethnal Green.

Surya FREE   If you want to feel good about yourself while shaking down your bad self, then the world's first ecological club should be your venue of choice. Technical wizardry means that the faster and harder you dance, the better it is for the planet, with all that carefully choreographed kinetic energy being used to supply a portion of the club's electricity. Further energy-saving devices include solar panels, a wind turbine, and minimum flush toilets. Best of all, your evening of dancing is completely free if you can prove you arrived via public transport.

56 Pentonville Road, N1. ✆ **020 7713 6262.** www.club4climate.com/surya. Tube/ Train: King's Cross.

9 Cabaret

Right now nothing in the capital seems as on-the-cusp fashionable as a bit of vintage. Retro clothes, decades-old records, and dances where you actually have to learn steps rather than just improvise a rhythmic shuffle, have never been so popular. Hand in hand with this taste for all things old-fashioned has come the decade-long rise of a new breed of burlesque and supper club offering period-themed, nipple-tasselled entertainment for adults—and not always at grown-up prices. There are plenty of free nights and cut-price shows among all the £35 dinner revues.

Bistrotheque   Don't go for the restaurant, which serves basic bistro food, but for the small adjoining cabaret room, one of London's finest current venues. Prices are usually in the £10 to £12 range, but occasionally drop to £3 to £5 for midweek shows by new acts or for works in progress by established stars. Seats 60.

23–27 Wadeson Street, E2. ✆ **020 8983 7900.** www.bistrotheque.com. Tube: Bethnal Green.

★ **Cellar Door**   For vintage entertainment, you need a proper vintage setting, and this (fully) converted Victorian lavatory is just the ticket. Entering the club steps down from the pavement feels like entering a secret society (the address is rather cool, too). Once inside, take your chance to try things you can't get at any other club—such as 'snuff', the socially acceptable, if rather sneezy, form of nicotine ingestion. There are several flavours to sample and staff will demonstrate the correct snorting method. Once nicotined up, concentrate on one of the kitschy-catchy acts who entertain the carefully manicured crowds nightly from Monday to Saturday: drag acts, cabaret, jazz performances, and so on. Entry is usually free on Mondays and Tuesdays. Shows start at 9pm.

Zero Aldwych, WC2. ✆ **020 7240 8848.** www.cellardoor.biz. Tube: Covent Garden, Temple.

TV & Radio Shows

The volume of TV and radio shows requiring a studio audience ensures that tickets for recordings are nearly always free. Most popular shows are snapped up well in advance, but it would be almost impossible not to find something to watch, even if that means attending the recording of a new or niche programme for a digital, cable, or satellite station. The BBC, the country's largest broadcaster, should be your first port of call. It lists upcoming shows—comedy panel games, live music performances, chat shows, cookery programmes, celebrity dance competitions—plus their availability on its website. In most instances, BBC TV tapings are at Television Centre in White City, while those for radio programmes take place at more centrally located Broadcasting House, just north of Regent Street. The other terrestrial broadcasters, ITV, Channel 4, and Channel 5, use a range of agencies to rustle up their audiences, as do the majority of cable and satellite broadcasters including Sky.

BBC

✆ **0370 603 0304.** www.bbc.co.uk/tickets.

ITV, CHANNEL 4, CHANNEL 5, SKY & CABLE:

Applause Store

✆ **020 8324 2700.** www.applausestore.com.

Clappers

✆ **020 8532 2770.** www.clappers-tickets.co.uk.

Lost in TV

✆ **020 8530 8100.** www.lostintv.com.

Standing Room Only

✆ **020 8684 3333.** www.sroaudiences.com.

Royal Vauxhall Tavern Money saved at the RVT's Thursday night drag-heavy cabaret will depend on how much effort you put in beforehand. Turn up in your usual weekday mufti and you'll have to pay the full price. Make the effort to dress for the occasion, however, which is usually era-specific (glam, 1950s, new romantic), and you'll get in for free. If dressing up isn't your thing, there is plenty of other entertainment at this established gay venue, including Monday night bingo (free entry, £1 a game), Saturday club nights (£5), plus Edinburgh previews in summer and occasional poetry 'slams'.

372 Kennington Lane, SE11. ℂ **020 7820 1222.** www.theroyalvauxhalltavern.co.uk. Tube/Train: Vauxhall.

★ **Volupté Lounge** It bills itself as the 'The Most Decadent Little Supper Club In Town'. Although to be honest it's more professional than debauched, the Volupté Lounge puts on some of the best cabaret and burlesque evenings in town, featuring plenty of long gloves, feather

> **Unemployed TV**
>
> You may, on occasion, come across a deal even better than 'free'. It has been known, in exceptional instances, for the BBC to post adverts in Job centres offering to pay people to attend one of their unloved shows. Being handed cash to watch telly… it doesn't get much better than that—even if the show itself is practically unwatchable.

boas, nipple tassels, and sultry singing. To keep prices down, you'll want to avoid dinner, good though it may be (mains £12–£22), and stay on your feet. From Tuesday to Thursday standing tickets are just £5 (£10 seated) rising to £10 on Fridays (£18 seated). Avoid the ultra-glamorous Saturday nights when seats are £25 to £30 with no standing option.

7–9 Norwich Street, EC4. ℂ **020 7831 1622.** www.volupte-lounge.com. Tube: Chancery Lane.

10 Spectator Sports

At the elite level, spectator sports can be one of the most expensive forms of entertainment going, with ringside tickets for big-name fights costing several hundred pounds, test match seats retailing at £50 to £90, and even average seat prices for Premier League football in excess of £50. Enjoying the elite is therefore out, to be replaced by a new-found appreciation for the amateur and less popular disciplines of the sporting world.

FREE THE BOAT RACE

It's a major event on the sporting calendar, attracting live TV coverage and inspiring dedicated pull-out supplements in the daily newspapers, and yet it's difficult to explain exactly why. After all, it's just a minor inter-university competition—and there's never any doubt who's going to get to the final. As with so many great British traditions, the boat race has acquired its status largely through longevity. Since 1856 the top eight-man crews from the universities of Oxford and Cambridge have been holding an annual rowing battle along a 4½-mile Thames course from Putney to Mortlake. And as the decades have passed, the country has grown ever more interested to find out who wins. Today the event attracts a huge following: an estimated 250,000 people line the riverbank to watch the opposing crews row it out each year. The best places to watch the straining competitors glide by, and sample the exuberant atmosphere, are Putney Bridge and Chiswick Bridge. For the record, Cambridge currently leads, with 79 wins to Oxford's 75 with one dead-heat.

www.theboatrace.org

CRICKET

Ticket prices at London's two premier grounds, Lords and the Oval, range from £50 to £90 for an Ashes Test down to just £10 for a 1-day Natwest Pro40 match (at the Oval; they're £16 at Lords). Tickets for the newest and increasingly popular form of the game, Twenty20, are (appropriately enough) £20. You can also watch one test match a year, usually the final one of the summer at the Oval, for free on a big screen in Regent's Park. The outer boroughs of the capital are also home to numerous amateur and semi-amateur clubs where you can watch this most archetypal of English sports for free, often from the comfort of a nearby pub.

Lord's

St John's Wood Road, NW8. ✆ **020 7616 8500**. www.lords.org. Tube: St. John's Wood.

The Oval

Kennington, SE11. ✆ **020 7820 5756**. www.britoval.com. Tube: Oval.

FOOTBALL

The biggest show in town. Football matches are the most popular sporting events—scrap that, the most popular form of entertainment—in the entire country. Come the weekend from August to May, more people entertain themselves with a bit of footie than with anything else. At the top end prices can be extraordinary. This is a sport where a restricted view seat for a mid-level Premiership side like West Ham

United can exceed £50. As you drop down the leagues, however, the prices come down with you. It's around £25 to £50 for a match in the Championship (the league below the Premier League) down to £10 and below once you reach the semi- and non-professional likes of the Ryman League Division 1 Blue Square Conference League South. The skill level at these matches is obviously lower, and the crowds smaller, but the atmosphere, the fervour, and the sense of hope desperately trying to overcome long and painful experience is as apparent as any-where. For details of your nearest non-league club, check out www. isthmian.co.uk and www.bluesqsouth.com.

WOMEN'S FOOTBALL

If all the misplaced passes, mistimed tackles, and woeful finishing of the lower leagues leave you pining for a touch of class and skill—but you just don't have the money to go the Premier League route—this is a bargain-priced alternative. Tickets for the top tier of women's foot-ball, the 12-team Women's Premier League, are usually a tenner or less. The games are slower, (slightly) less physical, and much less well attended than their male equivalents, but feature comparable skill and athleticism. There are currently four London teams playing in the top division.

Arsenal Ladies: www.arsenal.com/ladies.

Chelsea Ladies: www.chelseafc.com/page/ChelseaLadies.

Millwall Lionesses: www.millwallfc.co.uk/page/Lionesses.

Watford Ladies: www.watfordladiesfc.com.

FREE THE LONDON MARATHON

Though I've often dreamt of scoring the winner at Wembley or clinch-ing the crucial runs at the Oval, I have no such fantasies regarding the marathon. The physical brutality of this 26-mile slog makes it one of those events I'd *always* rather be watching than doing. Many disagree with me. In fact, so many thousands apply to run each year that places have to be allocated by ballot. There are numerous good spots along the route to watch the bobbing sea of humanity make its way from Blackheath to the Mall—from the elite athletes at the front to the charity runners in their rhino suits and deep-sea diving helmets at the rear. These include Greenwich Park, for good views of the start, Hungerford

Sporting Screens at Broadgate

If you decide not to splash out £90-plus for a ticket to the men's final at Wimbledon, it is possible to watch it for free on the big screen at **Broadgate Arena.** This purpose-built outdoor entertainment area in the City stages various events throughout the year, including concerts, beach volleyball (in summer, with imported sand), and ice skating (in winter, with imported ice), principally for the benefit of nearby office workers. The big screen is also wheeled into Broadgate Circle for big football and cricket matches.

www.broadgateinfo.net

Foot Bridge, to watch the riverside slog down the Embankment, and St. James's Park for the final push home. You'll have to claim your vantage point early if you're hoping to see anything.

www.london-marathon.co.uk

RUGBY

Though it's nowhere near the all-conquering entertainment juggernaut that is Premier League football, rugby has become increasingly popular in the past decade, particularly since the advent of professionalism and good England showings in two World Cups (first in 2003, second in 2007). Unfortunately, this success means that prices, once dirt cheap, have risen significantly: you can easily find yourself paying £30 to £40 for a matchday ticket in the Guinness Premiership, the top league. Bargains are still out there, however. Saracens, one of four London Premiership teams, offers a limited number for just £14.50, around half of what you'd pay for the very cheapest Premier League football tickets (www.saracens.com). As with football, however, aim lower to bag a real bargain. Three divisions below the Premiership, matches in the semi-professional National League 2 South are either free or cost just a few pounds. There are currently six London teams competing in the 16-team league: Barking, Barnes, Ealing, Richmond, Rosslyn Park, and Westcombe Park. The National Clubs Association can provide contact details for all (www.ncarugby.org).

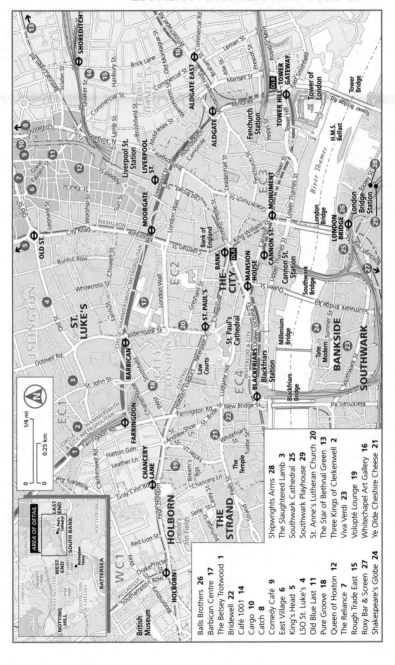

Balls Brothers **26**
Barbican Centre **17**
The Betsey Trotwood **1**
Bridewell **22**
Café 1001 **14**
Cargo **10**
Catch **8**
Comedy Café **9**
East Village **6**
King's Head **5**
LSO St. Luke's **4**
Old Blue Last **11**
Pure Groove **18**
Queen of Hoxton **12**
The Reliance **7**
Rough Trade East **15**
Roxy Bar & Screen **27**
Shakespeare's Globe **24**

Shipwrights Arms **28**
The Slaughtered Lamb **3**
Southwark Cathedral **25**
Southwark Playhouse **29**
St. Anne's Lutheran Church **20**
The Star of Bethnal Green **13**
Three Kings of Clerkenwell **2**
Viva Verdi **23**
Volupté Lounge **19**
Whitechapel Art Gallery **16**
Ye Olde Cheshire Cheese **21**

ENTERTAINMENT IN THE WEST END

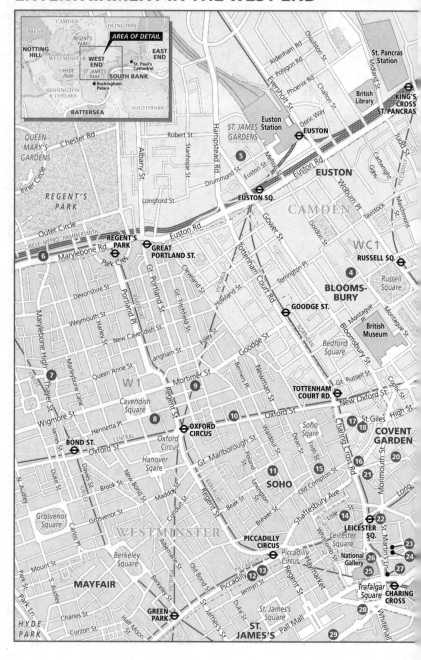

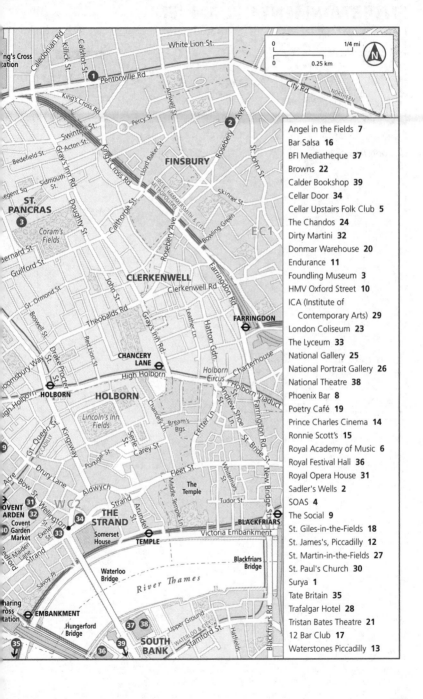

0   1/4 mi

0   0.25 km

N

King's Cross
Station

White Lion St.

Caledonian Rd.

Killick St.

Calshot St.

Pentonville Rd.

City Rd.

NORTHERN

King's Cross Rd.

Amwell St.

St. John St.

Rosebery Ave.

Percy St.

FINSBURY

Lloyd Baker St.

King's Cross Rd.

Swinton St.

Gt. Acton St.

Skinner St.

Bedeford St.

Grays Inn Rd.

Sidmouth St.

Calthorpe St.

Rosebery Ave.

Bowling Green

EC1

ST.
PANCRAS

Doughty St.

Coram's
Fields

Guilford St.

John St.

CLERKENWELL

Clerkenwell Rd.

Farringdon Rd.

Gt. Ormond St.

Theobalds Rd.

Grays Inn Rd.

Leather Ln.

Hatton Gdn.

Charterhouse

FARRINGDON

Boswell St.

Red Lion St.

CHANCERY
LANE

Holborn
Circus

Holborn Viaduct

Farringdon Rd.

HOLBORN

High Holborn

Andrew St. Shoe

St. Bride St.

New Bridge St.

Lincoln's Inn
Fields

Chancery Ln.

Fetter Ln.

Whitefriars St.

Fleet St.

The
Temple

Middle Temple Ln.

Tudor St.

Covent
Garden

Strand

Aldwych

Arundel St.

BLACKFRIARS

WC2

THE
STRAND

Somerset
House

TEMPLE

Victoria Embankment

Blackfriars
Bridge

Waterloo
Bridge

River Thames

Blackfriars Rd.

EMBANKMENT

Hungerford
Bridge

Upper Ground

SOUTH
BANK

WATERLOO & CITY

Stamford St.

Hatfields

Angel in the Fields	**7**
Bar Salsa	**16**
BFI Mediatheque	**37**
Browns	**22**
Calder Bookshop	**39**
Cellar Door	**34**
Cellar Upstairs Folk Club	**5**
The Chandos	**24**
Dirty Martini	**32**
Donmar Warehouse	**20**
Endurance	**11**
Foundling Museum	**3**
HMV Oxford Street	**10**
ICA (Institute of Contemporary Arts)	**29**
London Coliseum	**23**
The Lyceum	**33**
National Gallery	**25**
National Portrait Gallery	**26**
National Theatre	**38**
Phoenix Bar	**8**
Poetry Café	**19**
Prince Charles Cinema	**14**
Ronnie Scott's	**15**
Royal Academy of Music	**6**
Royal Festival Hall	**36**
Royal Opera House	**31**
Sadler's Wells	**2**
SOAS	**4**
The Social	**9**
St. Giles-in-the-Fields	**18**
St. James's, Piccadilly	**12**
St. Martin-in-the-Fields	**27**
St. Paul's Church	**30**
Surya	**1**
Tate Britain	**35**
Trafalgar Hotel	**28**
Tristan Bates Theatre	**21**
12 Bar Club	**17**
Waterstones Piccadilly	**13**

ENTERTAINMENT IN CAMDEN

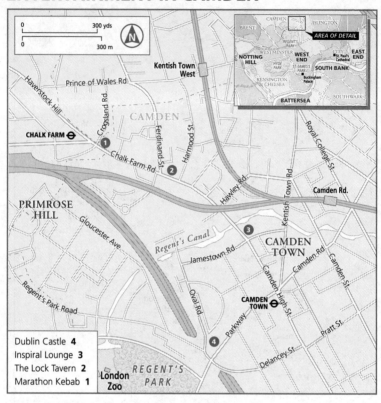

Dublin Castle **4**
Inspiral Lounge **3**
The Lock Tavern **2**
Marathon Kebab **1**

Pedestrians walking through the ever popular Borough Market.

FREE & DIRT CHEAP ITINERARIES

Itinerary 1: A South Bank Stroll

Where	The South Bank between London Bridge and Westminster Bridge.
How to Get There	Take the Tube or train to London Bridge. Exit via the main entrance and head towards the southern end of the bridge.
How Long to Spend There	It takes at least 45 minutes to walk the route, but this is a busy itinerary that could easily fill a day or more.
Best Times to Go	On a summer weekend, when the riverside walkway is littered with additional free entertainment in the form of buskers, jugglers, mime artists, and musicians. Or any Friday afternoon when you can finish the week enjoying one of the free concerts laid on by the Royal Festival Hall or Tate Modern (first Friday of the month only).

South Bank Stroll Costs

Free	
The River Thames, four bridges, a cathedral, a market, a ruined palace, roosting birds of prey, an art gallery, a tower, a lido, several theatres, an arts centre, concerts, exhibitions, and the Mother of Parliaments	£0
Dirt Cheap	
A pint of lager at the Anchor	£3.10
Second-hand paperback at South Bank Book Market	£2
Add-ons for Spendthrift Millionaires	
Coffee and cake at Borough Market	£4
The *Golden Hinde*	£6
Clink Museum	£5
Shakespeare's Globe tour	£9
Spin on the London Eye	£17
Tour of the Houses of Parliament	£12

① London Bridge

We may as well start where it all began, London Bridge. Now one of the world's great metropolises, London started in humble fashion as a small settlement that grew up next to a bridge across the Thames. The Romans founded Londinium during their A.D.1st-century occupation of Britain. The bridge remained London's only permanent river crossing until the mid-18th century, a bottleneck of humanity which in the Middle Ages was lined with houses and shops (the Museum of London has a model showing what it looked like; p. 105). The current bridge, erected in the 1970s, is a nondescript and almost ironically featureless successor. However, it does supply views of the chocolate-box turrets of **Tower Bridge** just downriver (p. 127), and *HMS Belfast,* a World War II cruiser turned floating naval museum.

② Southwark Cathedral

On the bridge's southern end, just north of the Barrowboy and Banker pub, take the narrow set of steps down to a cobbled street. These are known as the 'Nancy Steps', marking the spot where Bill Sykes murdered Nancy in the Dickens' novel *Oliver Twist*. Head west to Southwark Cathedral,

ITINERARY 1: A SOUTH BANK STROLL

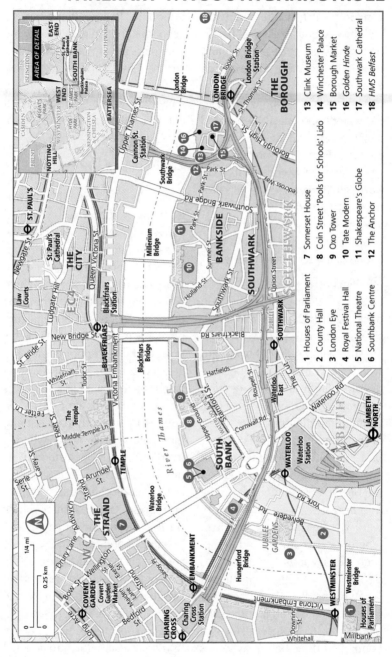

1	Houses of Parliament
2	County Hall
3	London Eye
4	Royal Festival Hall
5	National Theatre
6	Southbank Centre
7	Somerset House
8	Coin Street 'Pools for Schools' Lido
9	Oxo Tower
10	Tate Modern
11	Shakespeare's Globe
12	The Anchor
13	Clink Museum
14	Winchester Palace
15	Borough Market
16	Golden Hinde
17	Southwark Cathedral
18	HMS Belfast

London's first Gothic church, which was built over a 200-year period between the early 13th and early 15th centuries. The church was originally known as St. Mary Overie ('overie' meaning 'close to the water') and wasn't designated a cathedral until the early 20th century. Free organ recitals are given here on Mondays at 1pm. **Borough Market,** the capital's premier foodie haunt, lies just to the west (p. 90). If you're flush, fortify yourself with a coffee and a cake at one of the surrounding cafés.

③ Winchester Palace

Heading north-west takes you back towards the river and a full-size replica of the **Golden Hinde,** the surprisingly small ship aboard which Sir Francis Drake became the first Englishman to circumnavigate the globe in the 16th century (admission is £6, however). Continuing west takes you past the ruins of Winchester Palace, the medieval residence of the bishops of Winchester. In the Middle Ages this part of Southwark was the bad side of town, where locals came to indulge in such unsavoury practices as drinking, visiting prostitutes (known locally as 'Winchester Geese'), bear baiting, and, worst of all, going to the theatre. Most of London's principal playhouses were located along this stretch of riverfront. It was the job of the bishop to license these various licentious shenanigans. Today the only parts of his palace to survive are the Rose Window and a few sections of the former prison, which have been turned into a London Dungeon-style museum, the **Clink** (admission £5).

④ The Anchor Pub

Keep heading west until you reach the Anchor pub. It was from here that diarist Samuel Pepys supposedly watched the Great Fire engulf his city in September 1666. Another fire 10 years later did for the pub, which was then rebuilt over the next decade. Much of its higgledy-piggledy interior dates from this time, and the outdoor terrace is a great place to sit with a pint watching the comings and goings on the river. Numerous relics of Southwark's bawdy past remain, including Bear Gardens, where a bear-baiting pit once stood, Cardinal's Cap Alley, the site of a notorious brothel, and Old Theatre Court, an apartment block on the site of the original Rose Theatre. Look out too for the small seat embedded into the wall of the Real Greek restaurant, where medieval boatmen used to wait for custom. Prior to the construction of the city's modern bridges most traffic crossed the Thames in small boats.

5 Shakespeare's Globe

Your next stop is one giant, Technicolor historical recreation. Built in 1598, the original Globe premiered many of the Bard's most famous works, including *Julius Caesar, Hamlet,* and *Macbeth*. It burnt down in 1613 when, according to the story, an ember from a cannon fired during a performance of *Henry VIII* set fire to the thatched roof. It was rebuilt in the mid-1990s in a style as close to the original as safety standards allowed. Though something of a tourist trap, it is also a respected venue that stages year-round theatre (see p. 247 for details of attending a performance on the cheap). It costs £9 to take a nose around inside, so keep on walking.

6 Tate Modern & the Millennium Bridge

A short walk past the Globe takes you to the Tate Modern, the capital's pre-eminent gallery of modern art (p. 121). In front, a footbridge crosses the river to the City. Dubbed, rather hubristically as it turned out, a 'blade of light' by its designer, Sir Norman Foster, this elegant walkway opened in 2000. Unfortunately, as the first people began walking across, the bridge started shaking in such an alarming (and potentially dangerous) manner that the authorities were forced to close it. Newspapers and Londoners named it the 'wobbly bridge' rather than Foster's preferred moniker, and that's the label that stuck—though some engineering wizardry solved the problem and the bridge reopened, more or less wobble-free, in 2002. Today it offers expansive views up and down the Thames and north to the iconic plump dome of St. Paul's. From July to September you can also enjoy one of London's few impressive wildlife views, when the RSPB sets up free telescopes trained on a pair of peregrine falcons who roost atop the Tate chimney.

7 Oxo Tower

The walk's best (free) elevated views are available from the eighth floor viewing platform of the Oxo Tower (p. 125). The tower is owned by Coin Street Community Builders, a not-for-profit organisation that also runs nearby Bernie Spain Gardens: a small patch of lawn, Gabriel's Wharf (shops, restaurants, and craft stalls occupying converted garages), and, in August, a temporary lido, where free swimming lessons are available for all ages (advanced booking essential). Come summer the area also hosts various free events as part of the Coin Street Arts Festival (p. 18). As you walk along the riverfront look out for silver disks set into the ground. These mark the route of the 14-mile **Silver Jubilee Walkway** (p. 136).

8 The Southbank Centre

Keep heading south-west along the riverfront and you'll reach what looks like a grim housing estate. In fact these ugly, boxy, concrete buildings make up one of the country's most prestigious arts venues, the Southbank Centre, comprising various theatres, cinemas, and concert halls. Begun as part of the 1951 Festival of Britain's attempt to revitalise the postwar arts scene, the complex's brutally basic design was clearly influenced by the austerity of the time. Notwithstanding these exterior limitations, the complex's different elements offer a universally acclaimed arts programme with plenty of bargain opportunities, including cheap tickets for the **National Theatre** (p. 246), 'Watch This Space' free street performances in summer (p. 246), the free Mediatheque film archive at the NFT (p. 250), and the various free concerts staged at the **Royal Festival Hall** each weekend (p. 238).

9 Waterloo Bridge

Follow in the footsteps of Terry and Julie to Waterloo Bridge, which stretches across the 'dirty old' river just west of the National Theatre. From mid-span you look back towards the Southbank Centre (should you really want to) and across to the graceful 18th-century bulk of **Somerset House** (p. 126) on the north bank. As the song suggests, 'sunset' is the most picturesque time. Follow the bridge inland to the Waterloo Roundabout, at the centre of which stands the giant glass drum of the BFI IMAX cinema. The bridge was built soon after (and named in honour of) the Duke of Wellington's decisive battle over Napoleon in 1815. After falling into disrepair, it was rebuilt during World War II, largely by women who at the time made up the majority of the labour force. If it's raining, the small second-hand book market on the walkway beneath the bridge makes a great place to wile away half an hour (p. 211).

10 The London Eye

The next crossing along is Hungerford Bridge, a rail- and footbridge linking the Royal Festival Hall with the Victoria Embankment. It's a rather ugly construction, particularly when compared with its Isambard Kingdom Brunel-designed predecessor, dismantled in the early 1860s and used as the basis for the elegant Clifton Suspension Bridge in Bristol. Continuing south takes you past the rotating pods of the London Eye, a giant Ferris wheel erected for the millennium that has become part of the city's skyline. It's £17 for a spin, so you'll have to content yourself with views of the wheel itself, which are pretty impressive. In recent years it's become the focus of the capital's New Year firework display. Just south is the 1920s-built **County Hall,** former headquarters of the GLC (Greater London Council) and now home to a hotel and some pricey attractions, including the London Aquarium (£13.25), Dali Universe (£12), and the Muvieum, a museum on movies (do you see what they've done there? £15). You can safely ignore them all.

11 Westminster Bridge & the Houses of Parliament

Westminster Bridge provides postcard views of our walk's final destination, the Houses of Parliament (properly known as the Palace of Westminster). Most of this neo-Gothic building was constructed in the mid-19th century following a fire, although a couple of medieval sections survive, notably the 11th-century Westminster Hall. (Incidentally, 'Big Ben' is officially the name of the bell inside the clocktower, and not the tower itself, although it's a distinction observed by few these days.) It's free to attend debates in

One Last Look

When you're on Westminster Bridge, look back towards County Hall and the row of lions' heads embedded in the embankment. Each has a metal ring clamped in its mouth. Although they look like moorings, these are in fact traditional flood warnings, and gave rise to the local phrase 'when the lions drink, London is in danger'. Thankfully the opening of the Thames Flood Barrier in the 1980s (p. 127) means that our lions are likely to remain thirsty for the foreseeable future.

the House of Commons. Some tickets are available for walk-up visits each day, but you're safer to arrange a visit in advance either through your local MP or via your embassy. Many debates can, in truth, be sparsely attended, jargon heavy, and rather dull—and, unfortunately, they are the ones you're most likely to get tickets for. Try instead to get an invite to Prime Minister's Questions, held at midday on Wednesdays. It's a piece of raucous parliamentary pantomime, where government and opposition boo, hiss, and hurl insults at each other across the debating chamber. Tours of the building are available only when the MPs have gone home for their 2-month summer holiday, and cost a not inconsiderable £12.

South Bank Stroll Itinerary Index

The Anchor   34 Park Street, SE1. ℃ 020 7407 1577.

Borough Market   Borough High Street, SE1. ℃ 020 7407 1002. www.boroughmarket.org.uk. Thurs 11am–5pm, Fri midday–6pm, Sat 9am–4pm.

Clink Museum   1 Clink Street, SE1. ℃ 020 7403 0900. www.clink.co.uk. Mon–Fri 10am–6pm, Sat–Sun 10am–9pm.

Coin Street 'Pools for Schools' Lido   Riverside Walkway, by Gabriel's Wharf, SE1. ℃ 0844 357 2549. www.coinstreet.org. Aug only.

Golden Hinde   Pickford's Wharf, Clink Street, SE1. ℃ 020 7403 0123. www.goldenhinde.com. Mon–Sat 10am–5:30pm.

HMS Belfast   Morgan's Lane, Tooley Street, SE1. ℃ 020 7940 6300. http://hmsbelfast.iwm.org.uk. Mar–Oct daily 10am–6pm, Nov–Feb daily 10am–5pm.

Houses of Parliament   Parliament Square, SW1. ℃ 020 7219 4272. www.parliament.uk. When parliament is sitting, Mon & Tues 2:30–10:30pm, Wed 11:30am–7:30pm, Thurs 10:30am–6:30pm, Fri 9:30am–3pm.

London Eye   Riverside Building, County Hall, SE1. ℃ 0870 990 8883. www.londoneye.com. May–June & Sept daily 10am–9pm, July–Aug daily 10am–9:30pm, Oct–April daily 10am–8pm.

Oxo Tower   Oxo Tower Wharf, Bargehouse Street, SE1. ℃ 020 7021 1600. www.coinstreet.org/oxotower_wharf.aspx. Daily 11am–6pm.

Shakespeare's Globe   21 New Globe Walk, SE1. ℃ 020 7902 1400. www.shakespeares-globe.org. Mon–Sat 9am–5pm, Sun midday–5pm.

Southbank Centre   Belvedere Road, SE1. ℃ 020 7291 0823. www.southbankcentre.co.uk.

Southwark Cathedral   Montague Close, SE1. ℃ 020 7367 6700. http://cathedral.southwark.anglican.org. Daily 8am–6pm.

Tate Modern   Bankside, SE1. ℃ 020 7887 8888. www.tate.org.uk/modern. Sun–Thurs 10am–6pm, Fri–Sat 10am–10pm.

Itinerary 2: A West End Wander

Where	The West End between Green Park and the Strand, by way of tourism central: Buckingham Palace, the Mall, Trafalgar Square, and Covent Garden.
How to Get There	Jump off the Tube at Green Park.
How Long to Spend There	The walking itself will take at least an hour, but with a few stops leave at least a half-day in total.
Best Times to Go	Late morning so you can catch the Changing of the Guard at Buck House and a free lunchtime concert at the Royal Opera House.

① Green Park

Take the left-hand exit from Green Park station up to the pavement, then a sharp right off Piccadilly into the park itself. This is a great place for a relaxing wander or a lie on the grass (weather permitting), even if it is the least well equipped of London's royal parks: there's no lake or bandstand, just lots of lawn and trees, hence the name. But then it's probably best that they don't do too much digging around here: according to legend, the park was laid out over the site of a medieval leper colony (see also p. 130).

② Buckingham Palace

Pass out of Green Park's southern side to watch the watchers at Buckingham Palace. The grand, if rather staid, 19th-century building is never without a contingent of camera-toting tourists furiously snapping everything (and nothing) through the railings. It's at its busiest at 11:30am for that terribly English piece of postcard pageantry, the Changing of the Guard (daily April–July, alternate days the rest of the year; p. 14). Before you depart, be sure to check the palace's flagpole. If the royal standard is flying, the Queen is at home. It's a fairly regal £15.50 to visit the State Rooms in summer.

③ The Mall

Head north-east, around the roundabout and up the Mall, a stately (and very pink) tree-lined road leading to Admiralty Arch. The statue in the centre of the roundabout is the **Victoria Memorial.** The gold figure on its top is a representation of Victory, not Queen Victoria herself (she was much less lithe, and didn't have wings). Bordering the Mall on the right is **St. James's Park,** one of the capital's prettiest open spaces. In the 17th century it held several aviaries, hence the name of the road on its southern

ITINERARY 2: A WEST END WANDER

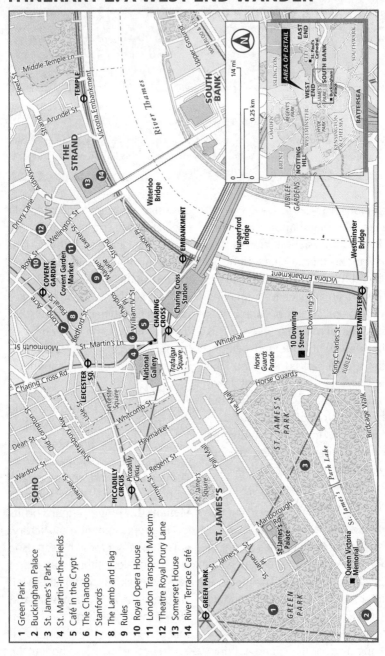

1 Green Park
2 Buckingham Palace
3 St. James's Park
4 St. Martin-in-the-Fields
5 Café in the Crypt
6 The Chandos
7 Stanfords
8 The Lamb and Flag
9 Rules
10 Royal Opera House
11 London Transport Museum
12 Theatre Royal Drury Lane
13 Somerset House
14 River Terrace Café

West End Wander Costs

Free	
Two parks, the Changing of the Guard, a gallery, a church, a market, street performances, lunchtime concerts, and river views	£0

Dirt Cheap	
Full English breakfast at Café in the Crypt	£6.25
Pint of lager in the Chandos	£2.15

Add-ons for Spendthrift Millionaires	
Tour of Buckingham Palace	£15.50
London Transport Museum	£8
Theatre Royal backstage tour	£11.50
Coffee at Somerset House	£1.60

edge, Birdcage Walk. Today its central pond is still home to numerous species of wildfowl, including pelicans (p. 133). At the Mall's northern end stand the three arches of Admiralty Arch, which lead through to Trafalgar Square. Pass through the left-hand arch and look out for 'the nose', a human-sized metal replica of a nose stuck on the wall about half-way up. Who put it there, and why, is a bit of a mystery, but it's rubbed for luck by anyone passing through on horseback—for whom it sits at about waist-height.

4 Trafalgar Square

Grim, grey, and full of pigeons, for years Trafalgar Square was a bit of an embarrassment, particularly compared to the elegant piazzas of Europe. Now, thanks to a bit of remodelling, pedestrianising and most importantly de-pigeonising, it's a nicer place. Not world class, but nicer, with gurgling fountains and elegant facades (the **National Gallery,** to the north, p. 118; **St. Martin-in-the-Fields** to the east, p. 125), all under the heroic gaze of Nelson on his column. Most major parades and marches, including St. Patrick's Day, the New Year's Day Parade, and Pride London, end up here—as do many political rallies. It's also the site of a few unusual attractions: the empty fourth plinth; an equestrian statue of Charles I from where all distances from London are measured; and, in the south-west corner, the world's smallest police station (it has room for just one, rather lonely, officer).

- **Mealtime** St. Martin-in-the-Fields boasts an atmospheric, subterranean eating choice, the

Café in the Crypt, where you can get a full English breakfast for £6.25, plus reasonably priced lunch options. If you come on a Monday, Tuesday, or Friday, you can enjoy a 'free' recital of classical music ('free' in this instance means a donation of £3.50). For anyone in need of something stronger, **The Chandos,** just north-east on Chandos Place, does a decent, cheap pint (p. 260).

⑤ Stanfords
Exit the square by its north-east corner and head up Charing Cross Road until you reach Leicester Square station. To the west are the cinemas, clubs, and half-price ticket booths of Leicester Square, plus the restaurants of **Chinatown,** while to the north are the second-hand bookshops of Charing Cross Road (p. 208). We, however, are heading east along Cranbourn Street, across the junction, and then up Long Acre. On your right is Stanfords, the capital's leading guidebook and map shop, and a great place to browse away an hour. If they don't have a particular country in stock here, it probably hasn't been discovered yet.

● **Mealtime** Just past Stanfords, alongside Next, is a narrow alley leading through to the **Lamb and Flag** pub. It's one of the area's oldest boozers, dating back at least 300 years, and a fabulously unreconstructed place of bare wood floors and shadowy corners where everything is a bit bent out of shape. The bar serves an old-fashioned menu of sandwiches, jacket potatoes, and other pub staples for around £5 to £7.

⑥ Fruit, flowers & free street performances
Keep heading east on Long Acre till you reach Covent Garden Tube station; a right down James Street leads to the Garden itself. This was once London's main fruit, vegetable, and flower wholesale market, and was the setting for the early scenes of *Pygmalion*—this is where Professor Higgins first encounters the flower girl, Eliza. Congestion forced the market to de-camp to Nine Elms in the early 1970s (p. 195). The grand old buildings were revamped and now hold a hotchpotch of arty-crafty shops, a touristy market, and the excellent, if pricey, **London Transport Museum** (£8). The Garden has also become London's unofficial busking and street performance hub. Jugglers, unicylists, and physical comedians entertain the crowds on the Piazza, while on the ground floor of the market building opera singers warble stridently for cash. Maiden Lane, behind the square's

West End Wander Itinerary Index

Buckingham Palace   The Mall, SW1. ℂ **020 7766 7300.** www.royal collection.org.uk. Late July–Sept daily 9:45am–6pm.

Café in the Crypt   St Martin-in-the-Fields, 6 St. Martin's Place, WC2. ℂ **020 7839 4342.** www2.stmartin-in-the-fields.org/page/cafe/crypt/ crypt.html. Mon–Wed 8am–8pm, Thurs–Sat 8am–9pm, Sun 11am–6pm.

The Chandos   60 Chandos Place, WC2. ℂ **020 7836 0060.** Mon–Sat 11am–11pm, Sun 11am–10:30pm.

Green Park   Piccadilly, W1. ℂ **020 7930 1793.** www.royalparks.org.uk. Daily 24 hours.

Lamb and Flag   33 Rose Street, WC2. ℂ **020 7497 9504.** Mon–Sat 11am–11pm, Sun midday–10:30pm.

London Transport Museum   Covent Garden Piazza, WC2. ℂ **020 7379 6344.** www.ltmuseum.co.uk. Mon–Thurs & Sat–Sun 10am–6pm, Fri 11am–6pm.

River Terrace Café   Somerset House, Strand, WC2. ℂ **020 7845 4646.** www.somersethouse.org.uk. Summer 11:30am till late (weather permitting).

Royal Opera House   Covent Garden, WC2. ℂ **020 7304 4000.** www.roh. org.uk.

St. James's Park   SW1. ℂ **020 7930 1793.** www.royalparks.org.uk/ parks/st_james_park. Daily dawn–dusk.

Stanfords   12–14 Long Acre, WC2. ℂ **020 7836 1321.** www.stanfords. co.uk. Mon, Wed & Fri 9am–7:30pm, Tues 9:30am–7:30pm, Thurs 9am– 8pm, Sat 10am–8pm, Sun midday–6pm.

Theatre Royal Drury Lane   Catherine Street, WC2. ℂ **0844 412 4660.** www.reallyuseful.com/theatres/theatre-royal-drury-lane.

southern edge, is home to **Rules,** London's oldest restaurant, which first opened way back in 1798. Its menu has apparently changed little since.

7 Bow Street

Walking east out of Covent Garden takes you to Bow Street and the **Royal Opera House.** First erected in the 18th century, it's been much rebuilt and remodelled since. It now boasts a glass and stone exterior which makes it look a bit like a cross between a classical temple and the Crystal Palace. Though often held up as the epitome of cultural exclusivity, not everything the ROH stages is expensive. Come at lunchtime and you may be able to enjoy a free classical recital (p. 237). London's first professional police force, the Bow Street Runners, operated out of a building opposite the Opera House. Founded by the author and magistrate, Henry Fielding, in 1749, the force was sent out into the mean streets on the hunt for criminals. Alas, as there were only eight of them, it's doubtful they were particularly effective in tackling either crime or the causes of crime.

⑧ Onwards to Somerset House
The country's oldest theatre, the **Theatre Royal,** is just east of Bow Street on Drury Lane. The present building dates from the early 19th century; it replaced one built in 1663, just after the Restoration of the monarchy, when plays were once again performed following the puritan interval of Oliver Cromwell's rule. Backstage tours are available for £11.50. Finish the walk with a stroll south to the Strand and treat yourself to a tea (£1.65) or a coffee (£1.60–£2.25) and view out over the Thames from the elegant confines of Somerset House's **River Terrace Café.**

Itinerary 3: A Fiery Sojourn, from Pudding Lane to Pye Corner

Where	The original City of London, from the source of the Great Fire (the Monument and Pudding Lane) to its end (Pye Corner).
How to Get There	Take the Tube to Monument, or the Tube/train to London Bridge then cross the water to the north side.
How Long to Spend There	The walk will take at least an hour at marching pace, but can comfortably fill a half-day with stops.
Best Times to Go	Late morning or early afternoon. If you come on Friday morning, you could add a preliminary detour to Bermondsey Antique Market (p. 199). Avoid the weekend when many of the attractions, shops, and pubs are closed.

Tracing the course of the Great Fire, this walk takes us through the commercial heart of the capital (the City, or 'the Square Mile'). Primarily known today as a financial district, it was once London's main market area—and almost obliterated in the September 1666 blaze. Only in the aftermath of the Great Fire, when wooden stalls were banned from the centre, did market trading cease to be the most visible form of business taking place on the original site of Roman Londinium. From the 18th century onwards, it was the great banking and stock-trading institutions that came to dominate both the skyline and the business of the City of London.

1 The Monument

The walk begins at the northern side of London Bridge where, just to the east, you'll find the Monument. Designed by Sir Christopher Wren to commemorate the Great Fire, it also symbolises the historical break between the old and new Londons (p. 115). Just to the east is **Pudding Lane:** it was here, on the night of 2nd September 1666, that the conflagration began. Three days later it had accounted for 13,200 houses, 87 churches, but just six lives (according to official figures, although many historians now believe the toll must have been considerably higher).

2 Leadenhall Market

Head up Gracechurch Street, which runs over the epicentre of Roman London (the remains of Londinium's Forum lie beneath). Pass **Lombard Street**—named after Italian financiers who settled here in the 13th century and taught Londoners the theory of banking—then you'll reach the entrance to Leadenhall Market. London's oldest surviving retail market was established in the 14th century for traders from outside the capital to sell their wares, although it has only occupied its current iron and glass premises since the late 19th century. In truth, it's now more of an upmarket shopping arcade than a true market; most outlets are pubs, chain stores, and restaurants. Before you leave check out **Nicholson & Griffin,** a traditional barbers, where, in the basement, you can view the remains of the City's Roman basilica.

3 The Lloyds Building & 'Gherkin'

Take the market's north exit, turn right, and you'll come face-to-facade with one of the City's most distinctive offices, the Lloyds Building. Designed by Richard Rogers and opened in 1986, it is one of the archetypes of the back-to-front school of architecture. Many of what you might normally consider its interior features—pipes, ducts, stairs, lifts—are on the outside. To get the best view walk just to the north onto St. Mary Axe, where you'll find one of the City's other notable buildings, **30 St. Mary Axe,** more commonly known as the **'Gherkin'.** Since completion in 2004, it has become an icon as potent as St. Paul's, and one of

ITINERARY 3: A FIERY SOJOURN

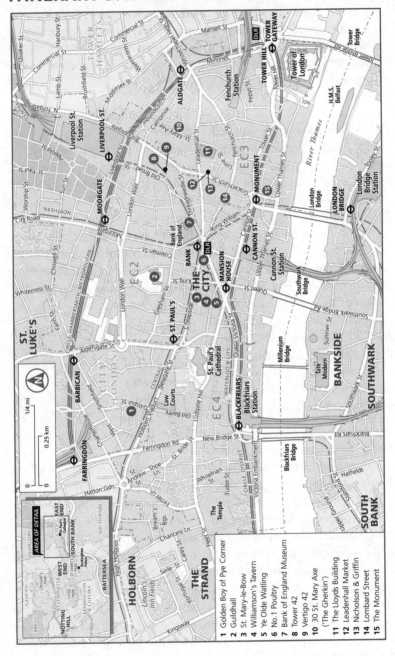

1 Golden Boy of Pye Corner
2 Guildhall
3 St. Mary-le-Bow
4 Williamson's Tavern
5 Ye Olde Watling
6 No.1 Poultry
7 Bank of England Museum
8 Tower 42
9 Vertigo 42
10 30 St. Mary Axe
   ('The Gherkin')
11 The Lloyds Building
12 Leadenhall Market
13 Nicholson & Griffin
14 Lombard Street
15 The Monument

Fiery Sojourn Costs

Free	
Two memorials to the fire, skyscraper views, a market, Roman remains, two museums, a library, an art gallery, medieval architecture, and the cockney church	£0
Dirt Cheap	
Pint of bitter at Williamson's Tavern	£2.75
Add-ons for Spendthrift Millionaires	
Climb the Monument	£3
Cheapest glass of bubbly at Vertigo 42	£12.75
St. Paul's Cathedral	£11

the most easily identifiable silhouettes on the London skyline. It actually looks better from a distance. Up close, it just looks tall (180m/590.5ft), curvy, and glassy, although the giant metal triangles forming the entrance are pretty cool. It was built on the site of the original Baltic Exchange, bombed by the IRA in 1992.

4 Tower 42

Trace your path back to Leadenhall Street, head west, and then north up Bishopsgate till you reach the junction with Threadneedle Street. Walk a little further up Bishopsgate and you'll begin to see Tower 42, the tallest building in the City, as it begins to poke its head above the rooftops to the left. If you fancy splurging all the cash you've so carefully saved up to now, there's a very fancy champagne bar on the top floor, **Vertigo 42,** which offers the highest accessible views in

London. If you've got your walking shoes on, another 5 minutes or so up Bishopsgate is rewarded with great views back to the Gherkin.

5 Bank of England

Wander down Threadneedle Street past the Bank of England, the bank to the banks, which sets the country's interest rates and holds its gold reserves. You can see a fraction of its treasure at the (free) **Bank of England Museum,** which provides an engaging overview of the development of banking over the past few hundred years (p. 104).

6 Cheapside

Carry on down Threadneedle Street to Poultry (that's its full name—it's not Poultry Street or Poultry Road, just Poultry). Pause to look at **No.1 Poultry,** an undulating, red and cream creation that looks like a stone ocean liner designed by Fisher Price. Next comes Cheapside, the heart of London's medieval market. At first glance there would seem to be little remaining of the City's street-trading origins. Where Cheapside would once have been bursting with market life (*Ceap* is the old Saxon word for market), it's now home to an interchangeable assortment of pale neo-classical buildings and chain shops. Echoes of the past, however, can be found in the narrow streets leading off, which retain both their original names— Ironmonger Lane, Wood Street, Milk Street, Bread Street—and their medieval layout. Following the Great Fire, the City was rebuilt more or less where it had stood: new stone buildings overlaid the sites of the burnt wooden ones. It was considered too expensive and time consuming to redesign London as a grid.

7 The Guildhall

From Cheapside, take a right up King Street to the Guildhall, the grand medieval meeting-house that represents what happens when market traders get organised. By the Middle Ages commerce had become so important to the City that representatives of the 12 most important trades (Mercers, Grocers, Drapers, Fishmongers, Goldsmiths, Skinners, Merchant Taylors, Haberdashers,

Salters, Ironmongers, Vintners, and Clothworkers—not an IT consultant among them) formed themselves into guilds. These became responsible, not just for the organisation of trade, but also for the political life of the town. Their headquarters, the Guildhall, became (and remains) the City of London's seat of government overseen by the Lord Mayor of London. The Guildhall was constructed in the 15th century and, although badly damaged in World War II, retains much of its original stonework and boasts London's largest surviving medieval **crypt.** Outside of official occasions, you can visit the Guildhall to see its crypt, **Great Hall** (London's largest medieval hall after Westminster), **Clock Museum** (p. 112), **Library** (p. 167), and **Art Gallery** (see p. 117).

8 St. Mary-le-Bow

Back on Cheapside, look out for the slender tower of St. Mary-Le-Bow church. It was designed by the great architect of London's post-fire reconstruction, Sir Christopher Wren, in the late 17th century on the site of an 11th-century original. St. Mary-le-Bow is also known as the 'Cockney Church' because, according to tradition, to be a 'real' Cockney, you must be born within the sound of its bells. Just east of the church is Bow Lane, a

Fiery Sojourn Itinerary Index

Bank of England Museum   Threadneedle Street, EC2. ℂ 020 7601 5545. www.bankofengland.co.uk/education/museum. Mon–Fri 10am–5pm.

Guildhall   Gresham Street, EC2. ℂ 020 7606 3030. www.guildhall.city ofllondon.gov.uk. May–Sept daily, Oct–April Mon–Sat, 10am–5pm.

Leadenhall Market   Gracechurch Street, EC3. ℂ 0845 226 1150. www. leadenhallmarket.co.uk. Mon–Fri 11am–4pm.

Nicholson & Griffin   90 Gracechurch Street, EC3. ℂ 020 7283 0075. www.nicholsonandgriffin.com. Mon–Fri 8am–7pm.

St. Mary-le-Bow   1 Bow Lane, EC4. ℂ 020 7248 5139. www.st marylebow.co.uk. Mon–Wed 7am–6pm, Thurs 7am–6:30pm, Fri 7am–4pm.

Vertigo 42   Tower 42, 25 Old Broad Street, EC2. ℂ 020 7877 7842. www. vertigo42.co.uk. Mon–Fri midday–3pm & 5–11pm.

Williamson's Tavern   1 Groveland Court, EC4. ℂ 020 7248 5750. Mon–Fri 11am–11pm.

Ye Olde Watling   29 Watling Street, EC4. ℂ 020 7248 8935. Mon–Fri 11am–11pm.

bustling pedestrianised alleyway that, though rather gentrified and quaint these days, nonetheless supplies some idea of what medieval London must have looked like. Still occupying their original positions are two famous 17th-century pubs—the **Williamson's Tavern** and **Ye Olde Watling.**

9 St. Paul's Cathedral

Continue south until you reach Watling Street, London's oldest surviving street, which 1,900 years ago was the main Roman artery between Dover and St. Albans. Head west until you reach the grounds of St. Paul's Cathedral. Wren's masterpiece didn't simply redefine the city's skyline, it also helped to re-cast the role of the cathedral itself. The medieval version, destroyed in the Great Fire, had been as much a public meeting place and market as it had a house of worship. It was even felt necessary in the 14th century to issue formal edicts banning ball games, wrestling, and beer selling. Bishop Pilkington described it thus in

1560: 'The south side for popery and usury, the north for simony; and the horse-fair in the midst for all kinds of bargains, meetings, brawlings, murders, conspiracies; and the font for ordinary payments of money, as well known to all men as the beggar knows his bush'. The modern cathedral, while undoubtedly beautiful, is a much less exciting place. It's also a good deal too expensive for the purpose of our tour (£11), although its western entrance makes for a great photo opportunity and its churchyard is a nice spot for a picnic.

🔟 The Golden Boy of Pye Corner Just west of the cathedral, along Newgate Street and up Giltspur Street, is the Golden Boy of Pye Corner. This small, gilded statue marks the spot where the Great Fire finally petered out, on Wednesday 5th September. According to the inscription, the blaze was 'occasion'd by the sin of gluttony'—it started in *Pudding* Lane and ended at *Pye* Corner.

Itinerary 4: A Sunday Market Meander

Where	The markets of the East End—Spitalfields, Petticoat Lane, Brick Lane, and Columbia Road.
How to Get There	Ride the Tube or train as far as Liverpool Street.
How Long to Spend There	A Sunday morning and into the early afternoon.
Best Times to Go	Sunday: it's the only day when all four markets are open simultaneously.

This walk neatly demonstrates the variety of London's markets. Within around a square mile you can browse cheap clothing (Petticoat Lane), household goods (Brick Lane), arts and crafts (Spitalfields), and flowers (Columbia Road). Each of the markets is always full of noise and bustle, with stall-holders entreating the crowds with impassioned testimonials as to the bank-breakingly cheap nature of their produce.

① Spitalfields Market Exit Liverpool Street station at the eastern end, onto Bishopsgate, then turn north. A couple of minutes' walking brings you to Brushfield Street. Turn right and head down to Spitalfields. You enter through a modern, glass development, full of high-end shops, restaurants, and delis, beyond which is the reduced but still thriving craft market. This venerable institution has undergone various renovations and rebirths over the course of its 350-year history. The small-scale

Sunday Market Meander Costs

Free	
Five markets and a farm	£0
Dirt Cheap	
Three pairs of socks from Petticoat Lane Market	£1
Hot salt-beef bagel from 24-hour Beigel Bake	£2.60
Add-ons for Spendthrift Millionaires	
Pizza Funghi and a glass of wine at Stingray Globe	£9

market founded here in the mid-17th century was, in the late 19th, turned into a large fruit and veg wholesale market, which lasted until a 1991 relocation to Leyton. Part of the fine Victorian building was demolished to make way for offices in the late 1990s (see also p. 201).

2 Petticoat Lane

Head out the back of Spitalfields onto Commercial Street and then south for a minute or so till you reach Petticoat Lane Market—you can't miss the vast array of clothes stalls. Despite what the gates guarding this pedestrianised stretch say, there's no longer such a place as 'Petticoat Lane', officially speaking at least. First established more than 400 years ago by French Huguenots who sold lace—including the eponymous undergarments—the market street's name was changed to Wentworth Street in the 19th century, so as to avoid offending delicate Victorian sensibilities. Traders have long memories,

however, and so London's premier cheap clothes market continues to be known by its slightly saucier moniker. It can be a real scrum here on a busy Sunday afternoon (see p. 197).

3 Brick Lane

Now suitably attired, head along the eastern stretch of Wentworth Street to the intersection with

An East End Pit Stop

At no. 159, at the north end of Brick Lane, is the 24-hour **Brick Lane Beigel Bake.** A visit here is a rite of passage for Brick Lane Market newbies. It stocks an array of filled doughy circles— salt beef or salmon with cream cheese are the traditional choices—plus a selection of breads and cakes. Queues often spiral out of the door. If you fancy something a little heartier, not to say hotter, the southern stretch of the Lane is known for its curry houses.

ITINERARY 4: A SUNDAY MARKET MEANDER

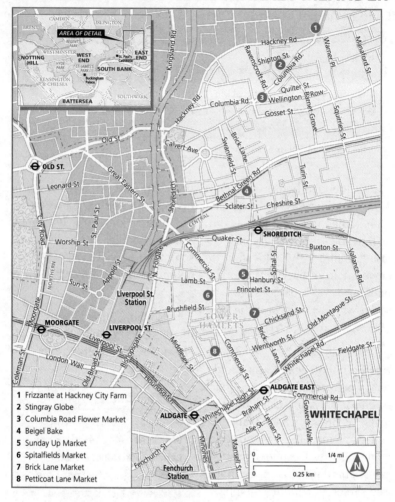

1 Frizzante at Hackney City Farm
2 Stingray Globe
3 Columbia Road Flower Market
4 Beigel Bake
5 Sunday Up Market
6 Spitalfields Market
7 Brick Lane Market
8 Petticoat Lane Market

Brick Lane. Every Sunday you'll find a vibrant, sprawling flea market: stalls sell everything from furniture, clothes, and electrical equipment to CDs, DVDs, and bric-a-brac (p. 196). Brick Lane seems a throwback to markets of times past. It's the sort of place that wouldn't have been out of place in 19th-century London—noisy, chaotic, and in parts a bit dodgy. About halfway down is the Old Truman Brewery, built in the early 18th century, and at one stage the largest brewery in the capital. The brewery closed in the 1980s and is now home to the **Sunday Up Market,** filled with stalls selling arts and crafts, vintage clothes, and fashions and jewellery by new designers, as well as a selection of hot food (see p. 90).

④ Columbia Road

Keep heading north along the upmarket section of Brick Lane, all boho cafés and fashion shops, to the point where the road disappears into an estate. Turn left, then right, after which it's a little wiggle up a couple of roads to Columbia Road for its famous flower market. Every Sunday, from the early morning till early afternoon, the street is packed out with stalls selling colourful and fragrant blooms (p. 193). It's a pleasant place to come during the rest of the week, too, albeit not quite so heady. There's a well-to-do selection of galleries, cake shops, delis, vintage clothes stores, and restaurants.

● **Mealtime   Stingray Globe,** at no. 109, makes a well-priced lunchtime pit stop: a pizza and a glass of wine comes in under a tenner. You can also get a very hearty, very free range, largely locally grown and reared breakfast from **Frizzante** just north of here at Hackney City Farm (p. 135)—£6.75 gets you two eggs, two bacon, two sausages, mushrooms, tomatoes, and two toast. Should you feel like doing anything once you've polished off that lot, wander among the paddocks and say hello to the resident sheep, pigs, donkeys, and cows, and perhaps buy some of the farm's produce at the shop.

The Tourist Information Centre outside St. Paul's Cathedral in the City of London.

LONDON BASICS FROM A TO Z

1 Information Central

VISITOR INFORMATION

There are seven official tourist information centres in central London, plus another dozen across Greater London. Most of the major train stations have one, including Victoria, Euston, and Liverpool Street, although much of the information they provide is also available from the official website, www.visitlondon.com. The site also has a bookable accommodation section—with enhanced content in the form of TripAdvisor customer reviews—as well as sections devoted to tourist attractions, sport, travel, and more.

Britain and London Visitor Centre   The biggest and most useful of the capital's visitor centres.

1 Regent Street, SW1. ℭ **0870 156 6366.** Apr–Sep Mon 9:30am–6:30pm, Tues –Fri 9am–6:30pm, Sat 9am–5pm, Sun 10am–4pm; Oct–Mar Mon 9:30am–6pm, Tues–Fri 9am–6pm, Sat & Sun 10am–4pm. Tube: Piccadilly Circus.

City of London Tourist Information Centre   The newest tourist information centre opened in 2008 in a swish building next to St. Paul's Cathedral. It holds lots of free information on City-based walks and tours.

St. Paul's Churchyard, EC4. ℭ **020 7332 1456.** Mon–Sat 9:30am–5:30pm, Sun 10am–4pm. Tube: St. Paul's.

INTERNET ACCESS

The spread of affordable Wi-Fi has increased public internet availability tenfold over the past few years. Many cafés and hotels and most public libraries (p. 165) now provide it, either free (in cafés usually to paying customers only) or for a small charge. See http://londonist.com/2007/05/free_wifi_in_lo.php, which has a constantly updating map of free hotspots, or www.wi-fihotspotlist.com, which has a (far from comprehensive) list of some of the current places offering access. If you're a vinyl kind of person and hanker after that internet café experience, there are still a few around offering online time for less than a pound an hour. You'll find an exhaustive list at www.allinlondon.co.uk/directory/1166-2.php; www. easyinternetcafe.com can also point you in the right direction.

Netstream-London   Twenty-four-hour café with 20 computers in Soho, a couple of minutes' walk from Oxford Street.

St. Anne's Court, W1. ℭ **020 7434 2525.** www.netstreamlondon.com. Daily 24 hours. Tube: Tottenham Court Road.

2 Getting to London

ARRIVING BY PLANE

London is served by five major airports; in descending order of size: Heathrow, Gatwick, Stansted, Luton, and London City. Only two, Heathrow and City, are within the M25, and only one, City, is anywhere near central London—frustratingly, it also handles the fewest flights. With Luton, Gatwick, and Stansted all over 30 miles from the centre, getting into the capital after you land can add significantly to the total cost of your door-to-door journey. The cheapest options for each are listed below. If you're thinking of jumping in a taxi—£100-plus from Gatwick, for example—this is not the book for you.

Gatwick The **Dot2Dot** coach service, which deposits you at your door, costs £26 one-way; the 30-minute **Gatwick Express** to Victoria costs £16.90 one-way. That leaves two options for bargain-hunters. Slightly slower trains operated by Southern (www.southernrailway.com), typically 35 to 50 minutes depending on stops, cost £11 one-way; it's just £3 to £7.50 if you book online, but you have to nominate the *exact* service you'll be using—a risky option on the return journey, when you're at the mercy of your airline's punctuality record. The **National Express** coach, meanwhile, costs £7.30 one-way and takes between 65 and 85 minutes, depending on the time of day (www.nationalexpress.com).

30 miles south of central London. ℂ **0844 335 1802.** www.gatwickairport.com.

Heathrow The **Heathrow Express** to Paddington takes just 15 minutes, but costs £16.50 one-way. Cheaper methods take a little longer to get into town. The **Heathrow Connect** train (£7.40 one-way) takes 30 to 40 minutes to reach Paddington, depending on what terminal you land at, making half a dozen stops en route. A Piccadilly Line Tube into central London costs a flat rate £4 (£3.80 with an Oyster Card) but takes nigh on an hour. If you plan to make further journeys by public transport after your arrival, it may be worth getting an Oyster Card or a Travelcard (see below).

15 miles west of central London. ℂ **0844 335 1801.** www.heathrowairport.com.

London City If you're lucky enough to fly into London City, you'll find getting into town an absolute doddle. Just hop aboard the DLR for the 20-minute journey to Bank—the walk-up fare is £4; £2.20 to £2.70 with an Oyster Card.

9 miles east of central London. ℂ **020 7646 0088.** www.londoncityairport.com.

Luton If catching a train, you'll first need to take the bus (£1) from the airport to Luton Airport Parkway train station from where it's £12.90 one-way (£13.80 before 9:30am) to London St. Pancras. Coaches, operated by **EasyBus** (www.easybus.co.uk), **Greenline** (ℂ **01582 584478,** www.greenline.co.uk), and **National Express** (ℂ **0871 781 8181,** www.nationalexpress.com), are marginally cheaper at £10 to £12.

30 miles north-west of central London. ℂ **0158 240 5100.** www.london-luton.co.uk.

Stansted   The **Stansted Express** to Liverpool Street costs £18 one-way and takes 45 minutes, while fares for regular **National Express East Anglia** train services to Stratford, in East London, are in excess of £19 and the journey takes 1 hour. The cheapest options are the bus services operated by a raft of companies, including **EasyBus** (www.easybus.co.uk), **National Express** (✆ **0871 781 8181,** www.nationalexpress.com), and **Terravision** (✆ **01279 680 028,** www.terravision.eu). These cost £9 to £11 and can take anything from 55 minutes to 2 hours.

35 miles north-east of central London. ✆ **0844 335 1803**. www.stanstedairport.com.

ARRIVING BY TRAIN

Eurostar trains from the continent arrive at the shiny new terminus at St. Pancras station, adjacent to King's Cross. Here you can connect to

Budget Airlines

BMI Baby   Connects London Stansted with several European countries, including the Czech Republic, France, the Netherlands, Portugal, Spain, and Switzerland.
✆ **0905 828 2828**. www.bmibaby.com.

Easyjet   Based in Luton but also flies out of Gatwick and Stansted to numerous European countries including France, Greece, Italy, and Spain, as well as further afield to Israel and Morocco.
www.easyjet.com.

Flybe   Flies from Gatwick and Luton to France, Ireland, Italy, Spain, and Switzerland among others.
✆ **0871 700 2000**. www.flybe.com.

Flythomascook   Cheap flights out of Gatwick, Luton, and Stansted to Europe, and beyond, including the USA, Canada, Brazil, Egypt, and Kenya.
http://book.flythomascook.com.

Ryanair   The biggest budget carrier currently flying out of the UK. Connections from Gatwick, Luton, and Stansted to Finland, France, Germany, Ireland, Italy, the Netherlands, Norway, Portugal, Spain, and Sweden.
✆ **0871 246 0000**. www.ryanair.com.

the capital's rail, bus, and Tube networks. See the relevant passages in 'Getting Around', below, for details. King's Cross is in Zone 1.

ARRIVING BY COACH

Travelling by coach is by far the cheapest way of covering long distances in the UK, with fares for many inter-city routes costing just a few pounds. However, savings made have to be weighed up against comfort lost—coach journeys can take a long time and are often crowded. Victoria coach station, just south of the rail and Tube hub, is the main London terminus for coaches from all over the UK and Europe. See the relevant passages in 'Getting Around' for details of fares from Victoria (which is in Zone 1).

Cheap Flight Websites

www.cheapair.com
www.cheapflights.com
www.cheaptickets.com
www.expedia.co.uk
www.flights.com
www.fly.com
www.lastminute.com
www.skyscanner.net
www.travelocity.co.uk

LOW-COST COACH COMPANIES

Megabus

℗ **0845 712 5678.** www.megabus.com.

National Express

℗ **0871 781 8181.** www.nationalexpress.com.

3 Getting Around London (Cheaply)

The body in charge of London's public transport system, **Transport for London** (℗ **020 7222 1234,** www.tfl.gov.uk), has an excellent website with a journey planner, timetables, route maps, and live travel updates. For information on regular rail services, including timetables, contact **National Rail** (℗ **08457 484 950,** www.national rail.co.uk).

REDUCED-FARE TICKETS

The UK's public transport costs are the highest in Europe, and increasing by the year, so this is an area where you'll need to do your research. Buying single fares as and when you travel is by far the most expensive way of getting around. To bag the biggest savings invest in either an Oyster Card or a Travelcard, depending on the sorts of journeys you want to make.

OYSTER CARDS

Oyster is a pre-paid, electronic smartcard that you can use to get reduced-price journeys on the Tube, buses, Docklands Light Railway (DLR), London Overground, and all National Rail services within Greater London. Buy one from (and top it up at) Tube stations, some newsagents, or travel information centres located inside major railway stations, including Euston, Liverpool Street, and Victoria. The smartcard itself is free, although Oyster demands a £3 refundable deposit on purchase. Your Oyster will have to be loaded with pre-paid credit before you can use it—the only exception is the **Visitor Oyster,** aimed at tourists, which comes pre-loaded with credit and can be purchased at airports and aboard Eurostar and National Express services. Oysters can also be topped up online.

Unfairs

If the fares on London's public transport network strike you as expensive, just wait till next year. Fares are usually raised in January, often well above the rate of inflation. Train prices tend to see the most signficant hikes. However, Oyster prices are often frozen or rise only minimally.

Oyster savings can be significant. For instance, the fare from Heathrow to central London, £4 if you pay by cash, drops to £2.20 outside peak periods (Mon–Fri 6:30–9:30am and 4–7pm). If you make several journeys in a day, the amount you spend is capped at 50p less than the price of a 1-Day Travelcard (see below). Remember to swipe your Oyster over a yellow station reader at both the start and end of your journey.

TRAVELCARDS

These offer less generous savings than an Oyster Card, but are the best option if you need to use National Rail services, many of which still don't accept Oyster. Travelcards are valid on all of London's various forms of public transport—trains, Tube, buses, DLR, and trams—within a certain time period, either a day, 3 days, or a week, and within certain Zones. For validity periods over a week, you need a photocard ID.

Travelcards come in two types. The cheaper, off-peak version allows unlimited travel within your designated Zone(s) after 9:30am Monday to Friday and all day Saturday and Sunday until 4:30am the next morning. An 'anytime' version which, as the name suggests, has no time restrictions is considerably more expensive. A 1-day off-peak Travelcard costs £5.60 for Zones 1 to 2 and £7.50 for Zones 1 to 6, while the anytime version is £7.20 for Zones 1 to 2 and £14.80 for

> ### Fare Zones
>
> If you're paying with cash as and when you travel, Tube and bus fares are set at a flat rate. However, for the purposes of working out fares for Oyster and Travelcards, London is divided into six concentric zones—Zone 1 is the centre, Zone 6 the outskirts. The fare is then worked out according to the distance travelled within and between these Zones.

Zones 1 to 6. A 3-day Travelcard for Zones 1 to 2 is £21.20 off-peak, and £42.40 anytime for Zones 1 to 6. If you're staying a week, the value option is to go for the 7-day Travelcard: it costs £25.80 for Zones 1 to 2, and just £47.60 for Zones 1 to 6, and is valid at all times.

BY TUBE

The London Underground network, or 'Tube', offers its most generous discounts to Oyster Card holders. A single walk-up fare of whatever length, be it one stop or 30, is a flat-rate £4. For a journey across all six Zones an Oyster Card brings this down to £3.80, Which is okay, but not as good as if you were travelling solely within Zone 1, when the single Oyster fare is just £1.60. Under 11s travel free on the Tube network at all times.

BY TRAIN

Just to make things interesting, London has two separate rail networks. London Overground, which operates four railway lines in North London, accepts Oyster Cards on all its routes. Network Rail co-ordinates a number of different operators whose trains serve the capital, not all of which accept Oyster. For these a Travelcard is the cheapest option (see above). For now, at least, all of the capital's rail operators are due to become Oyster enabled in the next couple of years. See www.nationalrail.co.uk/times_fares/london/OysterPAYG.pdf for a list of stations currently accepting Oyster Cards.

BY DOCKLANDS LIGHT RAILWAY (DLR)

This 1980s-built East London metro system connects with the Tube at several points, notably Tower Gateway and Bank. If your travel uses both the Underground and DLR networks, then the equivalent Tube fare applies—a £4 flat rate with the relevant Oyster saving. However, if your journey is solely on the DLR, then a ticket costs just £1.60 walk-up, £1.10 with Oyster.

BY BUS

A huge variety of buses operate in the capital, including single-decker, double-decker, and articulated 'bendy' buses as well as a couple of old-fashioned Routemasters serving 'heritage' routes (no. 9 and no. 15). All are red, of course. Despite the equally varied range of operating companies, prices are held consistent across the network. A single walk-up fare, of whatever length, costs £2. The Oyster fare is just £1, and the daily cost of unlimited bus travel on your Oyster is capped at £3.30. A 1-day bus and tram pass is £3.80. In outer London you may pay your fare to the driver upon boarding. However, in Zone 1, you *must* buy a ticket before boarding at the machine, provided it's working, by the bus stop. Oyster users, of course, needn't worry about such trifles; just remember to keep your smartcard charged with money.

For details on how to arrange your own DIY bus tour of London, see p. 137.

BY TRAM

London's Tramlink service, which runs between Beckenham, Croydon, and Wimbledon, has the same fare structure as the buses: £2 for walk-up fares, £1 for anyone with an Oyster Card. Travelcards and bus passes are valid on all trams.

BY CAR

The long list of reasons not to drive in London includes the following: congestion, high car-hire rates, limited and hideously expensive parking, baffling one-way systems, bus lanes with CCTV and heavy fines for even accidental encroachment, and an £8 congestion charge levied on every vehicle entering the centre between 7am and 6:30pm (Monday to Friday). It's really not a budget option. However, if you simply must drive, try joining a car-sharing service operated by

Zipcar (© **020 7669 4000,** www.zipcar.com) or **Streetcar** (© **0845 644 8475,** www.streetcar.co.uk). These give you driving access to a number of cars parked across the capital, from £3.95 an hour (fuel, insurance, and the C-charge included) plus an annual £50 membership fee.

BY BOAT

Taking a boat up the Thames is more a sightseeing trip than a convenient means to get around, although some commuters do take the watery route to work. **Thames Clippers** (© **020 7001 2222,** www.thamesclippers.com) runs a service between Waterloo Pier and Royal Woolwich Arsenal Pier, stopping at London Bridge, Tower Pier (for the Tower of London), Canary Wharf, and Greenwich. It also operates a service between the two Tate museums (p. 120) as well as an express between Waterloo and the O2 venue, which can come in very handy if you're catching a concert on a weekend when various Tube lines—invariably including the Jubilee—close for maintenance. Fares are a not-exactly-bargain £5 one-way, although this comes down to £3.35 for Travelcard (but not yet Oyster) holders. If you fancy heading upriver, **Westminster Passenger Service Association** (© **020 7930 2062,** http://wpsa.co.uk) runs daily services from April to October between Westminster Pier and Kew, Richmond, and Hampton Court. Fares are a stiff £10.50 to £13.50 one-way, reduced by a third for Travelcard holders.

BY TAXI

There are two options here: black cabs and minicabs. Black taxis are a beloved London institution, albeit a rather pricey one. In order to qualify, prospective drivers must know every street in central London, plus more than 400 designated routes. This astounding feat of learning, known as 'The Knowledge', takes on average 2½ years to complete and should ensure that your cabbie never gets lost. In return, however, expect to pay in the region of £10 for a journey of less than 5 miles; more after 8pm when a higher rate applies. It's £2.20 just to sit down, after which your meter will begin clicking on with indecent haste. To book a black cab (add another £2 booking fee) call **Taxi One-Number** on © **0871 871 8710.** Alternatively, if the orange sign is illuminated, it means a cab is free to hail from the street.

The other option is to take a minicab. These are cheaper, but slightly less reliable—although the advent of sat nav has improved a previously erratic standard of route finding. Only book through licensed firms—cabs should have the appropriate badge displayed in their front window. Never use one of the illegal (and possibly dangerous) independent operators who tout for business in the West End. To find a licensed minicab text HOME to Transport for London on 60835. TfL will then text you the phone numbers of your two closest licensed operators. Expect to pay half to two-thirds what you would for the equivalent journey in a black cab.

ON FOOT

London comes in two different sizes: Greater London, which is huge—28 miles north to south, 35 miles east to west—and central London, which isn't very big at all. Touring on foot is the best and cheapest way to get to know the smaller version. Do note, however, that London was created piecemeal over many centuries; its layout adheres to no comprehensible grid or plan. In other words, it's very easy to get lost. Take a copy of the *A–Z*, London's street atlas, when you're out pounding the pavements. If you fancy putting in major miles, see p. 280 for some suggested walking routes.

4 London Resources A to Z

TRAVELLERS WITH DISABILITIES

London's provision for the disabled is by no means perfect, but it is improving. Designs for all new public buildings have to take the needs of disabled visitors into consideration, and the majority of museums, galleries, and other attractions, even those occupying old buildings, offer reasonably good accessibility. The **Access Project** publishes a slightly out-of-date (2003) guide to accessibility in London which you can order for a £10 donation: e-mail gordon.couch@virgin.net or write to the Access Project (PHSP), 39 Bradley Gardens, West Ealing, W13 8HE, (www.accessinlondon.org).

The past decade has seen a marked improvement in disabled provision on public transport. All buses are now wheelchair-accessible, as are Tramlink and DLR vehicles. The situation on the Tube system, however, is not so positive. Most stations provide access via stairs or escalators, and only a handful have lifts—those that do are marked with a blue symbol on the tube map. There are various resources available for disabled travellers on the Transport for London website (ww.tfl. gov.uk), including a downloadable 'Getting Around London' guide in PDF format: www.tfl.gov.uk/gettingaround/transportaccessibility/1167. aspx.

EMERGENCIES

In the event of an emergency requiring the police, fire brigade, or ambulance service, call ✆ **999** or ✆ **112.** Calls are free.

If you need advice on a particular malady, you can call the National Health Service's free helpline, NHS Direct, on ✆ **0845 4647** or go online at www.nhsdirect.nhs.uk.

LGBT RESOURCES

LGBT London   An online directory listing lesbian, gay, bisexual, and transgender resources across the capital.

http://lgbtlondon.ning.com.

London Lesbian & Gay Switchboard   Helpline providing information and support for lesbian, gay, bisexual, and transgender people. It's open 7 days a week 10am to 11pm.

✆ **020 7837 7324.** www.llgs.org.uk.

LOST PROPERTY

All of London's airports have lost property offices where you can reclaim lost items. However, don't get too excited yet; you'll probably have to pay a 'storage' fee of £5 to £10 before they'll be handed back to you. For information, call the following:

Gatwick Airport, ✆ **01293 503162.**

Heathrow Airport, ✆ **020 8745 7727.**

London City Airport, ✆ **020 7646 0000.**

Luton Airport, ✆ **01582 405 100.**

Stansted Airport, ✆ **01279 663 293.**

Items lost on the bus or in the back of a black cab may turn up at the **Transport for London Lost Property Office,** 200 Baker Street, NW1. ✆ **0845 330 9882.** Mon–Fri 8:30am–4pm. Tube: Baker Street.

MEDIA

NEWSPAPERS

As well as the *Evening Standard*, London's weekday evening rag, there are two other free daily papers, distributed at Tube and train stations: *Metro* and *London Lite*. Aimed at occupying commuters' minds during a journey, they fill what few pages they print with brief summaries of the day's events plus lots of celebrity tittle-tattle.

RADIO

Given that there's no whopping cable or Sky bill for accessing our airwaves, radio remains an invaluable free resource. In addition to the stations listed below, which are available on traditional wavebands, there are a number of new stations broadcasting exclusively

News for Free

Newspaper circulations have been falling for years. The paid-for printed word is facing an onslaught from all angles: falling advertising revenues since the downturn, the growth of free online news sites, the (mixed) success of Free-sheets—the launch of *Metro* in 2006 represents one of the few genuine success stories to have come out of Fleet Street in recent years. However, one of the greatest threats of all is largely self-inflicted: the newspapers' own websites offer all the content of the print editions, plus a good deal more, for free. Most in the newspaper industry agree that if they are to survive in current form, they are going to have to start charging for online content. Trouble is, no one has yet worked out a viable model of how this might work. Which means that right now we could be living in the greatest era of free information in human history—so get online and get informed before someone figures out how to make money out of it. The best news sites include left-leaning www.guardian.co.uk, which is particularly good for live coverage of sporting events; the more right-wing, Eurosceptic www.telegraph.co.uk; www.ft.com, the leading source of business news; and Rupert Murdoch-owned www.timesonline.co.uk, which, if the pronouncements of its proprietor are to be believed, will probably lead the content-charging revolution.

Papers & Prices

Weekday Title	Mon–Fri Price	Saturday Price	Sunday Title	Price
The Times	90p	£1.50	Sunday Times	£2
The Daily Telegraph	90p	£1.60	The Sunday Telegraph	£1.90
The Independent	£1	£1.60	The Independent on Sunday	£1.80
The Guardian	90p	£1.60	The Observer	£2
The Financial Times	£1.80	£2.30	N/A	
The Express	40p	70p	Sunday Express	£1.30
The Daily Mail	50p	80p	The Mail on Sunday	£1.50
The Mirror	45p	65p	Sunday Mirror	£1
The Star	20p	60p	Star Sunday	90p
The Sun	30p	60p	News of the World	£1

on digital (DAB) radio and/or online. Come the weekend FM frequencies also play host to a fleeting array of pirate stations which flicker in and out of existence, usually playing specific niche music—such as UK garage and grime—and providing details of friends' parties.

BBC London, 94.9 FM   News, sport, phone-ins, a bit of music, and Danny Baker.

http://news.bbc.co.uk/local/london/hi/tv_and_radio.

Capital FM, 95.8 FM   London's leading commercial broadcaster—popular music and fluffy chat about the day's events.

www.capitalradio.co.uk.

Heart, 106.2 FM   Like Capital, but more so.

www.heart.co.uk.

Kiss FM, 100 FM   London's leading dance music station.

www.totalkiss.com.

LBC, 97.3 FM   The best channel for 'Broken Britain', 'political correctness gone mad', 'justice turned on its head' ranting phone-ins.

www.lbc.co.uk.

Smooth, 97.3 FM   Gentle sounds, of the Luther Vandross, Paul Simon, Lionel Richie variety, plus a bit of jazz.

www.smoothradio.com

XFM, 104.9   The capital's favourite indie music.
www.xfm.co.uk.

Magazines & Listings

TimeOut is still the pre-eminent source of capital listings. It's out weekly, every Tuesday, and costs £2.99 (or free online at www.time out.com/london). Several daily newspapers also publish entertainment guides with their weekend editions, the best of which is the *Guide*. It comes inside Saturday's *Guardian*. If you're a sports fan also look out for *Sport*, a free weekly magazine distributed on Fridays at Tube and train stations (www.myfreesport.co.uk).

PHARMACIES/CHEMISTS

Chain pharmacy Boots (www.boots.com) has dispensing chemists in many of its stores across the capital. Several large supermarkets, including Tesco (www.tesco.com), also operate dispensing services.

Boots   Late opening branch of the nationwide chain.

Piccadilly Circus, 44 Regent Street, W1. ℂ **020 7734 6126.** Mon–Fri 8am–midnight, Sat 9–midnight, Sun midday–6pm. Tube: Piccadilly Circus.

Zafash Pharmacy   Round-the-clock dispensing.

233–235 Old Brompton Road, SW5. ℂ **020 7373 2798.** www.zafash.com. Daily 24 hours, 365 days a year. Tube: Earls Court.

SMOKING

Smoking has been banned in all enclosed public spaces since 2007, including cafés, restaurants, pubs, and clubs. Many venues provide outside facilities for smokers—most London pub beer gardens allow smoking.

TIPPING

Tipping is common in the UK, but not as standard as in some other countries, notably the USA. I would normally tip my waiter in a restaurant or a café—typically 10 to 12.5%—if I thought the service was worth it (although I check that a service charge hasn't already been added; see p. 62 for more on restaurant tipping). I would also tip a porter or chambermaid in a hotel, assuming I could find a budget hotel that employed either. However, I would not normally tip a bartender, even if some central London bars give change on a little tray so as to encourage me to leave a few coins behind. These are designed to catch American auto-tippers who haven't worked out how things work yet—no one looks at you askance if you trouser all the money. If a taxi driver helps to carry your luggage or generally goes beyond the call of duty, then tip away, but for a straightforward journey, particularly in one of the capital's expensive black cabs, it's not necessary.

If you leave a tip in a restaurant, be clear in your mind who you're leaving it for. Is it for the establishment—to thank them for the dining experience—or is it for the waiter who attended to you? If it's the latter, then leave your 12.5% in cash and hang around to make sure it's picked up by the right person. In an unfortunate sign of the times, many restaurants (particularly chains) do not distribute tips paid on cards to their staff, but rather put the money towards paying (extremely) basic salaries. It's not cricket, but unfortunately it's not illegal, so there's no chance the practice will cease soon.

TOILETS

London is not exactly overburdened with public lavatories. The days when every high street had its own council-run facilities are gone. Still, there are options available when you get caught short. Many of the capital's train and Tube stops have public lavatories; download a list from www.tfl.gov.uk. Those at rail stations usually charge around 30p. Other likely candidates include museums, galleries, and arts centres, most of which are free, and offer clean facilities, as do public parks. Department stores are another good bet, as are McDonald's and Burger King. Come the evening, however, your best option may be to nip into the nearest pub—but be discrete. Although many establishments have signs in their windows declaring that their facilities are 'for the use of patrons only', it's usually easy to sneak in and do what you have to do, particularly if they're busy. I wouldn't try it in a restaurant, though. The following website has a number of public loo suggestions: http://golondon.about.com/od/londonforfree/tp/freetoilets.htm.

USEFUL WEBSITES

www.freelondonlistings.co.uk

Free and nearly free events across the capital.

www.gumtree.com

London's leading online noticeboard and source of classified ads.

www.hiddenlondon.com

Guide to London attractions off the beaten path.

www.london.gov.uk

Website of the Mayor of London, the London Assembly, and the Greater London Authority.

www.london-footprints.co.uk

Capital walks to print out and tread for yourself.

www.londonforfree.net

Suggestions for gratis activities and day trips in the capital.

http://londonist.com

A blog celebrating London. Its regular 'London on the Cheap' features bargain events taking place across the capital.

www.london2012.com

The official London Olympics website.

http://london.unlike.net

Self-consciously hip guide to the capital, designed to be displayed on a mobile phone (so you can access location-specific content as you move around). It's also available as an iPhone app.

www.moneysavingexpert.com

The website of Martin Lewis, a financial journalist, specialising in ways to save money. The site contains sections devoted to shopping, credit cards, banking, travel, and utilities, as well as forums where members of the public offer their own money-saving tips—many of which relate to London.

http://news.bbc.co.uk/local/london/hi

The BBC's dedicated London section with news, sport, and cultural features.

www.royalparks.org.uk

The facilities, attractions, entertainment, and events taking place at London's nine royal parks.

http://stonch.blogspot.com

Pro-real beer, pro-local pub blog written by the landlord of the Gun-maker's Arms in Clerkenwell with reviews and information about the capital's best boozers.

www.storyoflondon.com

A website dedicated to the history of the capital featuring historical accounts of famous events.

www.tfl.gov.uk

Website of Transport for London, the body in charge of the capital's public transport.

www.visitlondon.com/people/budget

The London Tourist Board dedicates a whole section on its website to budget travellers, with sections on restaurants, family days out, pubs and bars, and the theatre.

INDEX